DEFENSE AND DÉTENTE

STUDIES IN GLOBAL SECURITY
Alan Ned Sabrosky, Series Editor

DEFENSE AND DÉTENTE
U.S. and West German Perspectives on Defense Policy

Joseph I. Coffey
and Klaus von Schubert

with Dieter Dettke, James R. Golden,
and Gale A. Mattox

Westview Press
BOULDER, SAN FRANCISCO, & LONDON

For our children

Studies in Global Security

This Westview softcover edition is printed on acid-free paper and bound in softcovers that carry the highest rating of the National Association of State Textbook Administrators, in consultation with the Association of American Publishers and the Book Manufacturers' Institute.

Published in 1989 in the United States of America by Westview Press, Inc., 5500 Central Avenue, Boulder, Colorado 80301, and in the United Kingdom by Westview Press, Inc., 13 Brunswick Centre, London WC1N 1AF, England

Library of Congress Cataloging-in-Publication Data
Coffey, Joseph I.
    Defense and détente: U.S. and West German perspectives on defense
policy/Joseph I. Coffey and Klaus von Schubert, with Dieter
Dettke, James R. Golden and Gale A. Mattox.
        p. cm.—(Studies in global security)
    Bibliography: p.
    Includes index.
    ISBN 0-8133-7722-6
    1. United States—Military policy. 2. Germany (West)—Military
policy. 3. United States—Military relations—Germany (West).
4. Germany (West)—Military relations—United States. I. Schubert,
Klaus von. II. Title. III. Series.
UA23.C575   1989
355'.0335'73—dc19   89-30341
                                                                                        CIP

Printed and bound in the United States of America

The paper used in this publication meets the requirements of the American National Standard for Permanence of Paper for Printed Library Materials Z39.48-1984.

10   9   8   7   6   5   4   3   2   1

Contents

Acknowledgments

This book is the product of many minds and many hands. In some cases both belonged to the same person: thus, credit must be given to Dr. Dieter Dettke, Executive Director of the Friedrich Ebert Stiftung; to Colonel James R. Golden, U.S. Army, Professor of Economics and Deputy Head of the Department of Social Sciences, United States Military Academy; and to Dr. Gale A. Mattox, Associate Professor of Political Science, United States Naval Academy, not only for the chapters of which they are authors but also for their insights into the issues discussed elsewhere in the text and their constructive criticisms of the work performed by other contributors. In some instances, the inputs were more purely intellectual, as was true of that by Dr. Catherine Kelleher, currently Professor of Political Science and Director of the International Security Project at the University of Maryland; in fact, Dr. Kelleher's insights and suggestions were instrumental in giving the book the form it now has. And somewhere between the two lie the contributions of Mme. Francoise Paublant, Research Associate at the University Center for International Studies (UCIS), University of Pittsburgh, who served as Executive Editor; Ms. Lisa McAnany of Carnegie Mellon University, Editorial Assistant; Mr. Alan Dieter, Jr., Mr. Andrew Hoehn, Mr. James Libbey, Miss Robin McLeister, Mr. William Pierce, and Mr. Kenneth Ruby, all Research Assistants at UCIS; and Mr. Jurgen Wiesner, Research Assistant at the Armed Forces University, Munich. At the administrative level, mention must be made of Mrs. Gertrude Whitman-Gordon, Mrs. Rosemary Anderson, and Frau Frauke Greifenstein, who typed and retyped seemingly innumerable drafts in several languages and who handled all the voluminous correspondence associated with a trans-Atlantic enterprise. Ms. Glema Burke, Assistant Director for Management of UCIS, and Dr. Friedhelm Solms, Senior Research Fellow of FESt, managed the even more difficult task of keeping track of finances during a period of sweeping changes in dollar-DM ratios; moreover, Dr. Solms also made all arrangements for the 1984 conference at which 28 American and West European participants reviewed the first draft of our manuscript.

Our research required not only "blood, sweat, toil and tears," which we provided in good measure, but also money. We are grateful to the University Center for International Studies (of which Dr. Burkart Holzner is Director) for substantial administrative and clerical support; to the Office of Private Sector Programs, United States Information Agency, which paid for the travel of some American participants to the Heidelberg Conference, and to Dr. Gregory Winn of that office, who himself participated in that conference, at his own expense; and to the Volkswagen Foundation, whose generous grant underwrote most of the costs of the project. We are particularly grateful to Dr. Alfred Schmidt of that foundation, who not only monitored the project but, by his penetrating questions, also helped to shape its scope and its thrust. His constant encouragement and support facilitated the book's completion.

Were we to list all those deserving of thanks, this section might be longer than the rest of the book! Let us, then, simply say of our unnamed helpers that they are not "unwept, unhonored, and unsung"; on the contrary, they share with those specifically mentioned our appreciation and our gratitude.

Joseph I. Coffey
Distinguished Service Professor
 Emeritus of Public and Inter-
 national Affairs
Senior Research Fellow, UCIS
Pittsburgh, Pa., USA

Klaus von Schubert
Director, Forschungsstätte der
 Evangelischen Studiengemein-
 schaft (FESt)
Heidelberg, FRG

Introduction

A Changed World

The two World Wars in the first half of the twentieth century had an impact almost without parallel in history; the consequences for Europe can only be compared to those resulting from the fall of the West Roman Empire in the Fifth Century. Political institutions were shattered, social systems changed, and economic relations altered almost beyond recognition. Europe itself was twice devastated and greatly weakened, empires were overthrown, and the successor states, like amoebas, changed appearance with every glance. More importantly, in the post-war period some of these successor states, like some of the continuing ones, came under the sway of external influences; far from radiating authority, Europe in some sense became subject to it.

The changes in Europe were paralleled by changes in the world at large as sweeping as those brought about by the rise of Islam in the Seventh and Eighth Centuries or the extension of West European influence, which began in the Sixteenth Century. For one thing, Europe itself ceased to be as important in the international system: Vast areas once under European domination re-emerged as independent states; the focus of world economic activity shifted from Europe, which no longer monopolized trade with (or controlled development in) the former colonies; and European power and influence declined both relatively and absolutely. For another, new actors appeared upon the international stage: Today there are more than 150 sovereign states, compared with fewer than 50 at the end of World War II, to say nothing of dozens of international businesses that command more resources and exercise more influence than do many of the national actors. For a third, two of the old actors became superpowers, whose extensive territories, vast resources, strong economic-industrial bases, and formidable military machines give them enormous advantages over other states; even if they had not developed nuclear capabilities far superior to those of any other country, the United States and the USSR would be virtually un-challengeable.

Moreover, other factors combined to shape a "new international order" significantly different from the old one. One such factor is the advent of nuclear weapons, which transformed both the bases of power and the nature of war, thereby affecting significantly the behavior of even the most powerful actors. As Raymond Aron phrased it, "The [possibility of a] recourse to nuclear arms remains an ever-present reality influencing all levels of conflict."[1] Another factor is the emergence of what Zbigniew Brzezinski dubbed "local leviathans," powers such as Japan, the People's Republic of China, India, Brazil, Nigeria, South Africa, Israel, and Saudi Arabia, which can and do make their influence felt. A third factor is that these states generate influence not only by their military capabilities (which are in some instances quite small) but by their economic capacity, their level of industrialization, and/or their control of natural resources; in some instances economic power is more useable than, and for some purposes more important than, military power. A fourth factor is that old states and new are increasingly interdependent, with Japan buying oil from the Middle East and financing its purchases from exports to the United States and Western Europe; with American and West European banks underwriting Brazilian development with recycled Kuwaiti oil revenues; and with American, British, French, German and Japanese economists, industrialists, and technicians, together with hundreds of thousands of Egyptians, Iranians, Pakistanis, and Palestinians, involved in an ambitious plan for the modernization of Saudi Arabia. And a fifth factor is the creation of a web of legal, political, and psychological barriers to the use of force—no longer is intervention sanctioned by international law nor war regarded as "the ultimate argument of kings."

Taken together, these changes have enormously complicated the task of insuring national security, i.e., of preserving the territorial integrity, political independence, and economic viability of a state. The mere existence of a superpower adversary means that the United States and its allies are in peril—as are the Soviet Union and its allies. The fact that other states cannot compete militarily with the United States or the USSR leads some to seek the support of one superpower against the other—or against their local rivals—and some to try and constrain the use of force. The fact that these constraints apply unequally to superpowers and to lesser powers, in Europe and in Africa, or to indirect uses of force as against direct ones, means that conflict, to paraphrase Clausewitz, "continues by other means." The fact that the world consists of many states, some weak and others strong, some internally stable and some divided or disrupted, some at peace with their neighbors and others at war, guarantees that opportunities to use these "other means" will be plentiful. Thus Saudi Arabia can underwrite the Iraqi war against Iran, Cuba can send troops to buttress the government of Angola, and the United States can organize and direct "covert" operations designed to undermine that of Nicaragua.

Differing Responses

Obviously, how nations attempt to enhance their security and achieve their interests in this changed and changing world depends on many factors: the definition of those interests, perceptions of threat, perspectives on the international environment, power to affect that environment, and domestic support for the exercise of that power and the ways in which it is employed.

Equally obviously, different nations will have different interests, perspectives, concerns, and power—as well as constraints on the exercise of that power; hence they will also pursue different policies. This is true even of close allies such as the United States and the Federal Republic of Germany, which in the past thirty years have differed over issues as varied as the sale of nuclear reprocessing systems, the value of détente, and doctrine for the defense of Western Europe. Nor are all those issues behind us; as any scan of the press will show, the two allies are still at odds over burden-sharing within the Atlantic Alliance, over the best way to implement the concept of "flexible response," over ways of dealing with the "out of area" problem, and over the desirability of arms control, both as an end in itself and as a means of promoting détente.

This study will attempt to define precisely the nature of the differences between the United States and the FRG with respect to a particular set of issues arising out of the policy of "Defense and Détente," which is intended to insure peace and security in Europe. More importantly, it will also try to uncover the reasons for those differences, in order to see whether, to what extent, and by what means the policies of the two countries can be brought closer together. In short, this study is an attempt at policy prescription, based on an analysis of factors influencing previous policies and programs.

In carrying out this project we will begin by singling out in Chapter 1 those factors in the international and domestic environments that seemingly have had the greatest impact on U.S. and/or West German security policy and discussing briefly their effects. We will then turn, in Chapters 2 and 3, to overviews of U.S. and West German foreign and defense policies in the post-war period, with particular reference to significant changes in those policies and the factors influencing those changes. Next we will, in Chapters 4 through 7, take up in turn a number of specific security issues, reviewing briefly the development of U.S. and West German measures to cope with these issues, examining the similarities and differences in their approaches and suggesting reasons for them. Chapter 8 will present in summary fashion our findings, and Chapter 9 will set forth our recommendations for change, based on an assessment of those influences that are transitory and those that are enduring. The first step, however, is to identify those influences.

J.I.C.
K.v.S.

Notes

1. Raymond Aron, "The Evolution of Modern Strategic Thought," in *Problems of Modern Strategy, Part 1, Adelphi Papers* 54 (London: International Institute for Strategic Studies, 1969), 9.

1

Factors Influencing
Security Policy

Joseph I. Coffey and Klaus von Schubert

Broadly speaking, defense and other policies are supposedly aimed at securing national objectives, which in turn are a means of advancing national interests. These policies (and to a lesser extent, objectives) are influenced not only by national values but by the threats to interests and by the environment in which policies must be formulated and implemented. Obviously, some aspects of that environment are both more significant and more enduring than others, and some of these will impact more strongly and more directly upon defense policy than will others. The purpose of this section is to single out those which, in our opinion, meet this latter criterion and to suggest ways in which they have affected defense policy.

Any assessment of the implications for security—and security policy—of the post-war environment is necessarily subjective, in that both perceptions of that environment and estimates of its effects will differ. Although that subjectivity can never be eliminated, we have tried to reduce it by using two separate methods of determining implications, one deductive and one inductive, carried out by different people.

The deductive approach involved a survey of relevant literature on both foreign and defense policy in order to ascertain those factors in the international and domestic environments which experts deemed important.[1] These factors were then classified according to duration, magnitude of impact, whether this impact fell directly on defense policy or indirectly, and whether it was continuous or intermittent. The inductive approach involved an historical survey of U.S. and West German defense policy, by different members of the Research Team, who singled out those factors that seemed to have had the greatest and longest lasting effects. The results of the two approaches were compared at a meeting of the Research Team and those factors which seemingly applied to both the United States and the Federal Republic, or which had had a major impact on the security of one country or the other, were selected for more detailed analysis. The twelve factors discussed below were derived from this comparative analysis and although they do not exclude consideration of other influences on defense policy, they will constitute the framework for our analysis.

Significant Influences
from the International Environment

The "Island Continent" and the Land Power

The U.S. is geographically an "island," thousands of miles away from Europe across the Atlantic and thousands of miles away from Asia across the Pacific. Historically, this has been very important both militarily and politically. Beginning with the American War of Independence, foreign powers have had to travel across great oceans to wage war against the United States, which has therefore remained relatively safe from invasion. Add to this a great abundance of natural resources, a "manifest destiny" which turned inward rather than outward and historical domination of the hemisphere and it is understandable that the United States remained rather isolationist until WWI and even beyond it.

The success of this isolationist policy depended, however, on the existence in Europe of a balance of power; long before the eminent geopolitician Sir Halford Mackinder pointed out that "Who rules the World Island commands the World,"[2] Thomas Jefferson was writing that the United States should throw its weight against the potential winner in the Napoleonic Wars, lest the conqueror of Europe become a threat to this country.[3] Twice, in 1917 and in 1941, the United States did just that, and it is prepared to do so again in order to prevent Soviet domination of Eurasia; even if Russia were still ruled by the Czars, the U.S. would be seeking to keep it from overrunning Western Europe.

In terms of defense policy, both geography and international politics inclined the United States (like Britain before her) to emphasize naval (and air) forces, which could both safeguard it from invasion and allow it to project power when its interests so required. Land forces were decidedly secondary, in terms of capabilities, readiness and mission; it is worth recalling that General Eisenhower was appointed in 1943 to the command of the Allied *Expeditionary* Forces in Europe. And though World War II established a more or less permanent American military presence in various parts of the world, and necessitated a second mission of defending key areas such as Western Europe and Japan, the old role of serving as "forces of intervention" is at least as important.

As suggested above, the political consequences of geographic isolation have always been modified by a concern for the security of the Western hemisphere and for the global balance of power. The military effects have to some extent been altered by the events of the past 40 years: a divided Europe, a global role for the United States, competition with the USSR and, above all, the development of nuclear weapons. Some of these, like the first, have resulted both in "entangling alliances" and in a more or less permanent U.S. presence in Europe. Others, however, have reinforced the tendency to rely heavily upon naval (and air) forces, to eschew fixed positions save as these serve military purposes (as do the bases in the Phillippines) and to make every effort to keep war distant from the homeland—an objective which is served both by U.S. concepts for the defense of Europe and by U.S. strategic doctrine and strategic programs— most notably and most recently the "Star Wars" proposal for shielding the United States against ballistic missiles.

Conversely, West Germany is a land power *par excellence*, with only short coastlines fronting on small and partially closed seas. Its position on the Great European Plain, between the Baltic Sea and the Alps, has made it a pathway for East-West migrations in earlier times and for the surge of armies in more recent ones. Politically, economically and culturally it has been part of the European Continent, with all that that entailed. And this role has been enhanced in the post-war world by the division of Germany, which left the FRG on the border between the two alliances, with an exposed outpost in Berlin.

Historically, the German response has been to try to establish a solid base of power in Central Europe, through which it could safeguard its own people and from which it could pursue its own interests, singly or in concert with others. Historically, the army has been the most essential and the most effective component of military power, the instrument by which Prussia expanded and thanks to whose successes a unified Germany was formed. Until the end of the 19th Century, the navy was small, so small that in 1870-71 only a British guarantee prevented the French Navy from smashing it. (Even its great accomplishments in World War I and II were made by a particular and peculiar weapons system: the submarine.) Thus, geography, history, experience and the nature of the threat all combine to focus attention on German land (and air) power, despite the maritime orientation of the alliance to which it belongs.

The post-war environment has largely reinforced these trends towards security through involvement and through land power. The vulnerability of West Germany to threats from the East, and the sense that its political aims could best be realized through association with the West, prompted it to seek an American guarantee, to join the Atlantic Alliance and to contribute to that alliance an army which is perhaps the strongest of any European member. For the same reasons, it has eschewed any global role, made no effort at "power projection" and sought instead to satisfy both political aspirations and security needs through a focus on regional issues.

A Global Power and a Regional One

As suggested above, political as well as geo-economic factors have limited West Germany's role to that of a regional power. A major objective is to re-unify (or at least re-constitute) Germany, an objective which demands both concentration on local matters and the promotion of good relations with the USSR; both as a means to the attainment of this objective and because of the market opportunities, the FRG has expanded its trade with Eastern Europe and the Soviet Union. Its major focus is, however, on Western Europe, eleven of whose countries have joined with it in the European Community to form the world's major trading area, and fourteen of whose states are associated with it in the Atlantic Alliance, the Western European Union, or both; thus the FRG is definitely Euro-centered.

While this is partly a matter of choice, it is also partly a matter of necessity. Germany's brief essay at being a global power, with colonies in Asia and Africa and interests which extended beyond Europe, ended with World War I. The attempts of the Third Reich to gain influence in Latin American and the Middle East were largely linked to its conduct of its operations in Europe and ceased even before its demise. The Federal Republic had, therefore, neither historical interest in playing a global role nor any basis from which to start. Furthermore, the West German economic base, while strong, is insufficient to sustain its socio-economic system, to maintain its land and tactical air forces and to develop the fleets, the long range planes and the network of bases required to operate globally. Moreover, it has bound itself not to produce the nuclear weapons which could shield it against the untoward consequences of any conflict outside Europe. In brief, the Federal Republic, despite its world-wide economic interests, does not desire to play a global role politically and could not sustain it militarily.

To the contrary, World War II resulted in the involvement of the United States throughout the globe, with new responsibilities for replacing the weakened allies as they withdrew from Asia and Africa, for assisting in the political and economic development of newly-emerging countries and for coping with the post-war transformation of the international system. These responsibilities were augmented by those deriving from the missions of checking Communist "expansionism" in its various forms and of competing with the Soviet Union for influence in the Third World. Whether they were always wisely assumed or properly discharged is perhaps debatable but of their existence and their implications there can be little doubt.

Given its global role and global perspective, the United States is almost bound to differ from its allies with respect to defense policies and programs; even though Western Europe may be the most important area in the world, it is not the only one. Thus, although a large share of the U.S. defense effort has been devoted to weapons and troops in or earmarked for Europe, other portions have gone to support strong forces in the Far East, to maintain sizeable fleets in the Mediterranean Sea and the Indian Ocean and, more recently, to organize and equip a Rapid Deployment Force as large as the garrison in Europe. This global mission again reinforces the U.S. notion, derived from its geographical position, that naval and air forces have primacy and that land forces have an expeditionary role at least as important as that of static defense in a particular theate.

Moreover, the United States is not only a global power but a global *superpower*; none of the allies has the resources, the economic base or the military capacity to match the American (or the Soviet) presence in the Third World. This means that in some instances threats to their interests (such as denying access to oil in the Middle East) can be countered only by the United States—which may not perceive either interests or threats in quite the same way these allies do. It means also that the U.S.-Soviet competition takes a form and reaches an intensity which the allies cannot directly influence. Hence, for countries which, despite their world-wide economic interests, are still essentially regional powers, the global interests and involvement of the United States are not unmixed blessings.

Superpower Rivalry and Defense Policy

As suggested above, the rivalry between the two superpowers has magnified and multiplied U.S. involvement throughout the globe; what might have been a transitory phase, devoted largely to coping with the immediate consequences of World War II, has been extended both temporally and geographically. As the Soviets attempted to woo the governments (and the anti-government forces) in Black Africa with economic, technical and military assistance, the United States increasingly employed the same instruments for the same purposes. As Soviet "forces of intervention" and their Cuban and East German proxies began to train, equip, and staff the forces of Angola and Ethiopia, South Yemen, Egypt and Syria, Cuba and Nicaragua, the United States devoted increasing attention to providing similar support to "threatened" neighbors: Zaire, Somalia, North Yemen, Israel, Honduras. When Soviet aircraft from Dakar began reconnaissance flights over the South Atlantic, and when Soviet warships began to operate from Cam Ranh Bay in Vietnam, the United States augmented its own surveillance efforts in these areas. And of course it responded to Soviet or Soviet backed "aggression" against Afghanistan, South Korea and South Vietnam, as well as to what it claimed were Soviet-sponsored efforts at subversion in Thailand, the Sudan and El Salvador.

This is not to suggest that all U.S. policies and programs are re-actions to the efforts of the USSR to extend its influence, only that this has had a significant influence upon defense policy: U.S. strategic nuclear forces are designed to deter those of the USSR, U.S. theater nuclear forces are aimed (primarily) at the Soviet Union, and U.S. conventional elements are trained, organized and equipped to do battle with the Soviet Army, Navy and Air Force.[a] Furthermore, this superpower rivalry has influenced in large measure deployments overseas, and, more particularly, the training and equipping of allied forces—though more for defense against "proxies" such as North Korea or Syria than for operations against Soviet units themselves. Finally, the existence of a Soviet "threat" has generated wide political and public support for defense programs—even though there is a countercurrent of feeling that the Americans should be negotiating arms reductions with the Soviets rather than competing with them in arms buildups.

These public attitudes derive in part from the dual nature of that threat. There is considerable historical evidence that "great powers" tend to behave in similar fashion: seeking to expand territorially, attempting to set up client states, maneuvering to put down rivals and turning to the use of force as an instrument of policy; in this respect, the Soviet Union of today is no different from the Germany of the 19th Century, the Britain of the 18th Century or the Holland of the 17th. But while Soviet efforts to achieve a degree of influence commensurate with their status as a superpower might in themselves be enough to generate American opposition, the ideological differences between the two countries make rivalry both inevitable and bitter: each sees in the other the antithesis of what it strives to be and to achieve.

The Federal Republic also acknowledges the two faces of the Soviet threat, though it draws different implications concerning their meanings. Communist ideology is seen not so much as a force aimed at eroding the underpinnings of the Western world as a legitimizing factor in the Soviet system—albeit one which, if it exerts a significant influence on Soviet policy, will make difficult any resolution of the East-West conflict, any true détente[4]. If, however, the Soviet Union is regarded more as a traditional power—even as a traditional "great power"—then an accommodation which takes account both of its security interests (especially in Europe) and of its desire to have an "equal voice" in world affairs is possible.[5]

To some extent, this differing interpretation may spring from different circumstances: the regional perspective of the FRG, its abjuration of any global role and the fact that its interests outside Europe are largely economic. To some extent, it may reflect the fact that a degree of recognition of Soviet interests may not only enhance West German security (by reducing fears and tensions that could lead to war) but also increase the possiblity of accommodation with the GDR. In any event, the FRG, though clearly on the side of the United States, is not prepared to support the latter in all of its anti-Soviet measures; instead, that support is selective, both as to its nature and as to the circumstances under which it will be given. And occasionally, as in the case of El Salvador, that support is withheld as an expression of desire for a very different American approach.

The Correlation of Forces and Defense Policy

A related factor is that of the "correlation of forces," i.e., the assessment of relative economic, political and military "balances" and of trends in the international system[6] which the Soviets employ in determining "Who's ahead." There is no doubt that the increase in Soviet economic capacity and the steady growth of Soviet military capabilities (for which see Chapter 4) have enhanced Soviet power, both absolutely and relative to that of the Western Alliance—though the latter still has a commanding economic lead. Nor is there a doubt that the USSR has utilized these resources to enlarge its influence throughout the world, most notably in Asia and Africa. And though Soviet efforts have not been uniformly successful, Soviet control over some of its client states may be tenuous, and Communism may have lost some of its appeal in and out of the USSR, many will argue that the political balance has also tilted against the West.

Partly because of its global interests and partly because of its rivalry with the USSR, this shift in power and influence has aroused widespread concern in the United States and has spurred American efforts to check that growth, to counter that influence and to maintain the American position in the world. Economically, these efforts have taken the form of constraints on technology transfer and on the advancement of credits to the USSR, as well as the provision of economic, technical and financial assistance to friendly countries, with some emphasis on those threatened by, or wooed by, the Soviet Union. Politically, they have included both measures to enhance regional stability and measures to deny the USSR a voice in regional affairs. (In the Middle East, for example, the United States has sought to resolve differences between Israel and Egypt, to link the latter country, Jordan and Saudi Arabia in a loose arrangement intended to make available forces and/or bases for operations in the region and to settle matters in Lebanon without Soviet participation.) More significantly, the United States has also aided countries such as El Salvador which seem likely targets of Soviet or Soviet-supported operations and has engaged U.S. troops against Soviet "proxies," most recently in Grenada.

By far the biggest impact has, however, been on U.S. defense programs, which are seen by many as the key component of the balance of power. Increases have been particularly pronounced in "high tech" fields such as space-based systems, where prestige as well as power flow from accomplishments, and in the area of strategic nuclear forces, where, as then Secretary of Defense Brown once said, "the United States must not be, or be seen to be, inferior in performance to the Soviet Union."[7] They have also, however, taken the form of constructing and deploying forces for "global power projection," in an effort not only to offset the growth of the Soviet Navy but also to have available a military counter to further Soviet efforts to upset local or regional stability.

The problem is, of course, that estimates of the "correlation of forces," even those having to do with relative military capabilities, are essentially judgmental—and hence are subject to vast uncertainties. This is, of course, true of all assessments in foreign and defense policy, with the difference that many made by Americans (and Soviets) are colored by the ideological biases mentioned earlier.[8] This sometimes results in inflated requirements for military forces whose purpose may be largely to demonstrate that America is "standing tall," or to hasty steps to buttress countries such as North Yemen, whose importance to the United States may be less than outstanding. Thus, while there is every need to take into account changes in the "correlation of forces," there may be some question about either the accuracy of the assessments or the judiciousness of the responses.

Entirely aside from these concerns, there is the further one that West German perspectives—and hence West German responses—are very different. While some officials in the FRG express alarm over the growth of

Soviet Rocket Forces and of the Soviet Navy,[9] their fixation is much more upon Europe. In the economic field, they see the Soviet Union as a "struggling giant," whose outmoded planning process, rigid bureaucratic controls and largely unmotivated work force result in an inefficient, high cost industrial base and an agricultural system that is a model of what not to be. And in looking at the political situation, they are much more prone than are Americans to stress that Soviet failures in Eastern Europe—most notably in Poland —point up the weaknesses and flaws in Soviet policy. From all this, they draw the conclusion that the Soviet Union, while it still poses a formidable military threat, is by no means riding the crest of the wave.

They are not, therefore, as concerned as their American counter-parts with Soviet efforts to create a power base in the Third World—though they are even more supportive of efforts to alleviate the poverty and injustice which make some peoples susceptible to Soviet blandishments. And in coping with the element of greater concern, Soviet military capabilities, they would prefer to "level down" rather than to "level up;" as Karsten Voigt put it, "Without neglecting the defense capability of either side, armaments control measures should be given priority over one-sided armaments efforts. . . . "[10]

The Disparity Between Power and Its Applicability

Another factor influencing security policy in the post-war world is that economic and military power does not necessarily translate into political influence. One reason for this is that economic power is widely diffused, with a number of states like Brazil, India and South Korea having sizeable industrial bases of their own. Another is that the industrialized states are competing among themselves for access to raw materials, for markets and in some instances for political influence, which means that less developed countries can minimize external influences by diversifying sources of support. A third is that states controlling critical natural resources such as oil, copper and chromium can themselves exert pressures against more industrialized states, as shown by the Arab oil embargo of 1973. But the fourth, and most important, is that interdependence makes difficult the use of economic power for punitive purposes; how can the Federal Republic of Germany, one-third of whose goods and services goes to foreign markets, cut off any sizeable proportion of its trade without great harm to its economy?

As for the use of military power, this is constrained in the first instance by the costs and the risks of war, which in the nuclear age must include the risk that any clash between the superpowers (or between one superpower and a close associate of the other) may well escalate to nuclear war. It is also constrained by the relative increase in the military capabilities, economic resources and political backing of other actors; if the United States had attempted to blockade Iran in 1978, as some proposed, the task would have been costly and difficult, if not impossible. A third constraint, which would also apply in the case above, is that international norms inhibit the use of military power, particularly by the major powers, or at least exact heavy political costs for that use, as the Soviets found out in Afghanistan. Thus, entirely aside from the fact that each superpower can—and frequently does—counter the attempts of the other to achieve political gains through economic pressures or military actions, the environment itself limits the application of force.

In the case of the United States, the lessons drawn from this have been mixed. On occasions, it has employed force and shouldered the costs, which in the case of Vietnam were indeed heavy. On other occasions, as during the Iranian hostage crisis, it has sat by in humiliating impotence. In still others it has relied on proxies, as with the South Africans in Angola; however, it is not always possible to find such proxies, as successive failures to create a Jordanian "strike force" for operations along the Persian Gulf have demonstrated. Most recently it has augmented the forces available for operations outside Europe, both as a means of suasion and as a hedge against efforts by others to use force. Whether, however, even the considerable increase in military power sponsored by the Reagan Administration will bring comparable political benefits is at best doubtful.

In the economic field, the lessons also have been mixed. The principal result of embargoes aimed at influencing political behavior, such as that on grain sales to the Soviet Union and that on trade with Nicaragua, has been to encourage these countries to turn to other sources of supply.[b] Seizures of assets and freezes on credit (as with Iran and Poland) have certainly affected the economic well-being of those countries but have had little impact upon their policies. Better success has been achieved with economic and military assistance, which has been used to reward old friends and to encourage new ones (such as Egypt, which had at one time been heavily dependent on the USSR), to buttress sagging regimes (as in the Sudan or in Zaire), to persuade associated states to support U.S. programs (as in the case of Pakistan, through which passes American aid to the Afghan "freedom fighters") and as an implicit *quid pro quo* for base rights, as with the Philippines and Somalia. By and large, however, the political influence gained by economic suasion or dissuasion is markedly disproportionate to the absolute and relative economic power of the United States, which still accounts for 40% of the world's gross national product.

As for the Federal Republic, it is fully conscious of the disparity between West German military power and its application, which in Europe is impossible except within the framework of the Atlantic Alliance and then only if attacked. By design, it has few capabilities for power projection elsewhere and little interest in expanding them. While it is cognizant of the new challenge arising in the Third World, from Soviet "dynamic offensive operations" as well as from intrinsic causes, it relies upon its allies, and especially upon the United States, to meet those challenges. Its own efforts are almost entirely in the economic field, where trade, aid and technical assistance are utilized both to serve West German interests and to promote economic development and political stability, thereby reducing the likelihood that other threats will materialize. If they have so far had little success in the latter endeavor, this may reflect the intransigence of the problem as much as the relevance of the economic instrument.

The Division of Europe

In some measure this is because Germany, in the heart of a divided Europe, is itself divided; both West German interests and threats to those interests are primarily Euro-centric. Moreover, because one-half of Europe is under Soviet influence and the other, albeit less completely, under that of the United States, the FRG finds itself caught up in the rivalry between the superpowers, in the confrontation between the two blocs.

West Germany has sought to accommodate itself to this situation by attaching itself firmly to the United States, by integrating its forces into NATO and by developing its security policy within the framework of the Atlantic Alliance; in this way, it hopes both to shelter under the "nuclear umbrella" and to guard against the possibility of Soviet aggression or, what is feared more, Soviet political pressures backed by the threat of force. At the same time, it has sought to resolve the "German question" by maintaining close economic ties with the GDR, by bending every effort to ameliorate the conditions of citizens of that state and by probing for ways in which a closer association can be formed. This *Ostpolitik* extends also to relations with the Soviet Union, in part because its acquiescence in any "coming together" of the two German states is essential, in part because détente is viewed as enhancing security.

In pursuit of these two goals the FRG has tailored its forces to meet NATO requirements, has assigned those forces to NATO, and has refrained from developing weapons or undertaking missions (such as that of protecting access to the Persian Gulf) which might, to Soviet eyes, suggest larger West German aspirations. Simultaneously it has, in concert with its NATO allies, sought to alleviate Soviet (and East European) fears by promoting arms control measures in Europe, with particular emphasis upon mutual and balanced force reductions and confidence-building measures. In short, the FRG has espoused the concept of "defense and détente" as the best way of coping with its particular situation.

To the United States also the division of Europe, which brought half a dozen states under Soviet influence and placed Soviet troops in the heart of Germany, had enormous consequences. To cope with this alteration in the balance of power, the United States abandoned its policy of "no entangling alliances" and formed NATO, undertook to assist the member nations in improving their defense capabilities, itself maintained large forces in Western Europe, and assumed primary responsibility for the military leadership of the Alliance and for its defense policy. This is not the place to discuss all the nuances of that policy (for which see Chapter 2,) but only to point out its implications. For one thing sizeable elements of the U.S. armed forces were deployed in, or earmarked for potential use in, the

European theater and as much as half the defense budget was spent on those forces. For another, the weapons, the forces and the doctrine of the Army, the Tactical Air Force and large portions of the Navy were tailored primarily to the conduct of war in Europe. For a third, the likelihood of such a war was a major influence on decisions on other politico-military issues; thus, one contingency that worried planners during the Cuban Missile Crisis was that the Soviets might seize West Berlin if the Americans invaded Cuba. And for a fourth, many of the programs for strategic nuclear forces, and the concepts for their employment, stemmed from the desire to maintain the credibility of the deterrent against Soviet attacks on, or pressures against, Western Europe. Hence, militarily as well as politically the focus on Europe impacted significantly on American security and security policy.

"High Tech" and Defense Policy

The "technological revolution" in weaponry which began with the invention of radar and the development of nuclear weapons before and during World War II also had a marked effect. The latter event has vastly altered the bases of military power, overcome limitations of time and space, and exposed countries to new dangers, against which the traditional virtues and the traditional programs offer no defense.

This is as true of the United States as of any other country, in that the safeguards afforded by distance and oceans no longer exist: in less than 24 hours the Soviet Union could, if it so chose, destroy the United States as a functioning entity. That the U.S. could, before or after such an attack, wreak similar damage upon the USSR only emphasizes the impact of technology upon security.

As far as the United States is concerned, this had led to reliance upon deterrence rather than upon defense, at least at the continental level, and to a consequent preoccupation with the size, capabilities, vulnerabilities and responsiveness of strategic nuclear forces. It has led to an equal preoccupation with ways of minimizing the likelihood of all-out nuclear war while still preserving the credibility of the nuclear guarantee to the allies, and this in turn to experimentation not only with weaponry but with doctrine, as in the concept of flexible response. Thus, the post-war vulnerability of the United States has induced far-reaching changes in both policies and programs.

Technological innovations have, however, neither begun nor ended with the first nuclear explosion: they have resulted in space-based reconnaissance vehicles, global communications systems, deep diving submarines, laser aiming devices and a host of other developments that have drastically affected the capabilities and the costs of armed forces. As far as the United States is concerned this has led first of all to an emphasis upon "high tech" in the design of weapons, partly to offset the numerical superiority of Soviet conventional forces, partly to meet the manifold requirements of its global mission. It has encouraged the development of far-reaching command, control, communications and intelligence (C³I) systems, and military doctrines (as for Airland 2000, for "protracted nuclear conflict" and, most recently, for the Strategic Defense Initiative) which would be impossible without these systems. It has induced a "technology race" with the USSR in which each side seeks to obtain advantages or to blunt the other's edge in weaponry, with consequent difficulties in negotiating arms limitations. And it has meant that here again the United States, by virtue of its resources and its priorities, fosters dependency on the part of the allies, who can compete only in limited areas and who frequently find that modernization of their armed forces is contingent on willingness to "Buy American."

Both aspects of the "technological revolution" have also had a marked impact on the security policy of the FRG. The advent of nuclear weapons has left West Germany vulnerable to a threat against which it can muster neither deterrent nor defense, leaving it totally dependent on the U.S. nuclear guarantee. Even if it were to overcome the political and psychological obstacles to nuclearization (which is unlikely in the near future) it would have a long way to go in building forces which could carry out even the limited mission of the French *force de frappe*: "to tear off an arm" from an attacker. Hence, the FRG is inextricably caught up in schemes to bind other nuclear powers to its defense, of which the "double-track decision" on the deployment in Europe of intermediate-range nuclear weapons is only one example.

Other technological innovations such as precision-guided munitions, cluster bombs, laser directed artillery and antitank weapons, hand held anti-aircraft missiles like the Stinger, and so on, may make a more positive contribution to West German security by enhancing the advantages of the defender over the attacker—though this is not yet certain. Such innovations are, however, costly to develop and even more costly to produce and maintain; moreover, West Germany lacks the research and development base essential to an accross-the-board effort as well as the resources to enlarge it. (Although comparative dollar figures may be misleading, the Pentagon in FY 1986 spent on R&D alone almost $30 billion, a sum half again as large as the defense budget of the FRG.) Thus the Federal Republic has been unable to take full advantage of technological innovations to offset the superiority in numbers and equipment possessed by an adversary who is also qualitatively improving his forces.

The International Economic System

As indicated earlier, the international economic system has changed greatly from that of fifty years ago, when a handful of (largely European) states dominated the system: the diffusion of industry, the internationalization of business, and the use of international financial institutions—to say nothing of the transformation of former colonies into independent states—have all had their effects. This system is marked not only by new players, such as the Soviet Union, Saudi Arabia and Brazil, but also by new rules, with close attention paid to the political and social effects of economic decisions, whether these be with respect to loans and grants, to investments in other countries, to the stabilization of commodity prices or to a host of other settlements by intergovernmental bodies, by governments, by multinational corporations and by trade associations. One does not have to be a Marxist to acknowledge that while economics may not determine politics it certainly influences it—a fact of which both the United States and the Federal Republic are highly aware.

In the case of the United States, its increasing stake in economic activities overseas, its growing dependence on foreign markets and foreign resources (for which see below) and its consequent reliance upon freedom of access for itself, its trading partners and its allies, all multiply American global interests and generate greater U.S. involvement in an increasingly interdependent world. At the same time, the heightened level of international economic activities, the growth or re-vitalization of other economies and the establishment of new trading patterns all mean that the once dominant position of the United States in the international economy has diminished—with a consequent diminution in its ability to utilize its economic power for the promotion of national interests. Hence, economic policy is more important than ever, both in and of itself and because of its implications for security.

By and large, the United States aims at creating and maintaining a world in which its basic national needs (as for access to resources) can be met, in which its economy can flourish and in which its economic institutions can function effectively. To a large degree the U.S. relies on economic and political measures to insure that its needs for raw materials and for access to markets are met, but it also offers military inducements to states controlling essential resources, just as it does to states occupying strategic geographic positions or possessing forces which could be utilized to serve common interests. In both cases economic support is frequently linked to, or followed by, military aid, including the provision of equipment, the construction of facilities, the dispatch of trainers, etc.; in fact, in many instances, economic assistance is designed to help support a larger or more modern military establishment than a country could otherwise manage. While economic interests may in some instances determine security interests, they are frequently juxtaposed, and the instruments for achieving them are virtually indistinguishable.

The foreign economic policies designed to promote growth take many forms: loans to exporters, tax credits, anti-dumping laws, mutual reductions in tariffs, etc. Because of the pattern of U.S. trade and the nature of the opportunities for U.S. investment, most of these involve allies or neutrals rather than adversaries. Their impact on security is largely indirect, as when disputes over the "dumping" of steel products, or concerns over high interest rates, cause divisions among the allies. And while these can be serious, they are usually less disruptive of cohesion than specific policies aimed at achieving specific politico-military objectives, such as barring the transfer of advanced turbines for gas pipelines to the USSR or precluding any non-nuclear powers from obtaining the equipment required for reprocessing spent fuel rods, thereby obtaining weapons-grade dissionable materials.

The third economic interest, that of maintaining a world in which U.S. economic institutions can function effectively, has perhaps more of an effect on security. One reason for this is that efforts to create such a world involve the United States in disputes with countries espousing different economic philosophies or emphasizing government-controlled corporations rather than privately-owned ones, which was a factor in the differences over exploitation of ocean resources at the Law of the Sea Conference. Another is that one of the favored institutions, the multinational corporation, is often viewed as an instrument of American imperialism designed to exploit local labor and resources, to channel investment into areas preferred by the United States and to enhance U.S. influence[11]. A third is that efforts to shape the world to the U.S. fashion, and/or to support multinational corporations abroad, have led to the utilization of non-economic instruments of policy, as when the United States supported the overthrow of President Salvador Allende of Chile, who was proposing to nationalize mines owned by Anaconda Copper. And although the United States has not so far used force to alter the economic systems of other countries, a policy of opposition to "Marxism" and "totalitarianism" sometimes induces actions which could ultimately have this effect.

The Federal Republic of Germany, even more than the United States, must live within and work within this new economic system. Its resource base is smaller than that of the United States, its dependence on imports of oil and other critical raw materials is much greater and its reliance on foreign trade, both to finance imports and to stimulate the domestic economy, is much higher. If, however, its needs are relatively more pressing than those of the United States its aspirations are more modest and its policies less ambitious.

In the first place, the Federal Republic is concerned primarily with improving its economic position rather than with achieving political objectives through economic means; only in the case of the German Democratic Republic does politics clearly govern economics. In the second place, the FRG could not, even if it would, exert the same degree of influence on the international economic system as does the United States, largely because of the difference in the sizes of the two economies, in the extent of investment overseas and in the impact on international finance. In the third place, West German aid programs are much less security-oriented than are those of the United States, with arms sales rigidly controlled and economic assistance more largely directed to the promotion of economic growth and social justice in recipient countries; although there are (as with Turkey) instances when security interests clearly dictate priorities in allocations, the FRG even then focuses almost entirely on non-military assistance. In short, although the Federal Republic also aspires to the maintenance of a world in which its economy can flourish, its means of achieving this objective differ markedly from those employed by the United States.

Major Influences from the Domestic Environment

The Geo-Economic Base

The Federal Republic of Germany. The Federal Republic crams over 60 million people into an area roughly comparable to that of Oregon, an area which contains the fourth largest industrial base in the world and supports a foreign trade which amounts to almost one third of gross industrial product. Futhermore, the territory occupied by the FRG is singularly lacking in the raw materials essential to the maintenance of such a base; save for coal and some chemicals, the FRG must import virtually everything needed to keep its industry going.

Obviously, West Germany is exceedingly vulnerable to any stoppage of its foreign trade, and especially of its imports of oil and other critical raw materials. There is, however, little that it can do about this, as it lacks both the political influence to head off such interruptions and the military forces to deter them; even if the Basic Law (the equivalent of the American Constitution) did not preclude the dispatch of armed forces outside the NATO area, the Federal Republic has neither the ships and aircraft required for "power projection" nor the bases essential to their operation. In peacetime, therefore, it leaves largely to the United States the responsibility for coping with any threat to its economic lifelines and in wartime it relies on its NATO Allies to safeguard these same lines of communication. This is not, however, the only respect in which the West German economic base is vulnerable, since as few as twenty 5-megaton weapons could virtually destroy the principal centers of population and industry.

Since this disastrous outcome can only be avoided if nuclear war never comes, the West German emphasis on deterrence is understandable. So is the emphasis on checking any conventional attack as far forward as possible, as 30% of the people live in a strip 100 km deep along the intra-German border, a strip which also contains 25% of German industry.[12] To insure that this territory will not be overrun, the FRG has insisted on, and the Alliance has adopted, a strategy of "Forward Defense," involving the stationing close to the border of most of the forces available to NATO and the maintenance of those forces in a high state of readiness.

Although the West Germans insist that the principle of "Forward Defense" does not preclude mobile operations, it is obvious that they are thinking of these in tactical terms. Many planners are uncertain that what amounts essentially to a linear defense can be maintained against the tank-heavy mobile forces the WTO can bring to bear, especially if these are used to penetrate and disrupt NATO defenses, as seemingly envisaged. Accordingly, there have been differences between the West Germans and their allies—notably the Americans—both as to where the line should be drawn and how it should be maintained, a point which will be discussed further in Chapter 4.

The United States. For the United States, vulnerability presents a different problem, in that the concern is largely about a strategic nuclear attack. At various times, this concern has manifested itself in plans for counterforce strikes or in emphasis on passive and active defenses but it has usually subsided as the technical difficulties or the financial costs of attempting to limit damage have become evident. Recently, however, it has emerged again, in the form of proposals for layered defense systems incorporating space-borne anti-missile lasers or kinetic energy devices. If these proposals can be—and are—put into practice, the implications for the credibility of deterrence and for the prospects of survival would be enormous. So, too, would be the implications for the Alliance, some of whose leaders have questioned both the feasibility and the desirability of abandoning the strategy of deterrence for one of defense and others of whom have said that if anti-missile systems are to be deployed they should be extended to Europe—a problem of a very different nature. And so also would be the implications for the military competition between the U.S. and the USSR, which cannot be expected to stand idly by while the United States erects a shield against Soviet missiles.

This does not mean that the United States has no other worries. World War II hastened a process that had begun well before World War I: a change from exporting raw materials to importing them. By the mid-70s, U.S. "strategic dependency" in 23 critical minerals, based on their military and economic uses, world reserves, concentration of supply and substitutability, had risen to over 50%, and in some instances, as with cobalt, chromium and vanadium, this dependence was absolute.[13] Additionally, both proven reserves in, and production of, petroleum have been falling, and the United States has for some years been importing over half its requirements of this essential item. Furthermore, dependency is expected to increase over time, so that by the year 2000 the U.S. will be importing well over half its requirements of even comparatively common minerals such as copper, iron and lead.[14]

The meaning of these changes for security depends on whether one is thinking of demand in peacetime or in wartime, and whether that war is non-nuclear or nuclear. It also depends on whether any disruption is brought about by economic disputes, by civil strife (as happened in Zaire in 1978), by deliberate withholding (as during the Arab oil embargo of 1973) or by interdiction. Thus one study of the availability of, and circumstances that could interfere with, peacetime supply of several critical minerals found only a few isolated cases where large disruptions (50-100%) lasting over 6 months had a 25% probability of occurrence.[15] And these contingencies are, of course, those that are are guarded against by the U.S. strategic stockpile.

Nevertheless, American policy has aimed at avoiding serious disruptions by maintaining friendly relations with significant producers (including "par-

iah states" such as South Africa), by granting some of them dispropor-
tionately large economic aid and by providing limited assistance in the
development and exploitation of alternative sources of supply. More importantly, it has tended to view seriously political changes (such as the
election of Allende in Chile or the coming to power of Neto in Angola)
which seemed likely to jeopardize access to key raw materials, as well as
military actions, such as the bombing of tankers in the Persian Gulf, which
actually did so.

By and large, however, these kinds of disruptions do not place significant
demands on American military forces: the use of a wing of transport
aircraft to carry French and Moroccan paratroopers to Zaire or the movement of a carrier task force closer to the Straits of Hormuz are eminently
feasible. There are, however, two kinds of contingencies which would require
that the armed forces exert every effort to insure access to raw materials.

One of these is, of course, a major conventional war, which would
generate an enormous surge in requirements, especially if it were accompanied by Soviet attempts to destroy sources of supply or to launch air
strikes and submarine attacks against merchant vessels transporting materials to the United States (and its allies). Indeed, it is this possibility
which has both stimulated the stockpiling of critical raw materials (including oil) and led to the Navy's being given the mission of safeguarding the
sea lines of communication. In the past, neither of these functions has
received strong and consistent support, largely because any conflict involving the USSR was expected to "go nuclear" long before it would be
necessary, or feasible, to organize a regular flow of supplies to the United
States. If, however, the Reagan Administration tries seriously to prepare
for "protracted conventional conflict" this situation may change—and with
it the need for forces that could conduct large-scale and sustained operations
to safeguard both the sources and the shipment of critical raw materials.

The second contingency, is, of course, that of the seizure of the major
oil fields in and around the Persian Gulf, whether by local elements or, as
is more commonly assumed in the United States, by Soviet troops. Although
the immediate impact on the United States would be small, as only 5% of
its oil comes from that region, over a third of the supplies for Western
Europe and two-thirds of those going to Japan orginate in the Persian
Gulf; whatever the level of stockpiles, the effectiveness of cuts in consumption and the efficiency of measures for sharing resources, the economic
consequences for the Western world could be dire. So too would be the
political implications of a takeover, which the United States is pledged to
resist. And against the more dangerous, if less likely, possibility, that the
USSR would attempt such an operation, the United States is building a
Rapid Deployment Force which will ultimately surpass its present level of
4 1/3 divisions, 7 Air Force and 1 Marine Tactical Fighter Wings, 3 Carrier
Battle Groups and a host of ancillary and support elements.[16] Thus, protection of access to oil, through only one mission of the Rapid Deployment
Force, is important enough to generate substantial requirements-at sub-
stantial costs.

Economic Interests

The United States. As indicated previously, American security policy is to some extent influenced by the need to function in an increasingly interdependent international economic system and to cope with potential disruptions in that system which could adversely affect the U.S. economy, in peace or in war. By and large, there has been strong support for the general policy of insuring access to markets, opportunities for investment and the maintenance of "free" economies throughout as much of the world as possible. And there is recognition that this policy requires greater focus on the Third World than on Europe, which accounts for only a quarter of U.S. foreign trade and virtually none of its imports of oil and of critical raw materials.[17]

Conversely, attempts to adjust economic policy to meet security needs have run into significant opposition. Thus, some multinational corporations, who may deem their business interests best served by freedom of choice with respect to the location of factories and the transfer of technology, have not been entirely happy with the prohibition of loans to Poland, constraints on exchanges of information with subsidiaries in Europe or bans on the sale of nuclear reprocessing equipment to Brazil. Similarly, some domestic industries, arguing that "national security" requires a strong industrial base, have sought to limit imports of steel from the European Community or to restrict the number of automobiles that Japan can ship to the United States[c], measures which could have an adverse impact on relations with Allies. Thus there is a "pull and haul" between particular economic interests in the United States and those elements responsible for the formulation of security policy which makes that policy less cohesive and less constant than one might suppose.

However, a more direct influence on security policy arises from another economic interest, that of maintaining a strong, resilient and advanced base for the development and production of military equipment. One does not have to accept *in toto* President Dwight D. Eisenhower's warning against the "military-industrial complex" to recognize that the symbiotic relationship between defense contractors and the Pentagon involves the former in the design of weapons as well as in their production and in the support of defense programs from which they themselves benefit and the latter in a pattern of contracting which not only shields a dozen or so large aerospace corporations against competition but also rewards them for activities aimed at inducing the government to buy, or to buy more of, particular weapons systems.[18] At the micro-level, this loose alliance inhibits the development and procurement of weapons on an intra-alliance basis—as, to be honest, do its counterparts in other Western countries. At the macro-level, its members manifest a not-surprising congruence of views concerning the nature of the threat, the desirability of strong measures to cope with that threat and the need for a military posture which can both underpin and if necessary carry out those measures. Without arguing that these results are "good" or "bad" it is possible to say that they are important, to détente as well as to defense, and to arms control as well as to the effectiveness of the Atlantic Alliance.

There is another, if less powerful, interest which runs directly counter to that of the military-industrial complex: that of the groups which consider current defense programs detrimental to the economy. This opposition contains elements who argue that the diversion of scientific talent, the distortion of investment patterns and the sheer magnitude of the defense effort all act as drags upon the economy; in consequence, modernization is impeded, growth is slowed and unemployment remains high. And it contains others who argue that dollars spent for defense cannot be allocated to the refurbishment of the national infrastructure, to the clean-up of the environment, to the re-building of cities, to the improvement of education or to a host of other pressing needs. In brief, the opposition suggests that the maintenance of a strong and stable economic system, which is essential to security, requires a different set of priorities than those now governing.

This philosophical dispute over the allocation of resources at the macro-economic level takes on form and meaning at the micro-economic level, i.e., in the national budget. At this level, the differences show up primarily in the competition between the military and the civilian sectors: shall expenditures for defense or those for social security payments be frozen, shall monies for research be allocated to the National Institutes of Health or to the Strategic Defense Initiative Organization? They also show up, however, in debates over tax policy, where decisions on acceptable levels of depletion allowances, rates of depreciation of equipment, deductibility of state and local taxes and a host of other measures will affect the vitality of the private sector, the ability of organs of government to meet social needs and the welfare of people throughout the country. In the past six years, defense programs (and tax cuts) have received priority, even at the expense of sizeable budgetary deficits; now, opinion seems to be turning against that approach, with Congress and the Presidency seeking to cut deficits even if this results in a slow down in spending.

Although it is too early to say how these developments will affect the on-going modernization and strengthening of U.S. armed forces (and, some would say, the negotiations on arms control at Geneva) they have already opened up new possiblities. One is that high cost research and development activities will either be recommended for cancellation (as has the Sergeant York divisional anti-aircraft gun) or slowed, as has the Administration's program for "Star Wars;" indeed, a whole school of "modernizers" calling for simpler and cheaper weapons has emerged in the Congress and in some quarters of the defense establishment. Another is that strategic doctrines which are dependent on complex command, control, communication and intelligence systems, as would be true of FOFA (Follow-on Forces Attack) and "protracted nuclear conflict," may be questioned on the ground of cost. And a third, already in evidence, is that pressure may be put upon the Allies for larger defense contributions; indeed, many Americans feel that the Allies are getting a "free ride," both with respect to their relative defense expenditures and with respect to U.S. security policies designed to insure access to Third World markets and sources of supply, as in the Persian Gulf. And while there are at least two sides to this issue, as will be seen in Chapters 5 and 6, in this instance also "Perceptions are more important than truth."

The Federal Republic of Germany. As an industrial country dependent on exports, the Federal Republic of Germany is especially interested in access to markets throughout the world. This access is vital because an economy forced to turn back to a home market would quickly collapse. The common European market serves this interest, but it is also—and just as essentially—served by access to the American market and, in the context of this study, to that offered by Eastern Europe and the Soviet Union.

Wherever there is a conflict of economic interests in transatlantic trade, the conviction has always predominated on both sides of the Atlantic that the Alliance and common interests in security policy forbid tougher forms of West-West competition like mutual sanctions. It is more difficult, however, from a German point of view, to sustain a common embargo policy towards Eastern bloc countries. The high-tech goods on the COCOM list, classified in the NATO framework as being of military importance, are often difficult to identify and to distinguish from permissable items. Moreover, while the Federal Republic of Germany abides by the restrictions—agreed upon within the NATO framework—on the proliferation of advanced technology to Eastern bloc countries, the opportunity to trade with COMECON states plays a greater role than it does in the U.S.A. Furthermore, the suspicion that the COCOM lists are being used to obstruct West German trade with the East, thereby improving the competetive advantage of American industry in the global market, puts a strain on the German-American relationship.

From a West German point of view, East-West economic relations also affect security policy. Trade agreements, especially long-term ties, are seen as elements of mutual dependence which enhance general interest in peaceful relations and induce the participants to exercise moderation in crisis situations.

Arms production in the Federal Republic of Germany does not (yet) play such an important role as does the American arms industry. So far the "military industrial complex" cited by President Eisenhower in his farewell speech has not developed to the same extent in the Federal Republic of Germany. Nevertheless, there are more and more voices warning against the possibility of such a complex emerging in West Germany, too. This would mean that security policy and military technical decisions would be influenced, if not dominated, by industrial-political interests. (On the other hand, there are an increasing number of critics of the political economy in the Federal Republic of Germany who demand that economic behavior be adapted to meet ecological imperatives, an approach which could, if carried through, drastically limit some armaments industries.)

In the last few years the Federal Republic of Germany has developed into one of the greatest arms exporters in the world. Theoretically, German law forbids the supply of arms to areas of tension and the free export of arms is only possible within the NATO area. Increasingly, however, German weapons or component elements are also—via coproduction agreements and triangular deals—to be found in crisis areas throughout the world. If there should, in the foreseeable future, be widespread efforts to impose restrictions on the export of arms not only the U.S. but also the Federal Republic of Germany would have to be involved.

West German military expenditures have grown more consistently over the last two decades than has military spending in America, which shot up during the Vietnam War, then went down and, during the Reagan Administration, shot up again. Since the late sixties, when the *Bundeswehr* was established and equipped, both left- and right-wing governments have, fairly constantly, kept increases in the military budget slightly below the growth rate of public spending. In view of the economic and ecological tasks facing the national economy in the Federal Republic of Germany, a change in this policy is not to be expected; in other words, it is unlikely that military spending will be increased significantly. This means that there are limits to the growth of the arms industry, unless it expands through arms exports.

The emphasis on "high tech" also influences military production in the Federal Republic, where the arms industry has, in the three decades since the establishment of the *Bundeswehr*, greatly changed its production base. In the Federal Republic, too, there is a debate on whether large, expensive weapons like airplanes, ships and tanks should continue to be procured in ever smaller quantities, or whether cheaper equipment should be procured in larger quantities. Critics of defense procurement, like their counterparts in the United States, doubt the cost effectiveness of an arms policy which invests primarily in advanced weapons and equipment, to the detriment of simpler, more easily operable and more readily maintainable weaponry.

Political Structure and Defense Policy

The United States. Far more important than either of the economic influences mentioned above are the political ones, both structural and attitudinal, because these affect directly the nature and the durability of defense policy. In discussing the former, one must begin by noting that the political structure of the United States tends to fragment authority and to diffuse responsiblity, even in the area of defense policy. In part this is a result of the "separation of powers" enshrined in the Constitution, under which Congress and the President are called upon to play different but interrelated roles. Thus, the Congress passes the basic legislation organizing and governing the armed forces, appropriates money for their support, approves appointments of officers and senior officials, declares war and ratifies treaties of peace, while the President (with his staff) drafts enabling legislation, prepares the defense budget, selects officers and officials for key posts, serves as Commander-in-Chief of the armed forces and decides on their deployment and employment, in peace as well as in war.

In theory, therefore, the Congress and the President share responsiblity for defense policy but in practice that is not the case: over the years a number of things have combined to enhance the power of the President in this area. One has derived from the international environment itself, with its continuing instabilities and rapid changes; crises such as the invasion of South Korea in 1950 or the dispatch of Soviet missiles to Cuba in 1962 tend to enhance presidential authority as well as to increase presidential responsibilities. Another has stemmed from technological innovations; with the United States subject to devastating attack almost without warning the responsibility for coping with that attack falls upon the President, who must accordingly assure himself of the ability of the armed forces to provide that warning and to respond to that attack. A third has resulted from the (partial) establishment of presidential control over the policy-making process, through the National Security Council and its staff, and over the armed services, through the Department of Defense. A fourth has come from the sheer magnitude and complexity of security issues and security programs, with which a divided and fractionated Congress is ill-equipped to deal. And a fifth has derived from the ability of the President to influence public and elite opinions, by deeds as well as by words, an ability which that same Congress cannot match. Today, therefore, the President is paramount.

To say that the President is paramount does not mean that he is all-powerful: the structure of the Executive Branch, the nature of the Congress and the extent of public participation in decision-making all militate against a centrally-imposed defense policy. One barrier to such a policy is the existence of four separate armed services, Army, Navy, Air Force and Marine Corps, which compete among themselves for prestige and for resources and which tend to espouse military doctrines and defense programs reflecting the experience—and the interests—of their particular service; although the Department of Defense has gained power since its establishment some forty years ago, there are still limits on its ability to rule in its own house. Another barrier is that a similar situation exists at Cabinet level, with not only Defense but State, Treasury, the Central Intelligence Agency, the Federal Emergency Management Agency and other institutions all involved in the formulation and implementaton of national security policy. Although coordinating mechanisms such as the National Security Council also exist at this level, these cannot create policy nor even effectively monitor its conduct in the face of opposition by, or differences among, powerful agencies such as State and Defense.[19] And while there is little question that the President can, when he chooses, impose his will on these agencies, there is grave doubt as to his ability to do so on a continuous basis.

Moreover, Congress still serves as a reviewer and critic of policies, through its powers of inquiry and oversight, as an authorizer of legislation and as a provider of funds; indeed, congressional influence on security policy is greatest in budgetary matters, as mentioned earlier in the discussion of economic interests. Moreover, the Congress is able to act independently of the President because its members have a different political base: an indirect consequence of the federal system is that national political parties are agglomerations of state and regional parties, rather than cohesive entities, more or less responsive to central leadership, as is the case in parlimentary governments. At one level, this means that the President must woo individual congressmen and senators on particular issues, with due regard for the domestic implications of those issues, such as their impact on regional economies or on given communities. At another level, it means that it is difficult for the President to create and maintain a consensus on defense policy in terms of strategic concepts, force levels, weapons systems programs and budgets—and agreements on broad principles such as the centrality of deterrence are largely meaningless when agreement on operational requirements is lacking.

This difficulty of achieving consensus is compounded by the fact that the American system offers manifold opportunities for public participation in the policy process, both through political channels and outside them—and publics are both fickle and inconsistent. (Thus, according to one study, 56% of those polled in 1984 thought that "Wherever there's trouble in the world . . . chances are the Soviets are behind it," while 70% agreed that this idea is "a dangerous oversimplification."[20]) But though public opinion may set limits to defense policy, these limits tend to be broad and non-operational. Moreover, under normal circumstances, public opinion comes to bear on policy only indirectly, when political leaders incorporate it into their own decision-processes or when elites give it focus and mobilize it to support their own positions; only rarely, as during the Vietnam War, does public opinion directly and immediately affect policy.

More significant is the role played by elites, and particularly by public elites,[d] whose interest is high and whose involvement is both more pronounced and more effective. Through personal interactions, lobbying, dissemination of information, mobilization of particular publics and/or other influential elites, such as businessmen and clergy, public elites are able to influence local politicians and party leaders, legislators, staffs of senior officials and frequently those officials themselves; thus, Dr. Edward Teller, the "father of the H-Bomb," was apparently instrumental in persuading President Reagan of the feasibility and desirability of the Strategic Defense Initiative. In brief, public elites both participate in the formulation of policy and help to obtain its acceptance or rejection; they, rather than the media, constitute the "fourth branch of government" in the United States. And this "branch" frequently finds itself at odds with the President, the Congress, or both.

The Federal Republic of Germany. The difference between the German parliamentary cabinet system and the American presidential system is manifest in the decision-making process on security policy.

There is no figure in German politics with power comparable to that of the American president. The Federal Chancellor may, according to the consitution, determine policy guidelines, but important security policy decisions are made at government level in the Cabinet or the Federal Security Council. In the Cabinet the Minister of Defense and the Foreign Minister play the most important parts. Nor does the latter always play "second fiddle"; for example, the Foreign Ministry is responsible for all arms control matters and the Minister of Defense has only an advisory function in this area. The Federal Security Council consists of the ministers of the responsible departments, the Inspector General of the *Bundeswehr* and the Head of the Intelligence Service. Unlike the National Security Council, it meets regularly and discusses security policy decisions of general principle.

Parliament has little influence on individual security policy decisions. The only way the *Bundestag* can have a say in defense policy is via the budget. As a result of the experiences of German history, the consitution lays down that the strength and structure of the *Bundeswehr* must be fixed every year in the Budget Act. This means that the *Bundestag* Budget Committee has a strong position. The Defense Committee, as a body which only has an advisory function in security policy and procurement planning, is weaker. Its dependence on the information given to it by the Ministry of Defense does not allow it to make any forward planning in security policy. It can only implement policies for which the government has already prepared the ground; alternatives are seldom discussed.

On the whole, the parliamentary power in the Federal Republic of Germany is weaker than the executive. The government has such a lead in information and know-how that Parliament, which only has a tiny apparatus at its disposal, cannot catch up with it.

The political parties play a more important role in the development of informed political opinion in the Federal Republic than in the United States. They are a transmission belt between the politically active middle classes and political decision-making bodies. In the parties fundamental political questions are debated and—together with basic statements of the party's political program—passed as resolutions at party conferences. The parties also perform the function of grooming and selecting the politicians who will ultimately hold high posts in the Federal Government. For this reason discussions of security policy take place with the parties. In all the big parties, the SPD, the CDU and the FDP, there is at national level a security policy committee in which politicians, experts, scientists and also military adivisors discuss and formulate the basic line to be taken by the party in its statements on security policy and in its party conference resolutions.

Scientific expertise does not have such a broad basis in the Federal Republic of Germany as it does in the U.S.A. Institutes working in the field of security policy are not to be found on the scale of, for example, the RAND Corporation. On the other hand, the German institutes are not so dependent on the government of the day. Those which could be classified as being closest to the government are the *Stiftung Wissenschaft und Politik*

(Foundation for Science and Politics) near Munich and the *Deutsche Gesellshaft fur Auswärtige Politik* (German Society for Foreign Policy), in Bonn. The three peace research institutes (in Hamburg, Frankfurt and Heidelberg) are completely independent and in 1987 they presented, for the first time, a joint annual report on the policy of peace. With this report, independent institutes confronted government leaders with a scientific analysis and scientifically based options for security policy—not as a document of the political opposition but as a statement of alternative policies, seen from a scientifically detached point of view.

Domestic Support for Foreign and Defense Policy

The United States. The American political structure means that in the United States, even more than in other democratic countries, foreign and defense policies cannot long endure without domestic support. It means also that this support must come from publics and elites as well as from the Congress and from the group of officials and advisors in the Executive Branch who participate in the making of that policy.[21] It is therefore, essential that we know something about past developments and present trends in public and elite opinion—which, as already noted, sets limits to presidential (and congressional) freedom to act and helps determine the nature of particular actions.[22]

The first thing to note is that the American people "have always been able to find a glow of ethics in their foreign policy," deriving in part from the nature of American society and in part from a sense of mission which originated with the Republic. This has led, among other things, to a strong and continuing opposition to international Communism, with over 60% of the American people stating that the United States "should take all steps, including the use of force, to prevent the spread of communism."[23] In practice, however, different "steps" command different levels of support. Sizeable majorities (including a majority of those who deemed the Vietnam War "fundamentally wrong and immoral") would "send troops" to support Western Europe or Japan if these were invaded by the USSR—though leaders are far more willing than the public at large to endorse this course of action. However, this same willingness to help allies does not extend to non-Soviet military operations (such as a North Korean invasion of South Korea or an assault on Israel by the Arab States) nor, most emphatically, does it apply if "leftist guerrillas are about to defeat the government of El Salvador."[24] (Such reluctance to utilize U.S. troops to sustain a friendly government against internal threats is not new: in August 1953, 91% of those citizens polled disapproved of sending U.S. soldiers to help the French in their fight against "the Communists in Indochina.")[25] And it is paralleled by a similar reluctance to use force for other political purposes, whether these be the overthrow of Castro or the punishment of Iran for taking American citizens hostage.

Not surprisingly, this opposition to communism has been reflected in a concern about the military balance, with growing percentages of both publics and elites seeing a shift in favor of the USSR over the past 8-10 years)[26] and, to a lesser extent, in readiness to support programs to strengthen the armed forces. In the past a majority of Americans believed the United States should be stronger than the Soviet Union and to this end were willing to keep up or increase defense expenditures; however, a growing minority deems these too high—a trend which increasingly manifested itself under the Reagan Administration.[27] (Although this shift is more pronounced among those judging the United States equal to or superior to the Soviet Union, a majority of those believing the USSR stronger militarily also oppose further increases in the defense budget[28]— suggesting that factors outside the field of security may moderate opinions on defense spending.) More recently, opinion has shifted further, with more than 80% of those polled indicating that the United States cannot hope to regain nuclear superiority, as the Soviets would simply keep building weapons until they caught up.[29]

This judgment (and a concomitant one that a nuclear war simply cannot be won) has had two important consequences. One is that it has led to a reversal of earlier willingness to risk or to fight nuclear war rather than to accept Soviet domination; "nuclear war is no longer seen as a rational policy for the U.S. government to consider."[30] Over three-quarters of the public believe that the United States should not use nuclear weapons unless they are first used against this country or against its allies—and believe also that this *is* current U.S. policy.[31] The preferences are clear: for less rather than greater reliance on nuclear weapons.

Another consequence is an even stronger interest in arms control, across a spectrum of measures from destruction of all nuclear weapons through a mutual freeze on Soviet and American production to a cessation of the deployment of INF in Europe if the Soviets agree to limit their own forces. This propensity to seek limitations on armaments is hedged with many qualifications, such as the desire for equality in U.S. and Soviet Strategic Nuclear Forces and insistence on verification—the latter reflecting a long-term belief in the insincerity of Soviet proposals on disarmament and on their propensity to cheat. It is, however, indicative of a growing belief that Americans and Soviets are drifting toward catastrophe, that it is time for negotiation, not confrontation and that this must and should extend to over-all U.S. Soviet relations as well as to arms control itself.[32]

In looking at public and elite opinions on foreign and defense policies, a number of factors should be noted. One is that the publics generally tend to be more concerned with issues affecting them personally, such as protecting jobs, maintaining the tariff, etc., than with politico-military issues. Another is that the better-educated elements (i.e., college graduates or those with some college education) generally are more internationalist, less supportive of military spending, and so forth. In consequence there are serious gaps between publics and elites (and between publics and leaders) with respect to support for economic and military assistance, circumstances under which force should be used and enthusiasm for arms control.[33]

A third point to bear in mind is that the elites themselves are often divided over the policies to be pursued. The post-war consensus on foreign policy (which really reflected the temporary predominance of the "Cold War Internationalists")[34] has broken down and the existence of different (and largely incompatible) domestic and foreign policy belief systems among elites may make difficult the construction of any new consensus and the formulation of a "grand strategy" for a changing world.[d] Moreover, such congruence as does exist is between the "Cold War Internationalists" and the "Reindustrializers," whose joint efforts to rebuild U.S. economic and military power, and to re-employ it in pursuit of American interests as they define them, may alienate not only other elements in the United States but also some among our allies. Thus, public support for U.S. defense policy may be more divided and uncertain than usual.

This is true for another reason: such trends as are discernable show that the public was strongly opposed to key policies of the Reagan Administration. While that Administration was discussing a strategy for "protracted nuclear conflict," public opinion is moving in the direction of no nuclear conflict. While Ronald Reagan and his associates stressed the necessity to build weapons as "bargaining chips" in arms control negotiations, 84% of the public said that such a policy would not work. While then Secretary of Defense Caspar Weinberger was urging the President to cease observing the unratified SALT II agreement, the public was prepared for new, unilateral initiatives in arms control. By and large, there are similar differences between public opinion and current policy with respect to further increases in the defense budget, support for the "contras" and, above all, the use of American troops to stem "creeping Communism."

The mere fact that both opinions and policies co-exist suggests that the former have little impact on the latter and to some extent this is true. There have, however, been modifications in Mr. Reagan's position on issues such as arms control and détente, if not in the positions of some of his senior officials. More importantly, there have been significant changes in Congressional attitudes toward defense policies and programs, changes which parellel those in public opinion. Although the end is not yet, one or both chambers of the Congress have recently voted to set severe limits on the production and deployment of the MX, to cut back on R&D for "Star Wars," to freeze for a time the defense budget and otherwise to curtail future increases in defense programs. Moreover, the Senate resoundingly endorsed continued observance of the SALT II agreement when Mr. Reagan was considering abrogating or selectively modifying it. And while the Congress has by no means been opposed to every aspect of the administration's defense policy, nor been united when it was, there has been a marked change from 1980-1981.

What this suggests is that the Reagan Administration will be hard-pressed to continue the policies laid down during its first year in office; even where those policies (as for enhanced conventional force capabilities) may be continued, sizeable budgetary deficits virtually rule out large allocations of resources for their implementation. Only if and as it emphasizes negotiations rather than confrontation is the Administration likely to receive the approval of the "silent majority"—though even that majority may also be concerned lest the United States appear "weak" or seem to be falling behind the Soviets in technology or in weapons. What it suggests even more strongly is that *no* administration may be able to reformulate a consensus on defense policy, barring a change in the world situation which clearly favors either defense or détente. And if that is correct, then the future, like the recent past, is apt to be marked by spurts and starts, by contradictions and compromises, rather than by a coherent and steady policy on which friends and foes can both count.

The Federal Republic. As in the U.S.A., the general public only participates to a limited extent in the discussion of security policy. However, the debate starting in 1979 on NATO's double track decision showed that an unexpectedly large number of politically interested Germans—including members of the younger generation—can become active in security policy questions where there is a special cause. This commitment was manifested not only in demonstrations but also in countless work groups, public debates and active committees.

As is also true in the United States, the press plays a dual role in the Federal Republic of Germany. On the one hand, it educates its readers— within limits—in the complexities of security policy. On the other hand, newspaper, radio and television commentators have a direct influence on political decisions when they articulate a firm opinion. The big daily newspapers and the big radio and television stations have their own security policy correspondents, who can often be found in different political camps; thus, the scientific and political aspects of defense policy are largely inter-mingled.

Serious polls and the results of parliamentary elections show that there is, in the West German population, a broad and strong basic consensus on security policy, a consensus which includes quite explicity and simul-taneously support for the *Bundeswehr*, maintenance of the draft, member-ship of NATO and an active policy of détente towards the East. This basic consensus also helped to ensure the continuity of foreign and security policy and, simultaneously, defense and détente policy wherever there was a change of government—as in 1969, when the Social Democrats came to power, and in 1982, when the Christian Democrats took over.

This positive attitude towards the *Bundeswehr*, the Federal Republic's membership of NATO, and the U.S. presence in Germany has remained constant over the decades. Approximately 80% of the population consider the *Bundeswehr* to be important and believe that it makes peace more secure. Opinion polls since 1968 have revealed that the same percentage of the population believes that the Federal Republic should belong to NATO and that the percentage of those against NATO was well below 10%. The presence of American troops in Europe has also, since 1970, been considered by 70–80% of the population to be imperative, while fewer than 10% believe it to be detrimental.

It is, however, important to realize that, after the topics of jobs and conservation, that of disarmament in East and West is regarded as important by 88% of the population.[35] Thus, these indicators of public support for the American presence, like those for defense in general, must be seen in context.

A Summing Up

The United States

The factors discussed are by no means the only ones influencing U.S. defense policy, which is affected by everything from service rivalries to the level of unemployment. They do, however, seem to be among the most important, both in terms of their impact and in terms of their performance. For example, the geographic position of the United States, its global role and its global rivalry with the Soviet Union have all influenced the existing tendency to emphasize air and naval forces for both "power projection" and for defense against Soviet aggression, and to assign to land forces a secondary (though still important) role. Similarly, that geographic position, which essentially leaves the United States vulnerable only to nuclear attack, has encouraged a focus upon strategic nuclear forces and upon "high technology," as a way to control and direct those forces in the event of war and perhaps as a way to safeguard both forces and people against the effects of such a war.

In some respects, the mission of assisting in the defense of Western Europe represents a diversion from, and a threat to, the previous missions of safeguarding global interests and protecting the American homeland. It is a diversion in that it requires not only sizeable forces but different ones, many of which are less effective elsewhere than they could otherwise be. It is a threat in that it requires the United States to risk nuclear war for purposes other than the (comparatively simple) one of deterring direct attack; moreover, the strategic nuclear forces needed for extended deterrence may well be larger than would otherwise be necessary, and different in nature. Thus one would expect to find a perpetual tension between the two conflicting sets of requirements arising out of the global and the regional role of the United States—as is indeed the case.

This tension is exacerbated rather than alleviated by some of the domestic influences on defense policy. By way of illustration, both the increasing scarcity of resources and some economic thrusts heighten U.S. interest in, and involvement in, the Third World, yet public and elite opinion is strongly opposed to military intervention there, whether for the purpose of aiding friendly regimes or of overthrowing hostile ones. This stands in contrast to the continuing willingness to use U.S. troops should Soviet forces invade Western Europe or Japan, which suggests an emphasis upon regional requirements rather than global ones. Yet the Reagan Administration, as will be seen, has developed a global strategy which it has been seeking to implement by developing global capabilities.[36] Given the costs of this strategy something may have to give, though whether it will be the strategy itself, the (rather inchoate) public opposition to it or that part of the defense program earmarked for forces in Europe is an open question.

The Federal Republic of Germany

No such tension exists within the Federal Republic, which is a regional power with regional interests and concerns. Insofar as it concerns itself with global threats it does so indirectly, by arranging for other allies to cope with them—hopefully in ways which do not enhance the risk of war or run counter to West German interests in the Third World. Its forces are, therefore, tailored for their primary mission: contributing to deterrence by the ability to check a conventional attack should it come.

The problems for the Federal Republic arise from another set of factors. For one, the division of Europe not only enhances threats to security but stands in the way of a pre-eminent national objective: an end to the division of Germany. For another, the superpower rivalry and superpower competition undermine any prospects for ending that division. And for a third, technological innovations mean that West Germany must depend on others to safeguard it from nuclear attack and, to some extent, to help it make its conventional contribution to deterrence. Thus, the fate of the Federal Republic is in the hands of others to a degree that is not true of the United States. And while this is accepted as necessary, it is not relished, as evidenced by the strong public support for détente and for disarmament, as alternative routes to security.

Notes

1. William R. Pierce, "Factors Impinging on U.S. Defense Policy" (Internship Report, Graduate School of Public and International Affairs, University of Pittsburgh, June 1984), especially 1-13.

2. Sir Halford MacKinder, *Democratic Ideals and Reality* (New York: H. Holt & Co, 1942), 150.

3. Arthur Schlesinger, Jr., "Foreign Policy and the American Character," *Foreign Affairs* 62, 1 (Fall 1983), 2.

4. In this connection, see:
- Carl Luders, "*Ideologie und Machtdenken in der sowjetischen Aussenpolitik*," *Aus Politik und Zeitgeschichte, Beilage zur Wochenzeitung Das Parlament* 37 (1981).
- *Deutsche Gesellschaft fur Friedens—und Konfliktforschung (DGFK), Zur Entspannungspolitik in Europa* (Baden Baden: Nornos Verlagsgesellschaft, 1980).
- Wulf-W. Lapins, "*Zur Einschatzung sowjetischer Bedrohung in der westdeutschen Uberregionalen Tages- und Wochenpresse*" (Dissertation, Bonn, 1983).

5. The Federal Minister of Defence, *White Paper 1983* (Bonn: 1983), 33ff.

6. Wolfram F. Hanrieder and Larry V. Buel, *Words and Arms: A Dictionary of Security and Defense Terms, with Supplementary Data* (Boulder, CO: Westview Press, 1979), 29.

7. *Report of Secretary of Defense Harold Brown to the Congress on the FY 1982 Budget, FY 1983 Authorization Request and FY 1982-1986 Defense Programs* (Washington, D. C.: January 1981), 43-44.

8. For example, Ray Cline, in his assessment of the correlation of forces, put the Soviets behind in all categories save "will;" on the basis of his evaluation of this factor, he deemed the overall balance favorable to the USSR. *World Power Assessment* (Boulder, CO: Westview Press, 1977), 166-67.

9. *White Paper 1983*, 68.

10. Karsten Voigt, "German Security Policy and European Security Needs," *AEI Foreign Policy and Defense Review* 3 & 4, (March 1983), 25.

11. Robert Gilpin, *U.S. Power and the Multinational Corporation*(New York: Basic Books, 1975), 138-162, discusses this and other ways in which the multinational corporation has supported "American global hegemony."

12. *White Paper 1983*, 144.

13. C. W. Kegley, Jr. and P. McGowen, eds., *The Political Economy of Foreign Policy Behavior* (Beverly Hills, CA: Sage Publications, 1981), 196.

14. Robert Kennedy and Daniel S. Papp, *The Evolving Strategic Environment*, Strategic Studies Institute (U.S. Army War College: 1979), Tables 1 & 4.

15. L. L. Fischman, *World Mineral Trade and U.S. Supply Problems* (Washington, D.C., Resources for the Future 1980), 476-535.

16. *Report of Secretary of Defense Caspar W. Weinberger to the Congress on the FY 1984 Budget FY 1985 Authorization. Request and FY 1984-88 Defense Programs* February 1, 1983 (Washington, D.C., 1983), Table III. E. I., 195.

17. United States Department of Commerce, Bureau of Economic Analysis, *Business Statistics 1982* (Washington, D.C.: 1983), 75-80.

18. For a critical indictment of these practices, see S. Adams, *The Iron Triangle: Politics of Defense Contracting* (Council on Economic Priorities, New York: 1981).

19. Philip Tankman, "The Schultz-Weinberger Feud," *The New York Times Magazine* (14 April 1985), 50ff.

20. David Yankclovich and John Doble, "The Public Mood," *Foreign Affairs* 63, 1 (Fall 1984), 41-42.

21. Although definitions vary, publics include everyone, elites those with higher education and/or a predilection for tapping sources of information about policy issues and leaders those who play a significant role in formulating policy and/or in shaping the opinions of others concerning it. Thus, the 'public leaders' polled by the Chicago Council of Foreign Relations include members of Congress from committees on the armed services and foreign relations, officials with international responsibilities, business leaders, media representatives and oficials, members of foreign policy institutes and presidents and scholars from major colleges and universities. John E. Rielly, ed., *American Public Opinion and U.S. Foreign Policy*, 1983 (Chicago: The Chicago Council on Foreign Relations, 1983), 2.

22. This is especially true when the policy is highly salient and the time frame is long enough for public opinion to have an impact on official thinking and behavior. Bruce Russett and Harvey Starr, *World Politics: The Menu for Choice* (San Francisco, CA: Freeman, 1981), 248-249.

23. "Foreign Affairs: What's Past is Prologue," *Public Opinion*, 6, 4 (Aug./Sept. 1983), 31. See also Rielly, *American Public Opinion and U.S. Foreign Policy*, Table II-3, 13, showing that 59-60% of the public (and 44-45% of the leaders) polled in 1982 and 1978 deemed "Containing communism" very important—though not quite as much as "Worldwide arms control."

24. *Ibid*, Tables V-6 and V-7, 31. See also: "Defense and Offense," *Public Opinion*, 6, 2 (April/May 1983), 29.

25. "Foreign Affairs: What's Past is Prologue," 29. "Americans Assess the Nuclear Option," *Public Opinion*, 5, 4 (Aug./Sept. 1982).

26. Joseph I. Coffey and Alan T. Dieter, Jr., "Allied Perceptions of Threat," *International Forum (Sozialwissentschaftliches Institut der Bundeswehr*, Munich, 1983): Tables 3-24, 75 and 3-13, 48.

27. "Foreign Affairs: What's Past is Prologue," 30. See also Rielly, *American Public Opinion and U.S. Foreign Policy*, Table V-1, 28.

28. *Ibid*, Table V-2, 29.

29. Yankelovich and Doble, "The Public Mood," 37-38.

30. *Ibid*, 36.

31. *Ibid*, 45.

32. *Ibid*, 46.

33. Reilly, *American Public Opinion and U.S. Foreign Policy*, 38.

34. James H. Rosenau and Ole R. Holsti, "U.S. Leadership in A Shrinking World: Emergence of Conflicting Belief Systems," *World Politics*, 3 (April 1983), 392.

35. All opinion poll statistics are from Karl-Heinz Reubard, "Rearmament, NATO and the *Bundeswehr* Seen Through the Eyes of West German Citizens," in Wolfgang R. Vogt, ed., *The Military as Counterculture? Armed Forces in a Changing Society* (Opladen: 1986), 145 ff.

36. Joseph S. Nye, Jr., " U.S. Power and Reagan Policy," *Orbis*, 82, 3 (Summer 1982), especially 402-404.

Comments

a. Although there have been times when other countries were also viewed as adversaries, as was the PRC, this was largely because of their incorporation in "monolithic Communism;" when the monolith crumbled, so did (most of) the concern. And although there have also been times when some units were trained for other missions, such as intervention in Third World countries, the forces involved were miniscule; even now, the Army will designate only two of its 17 divisions as "light" and re-equip them for operations against non-Soviet forces-though, the proponents hasten to add, this does not mean that they could not carry out some missions in the European theater!

b. A secondary, but by no means unimportant, consequence has been to weaken the U.S. economy and to alienate powerful producer and trading groups, such as the farmers and the purveyors of oil drilling and pumping equipment.

c. This has been a major argument of the oil companies, who have maintained that tax and other incentives served to encourage exploration for the reserves which would be essential in time of war.

d. It is erroneous to suggest that consensus on foreign policy was an enduring feature of the republic; one has only to look at the War of 1812 (which nearly led to the secession of New England), the dispute over the American "imperialism" following the war with Spain, the differences over the League of Nations, etc., to realize that U.S. foreign policy is marked by bitter (and frequently partisan) controversy, not by agreement.

2

The U.S. Adaptation
to the Post-War World

Joseph I. Coffey

As indicated earlier a host of factors, both internal and external, will affect foreign and defense policy, frequently in contradictory ways. Yet if policy is to be viable, it must reflect these influences, even as it struggles to reconcile them. This is as true of U.S. efforts to adapt to the post-war world as it is of those of any other nation, in any other period of time.

In the following pages we will attempt both to record and to explain that policy, as a prelude to examining the issues still facing the United States as it tries, in conjunction with its allies, to maintain a peaceful and secure Europe. One reason for the review is our awareness of Santayana's axiom that "He who does not know history is condemned to repeat it"— a process none of us would like to go through. Another is that unless we can in some measure understand why previous decisions were taken, we will be in no position to say whether future ones should be made, much less what these decisions should be.

In this chapter, therefore, as in its parallel piece on the Federal Republic of Germany, we will first sketch in the national interests and objectives, next outline the foreign policy designed to promote those interests, then describe the threats to U.S. interests and finally discuss the defense policies designed to cope with those (changing) threats. And in the latter, and more detailed, inquiry we will attempt to analyze key changes in policy, as a basis for future assessments.

American National Interests
and National Objectives

In theory, at least, national policies (including defense policy) are aimed at achieving national objectives, which in turn are determined by national interests. If, therefore, one is to ascertain the sources of policies one must look at interests and objectives as well as at the geo-political, geo-economic and historical factors which influence all three.[1]

National interests, which Hanreider and Buel define as "a highly generalized concept of elements that constitutes a state's compelling needs . . . "[2], have the virtues of primacy and constancy, but they are not specific enough to serve as guides to policy. Hence, an intermediate step is to set forth national objectives ("fundamental aims, goals or purposes . . . "[3]), marked by greater specificity and closer attention to the threats, opportunities, and constraints imposed by the international and domestic environments. And national policies, broad courses of action or statements of guidelines, would be still more sensitive to environmental and other factors and in consequence still more malleable—as would be the programs intended to carry them out.[a]

As suggested by the preceding paragraph, national interests basically derive from the mere existence of a state and relate to perpetuating that existence; hence, Denmark, Germany and the United States might all list among their national interests territorial integrity, political independence, economic viability and military security. However, some states, at some times and under some circumstances, might go beyond these minimalist definitions to include the maintenance of regional hegemony, the establishment of a political philosophy or the creation of a world order in which its values could flourish—as have in their day, the Denmark of the 16th Century, the Third Reich and the United States of America. Theoretically, every state will attempt to uphold its minimal national interests, while those with the power to do so may seek to achieve the maximum ones, even at some risk.[4]

From its very beginning, the United States has had maximalist interests, deriving from its sense of mission and, paradoxically, from its sense of isolation in an absolutist world. Only rarely have these maximalist interests been reflected in U.S. foreign policy, but they do persist. Thus, while NSC-68, the basic policy guide of the second Truman administration, focused on preventing the hostile domination of Europe and Asia, in 1981 then Secretary of State Alexander M. Haig, Jr., speaking more recently, defined U.S. interests to include creating " . . . a world hospitable to our security and ideals, a world where peaceful change is the norm and nations can settle disputes without war"[5], a taller order by far. It is this swing between minimalist and maximalist definitions of national interests that led Lincoln Bloomfield to note a " . . . difficulty in distinguishing the exact nature of the United States: is it a territorial state in the European tradition, or is it a political organ, like the USSR, centered upon an idea?"[6] One cannot answer that question abstractly, as in and of themselves statements such as that by Mr. Haig may mean nothing: it is only as interests are reflected in objectives (and these in turn are furthered by policies and programs) that definitions of interest change from rhetoric to reality.

Objectives, then, make clear the values and the purpose of a state, as well as reflecting the nature of the environment within which it must safeguard its interests.[7] Because that environment is different from, and more susceptible to, the manipulations of different countries, the national objectives of states may vary more than their national interests. Since, moreover, both domestic and international environments will change, so should particular national objectives. This has not, however, been true of the United States in the post-war period, in that its objectives seem to persist almost unaltered; as former Secretary of State William Rogers said in 1971, though the role of the United States changed, " . . . we continued to adhere to the basic objectives which have characterized American policy for decades."[8]

What, then, are those "basic objectives?" As pieced together from various sources, they seem to be: prevention of Soviet expansion; protection of the industrial democracies against Soviet threats and pressures; accessibility of these democracies to essential raw materials; maintenance of an international economic system which facilitates trade and investment; and enhancement of peace and security in the Third World—with promotion of more responsive and responsible governments and improvements in socioeconomic conditions sometimes seen as means to this latter end and sometimes as ends in themselves.[9]

Though the objectives may have remained constant, the policies themselves have of course, altered. The reasons for this are not hard to see, given all the variables that impinge on policy choices, but an illustration of this may be helpful. When President Jimmy Carter took office in January 1977, he initiated a number of policies very different from those of President Gerald Ford. For one, he treated North-South relations as more important than East-West relations. For another, he tried to shift from a "militarist" to a "humanist" foreign policy, which meant not only (temporary) cuts in arms sales and increases in economic assistance but an emphasis on social justice and human rights. For a third, he announced that arms control was the most urgent and important item on his policy agenda, and produced a proposal for strategic arms limitations going far beyond any acceptable to Mr. Ford. Clearly, Mr. Carter saw differently from Mr. Ford the world in which they both lived, and hence acted differently, thereby indicating the importance of the idiosyncratic variable.

But before long the situation President Carter had inherited changed drastically, first with the seizure of U.S. hostages by Iran and secondly with the Soviet incursion into Afghanistan. In response, Mr. Carter shifted away from a "global agenda" towards a "Soviet agenda," marked by denunciations of the USSR, suspension of ratification of the SALT II treaty signed in 1979, a step-up in arms shipments to the Third World, significant increases in U.S. defense expenditures and the creation of a Rapid Deployment Force for possible employment in the Middle East.[10] In this case at least, the situational variable proved more important than the idiosyncratic one.

U.S. Policy in the Post-War World

Almost from its beginning, the foreign policy of the American Republic was based on two somewhat contradictory themes: isolationism and a sense of mission. The first militated against "entangling alliances" with other states, even for the pursuit of common objectives[b], while the second resulted not only in a general sympathy for national independence, for republican forms of government and for "free" economies but on occasion in the active support of means to those ends, as in President Woodrow Wilson's Fourteen Points. And while the United States did, in the forty years beginning with the Spanish-American War, itself acquire territories overseas, intervene militarily in the affairs of lesser American states, and behave in other respects like a great power, as late as 1939 it still clung tenaciously to the twin tenets which had guided its foreign policy for a hundred and fifty years.

World War II irretrievably ended American isolationism; as one study concluded, " . . . neither its power . . . nor its interests would permit it [the United States] to remain aloof from the political maneuverings of other nations, as it attempted to do after World War I."[11] If it was to promote the "Four Freedoms" (from war, hunger, fear and oppression) envisaged by President Franklin D. Roosevelt—or even if it were to secure the lesser goals of peace and stability—it had to shed its isolationism. Initially, this "new activism" took the form of cooperation with the USSR and other powers to make the United Nations an effective instrument for keeping the peace and promoting progress; to establish new international institutions, such as the World Health Organization and the International Monetary Fund; to stimulate and support economic recovery: and to mediate between warring elements, such as the Dutch and the Indonesians on Java and the Nationalists and the Communists in China.

The failure of this last effort, with the consequent "loss" of China to the Communists, unhappiness with Soviet rigidity and intransigence, and a growing realization of the fact that U.S. and Soviet interests were almost diametrically opposed, led to a switch of policy from cooperation to "containment." One element of that policy was reliance on other and less universal organizations (such as the OAS and the OECD) rather than on the United Nations, whose effectiveness had always depended on cooperation among the major powers. Another was establishment of regional alliances (NATO, SEATO and CENTO) directed against the USSR and/or the PRC, along with the signature of bilateral security agreements with over forty countries, from South Korea to Saudi Arabia. A third was a significant buildup of U.S. military power, triggered by the outbreak in 1950 of the Korean War but continuing even after its end. A fourth was the provision of military assistance to allies and client states so that these too could contribute forces for a collective defense against aggression, or, at the very least, provide for their own security against local threats, external or internal. And while the old idealism still manifested itself, in terms of opposition to colonialism, support for newly-emerging states, and programs of economic and technical assistance, even these were at times subordinated to the overall mission of containing Communism, as when the United States supported the French in Vietnam in 1949-54, channeled its aid largely to "threatened" allies such as Greece, Iran and Pakistan, or fostered coups against leftist regimes, as in Guatemala.

The focus of the post-war confrontation with the USSR was initially Europe, where the Soviets had gained control over most of Eastern Europe (including East Germany), maintained sizeable armed forces in advanced positions and attempted, by a combination of military threats and diplomatic pressures, to undermine the U.S. position in Western Europe. One American response was to provide economic assistance, first to Greece and Turkey and then, under the Marshall Plan, to other countries in Western Europe.ᶜ Another was to create, in conjunction with its West European allies, the North Atlantic Treaty Organization, which provided both a collective security guarantee and, ultimately, sizeable forces to back it up. A third was to alter the punitive policy toward Germany formulated during WW II, to encourage and assist in the creation of the Federal Republic of Germany and to bring a rearmed West Germany into NATO. In sum, the United States sought, in a variety of ways, to strengthen the countries of Western Europe, to bind them more tightly to itself and to each other and in this way to create a barrier to further Soviet encroachment. At the same time, it sought to diminish the likelihood of such encroachments, both by arms control measures which would reduce Soviet/WTO military capabilities and by the promotion of "détente"—though interest in both of these policies fluctuated markedly over time.

This does not mean that all American actions were motivated by anti-Communism nor all American programs designed solely to counter or undercut those of the Soviet Union and its associates; for example, the "Alliance for Progress" of the Kennedy Administration was a bold effort to stimulate economic development and social progress in a Latin America largely untouched by Soviet or Cuban activities and the "human rights" campaign of the Carter Administration was directed at "friendly" governments as well as unfriendly ones. Nor did it mean that the United States eschewed efforts to improve relations with the Soviet Union, or to reach agreement with it on matters of common concern, such as the danger of inadvertent war and the costs and risks of competitive arms buildups. But it does mean that there was, over most of the post-war period, a preoccupation with the Soviet "threat," a tendency to view developments in terms of their effects on Soviet power and influence, and a heavy reliance upon the military instrument of policy.

Whether or not this approach was sound is a matter of judgement, with some holding that it was both necessary and effective, others that the cost was too great and the results too small, and still others that it was, at least as applied to Vietnam, a clear manifestation of "super-power arrogance."[12] What is important to us is not its validity but its implications for defense policy and for relations with the allies. However, before looking at the ways in which the armed forces were employed in support of U.S. foreign policy, it may be useful to examine the threats to American interests which were one element in the development of defense policy.

Challenges to U.S. Interests

Clearly the United States faced a multitude of problems in furthering its interests, even in the early post-war years, when the USSR was comparatively weak. That country has, however, markedly increased its military capabilities, across the board, which means that its ability to pose particular threats, even if latent ones, has multiplied over time. Given the primacy in U.S. defense policy assigned to deterring or countering these threats, it seems essential to delineate them more clearly, as a basis both for understanding the nuances of that policy and for determining whether differing perceptions of threat led to different policies by the Federal Republic of Germany.

The Soviet Challenge

At the Strategic Nuclear Level. From 1945 until the late 1960s the Soviet Union found itself in a position of clear nuclear inferiority when compared with the United States. By the 1970s, however, Soviet advances in rocket propulsion, guidance systems, submarine platforms and warhead design, coupled with an extensive building program, had resulted in the establishment of essential parity with the U.S. in strategic weapons. This "rough equivalence" was formalized in the various SALT agreements, which acknowledged the Soviets' co-equal status.

Since those agreements, both sides have made improvements to their strategic capabilities. On the part of the USSR, these have included the deployment of a new missile submarine, the Typhoon, and a new SLBM (the SSN-20), the testing of new and/or improved ICBMs, the development of a new strategic bomber (the Blackjack) and of better air-launched cruise missiles (ALCMs), the continued strengthening of air defenses and extensive research in ballistic missile defenses, as well as the orbiting of additional space-borne reconnaissance and communications systems.[13] So far, the quantitative and qualitative changes in Soviet weaponry have not altered the essential equivalence attained during the 1970s—in large measure because of offsetting U.S. strategic nuclear programs. They have, however, posed a continuing challenge to American defense planners. For one thing, increases in the number and throw-weight of Soviet ICBMs, and in the number and accuracy of the re-entry vehicles these can carry, have led to concerns about the potential vulnerability to a disarming strike of U.S. land-based systems, and hence about the stability of strategic deterrence. For another, the over-all shift in the strategic balance, to the point where a meaningful American advantage no longer exists, has raised serious doubts about the credibility of the nuclear guarantee, and hence about the validity of extended deterrence. As we shall see, U.S. strategic doctrine and force planning have largely focused on efforts to cope with these two challenges, the second of which has also had a direct and significant impact on NATO planning.

At the Theater Level. Since the end of World War II the Soviets have deployed in Central Europe, and retained in their strategic reserve, large numbers of infantry and tank divisions, backed up by sizeable tactical air and air defense forces. The existence and the continuing modernization of these forces led the Allies to believe that the USSR might, or at least could, launch a massive conventional assault against Western Europe, one which NATO could neither deter nor resist without the threat to employ nuclear weapons. And as will be seen later, much thought and effort were devoted to obtaining that combination of conventional and nuclear capabilities which offered the best assurance of successful deterrence, before and during any conflict.

Beginning in the mid-fifties, however, a new element was added to the equation: Soviet theater nuclear forces. Their introduction, following close on the deployment of U.S. nuclear-capable tactical weapons systems, enabled the Soviets to threaten intra-theater nuclear strikes of their own, raised doubts about the ability of NATO to control escalation in the event of conflict, ultimately brought into question the validity of the U.S. nuclear guarantee and generated concerns about nuclear blackmail. Hence, Soviet theater nuclear forces enormously complicated the problem of deterrence and defense—a situation which will be altered, but not ended, with the projected removal of intermediate-range and short-range ballistic missiles under the so-called "double zero" agreement of 8 December 1987.[14]

On the Oceans. Perhaps the most widely recognized challenge to American interests is that deriving from the enormous growth in size and capabilities of the Soviet Navy since WW II. From a small, almost derisory coastal force, whose primary mission even in the early 1950s was that of checking Western amphibious operations, it grew successively to one aimed at countering carrier-launched nuclear strikes, to one intended to keep at bay short-range missile submarines and then to one designed to provide sanctuaries for Soviet Ballistic Missile Submarines (SSBNs). Since the mid-1970s there has been a shift away from ASW (Anti-Submarine Warfare) capabilities to those suited to protracted and possibly non-nuclear surface warfare. This has resulted in "a new generation of ships suitable for extended, open ocean deployments as part of battle groups which could be used against enemy aircraft carriers and amphibious groups and SLOCs [sea lines of communications]. . . . Such battle groups are obviously intended also to provide coastal bombardment in support of amphibious landings . . . "[15]

This design trend seems to indicate that the Soviet Navy is beginning to develop a powerful offensive capability, in contrast to its previous defensive one. At present that navy still lacks adequate logistic capacity and the organic aviation which is essential if it is to be truly wide-ranging. But the reported building of an aircraft carrier capable of carrying attack planes (as distinct from the helicopters and VTOL Forger aircraft which form the complement of the current ASW carriers) and the steady increase in foreign naval bases make it conceivable that in the future the Soviet

Navy may generate a surface threat to the U.S. Navy, along with that posed
by its large numbers of attack submarines and its long-range naval aircraft,
equipped with cruise missiles. But whether it achieves this capability or
not, the Soviet Navy has already demonstrated its capacity for "global
power projection" in support of other Soviet activities in the Third World.[16]

In the Third World. During the immediate post-WW II era, Soviet
activities at any distance beyond the borders of the USSR were limited by
its debilitated condition, the continued existence of Western colonial hegemony over wide areas of the globe, lack of the requisite naval and air
assets and, perhaps most importantly, by the enormous nuclear arsenal of
the United States. With the passage of time all of these circumstances have
been altered, and by the 1970s the world situation offered opportunities
for involvement in the independent but highly unstable Third World by a
Soviet Union which now had both the capacity and the desire to do so.

In large measure, this intervention has been traditional in nature, con-
sisting of political support, technical assistance, (limited) economic aid,
arms sales and so on. In some instances, the USSR has also provided
planners, trainers and even cadres for the armed forces of client states. In
a few instances—Cuba being the most noteworthy—the Soviets have placed
garrisons of combat troops for the protection of a regime against potential
"putsches" and in others (Egypt in the 1970s and Syria today), they have
manned anti-aircraft defenses, dispatched mechanized infantry units to
secure airfields and Surface-to-Air Missile (SAM) sites and/or landed nuclear-capable missiles as a deterrent to further advances by invading troops.

In some cases, support has gone not to friendly governments but to
friendly insurgents: in countries as diverse and as distant as Vietnam,
Mozambique, and the Sudan the Soviets have armed and supported "forces
of national liberation." So far as is known, they have not committed either
their own troops or those of their allies to these missions but they have
arranged for detachments of Cubans and East Germans to defend the
governments established by the insurgents against dissident elements, as in
Angola and Ethiopia. (Perhaps more importantly, they or their East European allies have also organized and staffed counter-intelligence and internal security operations, as in South Yemen.)

Soviet activities in the Third World, whether overt or covert, direct or
by proxy, have gained the Soviets numbers of *de facto* allies (Ethiopia,
Syria, Angola, Mozambique, Vietnam, etc.) and access to bases for Soviet
ships and aircraft. The availability of these bases enables the Soviets not
only to track Western naval and commercial shipping but also to threaten
vital world sealines of communication, such as the tanker route around
the Cape of Good Hope. Moreover, from the positions obtained, they or
their clients can extend their influence into neighboring areas, as from
Angola into southern Zaire or from Cuba into Central America.

In sum, the Soviets have tried to nibble away at Western positions,
employing the same instruments and techniques the Western powers used
to acquire these positions in the first place; as one Soviet analyst asked,

"What have we done that you [Americans] haven't done?" Although their successes have not been marked, and some of them have been transitory, their presence and their operations enormously complicate the task of safeguarding friendly states against external and internal threats to their security, of insuring access to resources and markets and of otherwise promoting American—and Western—interests in the Third World.

Other Threats to Security

It would be comforting to think that all threats to the security of the United States and its allies arose from the Soviet Union but this is not the case; indeed, the other threats posed, while perhaps less formidable, may be more imminent and are certainly more complex—as must be the means of coping with them. Among the most dangerous are the prospects that political developments may jeopardize vital economic interests, that local wars may engulf allies, if not the United States itself, and that internal instabilities may draw America into domestic conflicts, as in Vietnam, Lebanon and El Salvador.

Loss of Access to Raw Materials. As noted previously, the internationalization of the U.S. economy has made this country dependent upon foreign suppliers for an increasing percentage of crucial resources, such as oil, cobalt, bauxite, iron ore, etc., as well as for markets for manufactures— as is even more true of the European and Japanese allies. While the United States (and its allies) could probably withstand the closing of even major markets, it might not be able to compensate for the loss of a vital resource such as oil. The shock of a new Arab-Israeli war, the overthrow of the Saudi regime, even the closing of the Straits of Hormuz, as Iran has threatened to do, could all lead to higher prices, shorter supplies or temporary cut-offs of a magnitude sufficient to cause economic disruptions. And the passing of that oil into the control of a hostile state like the Soviet Union could have a drastic impact upon the economic well-being and the potential resilience of the allies.

Although most safeguards against temporary disruptions are economic, ranging from stockpiling and agreements to share available petroleum to establishing alternative sources of energy, such as the gas pipeline into western Europe, some would involve the armed forces. For one thing, a serious move by the Soviet Union to take over large parts of the Middle East, unlikely as that may be, could only be stopped by military action; in fact the U.S. Rapid Deployment Force was organized to meet just such a contingency. For another, attempted *coups d'état*, uprisings or incursions into key oil-producing states could well require intervention by American and/or other forces, at lower but still significant levels. (Indeed, this is why the United States is seeking to organize and equip a Jordanian "strike force.") And for a third, operations against Western shipping may require counter-operations, with consequent political side-effects and the possibility of expanded military actions; this indeed is the case today, with U S naval forces escorting Kuwaiti tankers re-registered under the American flag and

launching strikes against Iranian vessels and facilities used in attacking
shipping in the Persian-Arabian Gulf. And though none of these save the
first is likely to place extraordinary demands upon U.S. armed forces, all
require the ear-marking of some troops, if only on a contingent basis.

Local Conflicts. As noted earlier, the post-war environment has been
studded with small wars: between China and Vietnam, between India and
Pakistan, between Israel and her neighbors, between Algeria and Morocco
and even between Honduras and El Salvador, the so-called "Soccer War."
These can be of concern to the United States even if there is no (or no
significant) Soviet involvement, since such wars may lead to the defeat of
a friendly nation, to the loss of bases, to interruptions in the flow of raw
materials, etc. More significantly, as long as the United States looks to
international peace and stability either as ends in themselves or as means
to the larger goal of fashioning a world within which U.S. values can
flourish, such wars can be troublesome, if not disruptive.

Obviously, the United States cannot hope to "keep the peace" throughout
the world. Equally obviously, it cannot permit every local conflict to
continue unhampered to its (sometimes distant) conclusion. Although major
reliance has been, and should be, placed on diplomatic moves, singly or
in concert with others, these may not be enough to deter or dampen such
conflicts. Nor may arms sales and arms embargos (though the U.S. Government has tried both), economic boycotts (which have proven singularly
ineffective even when the United States has abided by them) and other
actions short of the use of force.

Involvement in these local wars poses a serious dilemma to U.S. policy
makers. They must tread a narrow path between the need to protect
American interests and the publics' clear reluctance to sanction such ex-
peditions—a point stressed in Chapter 1. They must face the fact that these
wars can, like Korea in its time, be long and bloody and that they carry
with them the risk of escalating into a superpower confrontation. Furthermore, even if the United States does not engage in combat operations, or
limits this involvement, as the Soviets did in Egypt, the cost of supporting
friends and clients can be enormous. Hence, one challenge to U.S. defense
policy is to provide units which are trained, organized and equipped for
rapid intervention in local conflicts, while simultaneously practicing restraint in their use.

Instability in the Third World. Instability is seemingly endemic in the
Third World, not only in terms of wars between nations but in terms of
upheavals within them. The causes are legion: ethnic conflicts, bureaucratic
and political inefficiency and corruption, socio-economic inequities stem-
ming from traditional practices or as a side-effect of rapid modernization,
economic hardships caused by acts of God or the vagaries of the international market, and foreign meddling. And they take a variety of forms,
from *coups d'état* to military uprisings, from small-scale guerrilla operations
to full-scale civil wars, as in Angola today.

The potential response of the United States may also take a variety of
forms, ranging from "benign neglect" through diplomatic and economic

support for the government to the actual utilization of American troops, either in a support role (as was the case when the U.S.A.F flew French paratroopers into Zaire) or in actual combat. Which roles (if any) are played depend upon a number of factors, ranging from judgments about the causes of instability to views of its potential impact upon U.S. interests. For example, those who see this unrest as symptomatic of the immaturity and inefficiency of socio-political institutions in newly emerging countries, or of their levels of economic development, are more likely to rely on preventive medicine in the form of economic and technical assistance then on doses of lead; conversely, those who see internal upheavals as instigated by or exploited by the Soviet Union and its associates are more likely to feel that this political cancer must be excised. In either case, the granting of aid or the dispatch of troops may be affected not only by the economic or geo-political importance of the country but by the loftiness of one's aspirations for universal peace or one's dedication to the creation of "the American Century." Thus, the challenge to American security interests posed by instabilities can be seen variously and responded to in very different fashion.

Since, however, that fashion may include the use of force, such means must be available. One problem is that some manifestations of instability, such as the overthrow of the Hashemite dynasty in Iraq in 1958 or the ouster of the Tubman regime in Liberia, can be reversed only by a large-scale invasion, if that. Only by providing "palace guards" to threatened rulers could one hope to preclude violent changes of government—and this does not seem either feasible or desirable. Another is that even small-scale guerrilla operations can be difficult to suppress, especially since most local forces are woefully unprepared for this assignment and many local governments are unable or unwilling to make the reforms which might deprive the guerrillas of support. And though the United States does have troops trained for counter-insurgency operations, they are few in number and not universally knowledgeable. A third is that once dissident elements have gained sufficient strength to organize armed forces of their own, the kinds and numbers of troops required to suppress them, and to re-establish control over territories they have occupied, changes markedly—as the United States found out in Vietnam. Hence, the military means required to cope with that threat may vary from small, highly mobile units like Ranger Battalions and Special Forces Groups up to light divisions, with air support, with consequent impact upon the ability to carry out other missions.

American Defense Policy in the Post-War World

As suggested above, some threats to U.S. interests, such as can arise from internal instabilities or local wars, have been "hardy perennials" while others have varied significantly over time; no American planner of the 1950s had to concern himself with a Soviet "global presence," as today's planner must. Moreover, not only threats but circumstances have varied, with France leaving the NATO establishment in 1967 and moving cautiously toward closer cooperation with its allies ten years later, with domestic support for active American defense policies falling in the late 1960s, as the Vietnam War dragged on, and rising again in the late 1970s.

In this section, we will try to give a general overview of these policies, which necessarily covers the provision of elements intended for operations in the Third World as well as troops for Europe, the modernization of strategic and theater nuclear forces as well as measures for the limitation of those forces and the allocation of resources to these and other require- ments. And we will try to indicate those changes in threats or those alterations in circumstances which impelled a reconsideration of policy, as well as the factors influencing the decisions reached.

The Early Years

World War II marked a watershed in U.S. defense policy, as well as in foreign policy. Both had to deal with a shattered world, in which the United States was inevitably and inextricably involved, in a new and prominent role, in which it was confronted in time of peace with challenges such as it had previously had to face only in time of war. Both had to deal with alterations in the power and the roles of many actors, some of them, like France, friendly but weakened, some, like the Soviet Union, hostile and growing in power, others, like India, non-aligned and still developing. And both had to recognize that the emergence of the United States as an economic and military giant placed new demands upon it, even as this development afforded American leaders an unparalleled op- portunity to reshape the world, if not to their heart's desire at least to something different from before.

The Truman Administration both accepted the challenge and seized the opportunity; in fact, it is no exaggeration to say that American foreign policy is still cast in a mold of President Harry S Truman's making. Almost immediately after succeeding to office, he began to take a tough line toward the Soviet Union; he shortly initiated post-war aid programs, with military as well as political and economic considerations in mind;[17] he extended military assistance to allies fighting Communist-controlled insurgents, in- cluding the Greeks, the French (in Indochina) and, for a time, the Chinese Nationalists; he sent military advisers to these and other areas and, most important of all, he participated in the formation of the North Atlantic Treaty Organization. This latter move was unprecedented in American history; not since its treaty with France in 1778 had the United States entered into such an "entangling alliance," to use Robert Osgood's felicitous phrase. Thus, Mr. Truman truly revolutionized American foreign policy.

By rights, "a revolution in . . . American military policy" should also have occurred, as the armed forces tried simultaneously to support these new global interests and responsibilities and to implement a strategy of deterrence,[18] i.e., one aimed at the "prevention or inhibition of conflict" rather than at war-fighting. This did not, however, happen immediately, for a number of reasons. One was that the United States attempted initially to insure collective security through the United Nations; only after this failed did the Truman Administration conclude that the "contemplated structure for the maintenance of world peace in the era after the war depended on the West retaining its military strength."[19] For another, the United States initially proposed, in the Acheson-Lilienthal and Baruch plans, to establish controls over all facilities which could produce nuclear weapons and to ban the latter, and only after the Soviets rejected U.S. proposals (which, they argued, would have left the USSR in a condition of technical and military inferiority) did American nuclear programs pick up speed.

More important than these events was the fact that the military implications of atomic weapons were neither recognized by, nor accepted within, the Army and the Navy. Although the newly created Air Force emphasized strategic bombing, both as a deterrent and as a means of waging war should deterrence fail, the Army and the Navy planned to seize the overseas bases from which aerial assaults could be launched, occupy the vast territories of the Soviet Union if strategic nuclear strikes proved successful and fight the vast forces of the Soviet Union if they did not. This thinking about the proper roles of the armed forces prevailed throughout most of the Truman Administration, and though the Army and the Navy never received the resources they deemed essential for such a formidable task, even after Korea, this was largely the result of budgetary restraints rather than of doctrinal disputes.

By the early 1950s, however, a number of factors combined to force changes in military policy. One was the Soviet acquisition of nuclear weapons, which ended the U.S. monopoly and threatened to place in jeopardy both American bomber bases and American cities. Another was the Korean War itself, which drove home the lesson that deterrence could never be absolute and that the United States would have to be prepared to fight limited conventional wars, if not major ones. A third was the increasing scale of operations by guerrilla forces, which, even when unsuccessful, caused enormous difficulties and placed new and different demands upon security forces, as the British found in Malaysia and the French in Indochina. A fourth was a revulsion of popular opinion against the human and financial costs of the conflict in Korea. Thus the United States had to create policies and programs which would insure strategic stability, enhance the credibility of deterrence and enable limited operations against regular and paramilitary forces, to say nothing of maintaining an American military presence in key areas, hopefully in ways which would both decrease defense costs and increase public support for defense programs.

The "New Look" of 1953

The response of the Eisenhower Administration was to change the way in which both all-out and limited wars would be deterred—and if necessary, fought. Essentially, conventional forces were downgraded in favor of nuclear ones, which in Europe meant planning to use nuclear weapons in time of war, regardless of whether the USSR employed them. (As President Eisenhower noted in his memoirs, " . . . In view of the disparity in the strengths of the opposing ground forces, it seemed clear that only by the interposition of our nuclear weapons could we promptly stop a major Communist aggression in the area. Two more divisions or ten more divisions, on our side, would not make very much difference against this Soviet ground force."[20]) In consequence, theater forces were assigned the role of "shielding" Western Europe from any Soviet attack while strategic bombing of the USSR shattered the bases of Soviet military power and, if necessary, the urban-industrial complex.[21] And although the "shield" was comprised largely of conventional forces, it also contained large numbers of tactical nuclear weapons, which were readied to launch strikes deep into enemy territory, as well as to conduct operations on the battlefield.

Outside Europe, the approach was similar. Emphasis was placed on the buildup of indigenous forces, some of which were intended for counterguerrilla operations, some of which were earmarked for local defense or for contributions to regional security. Given, however, the distance separating, say, Manila and Islamabad, and the inability of many countries to supply troops trained and equipped for modern warfare, it was obvious that only the United States could back up regional arrangements and the bilateral agreements binding together the allies. It was equally obvious that the United States did not propose to do this by providing massive ground forces, as it had in Korea; instead it chose to rely largely on mobile air and naval elements and on its ability "to respond vigorously at places and with means of its own choosing . . . "[22], including nuclear weapons.

This approach relied heavily on the ultimate sanction of the Strategic Air Command. By the mid-fifties both on-going programs and advancing technology had enabled the United States to achieve nuclear delivery capabilities so large and so diversified as to give it virtually unchallengeable advantages over the USSR. Accordingly, the Eisenhower Administration assigned to strategic nuclear forces the mission of executing "massive retaliation" against Soviet military targets and the economic bases of Soviet military power should the USSR choose to attack the United States or its allies; in short their role was one of war-fighting.[23] In view of the overwhelming capabilities of these forces, there was no doubt as to their ability to carry out their assigned mission, while Soviet retaliatory strikes could inflict little or no damage on the United States. Hence, deterrence was (according to the rational model) assured, as was victory in war.

Somewhat surprisingly, in view of the emphasis on strengthening Western defenses, the Eisenhower Administration also undertook negotiations on arms limitations. In a shift from previous (and unsuccessful) efforts to achieve nuclear disarmament, the United States, under some pressure from its allies, attempted to work out arrangements for reductions in conventional forces; these, however, foundered over differences within the administration, as well as with the Soviet Union. Nor did specific attempts to end nuclear testing, to provide safeguards against surprise attack or to cut off further production of fissionable materials fare any better. Thus, despite significant and far-reaching efforts, the arms control policy of the United States achieved nothing and security was, as before, dependent largely on power.[24]

As one means of enhancing that power, the United States further extended its system of alliances, establishing the Central Treaty Organization (Britain, Turkey, Iraq and Pakistan), with the United States as an associate, and the Southeast Asia Treaty Organization (Britain, France, the United States, Australia, New Zealand, Pakistan, the Philippines and Thailand), as well as signing a number of bilateral agreements. More importantly, NATO was expanded to include Greece, Turkey and a re-armed West Germany. Whether these measures amounted to "Pactomania," as some charged, or a prudent desire to make clear to potential aggressors the consequences of their actions, as others maintained, there can be little doubt that one basic trend of U.S. defense policy during the Eisenhower years was membership in a system of alliances.[25]

Another trend was that the costs of defense should be cut back. As indicated earlier, allies throughout the world were expected to take greater responsibility for their own security. This shift of responsibility and the advent of the "New Look" enabled the Eisenhower Administration to cut the armed forces from 3.6 million men in 1953, at the end of the Korean War, to 2.5 million in 1960 and to reduce the defense budget by one-quarter during the same period.[26] As part of this process, economic and military assistance was slashed in half, largely by phasing out support for most of the European allies. And though the draft was retained, it operated more as a stimulus to recruiting than as a sizeable source of manpower for the armed forces.

Although both the policies and the programs of this period were affected by a host of factors, several seem to have had particular importance. One of these was the division of Europe, whose presumed vulnerability to Soviet attack led both to the massive buildup of strategic and theater nuclear forces and to the efforts to bring a re-armed Germany into the Western Alliance. Another was the pace of technological innovation, which made possible the maintenance of significant American advantages in nuclear weapons and delivery capabilities. A third, already noted, was that the American people were unwilling to support further U.S. involvement in local conflicts or the kinds of defense expenditures needed to support the military programs of the Truman Administration. By far the most significant factor was, however, President Eisenhower himself: a former general with a detailed knowledge of the military and a reputation in the field that no one could successfully challenge. Since Mr. Eisenhower was also preoccupied with the long-term economic burden of defense expenditures, he adopted a program which would reduce them. Since he was aware not only of public *malaise* over the Korean War but of the frustrations of the armed forces with that costly stalemate, he was eager to avoid any repetition of such an experience.[27] And given both the power of the Presidency and his own popularity, he was able to take a "New Look" at defense programs, despite the opposition of some Army generals and the criticism of a number of analysts.

These criticisms took a number of forms. One was that strategic nuclear forces did not "constitute a credible deterrent to the broad range of aggression,"[28] since the growth of Soviet strategic nuclear forces could enable that country to place in jeopardy the nuclear delivery systems of the United States (thereby leading to strategic instability) and to threaten retaliation against the American homeland should those systems ever be employed. Another was that the cutbacks in conventional capabilities left the United States unable to deter or defend against non-nuclear attacks and, more importantly, to engage in politico-military bargaining. A third was that Soviet-supported "wars of national liberation" could not be handled solely by local forces, which might require assistance by American troops.

The Kennedy Years, 1961-63

As a Senator and as a campaigner for the presidency, John F. Kennedy echoed these criticisms; accordingly, when Mr. Kennedy took office in January 1961, he initiated four major changes in U.S. defense policy. First, believing that a "missile gap" existed, he moved rapidly to increase the rate of production of ICBMs and SLBMs, as well as to continue deployment of the B-52 heavy bomber—although he subsequently cut back on the ultimate number of missiles to be built. Moreover, he (or his Secretary of Defense, Robert McNamara) planned to employ these augmented forces in a war-fighting role, prime targets being Soviet air bases, missile sites and submarine pens. (In fact, at one stage, Mr. McNamara even proposed that in the event of war the U.S. and the USSR should strike only at each other's nuclear forces—a contest which the United States was bound to win.) And though expectations of success in "counterforce operations" changed with the growth of Soviet capabilities, leading first to a "damage limiting program" and then to the ostensible abandonment of this concept,[29] the mission of striking at Soviet military installations remained a significant one.

The converse was true of TNF, whose mission changed drastically: from that of war-fighting to that of "demonstrating our will and intent" to employ nuclear weapons;[30] in fact, the shift was so pronounced that the last annual report by Secretary McNamara in February 1967 did not include a single reference to theater nuclear forces! Despite this lack of interest, and despite concerns that widely-dispersed tactical nuclear weapons enhanced the danger of inadvertent war, these weapons continued to accumulate, so that by the end of the Johnson Administration there were in Europe 7,000 nuclear warheads and well over two thousand delivery vehicles. Thus, there was little doubt that TNF could carry out their limited mission—though there was considerable doubt as to whether that *should* be their mission, especially as the Soviets inched toward strategic parity.

The third major shift was in the role assigned conventional forces. Despite the rapid increase in U.S. SNF, and post-election awareness that the "missile gap" did not in fact exist, President Kennedy believed that the employment of nuclear weapons by the United States would result in costly reprisals, and hence was undesirable. His idea, ably forwarded by Secretary McNamara and members of his staff, was that conventional forces should be strengthened to the point where they could cope with anything short of an all-out attack, thereby heightening the credibility of deterrence, reducing the necessity to escalate at an early stage of conflict and providing a basis for probes and demonstrations of force designed to make clear Western determination to defend key areas such as Berlin.[31]

Although Mr. McNamara followed up on this approach by (temporarily) moving two additional divisions to Western Europe, stockpiling equipment there, increasing supplies of spare parts and ammunition, etc., it is unlikely that the forces available could have achieved the desired end; partly for budgetary reasons, partly because they still relied on the strategic deterrent, partly because they wished to avoid another war in Europe, the Allies balked at taking corresponding steps. Moreover, while the lower assessments of Soviet conventional capabilities which led defense planners to embark on this course of action were probably valid, the leaders of the USSR certainly could have raised them, either in East Germany or overall.[e]

The fourth—and in retrospect the most important—decision made by Mr. Kennedy was with respect to para-military forces. Convinced that "wars of national liberation" constituted a dire threat to American allies and interests, he expanded the modest internal security program of his predecessor into a full-fledged "counter-insurrectionary" effort, involving enlargement of the Special Forces, re-creation of Ranger battalions, and assistance to other countries attempting to cope with revolutionary elements. More importantly, he employed the "Green Berets" in actual anti-guerrilla operations, notably in South Vietnam. And this legacy, unlike others, was not treasured by his successors.

Mr. Kennedy also moved to transform the Arms Control Administration set up by Mr. Eisenhower into a full-fledged Arms Control and Disarmament Agency and to open negotiations on arms limitations with the Soviet Union, in abeyance since 1959. Progress in this area came only in 1963 in the form of a Partial Test-Ban Treaty and the construction of a "Hot Line" between Moscow and Washington but groundwork had been laid for subsequent developments such as the Non-Proliferation Treaty of 1968. Moreover, the Kennedy Administration adopted several unilateral measures intended to lessen the likelihood of inadvertent war, among them the withdrawal from Europe of the nuclear-capable Davy Crockett 4.2-inch mortar and the placement of locking devices on nuclear warheads in that theater, a measure which subsequently developed into the system of "Permissive Action Links."

Most of these moves, and the concomitant bettering of U.S.-Soviet relations, came only late in Mr. Kennedy's term of office, the first part of which was marked by an abortive summit meeting with Khrushchev, another Berlin crisis and, in 1962, the Cuban Missile Crisis. All of these placed strains upon the Atlantic Alliance, as did early moves toward adoption of the concept of flexible response, but these were weathered, thanks in part to Mr. Kennedy's strong personal interest and involvement in European affairs. Elsewhere, little change took place, with Mr. McNamara remarking later that "this system of alliances has substantially achieved its purpose. . . . the outward thrust of Soviet and Red Chinese pressure had generally been contained and the independence of even the smallest member of the alliance has been achieved."[32]

All this did not come cheap: both the size of the armed forces and the military budget rose by about 10% during the Kennedy years. By 1964 the United States was devoting approximately 50% of governmental expenditures (exclusive of transfer payments) and 8.3% of its gross national product to defense. Moreover, it had made large call-ups of National Guard units, and to a lesser extent of reservists, particularly during the Berlin Crisis of 1961. Whether or not these measures slowed economic growth, as some maintained, they certainly imposed social and economic costs, both directly and by pre-empting government revenues which could have been used for other programs.

In brief, the Kennedy Administration undertook both a major buildup of U.S. forces and a significant redirection of their missions, particularly with respect to conventional and para-military operations. These moves were seemingly motivated by an enhanced sense of the global competition with the Soviet Union, with Europe as the most important but not the only focus of activity. They also stemmed from the dynamics of technology, which changed the "correlation of forces" between the U.S. and the USSR, especially in the nuclear field. A robust economy made possible the expansion of defense programs without sizeable budgetary deficits or significant inflationary pressures but economic issues were not foremost in Mr. Kennedy's thinking. And the vulnerability of the geo-economic base became salient only during the Cuban Missile Crisis, after which Mr. Kennedy became more interested in measures for the control of armaments and began to seek a *modus vivendi* with the Soviet Union.

Perhaps the two most significant influences on policy in the Kennedy years were Mr. Kennedy himself and the political environment in which he moved. John F. Kennedy was a liberal, an internationalist and an activist, with a strong affinity for the traditional American values and a corresponding dislike of Communism, whether of the Soviet, Chinese or Cuban varieties. He was clearly persuaded of the necessity for strong measures to "rebuild" American defenses and restore American power and influence. More significantly, he seemingly convinced the public and the Congress that these were necessary and reasonable actions; hence, despite failure to achieve all he wanted in the domestic field, he had no difficulty in obtaining approval for his defense policies. Here again, therefore, the idiosyncratic variable and the political structure which gives a charismatic and determined president a largely free hand in security matters were the most important factors in the Kennedy years.

The Nixon Doctrine

Basically, President Lyndon Johnson continued the Kennedy policies, save that the strategic nuclear program leveled off. This was partly because the United States was far ahead of the Soviet Union, partly because the latter had already achieved force levels so high that the United States abandoned the "damage limiting strategy" as a guide to force development, settling instead for the mission of "assured destruction."[33] Heavy reliance continued to be placed on conventional forces and the doctrine of "flexible response" was formally adopted by NATO (see Chapter 4). Meanwhile, the counter-guerrilla operations in Vietnam initiated by Mr. Kennedy grew into a large-scale and costly conventional war, which absorbed half-a-million U.S. troops and the full attention of the president and his principal advisers. This war had a traumatic effect on the European allies, many of whom doubted the utility of U.S. policy and all of whom resented being asked to shoulder the economic and military burdens resulting from the war. It also led to an erosion of support among the American people, who for years to come were unwilling to endorse the use of force in defense of national interests.

It was left for President Richard Nixon to bring this war to a close, which he did by a combination of punitive operations against Vietnamese forces throughout Indochina and negotiations for an armistice—which the North Vietnamese later violated. More importantly, he not only withdrew American troops from Vietnam but, in the so-called "Nixon Doctrine," returned to the Dulles-Eisenhower concept of arming allies to provide for their own local (and internal) security, reserving U.S. forces to cope with major, overt assaults.[34] This shift both ameliorated many of the difficulties with the European allies and also, by signaling a change in U.S. perspectives, paved the way for the historic Nixon visit to China and the pursuit of détente.[35]

Mr. Nixon (or, to be more precise, Secretaries of Defense Melvin Laird and James Schlesinger) also made significant changes in strategic doctrine and force postures. One such change was the adoption of the concept of "sufficiency," under which U.S. forces were supposed to be able to inflict on the USSR damage equal to that which the Soviets could inflict on the United States—a requirement which, given the respective distributions of industry and population, greatly expanded the force requirements. Another, which affected both numbers and types of weapons required, was the development of "flexible options," which would enable the United States to strike at selected sub-sets of targets, sequentially or simultaneously, rather than engaging all targets at once, under the Single Integrated Operations Plan (SIOP).[36] When to these were added the continued rise in Soviet nuclear capabilities, which threatened the survivability of U.S. land-based systems, and the installation by the USSR of embryonic ballistic missile defenses, it was obvious that stronger U.S. strategic nuclear forces would be required.

Accordingly, the Nixon Administration began to deploy MIRVs (Multiple Independently Targetable Reentry Vehicles) on a new ICBM (the Minuteman III) and a new SLBM, the Poseidon C-3; these measures more than tripled the number of deliverable warheads in American hands and significantly increased the U.S. lead over the USSR in this category.[37] It also sought to expand and thicken the "light" ABM system proposed in the final stage of the Johnson Administration, with initial emphasis on the protection of ICBMs. And though only one cluster of ballistic missile interceptors was even installed, the strengthened U.S. forces were certainly capable of carrying out their assigned missions, even after a Soviet first strike.

This, however, would not in and of itself insure the credibility of extended deterrence, which depended in part on the effectiveness of conventional and nuclear forces in Europe. The withdrawal of France from the integrated military structure of NATO in 1967 and the drawdowns in U.S. troop strength and stockpiles resulting from the war in Vietnam had undermined conventional defenses in Europe, so that when Mr. Nixon took office in 1968 these were less formidable than they had been four years earlier. Although Mr. Nixon and Secretary of Defense Laird did improve U.S. conventional capabilities (and persuaded the Allies to upgrade their own forces) these combined efforts did not suffice to meet the stated goal of an initial (90-day) defense against a Soviet attack on Western Europe; indeed, rather than further increasing troop strength in Europe the administration had to fight off attempted drawdowns, either through the Mansfield Amendment (which called for the withdrawal of 100,000 men to the United States) or through the negotiations on Mutual and Balanced Force Reductions (MBFR), which supposedly aimed at establishing a common (and lower) ceiling for NATO and WTO ground forces in Central Europe. And outside Europe the Nixon Administration reduced both the requirements placed on general purpose forces (from meeting simultaneous Soviet and Chinese assaults to defending against one or the other) and the force levels, to a point below that attained in 1964.[38]

What Messrs. Nixon and Laird *did* was to make two changes in the roles of theater nuclear forces, one giving them the mission of enhancing deterrence of conventional aggression by the threat of escalation and the other assigning them that of "cop[ing] with each level of potential conflict at that level" by "hav[ing] a realistic option in the theater without having to rely solely on strategic nuclear weapons."[39] And Mr. Schlesinger, when he succeeded Mr. Laird as Secretary of Defense, carried this approach a step further by proposing that TNF be assigned a war-fighting role should deterrence fail. Since, however, the delivery systems available (which Mr. Schlesinger described as "a pile of junk") were neither modernized nor significantly expanded, their ability to carry out their assigned missions was questionable.

One reason for lack of progress in upgrading theater nuclear forces lay in the competition for funds within the Defense Department. The withdrawal from Vietnam had enabled Mr. Nixon to cut a million men from the armed forces and to reduce the defense budget from $65.4 billion in 1969 to $50.8 billion in 1972, in constant dollars. However, part of the monies saved by lowering manning levels went to pay the higher salaries and increased benefits associated with the "All-Volunteer Army," while other parts were devoted to re-establishing equipment levels and stockpiles in Europe and to improving strategic nuclear forces. Moreover, continuing inflation (which between FY 1968 and FY 1974 outran increases in the defense budget), the escalating costs of weapons systems and unforeseen contingencies such as the "Christmas Bombing" of North Vietnam in 1972 and the need to replace equipment lost by Israel in the "Yom Kippur War" of 1973 all placed severe strains on the defense budget.[40] Thus there were neither resources for other defense activities nor, if one looks at current dollars rather than constant ones, any "savings" from the end of the Vietnam War which could be devoted to social programs.

Far-reaching as these changes were, the major accomplishment of the Nixon Administration lay not in the military field but in the related one of arms control. Picking up what the Johnson Administration had begun before the occupation of Czechoslovakia cast a chill on U.S.-Soviet relations, Mr. Nixon negotiated two major arms control agreements:

1. the Interim Agreement on the Limitation of Strategic Armaments which, together with its Protocol, capped American and Soviet ICBM and SLBM forces at levels of approximately 1,700 and 2,400 SNDVs respectively;
2. the Treaty on Anti-Ballistic Missile Systems, which allowed each party only two clusters of one hundred interceptors each, one centered around the capital and one elsewhere in the country.[41]

And these were followed by a statement setting forth the Basic Principles of U.S.-Soviet Relations, which had been foreshadowed by the Quadripartite Agreement in Berlin and other moves toward détente.

In fact, it is for his détente policy rather than his defense policy that Mr. Nixon is remembered today. The latter, with its de-emphasis of conventional forces (especially outside Europe), its assignment of added responsibilities to TNF and its buildup of SNF was essentially a *reprise* of the "New Look." It was motivated primarily by awareness that domestic support for activist policies was lacking, an awareness enhanced by the (successful) public campaign against the deployment of ABMs, and by the consequent need for "military retrenchment without political disengagement."[42] It may also have been sparked by an awareness that the change in the strategic balance was irreversible and that the best thing one could hope for was strategic stability, preferably at lower cost; certainly that was the message conveyed by Secretary of State Kissinger.[43] In a larger sense, however, Mr. Nixon's policy represented an effort to ameliorate, if not to end, U.S.-Soviet rivalry, to follow up the stability achieved in Europe with some degree of stability elsewhere and in these and other ways to transform the global confrontation between the superpowers into one of cautious cooperation. And though events such as the Yom Kippur War of 1973 raised some debate as to how far this process could go, in June 1974, just a month before he resigned under threat of impeachment, President Nixon was in Moscow initialing a revision to the 1972 ABM Treaty and an agreement on a threshold test ban.[44]

The "Two" Presidents Carter

President Ford, who succeeded Mr. Nixon in 1974, made few innovations in defense policy; in fact, though he fired Mr. Schlesinger, he essentially retained the "Schlesinger Doctrine." However, Mr. Ford did, in the so-called Vladivostok Agreement, set overall limits of 2,400 on *all* U.S. and Soviet SNDVs and sub-ceilings of 1,320 on those carrying MIRVs.

This agreement—or, to be more precise the detailed papers implementing it—was set aside by President Carter, who in March 1977 proposed to Mr. Brezhnev drastically lower figures for SNDVs, MIRVed or not. This was in consonance with Mr. Carter's "ultimate goal—the elimination of all nuclear weapons from this earth." It also reflected two views on the part of the President and his advisers: that the military and political utility of nuclear weapons was less than commonly supposed and that arms control had not been pushed aggressively enough as a means of enhancing stability and promoting détente. Whatever the validity of these judgments, they ran afoul of the Soviet reluctance to "change agreements in the middle of the stream," so to speak. It was only after two years of negotiations that both sides finally signed the SALT II Treaty, which set over-all ceilings of 2,250 on SNDVs (lower than the Soviet force levels), and sub-ceilings of 1,200 on MIRVed missiles and 120 on bombers carrying ALCMs, which only the U.S. possessed at that time, and which introduced a number of qualitative constraints on weaponry.[45] But by that time political attitudes had changed and the Senate was reluctant to ratify the Treaty, which was eventually withdrawn following the Soviet intervention in Afghanistan.

The initial moves of the Carter Administration also reflected the opinions of the President and his advisers that while "perceived equality" in strategic forces was politically desirable, one need not worry very much about hard-target kill capabilities and other war-fighting measures. In line with this thinking Secretary of Defense Harold Brown defined two strategic requirements: maintaining a capability for "assured destruction"—reset at levels lower than those prescribed by his predecessor, Mr. Rumsfeld—and preserving "essential equivalence," a phrase of art first introduced by Mr. Schlesinger, which Mr. Brown defined as "a condition such that any advantages in force characteristics enjoyed by the Soviets are offset by other U.S. advantages."[46] Since the United States at that time held a two-to-one advantage in numbers of warheads, Mr. Brown must have felt that "essential equivalence" could easily be maintained; at any rate, he closed down the Minutemam III production line, deleted plans to modernize the Minuteman II missile, slowed down the procurement of Trident missile submarines (because of cost increases) and recommended to the President that he cancel procurement of the B-1 bomber in favor of utilizing B-52s with ALCMs (Air Launched Cruise Missiles) in a stand-off attack mode.[47] (As a result of these and other decisions, the number of deliverable U.S. warheads declined slightly from 1977-1979, while those carried by Soviet strategic forces increased from 3,900 to 5,900, though the United States still remained ahead.[48]) Similarly, the Carter Administration cancelled the planned deployment of ERW (Enhanced Radiation Weapons) to Europe and resisted for over a year pleas by the Allies for new intermediate range missiles to offset the SS-20, arguing that the real need was for improved conventional capabilities.

This the first—and second—Presidents Carter were indeed prepared to help provide. One of Mr. Carter's initial moves was to persuade the Allies to finance a Long-Term Defense Improvement Program, most of which went to buttress non-nuclear forces. Secretary of Defense Brown called for an adequate forward defense against a Pact conventional attack, including one with short warning, and the ability to respond rapidly in the event of aggression.[49] As applied to Europe, this meant the dispatch of two additional Army brigades, larger stockpiles of equipment for reinforcing units and an expanded air lift, financed by a 3% increase in budgetary allocations to forces earmarked for NATO, an increase which the Allies also agreed to make. Initially, however, despite proposals for a "deployment force of light divisions with strategic mobility"[50] little was done to augment forces for operations outside Europe; in fact, the Pentagon, in a continuation of Mr. Laird's policy, officially stopped preparations to cope with "a major two-theater attack."[51]

However, by the end of 1979, a "new" Carter had emerged, at least as far as defense policy was concerned. The abdication of the Shah of Iran, and the subsequent takeover of power by Islamic fundamentalists, focused attention on the Middle East, where additional naval forces were deployed and for which Air Force, Army and Marine units were earmarked. Additionally, headquarters for a Joint Rapid Deployment Task Force (JRDTF) were set up to plan for the utilization of these units and, after the Soviet occupation of Afghanistan in December of 1979, for the employment of other divisions and air wings allocated to the JRDTF. Moreover, the President gave purpose to these measures by enumerating the "Carter Doctrine," which stated that "any attempt by any outside force to gain control of the Persian Gulf region will be regarded as an assault on the vital interests of the United States of America and such an assault will be repelled by any means necessary, including military force."[52] And he accompanied them by stepped-up military assistance to the countries of the region, by the sale to Saudi Arabia of Airborne Warning and Control Aircraft (AWACS), temporarily manned by American crews, and by agreements with Egypt for the use of ports and airfields—first employed in the abortive attempt to rescue the U.S. hostages from Iran.

Nor were U.S. actions limited to the Middle East. Partly to restore the capacity for "flexible options," partly for political reasons, the Administration approved the deployment in Europe of 572 Pershing II SRBMs and ground-launched cruise missiles (GLCMs)—though the numbers and types of weapons were deliberately fixed below those required for a counterforce capability against their Soviet counterparts.[53] In 1980 it adopted a so-called "countervailing strategy," which added to the earlier requirements for "assured destruction" and "essential equivalence" one for "flexible options," defined as the ability to target selectively not only war-related industries but also centers of political and military leadership and control and Soviet military forces—including strategic nuclear delivery vehicles—and which aimed at improving the U.S. ability to wage a "protracted nuclear war."[54] In fact, Presidential Directive 59, which spelled out those options, plus the proposed deployment of 200 MX missiles with ten warheads each, and a step-up of work on the Trident II SLBM (one variant of which would have a hard-target kill capability) moved the Carter Administration a long way toward the war-fighting doctrine it had initially deemed unnecessary. And this change was justified in part by the argument that since Soviet military doctrine called for a war-fighting posture, the United States must be prepared to match or overmatch Soviet capabilities at any level of conflict.[55]

Obviously, these different policies had different impacts on the defense budget. In the first three years of the Carter Administration, both obligational authority and outlays, in constant dollars, went up only about 2% per year,[56] and much of that increase occurred because the actual rate of inflation exceeded that used in budgetary planning. Moreover, this rate of growth was insufficient to meet military needs, so that the Defense Department had to practice stringent economies in the procurement of new weapons, in purchases of ammunition and spare parts, in funds for training and in other categories affecting the readiness of the armed forces and their ability to engage in sustained combat. In the fourth year, as Mr. Carter and Mr. Brown moved to remedy existing deficiencies and to step up the rate of modernization, both current and projected expenditures increased sharply, to something like 7% per year, after allowing for inflation. Thus, even before the Reagan Administration came into office, there was a sharp rise in defense spending.

The initial approach of President Carter and his advisers was a blend of Kennedy-McNamara thinking about deterrence and Nixonian policy on détente. It was given both focus and intensity by Mr. Carter's own view that negotiations with the Soviet Union should "be guided by a vision— of a gentler, freer and more beautiful world" and that arms control could both facilitate the emergence of such a world and "increase the security of both sides."[57] This view was not widely held outside Mr. Carter's immediate circle (or even inside it, if one includes Mr. Brzezinski among that number), as the 1976 electoral campaign had indicated a shift to the right, both within the Republican Party and among the electorate as a whole. Accordingly, Mr. Carter's first defense policy represented an attempt to impose his own views on a public—and a Congress—that were not wholly sympathetic.

However, before the end of his term in office a "new" Carter had emerged, at least as far as defense policy was concerned. As one of his senior officials said, " . . . the Jimmy Carter of 1980 was a far cry from the Jimmy Carter who spoke during his election campaign of 'cutting five to seven billion dollars from the defense budget'[58] . . . " This shift in policy *circa* 1979-80 was apparently the result of three factors. The first was a further erosion of support for Mr. Carter's policies among both publics and elites, who by 1978 were beginning to express considerable concern over the Soviet military buildup and to call for increased defense spending.[59] The second was a feeling that even if the protracted negotiations on SALT II resulted in an agreement, it would do little to curb the growth of Soviet SNF and the consequent erosion of "essential equivalence;" hence, some means to enhance the credibility of the deterrent was essential. The third and most important was, however, the double shock administered by the Iranian takeover of the U.S. Embassy in Teheran and the Soviet move into Afghanistan. This latter led Mr. Carter to disavow publicly all his prior statements about the feasibility of reaching an acceptable understanding with the USSR and both together led him to call for stronger American forces and for significant increases in the defense budget.

It would, therefore, appear that a new awareness of the nature and the intractability of the superpower rivalry prompted a shift in U.S. defense policy. This was not, however, the only influence, since public opinion, economic interests (grounded in concern lest the Soviets next turn their attention to oil-rich Iran) and the prospect of an election less than a year hence all indicated the desirability of a sharp reaction to Soviet moves. That this reaction took the form of efforts to bolster forces in and available for the Middle East and to strengthen alliances there reflected the geo-political position of the United States. It also reflected the fact that in this region the U.S. was the only member of the Alliance with the strength to provide other than token forces; hence, the American predilection for unilateralism was furthered by its necessity. That these actions were accompanied by ones to strengthen SNF and plan for their employment in limited nuclear strikes is in large measure, however, coincidence, as the first hints of these developments had been given by Mr. Brown in May 1979, in his commencement address at the United States Naval Academy. Thus it would seem that continuing shifts in the strategic balance led to growing concern about the vulnerability of U.S. SNF and to a search for appropriate patterns of response; even if the Soviets had not invaded Afghanistan, Mr. Brown might have espoused a war-fighting doctrine as a means to effective deterrence and as a hedge against its failure.

The Two Reagan Administrations

Phase One. The measures taken by Mr. Carter were, however, widely criticized as "too little and too late," especially by Mr. Reagan and his supporters. These not only opposed the SALT II Treaty (which was never pushed to a vote in the Senate) but all previous arms control measures, which were deemed too favorable to the USSR, too restrictive on the United States and too likely to undermine support for essential defense programs. Officials argued that initiation of new Strategic Arms Reduction Talks (START) should await Congressional approval of a package of measures to restore and reinforce the deterrent capacity (both because of the intrinsic importance of this and because this "would make or break our arms control negotiations") and administration completion of the "hard . . . difficult . . . [and] interesting" intellectual problems of preparing for such talks.[60] The guidelines issued for these and other negotiations on arms control indicated that the acceptability of proposals to the Soviets should *not* be a criterion for their design. Hence, the initial position of the Reagan Administration can fairly be described as non-supportive of arms control.

This position proved, however, impossible to maintain, largely because of political pressures from the Allies. Accordingly, the Reagan Administration opened negotiations on INF in November 1981 and those on START shortly thereafter. Moreover, both President Reagan and his chief negotiators, notably Ambassador Paul Nitze, proved capable of tailoring measures which had some promise of Soviet acceptance, as well as considerable appeal to the Allies. Hence, the United States weathered the minor crisis caused by the Soviet walk-out from the INF negotiations in 1983 (and the indefinite suspension of the Strategic Arms Reduction Talks), waited out a Soviet return to the negotiating table and is now engaged in a fresh effort to curb armaments, as indicated below.

Whatever the questions about Mr. Reagan's intentions with respect to arms control, there can be none about those with respect to strategic nuclear forces: he started procurement of 100 B-1 bombers, increased the order for air-launched cruise missiles to 3,200, proposed to deploy 100 MX ICBMs in single silos and a small, single warhead ICBM thereafter, continued production of Trident submarines at the rate of one a year, stepped up development of Trident II SLBMs and ordered 400 nuclear-armed sea-launched cruise missiles, at a yearly cost of approximately $50 billion, for SNF alone.[61] More importantly, in March of 1983 Mr. Reagan announced that the United States would explore the technical feasibility of a space-based defensive system which could safeguard the United States against Soviet missiles and lead ultimately to the abolition of nuclear weapons;[62] as a means to this end the Administration initiated a $30 billion R & D program on "exotic weapons" and authorized service planning for multi-layered air and missile defenses. If carried out as planned, these initiatives would increase the number of deliverable warheads from about 9,000 when Mr. Reagan took office to 14,000 by 1990, in the process doubling and eventually tripling the hard-target kill capability,[63] and could provide a shield against Soviet disarming strikes, if not those directed at non-military targets.

One purpose of these changes was to redress the "margin of superiority" the Soviet Union allegedly possessed, thereby closing the "window of vulnerability."[64] Another was to insure that these forces should have, "throughout a protracted conflict and afterward," the ability to inflict very high levels of damage, so that the Soviets would seek termination of the war rather than deciding to strike at U.S. cities.[65] A third was to achieve a level of forces which could "prevail" in a protracted nuclear war, forces which should, according to the Report of the Scowcroft Commission that Mr. Reagan approved and adopted, have counter-force capabilities at least equal to those of the USSR.[66] Thus, the aim of the administration was to deter war by the prospect that, should it come, the United States would be able, in Secretary of Defense Weinberger's words, to "impose . . . war termination on terms favorable to the United States and its allies,"[67] i.e., to emerge victorious.

This too seemed to be the aim as far as conventional operations are concerned; to again quote Mr. Weinberger, "should our policy to deter aggression fail and conventional conflict be forced upon us, the United States would bend every effort to win the war as quickly as possible."[68] As one means to this end, the United States proposed not only to meet aggression where it occured but also to "launch counter-offensives in other regions and to exploit the aggressor's weaknesses whenever we might find them"[69], i.e., to practice "horizontal escalation." And this escalation might be used to "put . . . at risk Soviet interests, including the Soviet homeland"; in fact, then Secretary of the Navy John Lehman proposed operations not only against Soviet warships in all the oceans of the world but also against ports and naval installations in the USSR itself.[70] Since both these operations and others initiated by the Soviet Union and its proxies may take place anywhere, the United States must be prepared to "meet the demands of a worldwide war;" since the U.S. cannot count on such a war "ending within a few months," it must prepare for a protracted conflict.[71] In brief, the Reagan Administration initially planned to fight and win a conventional war, however long this took,[72] under the shield of strategic nuclear forces whose strength and durability would preclude the USSR from itself "going nuclear."

In this context, "forces of intervention" assumed new importance, as these would be used not only to insure access to raw materials and to defend Western interests in the Third World but also to attack Soviet outposts and proxies—including, in the event of a Soviet invasion of the Persian Gulf region, Cuba, Libya and Vietnam.[73] The same could not be said of TNF, whose mission, according to Mr. Weinberger, was that of "firmly linking strategic forces to our [U.S.] conventional capabilities". If, however, deterrence failed, then the Joint Chiefs of Staff would employ these weapons to "respond in kind to theater nuclear attack" or to escalate the conflict in a controlled fashion.[74] Indeed, given the emphasis on keeping a conventional war conventional, there is some question as to whether the operational definition of the role TNF are to play that was given by the JCS may not be more accurate than the political definition provided by the Secretary of Defense.

As one tries to understand the reasons for these radical alterations in defense policy and programs, a number of points stand out. One was the antipathy toward Communism, as embodied in the "evil empire" of the Soviet Union. Another was the sense of global rivalry with that empire, the threat from which was described as "at least as great as Hitler's."[75] A third was the belief that shifts in the "correlation of forces" have facilitated political gains by the USSR and have put not only American interests but the United States itself at risk. A fourth was the recognition that this latter risk is unacceptable; thus the efforts to reduce the vulnerability of the geo-economic base by emphasizing conventional war, building up superior strategic nuclear forces and if possible, establishing defenses against a Soviet nuclear attack.[76] A fifth was the seemingly greater pre-occupation with the Third World; although forces for Europe were strengthened, it was the Persian Gulf and Southwest Asia on which most attention was focused. A sixth is a belief that the accomplishments of American technology and the strength of the American economy would enable the United States to prevail in any "arms race" with the Soviet Union. And along with this went an assumption that "correcting imbalances in levels of weapons" was so important that neither enormous federal deficits nor growing public and political opposition to defense spending should affect proposed real annual increases of 9-10% in the defense budget. Since, however, that budget was, according to the Joint Chiefs of Staff, too small by half, and the forces it will generate fall short of those necessary, there is some doubt whether even the increases requested by the Reagan Administration would have given it what it needed in the way of enhanced military capabilities.[77]

Phase Two. There is, of course, even graver doubt that the administration will receive what it deems necessary, as public opinion has turned against further increases in military spending and the Congress has actually cut the defense budget in constant dollars. Faced with this opposition, and with the necessity to reduce the budget deficit, the Reagan Administration compromised on final appropriations for defense, even though it continued to ask for larger sums. In consequence, the Pentagon has twice been forced to adjust downward its five year plan and to slash its requests for new money, first under Mr. Weinberger and subsequently under his successor, Frank Carlucci. [78] Thus, it is highly unlikely that the 9% annual growth in spending achieved during the first four years of President Reagan's term of office will continue over the second four years; in fact, some analysts have predicted that defense spending at the close of Mr. Reagan's second Administration will be close to what it was at the beginning of his first one, in constant dollars.

Although a decline in appropriations for defense would not immediately halt the buildup of military capabilities, (which can be sustained for a time by monies not yet spent) it would certainly hamper the further development of the Rapid Deployment Force (now assigned to a newly-created "Central Command"), the construction of a "600-ship navy" and the implementation of options for "fighting on other fronts" in the event of Soviet aggression. Furthermore, it would appear that the $1.1 trillion expended during the first Reagan Administration, though it has led to improvements in the quality of personnel and in the resources necessary to sustain combat operations, did not generate significant increases in weapons procurement and has enabled only modest augmentations of combat units other than ships; for example, the total number of Air Force and Navy fighter squadrons increased only from 163 to 165.[79] Perhaps because anticipated capabilities have not been developed, perhaps because initial enthusiasms have been lost, one no longer heard Mr. Weinberger or his associates proposing in the event of a Soviet attack, to launch counteroffensives "against vulnerable points in the Soviet empire."[80] Moreover, the defenders on the Central Front have been given a more modest (if ambiguous) mission than was earlier assigned: that of deterring or defeating an attack or giving time for other decisions to be taken.[81] Thus neither the conventional force posture deemed necessary for the "Weinberger Doctrine" nor that doctrine itself is likely to be in place at the end of the second Reagan Administration.

Neither may the strategic nuclear forces required to "prevail" in a protracted nuclear war. Although these are reportedly being given priority in Pentagon planning,[82] the budgetary squeeze will undoubtedly affect them also, especially if expenditures for research on strategic defensive systems rise. Moreover, although the concept of a "population shield" has strong public support, the idea of "prevailing" in a protracted nuclear conflict does not; in fact, an overwhelming majority of the people don't believe there is any such thing as a "winnable nuclear war."[83] Furthermore, President Reagan himself has at least started on the process of cutting back on nuclear forces, beginning with the agreement to eliminate intermediate-range and short-range missiles signed on 8 December 1987 and looking forward to 50% reductions in strategic nuclear forces.[84] Hence, although the administration still proposes to conduct a controlled nuclear war, with emphasis on counterforce operations, one may see future adjustments in doctrine with respect to nuclear forces as well as with respect to conventional ones.

Whether these last moves reflect a change of heart is hard to tell; though Mr. Reagan, in the first flush of enthusiasm following the signing of the INF agreement, asserted that "Moscow has forsworn any thought of world domination,"[85] he emphasized his intention to deploy SDI , should this prove feasible. Nor is there any indication that he and his associates have changed their views about the primacy of force as an instrument of policy. They may, however, mark an adjustment to reality in terms of what force can accomplish, as well as in terms of what forces one can reasonably expect to create. They may also mark an awareness of the limits imposed

on even a charismatic and popular president by the political structure of
the United States; when over 80% of the public favor *rapprochement* with
the Soviet Union rather than confrontation and endorse limitations on
armaments[86] even a leader who holds differing views may well reconsider
his policies. And Mr. Reagan, though some may deem him an idealog, is
also a pragmatic politician.[87]

A Summing Up

Although this brief summation of developments over almost 40 years
cannot do justice to the efforts of American policy-makers to cope with
the problems facing them,[88] it may give a sense of the road they took.
After a brief period in which war-time doctrine underwent little change,
the United States, under President Eisenhower, emphasized deterrence
through the threat of nuclear retaliation, a threat which still underpins U.S.
defense policy. Over time there has, however, been a shift from a doctrine
of "massive retaliation," based on the ability to destroy the Soviet Union
almost without fear of consequences, to one of "assured destruction," in
which the threat to launch a potentially suicidal strike is made more
credible through the creation of "flexible options," coupled with local
defenses to heighten the "nuclear threshold" and/or triggering mechanisms
to raise the spectre of escalation, deliberate or inadvertent. Thus, an initial
strategic nuclear response to aggression (short of a direct nuclear strike
against the United States) will now be partial rather than total and delayed
rather than immediate.

Along with this change went two others particularly applicable to Europe,
one of which affected theater nuclear forces and concepts for their employment. Initially, these were to be used to supplement, or to substitute
for, conventional capabilities for the defense of Europe. When, however,
the USSR developed and deployed its own versions of TNF, the primary
mission assigned Allied units changed: first to that of destroying or degrading Soviet nuclear-capable elements in Eastern Europe, then to that of
deterring the use of these elements and finally to one of threatening
escalation, either as part of a nuclear strike against a variety of targets,
intended to show determination, or by employment against WTO conventional forces, on the battlefield or advancing toward it. And though intermittent efforts were made to upgrade TNF in Europe to the point where
they would have a significant war-fighting capability (as distinct from a
limited, emergency one), these foundered on the twin rocks of Allied
reluctance to wage a nuclear war in Europe and of infeasibility, given the
potential vulnerability of Western forces to Soviet attack.

The other change was in the role of conventional forces, which was
initially that of defending Western Europe while strategic bombing took
effect. In the next period, their function was primarily that of a "tripwire"
triggering a U.S. strategic nuclear strike—a function which in some European eyes is still the preferred one. However, with the advent of mutual

strategic deterrence, conventional forces in Europe were given responsibility for checking an initial assault by Soviet/WTO units, thereby deferring the time when nuclear weapons would have to be employed and giving the adversary time to reconsider the costs and consequences of continuing his military operations. Moreover, the United States has sought recently to move a step further, suggesting that precision-guided weapons and cluster munitions could be used to interdict the advance of Soviet reinforcements and to degrade Soviet/WTO tactical air capabilities and that NATO forces, properly armed, organized and equipped, could hold, if not defeat, even a massive assault—a subject which will be discussed at greater length in Chapter 4.

Outside Europe, however, the trend has not been so clear. Partly because the threat is more differentiated, partly because some of these threats have actually materialized, as in Korea, in Vietnam and, in different ways, in places like Angola, El Salvador and Lebanon, the responses have been much more variegated. Thus, the United States has sometimes been willing, when American lives were threatened, to use force, as it did in Grenada in 1983, sometimes eschewed its use, as against Iran in 1979; sometimes been prepared to employ troops against insurgents in friendly countries, as in Vietnam, and sometimes refrained from so doing, as in El Salvador; sometimes intervened to "keep the peace," as in Lebanon in 1972 and 1982, and sometimes left this task to others, as in Zaire in 1962 and in 1978. And while one can argue that these differing approaches reflect different situations, the correlation is not always evident.

Nor have U.S. policies on arms control been any more consistent than those on the utilization of the military instrument in the Third World. Both the Kennedy Administration and the Carter Administration were more opposed to nuclear proliferation than were others, and the Nixon Administration manifested a support for strategic arms limitations which the Reagan Administration only belatedly came to share. Furthermore, thinking about the desirability of curbing strategic defensive systems has gone full circle, from Johnson, who proposed such limitations, to Reagan, who opposes them. And though every President in the last fourteen years has supported the MBFR negotiations in Vienna, this may say as much about their poor prospects for fruition as about a common enthusiasm for lowering force levels in Europe.

All these responses seem to have been within a framework initially set by the division of Europe, the development of nuclear weapons and the rise of the USSR to superpower status; as the military balance shifted so did U.S. concepts and programs. Although intermittent efforts were made to accommodate to the changed position and power of the USSR, these did not extend to acceptance of the Soviet desire for an "equal voice" in world affairs and could not extend to toleration of Soviet efforts to extend their influence in the Third World. This meant that the global rivalry with the USSR not only continued but intensified, with consequent requirements for forces for "global power projection" and with consequent implications

for the confrontation in Europe. And if the disparity between power and
its applicability inhibited both the U.S. and the USSR from making the
gains they otherwise might have achieved, it did not lead either of them
to give up attempts to secure such gains, much less to put caps on the
forces they are employing for this purpose—though there are signs that
Soviet policy is changing in both respects.

The effects of U.S. domestic influences on this modern version of the
"great game" have been both mixed and variable. Some economic interests
have both urged and benefited from an activist foreign and defense policy,
while others have deemed it detrimental. ("War is not healthy for trade
and other growing things.") On some occasions, (as just before the election
of Mr. Reagan) publics and elites have supported the buildup and the use
of the armed forces while on other occasions, as in the aftermath of the
Vietnam War, they have balked. (One analyst suggests that the American
experience in Vietnam was so traumatic that some prominent officials in
the Carter Administration regarded the entire Third World as little more
than Vietnam writ large—a place devoid of vital U.S. interests and in
which the application of U.S. military power could lead only to trouble.[89])
The overriding factor, however, seemed to be that an activist president
could get (most of) what he wanted, from new missiles to new "allies"
like Somalia, South Africa and North Yemen.

This does not mean that all problems have been solved; in fact, in some
instances, policy options or programmatic choices may have made solutions
more difficult. Whether the reason for their existence is intractability or
bad judgment, a number of "hardy perennials" are still with us, as are a
number of new issues arising out of changed circumstances. In subsequent
chapters we will deal with the most important of these, following a discussion of West German approaches to defense policy.

Notes

1. For one illustration of this approach, see Donald E. Neuchterlein, "National
Interests and National Strategy: The Need for Priority," in Terry L. Heyns, ed.,
Understanding U.S. Strategy: A Reader (Washington, D.C.: National Defense Uni-
versity Press, 1983), 35-63.

2. Wolfram F. Hanreider and Larry V. Buel, *Words and Arms: A Dictionary of
Security and Defense Terms* with supplementary data (Boulder, CO: Westview Press,
1979), 79.

3. *Ibid.*

4. Jo L. Husbands, "Definitions of Security," in Charles E. Pirtle, Supervising
ed., *International Security: Concepts and Approaches*, an Introductory Course, (Center
for International Security Studies, University of Pittsburgh, 1979), 3.

5. Alexander Haig, "Relationship of Foreign and Defense Policies," *Current
Policy*, 302, Bureau of Public Affairs, United States Department of State (Washington, D.C.; 30 July 1981), 2.

6. Lincoln Bloomfield, *The United Nations and U.S. Foreign Policy: A New Look
at the National Interest*, rev. ed. (Boston: Little, Brown and Co., 1967), 28.

7. Charles L. Hermann, "Defining National Security," in John F. Reichart and Steven R. Sturm, eds., *American Defense Policy*, 5th ed. (Baltimore and London: Johns Hopkins University Press, 1982), 20-21.

8. William Rogers, *American Foreign Policy: Innovation and Involvement*, a reprint from United States Foreign Policy 1971: A Report of the Secretary of State (Washington, D.C.: 1971), v.

9. Bloomfield, *The United Nations and U.S. Foreign Policy*, 30; Heyns, *Understanding U.S. Strategy*, 223. For a more extensive listing see Neuchterlein, "National Interests and National Strategy," 38-41.

10. Robert E. Osgood, "American Grand Strategy: Patterns, Problems, and Prescriptions," *Naval War College Review*, 36, 5 (Sept.-Oct. 1983), 12.

11. Howard Bliss and M. Glenn Johnson, *Beyond the Water's Edge: America's Foreign Policy* (Philadelphia, PA: J. B. Lippincott Company, 1975), 65.

12. Ronald J. Stupak, *American Foreign Policy: Assumptions, Processes and Projections* (New York: Harper & Row, 1976), 154.

13. *Report of the Secretary of Defense Caspar W. Weinberger to the Congress on the FY 1985 Budget, FY 1986 Authorization Request and FY 1985-89 Defense Programs* (Washington, D.C.: 1 February 1984), 21-22.

14. For a recent assessment of Soviet theater forces available for operations in or against Western Europe see NATO Information Service, *NATO and the Warsaw Pact, Force Comparisons* (Brussels: NATO Information Service, 1984), 7-23, and 30-43. For the terms of the "double-zero" agreement and the weapons to be removed thereunder, see *The New York Times*, 9 December 1987, 10-11.

15. Armin Wetterhahn, "The Soviet Guided Missile Cruiser *Slava*," *International Defense Review*, 17, 1 (January 1984), 21-26.

16. Cf. *The Military Balance, 1984-1985* (London: The International Institute for Strategic Studies, August 1984), 13-22.

17. Although there was a humanitarian cast to these programs, there can be little doubt that they were intended primarily to further other objectives; as the Joint Chief of Staff stated, " . . . it is firmly believed that assistance should be concentrated on those countries of primary strategic importance to the United States." "United States Assistance to Other Countries from the Standpoint of National Security," JCS document 1769/1, 29 April 1947, quoted in Thomas H. Etzold and John Lewis Gaddis, eds., *Containment: Documents on American Policy and Strategy, 1945-1950* (New York: Columbia University Press, 1978), 83.

18. Russell F. Weigley, *The American Way of War* (New York: Macmillan Publishing Company, 1973), 368.

19. Bernhard Bechhoefer, *Postwar Negotiations on Arms Control* (Washington, D.C.: The Brookings Institution, 1961), 17.

20. Dwight D. Eisenhower, *Mandate for Change, 1953-56* (Garden City, NY: Doubleday and Company, 1963), 453.

21. David M. Schwartz, *NATO's Nuclear Dilemmas* (Washington, D.C.: The Brookings Institution, 1983), 32-34. See also Richard Halloran, *To Arm A Nation* (New York: Macmillan & Company, 1986), 271-274.

22. Secretary of State John Foster Dulles, Address to the Council on Foreign Relations , 25 Jan. 1954, quoted in Weigley, *The American Way of War*, 404.

23. In this context, war fighting is defined as "combat actions . . . designed . . . to prosecute wars," a definition which does not necessarily extend to the strategy or policy of being prepared "to fight any kind of war at any spectrum in the conflict level," as proposed by some analysts. Hanrieder and Buel, *Words and Arms*, 135.

24. For a good summary of developments during this period see John H. Barton and Lawrence D. Weiler eds., *International Arms Control: Issues and Agreements* (Stanford, CA: Stanford University Press,1976), 74-84.

25. Eisenhower, *Mandate for Change*, 446-447.

26. The budget declined from $60.7 billion in 1953 to $46.1 billion in 1960, in 1964 dollars. *Statement of Secretary of Defense Melvin R. Laird on the Fiscal Year 1972-76 Defense Program and the 1972 Defense Budget*, 9 March 1971 (Washington, D.C.: GPO, 1971) Figure 1 Eisenhower Strategy, 1953-1960, 155. (hereafter cited as Laird, *Annual Report, FY1972*).

27. Eisenhower, *Mandate for Change*, 449-458.

28. Robert S. McNamara, *The Essence of Security* (New York: Harper & Row, 1968), 69.

29. For example, then Secretary of Defense McNamara noted that even a full-scale program of active and passive defenses, plus augmented U.S. conterforce capabilities, could not reduce fatalities below 20 million, even if the United States struck first, and fatalities in other scenarios ranged up to 135 million. *Statement of Secretary of Defense Robert S. McNamara before the House Armed Services Committee on the Fiscal Year 1969-1971 Defense Program and 1967 Defense Budget*, (Washington, D.C.: 8 March 1966), 53.

30. "Remarks by Secretary McNamara, NATO Ministerial Meeting, 6 May 1962, Restricted Session," quoted in Schwartz, *NATO's Nuclear Dilemmas*, 161.

31. *Ibid.*, 139-142; See also 145-162.

32. McNamara, *Essence of Security*, 5.

33. "Assured destruction," required that the United States be able, under all circumstances, to inflict "unacceptable damage" upon the Soviet Union—a phrase sometimes defined as the devastation of 200 major Soviet cities, sometimes as the destruction of one-quarter to one-third of the Soviet people and two-thirds to three-quarters of Soviet industry and sometimes as inflicting such damage that "[Soviet] society would be simply no longer viable in the twentieth century terms." (*Ibid*, 52-53.)

34. Melvin R. Laird, "A Strong Start in a Difficult Decade: Defense Policy in the Nixon-Ford years," *International Security*, 10, 2 (Fall 1985): 20-23.

35. Raymond L. Garthoff, *Détente and Confrontation: American-Soviet Relations from Nixon to Reagan* (Washington, D.C.: The Brookings Institution, 1985), 248-261.

36. These "selected targets" were to include key industries on the outskirts of cities, critical military facilities and the air bases and missile silos of Soviet SNF, in increaseing order of importance. *Report of Secretary of Defense James R. Schlesinger to the Congress on the FY 1976 and Transition Budgets, FY 1977 Authorization Request and FY 1976-1980 Defense Programs* (Washington, D.C.: 5 Feb. 1975), I-11.

37. John M. Collins, *U.S.-Soviet Military Balance: Concepts and Capabilities, 1960-1980* (New York: McGraw-Hill, 1980), 458-459.

38. Testimony of Robert C. Moot, Assistant Secretary of Defense, (Comptroller), *Department of Defense Appropriations for 1972: Hearings*, Part 1, U.S. Congress, House, Committee on Appropriations, Subcommittee on Department of Defense, 92nd Cong., 1st Sess., 1971, 1131, cited in Colin S. Gray and Jeffrey G. Barlow, "Inexcusable Restraint: The Decline of American Military Power in the 1970's," *International Security*, 10, 2 (Fall 1985), 52.

39. Laird, *Annual Report, FY 1972*, 75-76.

40. Gray and Barlow, "Inexcusable Restraint: the Decline of American Military Power in the 1970's," 53-58.

41. The texts can be found in Roger P. Labrie, *SALT Handbook*, (Washington, D.C.: American Enterprise Institute for Public Policy Research, 1979) 15-23, followed by supporting documents and interpretations.

42. Robert Litwak, *Détente and the Nixon Doctrine*, (New York: Cambridge University Press, 1984), 54. See also *The Memoirs of Richard Nixon* (New York: Grosset and Dunlap, 1978), 395.

43. Press conference of Secretary of State Henry A. Kissinger, 22 July 1974, reprinted in Labrie, *SALT Handbook*, 225-227. See also *The Memoirs of Richard Nixon*, 415.

44. Garthoff, *Détente and Confrontation*, 425-427.

45. The texts of the treaty and of ancillary agreements (such as that concerning production of Backfire bombers by the USSR) will be found in Labrie, *SALT Handbook*, 621-660. An appendix (667-704) summarizes contrasting views on the treaty.

46. Department of Defense, *Annual Report, Fiscal Year 1979, Harold Brown, Secretary of Defense*, (Washington, D. C.: 2 February 1978), 56

47. *Ibid.*, 108-117.

48. Collins, *U.S.-Soviet Military Balance*, Table 8, 459-460.

49. Brown, *Annual Report, FY 1979*, 6-7.

50. Zbigniew Brzezinski, *Power and Principle* (New York: Farrar, Straus, Siroux, 1983), 177.

51. Brown, *Annual Report, FY 1979*, 13.

52. Jimmy Carter, *Keeping Faith* (New York: Bantam Books, 1982), 482.

53. Schwartz, *NATO's Nuclear Dilemmas*, 224-227.

54. Harold Brown, *Thinking about National Security, Defense and Foreign Policy in a Dangerous World* (Boulder, CO; Westview Press, 1983), 82.

55. *Ibid.*, 56-57.

56. *Report of Secretary of Defense Harold Brown to the Congress on the FY 1980 Budget, FY 1981 Authorization Request and FY 1980-1984 Defense Programs*, (Washington, D.C.: 20 January 1979), C-3, C-4.

57. "Remarks before the Southern Legislative Conference . . . 21 July 1977," reported in Labrie, *SALT Handbook*, 475 & 477.

58. Robert W. Komer, "What 'Decade of Neglect'?," *International Security*, 10. 2 (Fall 1985), 76.

59. John E. Reilly, ed., *American Public Opinion and U.S. Foreign Policy* (Chicago: The Chicago Council on Foreign Relations, 1983), 14 & 28.

60. Eugene V. Rostow, Director of the U.S. Arms Control and Disarmament Agency, *Hearings before the Committee on Foreign Relations on the Foreign Policy and Arms Control Implications of President Reagan's Strategic Weapons Proposals*, Part I, Nov. 3, 4 & 9, 1981 (Washington, D.C.: 1981), 76 & 80.

61. Congressional Budget Office, *Modernizing U.S. Strategic Offensive Forces: the Administration's Program and Alternatives*, (Washington D.C.: May 1983), xiii-xiv.

62. "President's Speech on Military Spending and a New Defense," *The New York Times*, 24 March 1983, 20.

63. Congressional Budget Office, *Modernizing U.S. Strategic Offensive Forces*, summary figure 1, xvi.

64. "President Ronald Reagan, Press Conference, 31 March 1982," *The New York Times*, 1 April 1982, 22.

65. Defense Guidance, FY 1985-1989, quoted by Richard Halloran, "Weinberger Angered by Reports on War Strategy," *The New York Times*, 24 August 1982, 8B.

66. *Ibid.*; Report of the President's Commission on Strategic Forces, 6 April 1983, 6, quoted in Robert Jervis, *The Illogic of American Nuclear Strategy* (Ithaca and London: Cornell University Press 1984), 112.

67. *Report of Secretary of Defense Caspar N. Weinberger to the Congress on the FY 1983 Budget, FY 1984 Authorization Request and FY 1983-1987 Defense Programs*, (Washington, D.C., 8 Feb. 1982), I-18.

68. *Ibid.*, I-16, I-17.

69. Testimony of Mr. Weinberger, *U.S. Congress, House Committee on Appropriations, Subcommittee on Defense, DoD Appropriaions for FY 1982, Pt 1, Hearings, 97th Congress, 1st Session, 1981*, 274-275, quoted in Keith Dunn and William P. Staudenmaier, *Strategic Implications of the Continental-Maritime Debate*, The Washington Papers, No. 10 (New York: 1984), 11.

70. Richard Halloran, "Pentagon Draws Up First Strategy for a Long Nuclear War," *The New York Times*, 30 May 1982, 17; U.S. Congress, House Committee on Armed Services, Hearings on the Military Posture and H.R. 5968, 97th Congress, 2nd sess., 1982, cited by Jeffrey Record, "Jousting with Unreality: Reagan's Military Strategy," *International Security*, 8, 3, (Winter 1983-84), 9-10. See also Weinberger, *Annual Report, FY 1983*, I-16.

71. *Ibid.*, I-14 & I-16.

72. FY 85-89 Defense Guidance, quoted by Richard C. Gross, "Pentagon Drafts Plan to Upgrade Strength," The *Washington Post*, 18 March 1983, 1.

73. Leslie H. Gelb, "Reagan's Military Budget Puts Emphasis on a Buildup of Global Military Power," *The New York Times*, 7 February 1982, 26.

74. Weinberger, *Annual Report, FY 1983*, III-71. See also Organization of the Joint Chiefs of Staff, *United States Military Posture for FY 1984* (Washington D.C.: 1983), 18.

75. "Interview with Mr. Weinberger," *USA Today*, 11 August 1983, 9.

76. Flora Whitt, "Weinberger: Star Wars' Defense Plan is No Fantasy," The *Washington Times*, 12 April 1983, 4.

77. Bill Keller, "As Arms Buildup Eases, U.S. Tries to Take Stock," *The New York Times*, 14 May 1985, 20. Also see Richard Halloran, "New Weinberger Directive Refines Military Policy," *The New York Times,* 22 March 1983, 18.

78. *The New York Times*, 23 September 1985, 1; *Ibid.*, 5 December 1987, 1 (N).

79. Congressional Budget Office, *Defense Spending: What Has Been Accomplished?* Staff Working Paper, April 1985, iii-iv, quoted in Komer, "What 'Decade of Neglect'?" 82; Benjamin S. Lambeth, "Pitfalls in Force Planning: Structuring America's Tactical Air Arm," *Ibid*, 88, Footnote 6.

80. Weinberger, *Annual Report, FY 1983*, 1-16.

81. *Report of the Secretary of Defense Caspar W. Weinberger to the Congress on the FY 1984 Budget, FY 1985 Authorization Request and FY 1984-88 Defense Programs*, (Washington, D.C.: 1 February 1983), 17.

82. *The New York Times*, 23 Sept. 1985, 1-15.

83. Daniel Yankelovich and John Doble, "The Public Mood," *Foreign Affairs*, 63, 1, 33-34.

84. *The New York Times.*, 9 December 1987, 10-11, 8.

85. *Ibid.*, 13 December 1987, Section 4, 9.

86. Yankelovich and Doble, "The Public Mood," 44.

87. Leslie H. Gelb, "The Mind of the President," *The New York Times Magazine*, 6 October 1986, 21.

88. For a somewhat more detailed treatment see Richard Smoke, "The Evolution of American Defense Policy" and the follow on, "A Summary of Developments since 1975," in Reichert and Sturm, *American Defense Policy*, 94-140.

89. Record, "Jousting with Unreality," 7.

Comments

a. In practice, of course, such an abstraction from reality is, like all models, grossly over-simplified. It does, however, provide a basis for analyzing comparative foreign (and defense) policies, which is our aim, and hence will be used here.

b. For example, when Great Britain in 1823 suggested that the United States issue a joint declaration warning other powers against intervention in Latin America, President Monroe refused—but then issued on his own authority the so-called Monroe Doctrine.

c. This aid was offered to, but rejected by, the USSR and the countries of Eastern Europe.

d. So, according to some analysts and officials, would a coordinated denial of access to oil, or an increase in prices so enormous as to threaten the economies of the industrialized countries; in fact, at one time scenarios leading to an American "take-over" of Saudi oil fields were bandied about so freely that the government of Saudi Arabia announced its own contingency plan: to blow up the pumps, pipelines and wells rather than to allow them to be seized by others.

e. During the Korean War Stalin raised the number of men under arms to over 5,000,000, a figure which Mr. Khrushchev halved between 1958 and 1962, during which time the USSR also withdrew from East Germany two of the 22 divisions stationed there.

3

The FRG's Adaptation to the Post-War World

Klaus von Schubert

As noted in the preceding chapter, at the end of World War II a strong, confident America was preparing to end its pre-war isolationism, to accept new challenges and responsibilities, and to assume a truly global role. The reverse was true of Germany, which was defeated, divided, and devastated; under these circumstances the eyes of all Germans were turned inward, not outward. Yet scarcely had the Germans cleared away the rubble, planted new crops, and begun (under close supervision and with a truncated industrial base) to produce essential goods and provide vital services than they had to turn again to questions of foreign policy.

One reason for this was that the four Occupation Powers (Britain, France, the Soviet Union, and the United States) were seeking to remake Germany after their disparate images, and the Germans wanted a voice in that process. Another was that these same powers fell out among themselves, with the consequent threat of a new war, which could have dealt a deathblow to Germany, and the reality of a "Cold War," which led to the division of Germany and required the Germans to choose between the two sides. The third reason was that the nation's choice among the existing powers would have fateful consequences for both German security and German nationhood, the most important influences on German policy during the past two hundred years.

German Security and German Nationhood

To say this is to acknowledge that a sense of nationhood came late to the Germans; down to the nineteenth century individuals associated themselves with Prussia or Bavaria, Saxony or Hannover, not with a still mythical Germany, and as nationals of these states they fought one another as frequently as they fought Frenchmen or Russians. But there was a strong sense that without a national base Germany would be neither complete or secure.

This belief was rooted in both history and geography. The area settled by Germans—largely lacking natural topographical boundaries to the East and the West—was predestined to be a watershed for transit traffic and violent encounter. In medieval times it was defended against external threats and kept more or less at peace internally by the Holy Roman Empire. In the age of the emerging European nation states the area was of indeterminate borders, an entity composed of small independent territories, largely engaged in fighting for supremacy. A war of unification finally led, under Bismarck, to a "small Germany," which though it left Austrians and other ethnic Germans outside its borders, was easier to define in terms of its security requirements.

As one nation-state among others, the Second German Reich was situated in the midst of neighbors who had also to be regarded as rivals—particularly in view of the annexations fatefully accompanying the founding of the Reich. Its security depended on the internal equilibrium of the European state system. The chief threat stemmed from the possibility of a war with one adversary which could extend to several, or even all, so great was the interlacing of interests among these nation-states and their coalitions. Situations of acute, anxiety-ridden conflict, did flare into war, in defiance of the security principle of balanced regional pluralism among nation-states. Nazi expansionism was ultimately born of anxiety as well and dealt the death-blow to this principle.

Adolf Hitler was defeated in World War II, but it was not possible to restore the old European pattern, nor the security system based on pluralism, balance and hegemonial restraint. The anti-Hitler coalition also crumbled after the removal of its immediate *raison d'être*, reforming, as noted earlier, into two opposed blocs.

Germany's ever-difficult central location in European political geography had altered drastically with the end of the World War II. If the East-West conflict is regarded as a relatively stable and—for the foreseeable future—lasting framework for the factors determining international relations, both the FRG and the GDR have moved to the periphery. This is due to the division of Germany and the shifting of power from Europe to the U.S. and Soviet poles. At the same time, the two Germanies are in the forefront of the East-West conflict in Europe and occupy a central position in a possible war.

German security as such disappeared with the total collapse of the Third Reich. The occupied zones, and subsequently the two German states, sought their own security—and their own nationhood. This raised few questions for the German Democratic Republic (GDR), owing to its much greater dependence on the Soviet Union. The Grotewohl and Ulbricht government hardly needed to worry about security since the Soviet Union had stationed many troops in the GDR and had helped the regime to establish a military-type police force to ensure that it kept the upper hand. Any large-scale opposition to that regime was out of the question, in the face of this military and police presence, as was any attack by the depleted armies of the West. Also out of the question was any attempt by the GDR to re-establish the German "nation," as it could take no independent political initiatives and was bound ultimately by Soviet decisions with respect to the future of Germany.

In their special situation the West Germans faced even greater difficulties in safeguarding their security. Unalterable factors affecting the security of the FRG are high population density, infrastructure and industrialization. The urbanization of whole regions; the closely interlocking road, rail, and aviation networks; telecommunications; electricity and water supply; and the sensitivity of modern industrial plants and their interdependence have made the FRG extremely vulnerable in all vital areas. This vulnerability is enhanced by the FRG's dependence on the import of food and partic-ularly of industrial raw materials and energy supplies. This general depen-dence on imports contrasts with its economically vital and irreplaceable reliance on exports. All these factors mean that war on German soil, using nuclear or even modern so-called conventional weapons, would strike at the country's heart. Thus today, as in 1949, the issue of "war avoidance" is paramount.

But, given the weakness and the vulnerability of West Germany, security could not be achieved by its unaided efforts. Nor could that country rely upon the United Nations; even had that organization lived up to the expectations of its founders Germany was not a member—and was, indeed, under severe strictures imposed by the UN Charter.

In endeavoring to keep West Germany at peace and, hence, secure, the political leaders of 1949 had three policy options: involvement in the Soviet sphere, neutrality in the East-West conflict with the possibility of German reunification (an option suggested in 1952 by Joseph Stalin himself),[1] or integration into the West. The feasibility of each option was heavily influ-enced by the prevailing international climate, the occupation status of the FRG, and the resultant perceptions of threat.[2]

The first option, integration into the Soviet sphere, was practically and politically unrealistic, given the predominance of the Western powers in their respective zones. Chancellor Konrad Adenauer's fundamental anti-Communism and SPD-leader Kurt Schumacher's vehement distrust of the Soviets precluded any involvement in the Soviet sphere. Observations of Soviet policies and administration in the East, including the heavy repar-ations and authoritative strictures levied on the East, strengthened the resolve to avoid this cooptation.

The second alternative, German neutrality, was not so easily dismissed and remained at the heart of the West German security debate. This option presupposed a guarantee of that neutrality by the two superpowers, an unlikely event in light of the escalating Cold War. Yet within the FRG this option was heatedly discussed, with the opposition SPD strongly supporting German neutrality if it led to reunification. The SPD, under the leadership of Kurt Schumacher, envisioned a neutral, reunified Germany residing in a collective European security system. Under this model, a reunified Germany would not belong to any military alliance, and neutrality would be guaranteed and overseen by the Allied powers. Security, however, was contingent upon German reunification within the 1937 borders. This was the concept articulated by Fritz Erler, the social democratic successor to Schumacher, when he spoke of a "security for and from Germany."[3]

Adenauer's security policy, based on the model of Western integration, predominated over the other two options. To Adenauer, German security meant unequivocally turning to the West and being integrated into the community of western European states and political traditions. Like the opposition, he believed in the concept of collective security, which in his eyes was to be found with the other Western European states. Unlike the opposition, however, Adenauer deemed any form of neutrality, even if it included a reunified Germany, an untenable surrender to Soviet expansionism, and therefore found it unacceptable. He envisioned integrating the FRG into a higher, even supranational, entity of western European states, embodied in the prototypical European Coal and Steel Community and the later unsuccessful European Defense Community. Integration had the advantage of credibly linking the need for security with a new political identity, replacing the tainted image of the past.

While both options sought to work within the framework of collective security, the Western integration formula placed a higher priority on the need for security, while the SPD formula for a neutral reunified Germany sought to first meet the need for national identity. The debate between the Government and the Opposition, notably between their leaders Adenauer and Schumacher, grew to a controversy over the method of foreign policy. While Adenauer assumed that a West German contribution to defense would lead to the FRG's achieving equality and sovereignty, through its own political weight, Schumacher wanted military participation to be the consequence of political equality, not the precondition. When a spokesman for the governing CDU-CSU coalition in the *Bundestag* referred to the raising of German troops as an "occurrence of genuine legitimation," an SPD politician bluntly retorted, "you don't die for an occupation statute." The dispute over method ended without resolution as the West Germans became members of the Western Alliance and got sovereignty simultaneously. This, however, was a West German solution. The question of German nationhood was left out altogether.

West German Perceptions of the East-West Conflict

The outcome of the debate on security policy within Germany was influenced by many things, one of which was German perceptions of the East-West conflict and particularly of the Soviet challenge to the West. This conflict takes many forms: political, economic, cultural and even military. It extends over the northern hemisphere with effects on the entire globe, albeit with foci on certain strategic areas, of which Germany is a major one. And it has a number of causes, which militate against resolving it, or even coping with it by one means or another.

What is this East-West (or West-East) conflict all about in the West German view?[4] First of all, since the October 1917 Revolution leading to the establishment of the Union of Soviet Socialist Republics, we have had a conflict of ideologies, i.e., of highly disparate political ideas. Since then this conflict has become more and more overtly a matter of rivalry between powers. It is difficult to determine the relationship between ideology and power politics as causes of conflict. On the one hand, it is undeniable that political doctrines have their own weight in policy-making. On the other, ideology regularly serves to justify moves which were not foreseen in Soviet ideology, having been made for pragmatic, i.e., power policy, reasons.

The power policy dimension of the conflict, embodied in the rivalry between the U.S. and the Soviet Union, came to the fore at the end of World War II, as Hitler's expansion from Central Europe had backfired and led to the weakening of this region. Power migrated westward and eastward, with Washington and Moscow becoming the new focal points. While quiet reflection and a look at the atlas might suggest to us that the U.S. could never conquer and occupy the Soviet Union, or vice versa, the power vacuum Hitler left behind him in Central Europe invited conflict about his legacy.

The new world powers were obviously unable to maintain their agreement over and beyond World War II. Instead of the "one world" called for by Roosevelt there followed the division of the world into spheres of influence and thus the formation of power blocs. Some people pinned their hopes on the intervening effect of the United Nations but that organization itself fell prey to the divisions between East and West.

If the division of the world into spheres of influence was to be regarded as a consequence of power politics, the ideological conflict between these spheres was openly declared in the aftermath of 1945. The very fact that the foreign ministers of the victorious powers were not able to agree on the political treatment to be meted out to the occupied regions shows the great variety of ideas about political order existing in Europe. "What does the Soviet Foreign Minister understand by democracy?" U.S. Secretary of State James Byrnes asked his Soviet counterpart, Vyacheslav Molotov, at one of these conferences. In 1947 President Truman, in his famous declaration to the U.S. Congress, accused the Soviet Union of imperialism, and the Soviet politician Andrei Zhdanov replied in the name of Stalin by returning the compliment. The Cold War was thereby declared.

For many years the ideological dimension was considered by both sides to imply political expansionism. In the West, people were always afraid of the violent spreading of world revolution, and of the power Karl Marx had predicted as necessary to the unfolding of history, but Vladimir Lenin had made the object of revolutionary strategy. Admittedly, the Soviet revolutionaries, like other successful ones before them, had primarily confronted the problem of maintaining power in their own country, but the West was not certain whether they might not one day try to export their revolution after all. In fact, Stalin had turned victory over Hitler into political dominance over the Eastern European foreground states, whose governments and societies were remodeled along Soviet lines. And though he had a geo-political rationale as well as an ideological one, the latter loomed large in Western eyes.

From the Soviet perspective, the very existence of states solving their problems by means of liberal economies and pluralist democracies was a challenge, particularly when they succeeded better than the socialist states. Couldn't this virus infect the Soviet Union or its immediate neighbors, any time, as was actually the case in 1953 in the GDR and in 1968 in Czechoslovakia? It is said that the day after a revolution all revolutionaries turn conservative, and the Soviet leaders used both ideological rigidity and images of political threats in order to consolidate their power at home and abroad. It is no surprise that the East-West conflict has added an ideological dimension to the traditional power rivalry even though the latter seems to be increasingly important.

This meant that the Germans, in choosing sides for the sake of security, had to commit themselves as well to an ideology: only if Schumacher's dream of a democratic, socialist Germany, guaranteed by both blocs but part of neither, were realized would they be spared this choice. Even though a democratic socialist state could certainly interact with the Western-bloc, it would have to avoid political and economic interdependence, as those who placed national unity above security recognized. Conversely, as will be seen, those who sought greater assurance of security than guarantees would provide had little choice but to opt for an alliance with the West.

The FRG's Foreign Policy as Security Policy in the East-West Conflict

Plotting a Westward Course

Even before its foundation in 1949 the FRG was totally enmeshed politically in the East-West conflict.[5] All decisions on questions of foreign policy, security and the armed forces were made with this conflict in mind, and interacted with it. As noted earlier, two different security concepts were conceivable for the Germans: (1) security through taking sides in the East-West conflict, in order to enjoy the protection of the respective leading power and its allies; (2) security through neutrality in the East-West conflict with the possibility of reunification of the two Germanies.

A preliminary decision against reunification had already been made through the founding of states in the western and eastern areas of the conflict zone. While the division was inevitable after German's unconditional capitulation, it was logical that the victor's rule should also entail the role of protector against a take-over by the competing power. The two German states were in the foreground of the spheres of influence of the dominant powers, and therefore a trouble spot and spectacular source of tension in the East-West conflict.

The interests of the powers responsible for Germany after the end of the war made for a perpetuation of the contradiction inherent in the German situation after 1949. This was to be expected as long as the Germans did not escalate the conflict themselves, which was hardly likely in view of their elemental fear of war. Their western neighbors, particularly France, showed little interest in resolving the contradiction. The U.S., in contrast to its behavior after World War I, pursued a policy of active containment, striving to consolidate the FRG as a "dike" against the East. The USSR pursued a foreground policy, creating a safety belt of dependent states just outside its own borders. The GDR was assigned the function of an armed outpost—though whether it would have really been available to impede enemy formations is an unanswered question.

In 1949 the Germans had no right or power to take action in the field of security or foreign policy. They could only grope for new freedom of action. They were not strong enough to remove the contradictions of their position by themselves, nor achieve reunification or a secure status for the Federal Republic. It was thus all the more important to correctly assess the international circumstances. The chief problem was to perceive and assess the Soviet policy towards the West. It was necessarily of central importance for the security of the FRG whether the Soviet Union's foreign policy would uphold an aggressive ideology throughout the world or whether it would continue the rather defensive tradition of Russian continental power. The national and international preconditions of German security appeared largely unclear and ambiguous to the political actors in the early years after 1945, in spite of the incipient Cold War positions.

The East-West conflict was heightened, with a tendency to clear the air, by the outbreak of the Korean War on 25 July 1950. The threshold from cold to "hot" war was thereby crossed in the Far East. The Germans wondered whether this could not be repeated on German soil at any time, for Korea was also a country divided in the context of the East-West conflict. The security question was instantly posed in urgent terms. Earlier suggestions of West German participation in Western defense efforts had always been immediately repressed in 1948-1949. The public now was abruptly reminded of security problems. The asymmetrical geography of the East-West conflict in Europe, the direct contact of the FRG with the Sovietized foreground of the USSR, including the GDR, and the behavior of its leaders in the current crisis combined with the prevalent anti-Communism in the West German public to awaken a politically effective anxiety syndrome.[6]

On 29 August 1950 the Federal Chancellor sent to the U.S. High Commissioner, John McCloy, two memoranda which he wanted to reach the September conferences of the Western foreign ministers and the NATO Council. The first, on the security of the federal territory, drawn up by a handful of staff and treated as confidential, contained Adenauer's description of the insecure situation of the FRG and was backed up by figures on the formidable Soviet military potential and on the GDR's police forces.

Adenauer urgently recommended—deviating from the position hitherto taken by the High Commissioners—that a "protective police force" be set up in West Germany. Apparently he considered there to be imminent danger of a Communist *coup d'état* with the support of the East German *Volkspolizei*, which would encounter only feeble Western resistance. Adenauer tried to mention the crucial sentence in passing—the offer "in the event of the formation of an international western European army to contribute in the form of a German contingent," which excluded a national army.[7] This sentence worried the conferees most. (To Adenauer's great regret it was soon given to the world press.) The second memorandum contained the demand that the western Allies dismantle the occupation regime step by step. The only function of the occupying power was to ensure external security for the foreseeable future. The FRG was to gradually acquire sovereign rights.

Adenauer's messages certainly reached their destinations. The NATO Council very soon spoke of the need for German participation in western defense, yet the Western Allies had varying interests, which led to a tug-of-war over the whys and wherefores of a German contribution. The U.S. call for a West German military contribution, officially presented at the New York NATO Council meeting in September 1950 by Secretary of State Dean Acheson, met with an extremely critical reception, by the French government in particular.

The French dilemma was that while they saw an urgent threat of Soviet attack towards the West, they also saw the Germans as a danger to their own country—for historical reasons. French Prime Minister René Pleven sought a way out of the dilemma with his (Pleven) Plan for German participation in western defense, but rejected any integration of independent German troops into NATO. German soldiers were instead to be integrated into a European army "on the basis of the smallest possible unit," and under "a unified political and military European authority."[8] This solution, emphasized French Foreign Minister Robert Schuman in Strasbourg, with an eye to French public opinion, could not be regarded as the rearmament of Germany, as it did not involve a national army. The argumentation corresponded to Adenauer's assertions in the security memorandum.

The British government was far from being as energetic in this matter as the French one. U.S. interests emphasized the improvement of the western defense capability in Europe, particularly as large American forces were tied up in Korea. The French were primarily interested in controlling German military potential, with weapons which—as English cartoonists noted—only went off to the east.

Adenauer had used the unexpected Korean War and struck while the iron was hot. The further fate of the proposed European Defense Community showed that his time was not unlimited. The EDC treaty was voted down in 1954 by the French National Assembly. What the FRG had regarded as an opportunity to find in Western European supranationality a new political identity after the catastrophe of 1945 was bound to hit the

French at their most sensitive spot—their sense of national independence, which re-asserted itself as Korea receded into the past.[9]

After the EDC failed, the alternative solution of allowing Bonn to join NATO was found surprisingly quickly. Although this is exactly what the French government had sought to prevent with its 1950 Pleven Plan, four years later it seemed to be the lesser evil. In October 1954 the London 9-power conference, attended by Great Britain and the U.S.A as well as the six continental states, adopted a package of draft treaties and statements, to be followed in the same month by the adoption of the "Paris Treaties." Even after the failure of the EDC, the basic dualism of defense contribution and granting of sovereignty remained the same, with NATO membership replacing the projected European Defense Community. (The presence of allied troops in the FRG was regulated by a separate stationing agreement.)

The Brussels Treaty concluded between France, Great Britain and the Benelux countries in 1948, before the founding of NATO, was used as an umbrella treaty, and endowed with a new function. The European connection was substituted for the safeguards against future German attacks that the Pleven Plan had envisaged. French security interests were accounted for through the FRG's assigning of its own troops to NATO. Above all, however, the treaty—in its enlarged form known as the Western European Union (WEU)—received the function of arms control in Europe and thus over the FRG. An arms control office was to oversee the quantities of West German arms laid down in appendices to the treaty. Finally, the FRG was admitted as the 15th member state to the North Atlantic Treaty Organization (NATO), founded in 1949.

Adenauer defined the FRG's security policy in these treaties, conceived in the precarious Korean summer of 1950 and ending in the western-oriented independence of the West Germans, in the following way: (1) closest political and military bonds with its western neighbors; (2) long-term linking of the U.S. political and physical presence to the continent of Europe; (3) special ties with the French after three Franco-German wars in 80 years; and (4) a clear-cut opting for the West in the East-West conflict, while avoiding any semblance of a seesaw policy between the two sides.[10]

What of the East?

In the face of the unmistakable fact that the integration of the FRG into the West in this way spelt a continuation of the division of Germany until further notice, there was an intensive search for alternatives and controversy over divergent policies. The fundamental question was whether there was any alternative to the FRG's close connection with the West. This question also applied to a reunified Germany, if it came into being, given the difficult historical situation of the East-West conflict and Germany's asymmetrical geographical position. Could it be safeguarded against invasion, pressure and hegemonial force in any other way than through strict western partnership?

This question was also addressed to the Soviet Union, from which a possible threat to the integrity of the FRG was expected and which more or less dominated the other German state. Moscow had to consider above all the elementary Western European need for security, if it wanted to constructively intervene in the post-war European order rather than merely consolidating a foreground of satellite states.

On 10 March 1972, just prior to the conclusion of the EDC negotiations, the three Western powers received a note from Stalin. This note could not be disregarded, since it contained an offer of German reunification on conditions which, while very vague and visibly tricky, seemed so fundamentally interesting as to merit closer inspection. According to Stalin, the reunified Germany was to have a neutral status, i.e., not be allowed membership in any alliance. This neutrality was to be armed, however, and Stalin proposed the establishment of a German national army.[11]

Stalin was undoubtedly concerned with preventing a Western European military bloc with a front against the Soviet Union. Was he willing to drop a satellite regime in the GDR and/or exchange it for the dissolution of the EDC? There is evidence to support this assumption but it cannot be proven as long as the Soviet archives are closed. And if the Kremlin had allowed reunification with free elections, the next question would have had to be answered: whether the neutrality of this Germany could have stood up to hegemonial pressure from the East in the long term.

Adenauer was convinced that this would not be possible; even before the note from Stalin he had told the Federal Parliament, "I believe that we will only attain the reunification of Germany with the aid of the three western Allies, never with the aid of the Soviet Union." It is questionable whether Adenauer's "policy of strength," formulated in the early 1950s, extended beyond a verbal flexing of muscles to avert domestic attacks on his foreign policy. However, despite the emphasis on a peaceful course, this phrase led to some misunderstanding of their role by German troops and to insinuations that German policy was revisionist.

It is questionable whether a serious Soviet interest in quadripartite negotiations on Germany, as presumed in 1952, still existed in 1953. After Stalin's death, and above all after the popular uprising of 17 June 1953 in the GDR, possible tendencies in the Kremlin to bargain about the East German regime seemed to have been eclipsed. The Berlin Conference on the German question of January 1954 was duly unproductive, despite interesting proposals. The West insisted on the FRG's being bound to it by treaty, although a revision clause was now included in the German Treaty. The East moved towards recognizing that Germany consisted of two states, after it was forced to realize that the forming of a complex of Western European alliances was not to be prevented.

Western policy regarding the FRG was mirrored in the Soviet Union's relations with the GDR; thus West German sovereignty was followed by East German sovereignty, Bonn's entering NATO by the founding of the Warsaw Pact.[12] Khrushchev's statement that reunification was up to the

Germans (made after returning home from the 1955 four-power summit on the GDR in Geneva) showed all concerned that consolidation of the respective blocs was the order of the day. The dynamic phase of the Cold War was now followed by a static phase.

The Addition of the Eastern Treaties

This did not mean that the German search for security had ended, only that it took a different form. With their integration into West European economic and political organizations, and their increasingly important role in the Atlantic Alliance, the West Germans sought a *rapprochement* with the East, i.e., they sought to employ détente, as well as defense, as a means toward their desired ends.

The building of the Berlin Wall in 1961 is an appropriate symbol of the turning point from the phase of Cold War confrontation to the phase of cooperation in détente. This is true despite the elements of détente visible in the 1950s and the occurrence of the decisive German contribution in the 1970s. The 1960s must be considered an interim period of reflection and reorientation for the FRG.

True, the test of strength between the two superpowers continued until the Cuban Missile Crisis of 1962, but following that there was a time of balancing self-estimates and perceiving mutual power, which then crystallized into a situation of equilibrium enabling initial practical steps towards détente. Strength through resistance and improved weaponry, plus flexibility through a new military strategy, enabled Kennedy to take safe and promising arms control initiatives. The Test Ban Treaty and the institution of the "hot line" between Washington and Moscow in Summer 1963 opened the era of cooperative arms control.

In the FRG, geographically and politically closest to events, the government hesitated to acknowledge the change, and it is not surprising that it reacted with uncertainty—recalling the Berlin crisis, the change of U.S. strategy in 1963, the past era of Eisenhower/Dulles and the beginning era of President Charles de Gaulle. Of all those involved in the Cold War, it remained to the Germans, with their ever more rigid division, to accommodate to the most grave "aftermath of war."[13] Germany continued to be regarded as a potential trouble-spot, whichever way one looked at it. In his final years of government. Adenauer, not quite certain of the continuity of U.S. support, tried to reduce the danger to the others and thus retroactively to the FRG. He made Nikita Khrushchev a direct offer of a ten-year truce. The Kremlin did not take it up, although Khrushchev referred to agreements along Rapallo lines in unusual talks with Bonn's ambassador to Moscow.

Several years later, when Ludwig Erhard was Chancellor, Foreign Minister Gerhard Schröder sought, through a policy of movement towards the East, to find a way out of the paralysis of nonpolicy or to shake off the policy of mutual negation. This, however, could not lead the FRG into the area of détente, as long as he sought a route via the smaller eastern

European states, bypassing Moscow and the question of intra-German relations. Schröder tried to build a bridge over bloc borders to the non-German East European states, in order to dismantle confrontation through cooperation, but to leave the German question open through isolating the GDR. He thereby increased slightly the FRG's international standing but did not succeed in his larger aim.

The Erhard government's "peace note" of March 1966 was backed by a broad consensus, but it was not able to achieve a breakthrough either. It contained, it is true, a proposal for the renunciation of force and expressions of understanding for East European security interests, but its positions on the German question remained unchanged, including a reference to the continuing validity of the borders drawn in 1937 until such time as a peace treaty would take effect.[14]

Helmut Schmidt criticized the lack of consistency and, in a long speech at the SPD party conference in 1966, developed the connection between policy towards the East, the German question and security.[15] He concluded that it was necessary to emerge from the isolation imposed by current German policy, by means of a fundamental rethinking of the positions of the 1950s. This had to be done in order to make the security connection with the superpowers' policy of détente, which otherwise could completely bypass German interests. From 1969 the Brandt/Scheel government was able to link up with the international détente process and set the stage for trans-bloc security structures, by revising goals and overcoming traditional liabilities.[16]

The growing awareness in the 1960s of the subsidence of the Cold War enabled the Social Democratic and Liberal coalition (elected to government in 1969) to neutralize the special German problem within the East-West conflict so that active security policy by Germans became possible as part of the superpowers' policy of détente. As in the case of the Western Treaties 20 years before, the Eastern Treaties were now to be legitimized by the public, above all in terms of security policy. After all, the security of the Federal Republic of Germany was the question at stake. However, there was no more talk on the FRG's basic stance in favor of West or East, or of neutrality. The Ostpolitik of the Brandt government was premised on the Westpolitik of the Adenauer era. On the basis of the bond with the West established in the 50s, and of the alliance structures existing within the West, the scope of political action could now be extended to eastern Europe. The aim was, alongside the protection from the West and deterrence through Western military power, to also base the FRG's security on contacts and partial cooperation with the East, i.e., to give equal weight to détente and defense.[17]

The Eastern Treaties declared two principles to be the foundation of political relations between the FRG and the eastern bloc states: renunciation of force and the recognition of the European status quo, with borders hardened through the Cold War. The renunciation of force was generally anchored in Section 2 of the UN Charter, with the Soviet Union having foresworn its right of intervention as a victorious power in World War II. (The Western powers had similarly committed themselves back in 1955.) Recognition of the borders by the FRG was of vital interest for Poland and the GDR, in particular, and was matched by the Soviet Union's recognizing the status of Berlin. The Four-Power Agreement gave West Berlin the needed guarantee under international law of its access routes and its political viability, including the freedom to develop its relations with the FRG[18]. The Basic Treaty with the GDR opened the way for the two Germanies to join the UN and thus share in international responsibility for conflict resolution at a new level.

The treaties' significance in security terms extends far beyond the immediate objects of agreement. Even though a residual German conflict persists in central Europe, it cannot fester into a threat to security, now that a *modus vivendi* has been arranged by treaty and political communication channels between West and East have been created which rely on mutual interests. The active German participation in the multilateral conference diplomacy on European security (for which see Chapter 7), is, like the conferences themselves, unthinkable without the specifically German contribution to security through the Eastern Treaties.[19]

On this basis the FRG was able to enter actively into the process of détente. It has contributed to strengthening the multilateral component and thereby to reducing at least relatively U.S.-Soviet bilateralism.

If at this point one restricts one's sights to German security interests again, it is possible to draw up an interim report. Besides the specifically German contribution to détente there has also been a specific German bonus. The security gained through alliances and treaties with the West initiated by Adenauer were supplemented by the reduction of confrontation through Willy Brandt's treaties with the East. Berlin, since 1948 an indicator of the East-West relationship and a lever for exacerbation of conflict in the hands of the Soviet Union, substantially lost this effect and gained security of status. The Eastern Treaties paved the way to the trans-bloc and multilateral politics of the European security conferences, at which the FRG can express its security interests in the requisite context. The political and military presence of the U.S. on the continent of Europe, which the FRG depends on as long as it has to fear hegemonial pressure from the Soviet Union, is no longer in question after U.S. participation in CSCE and MBFR. There has been no dissolution of the military alliances or loosening of alliance cohesion, so often feared by the West and so long aspired to by the Soviet Union. Western European political cooperation has even received crucial impulses through CSCE. In all, the West has by no means lost the possibility of action, but—on the contrary— held to the Harmel Study's strategy of the two pillars, defense and détente.

During the 1970s and early 1980s an awareness arose in the two Germanies that they were both jointly threatened and both responsible for peace. The incipient intra-German dialogue on questions relating to European security took a discreet and unspectacular course however. It only attracted public attention in the critical situation of 1980, after NATO had taken its two-track decision on holding talks and deploying intermediate-range nuclear weapons, and the Soviet Union had intervened in Afghanistan, at which time the two parties sought to minimize the potential consequences of these developments, both by continuous consultation and by endeavoring to restrain their allies. Today, in consequence, the FRG and the GDR can work together to exploit the new détente, just as they worked earlier to prevent the total breakdown of the old.

The Further Course of Policy

As indicated above, the choice made by the Federal Republic in 1949-1952 firmly fixed its security policy: Germany was a full member of the North Atlantic Treaty Organization, as well as of its subsidiary, the West European Union. Moreover, Germany occupied a unique position in the Atlantic Alliance, in that all its armed forces were assigned to NATO (and hence could not operate independently), unlike those of the other members, which came under operational control of NATO only in time of emergency. Thus, at the macro-level the security policy of Germany was inextricably linked with that of the Atlantic Alliance.

This does not mean that there were no differences between the Federal Republic and its fellow members, as evidenced by the debate over flexible response in 1961-1967, the backing and filling over MBFR in the early 1970s and the differences over the deployment of intermediate-range missiles after 1979. Nor did it mean that West Germany had no military relations outside the Alliance, for the Treaty of Friendship and Cooperation with France was aimed at keeping up joint planning and joint policy making with that country after it withdrew in 1967 from the integrated command structure of NATO. But unlike France, the United States and even Britain, the Federal Republic had no commitments outside Europe, no forces permanently deployed elsewhere and no competing strategies. Thus defense policy, as we shall see, consisted largely of efforts to prepare the *Bundeswehr* for its agreed NATO missions—the first and foremost of which was the defense of the homeland.

As for détente policy, the options were wider. Not only could West Germany press (as it did) for adoption by NATO of the Harmel Report in 1967 but it could also take initiatives of its own or with other like-minded states outside the alliance. As noted in the previous section, until the late 1960s these initiatives were taken sparingly and largely with respect to the non-German countries of Eastern Europe. Following the lead of the United States, the Federal Republic also embarked on direct negotiations with Moscow which led, as already noted, to the Eastern Treaties, to the CSCE and, ultimately, to the acceptance of the GDR as a second state within the German nation. Although there has been little substantial progress either in reducing armaments or in winding down the confrontation along the borders between East and West, German efforts at détente (which all governments, regardless of their composition, have pursued) have made peace a little more secure and conditions in Eastern Europe a little better.

There is, however, no sense that progress in détente is evidence of Soviet good will; it is seen as a pragmatic response by the Soviet Union and its allies to a situation wherein they too had something to gain by more conciliatory policies. Nor is there any illusion that politics alone can insure security; that requires, as the Harmel Report says, defense as well as détente—even where détente is expanded to include arms control. Thus, we will turn next to a consideration of German defense policy in the post-war years.

Defense Policy as Security Policy

The Founding of the Bundeswehr

The *Wehrmacht* ceased to exist as an organization in 1945, following its surrender. Even though five years had passed by 1950, it was still out of the question to simply pick up the pieces and continue. Whereas the Foreign Ministry was rather discreetly reinstituted in 1951, the reintroduction of an army could not possibly be done by sleight-of-hand. Public opinion in Germany and elsewhere would not allow the topic of rearmament to be handled casually. Foreign interest in the German military ranged from the Nuremberg war crimes trials to the aggression against other countries, from the unresolved status of the German nation to the German militaristic tradition. A long and winding road led from the Potsdam Agreement of 1945 through German demilitarization to the EDC Treaty of 1952.

The past weighed more heavily upon the armed forces than any other governmental institution in West Germany. Wasn't the judicial system deeply entangled in the illegality of Nazism? Yes, but its right to exist as an institution was not contested. Weren't the universities bound up with both the nationalism of the Kaiser Wilhelm era and the Nazism of the Hitler era? Yes, yet nobody seriously questioned their work or their right to exist. The German military, however, was inseparably linked to the catastrophe of 1945. People who preferred to forget about the fundamental turn around in German national policy under the Nazis regarded the surrender only in its obvious military aspects, and the subsequent occupation and division of Germany.

The dissolution of the army following its defeat forced a new beginning, which was indeed essential. The founders of the *Bundeswehr*, unlike the judiciary, could not return to the *status quo ante* of the Weimar Republic; they had to cope with four historical burdens:

1. the disproportionate influence of military thinking on politics, which in Prussian/German history has been termed militarism;
2. the use of the army by the monarchy as the "school of the nation" against democratic and republican opposition, and the degeneration

of military education to mere soldiering, still fresh in the memories of those who had served in the *Wehrmacht*;
3. the elevation of force to a doctrine of state by Hitler;
4. the possible use of the armed forces for purposes of dubious political morality, which had obviously been the case in Hitler's war of expansion.

The participants at the Himmerod Conference of Experts (1950) were aware of this problem. Here and in the following years of planning, people said over and over that the society had to receive brand new institutions, with the qualification that "tried-and-true" ones should be kept. A new army must not be allowed to become a "state within the state" like the *Reichswehr*. The German soldier of the future, says the Himmerod Memorandum, must "affirm the democratic way of life and government by his inner convictions." The organization of the German troops, it continued, must in no way be a reminder of the "Black *Reichswehr*;" it must be democratically legitimate and meet the approval of the opposition and also of the trade unions, a remarkable demand, considering the history of the *Reichswehr*.

The burdensome legacy of German militarism needed to be considered above all in its relation to constitutional and social policy. With this background, the new West German army was to be formed according to military statutes which would make it democratic, guarantee the paramount importance of the political decision-making process, and admit no doubt as to its sole purpose of safeguarding peace, as laid down in the Federal Republic's Basic Law. The leadership doctrine and internal structure of the new army should be based on and affirm the autonomy of the individual citizen. The leaders should not reject or simply tolerate the political system of the Republic, but be committed to it as active citizens. At the same time, the call to invest the President with supreme command, despite experiences under the Kaiser and the realities of the Weimar Constitution, shows how a shaky tradition was able to establish itself.

The need for experts and advisors in the Adenauer Administration was met only through a process of strict selection which took into account the degree to which the experts in question had been involved with the Nazi regime. July 20, 1944 (the uprising against Hitler), was important here, because it would have been much more difficult to introduce *Reichswehr* and *Wehrmacht* elites as *Bundeswehr* cadres without this event as an indication of these officers' ability to learn and to be reoriented. The 1945 defeat had not led to social revolution or a change of elites; there was nothing to do except to begin a selection process on the one hand, and a learning process on the other. Aware of these problems, the military advisors accepted the formation of a Personnel Evaluation Committee for officers, which was to act as a filter in setting up the *Bundeswehr*. This committee, installed by the *Bundestag*, reviewed all officers from the rank of colonel upwards until 1957, and issued directives for appointments to lower ranks.

Because of the provisions of former statutes, and because of historical experience, the legal status of a *Bundeswehr* soldier had to be carefully and thoroughly formulated. This was done for the most part in the Soldier Act. Civil rights and freedoms were to be limited only as far as utter functional necessity called for this; a soldier was not supposed to be an oppressed vassal, but a citizen defending his inalienable free right to political self-determination from outside attack. Thus for the first time in German military history *Bundeswehr* soldiers were given both the active and the passive right to vote; as members of political parties they could directly affect the formation of political power. Only the barracks themselves were considered off-limits for political activities so as to preserve the army's political neutrality.

The *Wehrmacht's* involvement in the Nazis' policies policies of violence, injustice, and indeed murderous extermination was behind the moral and legal limitation on mandatory obedience in the *Bundeswehr*. A legacy of the failed July 20, 1944, assassination attempt, the Soldier Act prohibited the execution of illegal orders instead of demanding unconditional obedience. Following unhappy experiences with swearing oaths to a person or to the constitution, the soldier's pledge of allegiance was to a free democratic order, thus forming the basis for the modern leadership practice of "internal guidance" employed by the *Bundeswehr*.

Fortunately, there was not nearly as much pressure to rapidly organize the *Bundeswehr* as there was for other government institutions, so that democratic principles could be formulated, introduced and learned. Right after Korea there were plans to set up a German contingent within a year and a half, yet it ended up taking six years for the first soldier to appear. Even in 1956, it was planned that twelve divisions be formed as quickly as possible; the process, however, took fully ten years. In contrast to the Weimar Republic, the Federal Republic as a state had a six-year head start on its army.

Both the size of the *Bundeswehr* and the issue of whether it was to be a conscript or a professional army were in dispute at first. A figure of 500,000 troops had already been given at a NATO Council session in Lisbon in 1952. This order of magnitude was based on universal conscription, which was also supported by the governing parties as a means of integrating the armed forces into republican society. In 1956, Adenauer reduced Defense Minister Theodor Blank's call for an 18-month term of compulsory service to 12 months as a campaign tactic in the face of the 1957 *Bundestag* elections. Franz-Josef Strauss replaced Theodor Blank as Defense Minister in the autumn of 1956 and considerably slowed down the *Bundeswehr's* growth on the basis of the shortened term of military service. Despite strenuous efforts, the Alliance's demands had proved to be impossible to meet for personnel, material, and infrastructural reasons. It was not until 1965 that Minister of Defense Kai-Uwe von Hassel could assign the 12th *Bundeswehr* Division to NATO. It took another two years until Gerhard Schröder, as Defense Minister of the Grand Coalition, declared a nearly complete *Bundeswehr* to be an instrument of NATO's flexible response strategy. Under Helmut Schmidt as Defense Minister of the Social-Liberal Coalition, the *Bundeswehr* even approached the magic number of 500,000 soldiers for a short period at the beginning of the seventies.

During the first decade, the *Bundeswehr* grew mainly by cell division, i.e., units which were already organized donated cadre personnel for the formation of new units. More and more of NATO's target figures were reached; with its increasing scope, the *Bundeswehr* also grew to become more and more an integral part of the Alliance. Whereas the top German representative in the NATO hierarchy in 1957 was General Hans Speidel, Supreme Commander of Land Forces in the Central European Command, West Germany had the chair of NATO's Military Committee starting in 1961 with its first Inspector General, Adolf Heusinger. In 1978, a post as a Deputy Supreme Commander of the Allied Forces in Europe was created for a German four-star general, the first of whom was Gerd Schmuckle.

Starting in the mid-1970s—the process of establishing the *Bundeswehr* lasted up to this period—the West German army entered the rather undramatic phase of normal bureaucracy. Whereas soldiers in the 1950s and early 1960s were regarded in public with a certain amount of mistrust or interested reserve, their social position was now characterized by benign indifference. The public saw the *Bundeswehr* as a normal government institution. The entire society, including soldiers themselves, described the army's political function unquestionably and exclusively as that of preventing war.

The Mission of the Bundeswehr

The mission of conventional defense has from the beginning been a primary one. It stemmed from the work of a conference of experts, convened in 1950 by Konrad Adenauer to examine the nature of a possible German contribution to a European army, and to draw up a concept for its employment. After one week of intensive work the officers handed in a paper which became the key document in the history of the *Bundeswehr*: the "Himmerod Memorandum." It contained basic requirements, such as the necessity for the Federal Republic, due to its geographic location, to be defended as far east as possible and for a West German defense contribution to be made in conjunction with the allied forces, and it was in this context that the question of how many divisions were deemed necessary, that is twelve, came up for the first time.

The *Bundeswehr* was not designed as an army using nuclear weapons during a conflict; rather, the German troops were to enable defense without nuclear devastation. The main reason for equipping the *Bundeswehr* with nuclear delivery systems from 1958 onwards was an agreement that the West German troops should be integrated into the Alliance on the basis of equality in principle, comparable armament and scale. The nuclear weapons as such remained the exclusive property of the United States.

This was a question of the political status of the Federal Republic within the Alliance, and of the homogeneous character of the divisions under European NATO control, but above all, of equality.

The role of the *Bundeswehr* as an army of the Alliance corresponded to the security concept laid down in the treaties, namely the closest possible interdependence with the Western neighbors. The *Bundeswehr* was not linked to the national question. The self-perception of the German soldiers was directed towards this Republic and its integration into the Western Alliance. The link rearmament—national reunification suggested itself but was contrary to the attachment of the Federal Republic to the Western Alliance.

West Germany and Nuclear Weapons

Since 1950 the role of the West German armed forces has been to conduct a defense of the homeland which had to begin as far east as possible. In the Himmerod Memorandum the nuclear weapons of the United States (Washington practically held the monopoly in nuclear weapons ready for use at the beginning of the 1950s) were described as nothing more than a shield, under which it was possible for a limited amount of time to pursue West German rearmament, without having to reckon with Soviet intervention. The strategic plans of NATO and the strategic role of nuclear weapons in this context were not officially known to the German military experts, who also knew little about them unofficially. Not until West Germany joined the Alliance in 1955 did they acquire access to these areas and only in the course of the following years, on the basis of the successive integration of *Bundeswehr* divisions into the Alliance, did they have the possibility of a limited say in Alliance strategies.

The public debate on the accession of the Federal Republic of Germany to NATO was hardly affected by the question of nuclear weapons because in the fall of 1954 at the Nine Power Conference in London Chancellor Adenauer had declared that the Federal Republic would not produce nuclear weapons on German soil and had explained the creation of the *Bundeswehr* and especially conscription by saying that a use of nuclear weapons would become less probable with strong West German ground forces. It was not until 1957, when German participation in NATO's nuclear strategy was considered, that a heated and persistent public debate about nuclear weapons began.

Leading German scientists, including Otto Hahn, Werner Heisenberg, Carl-Friedrich von Weizsacker and Albert Schweitzer, citing the effects of nuclear weapons, strongly opposed their use. In addition, the 1955 Carte Blanche maneuvers fanned the flames of domestic discontent when figures of millions of projected "casualties" caused by the simulated employment of nuclear weapons against targets inside Germany were released.

The government, in the person of Defense Minister Franz-Josef Strauss, explained that nobody was trying to get control over nuclear weapons and that nobody wanted their production in the Federal Republic, either. How-

ever, an apparent connection between the change of ministers Blank/
Strauss, a slower pace in the building up of the *Bundeswehr* on the one
hand, and the onset of a discussion about equipping it with delivery systems
for nuclear weapons cannot be denied. One can assume that Strauss changed
over to the Defense Ministry after having been Nuclear Minister knowing
that the possibilities of nuclear energy both in the military and in the civil
sector were a decisive factor in the political status of a country. Adenauer
had considered the question of equipping the *Bundeswehr* with nuclear
arms an internal NATO problem and a problem of its relation to the
Soviet potential. However, by the spring of 1957 it was the emotional effect
on the upcoming *Bundestag* elections that concerned the CDU/CSU leaders
the most. The election was won handily, with surprisingly little voter
concern over the nuclear issue despite the "fight nuclear death" campaign
and the opposition of the SPD and trade unions.

After the unavoidable German declaration on the renunciation of the
production of nuclear weapons, the following possibilities of a German
participation in the nuclear arms potential were conceivable: co-ownership,
a say in the use and participation in planning the use.

The possibility of co-ownership of the American nuclear arms potential
was contained in the plan of the Alliance's Supreme Commander in Europe,
General Laurie Norstad, who had proposed to make NATO the fourth
nuclear power by creating a joint weapons pool. Strauss, who had had the
Bundeswehr leaders stress the necessity of equipping the armed forces with
nuclear weapons, was quite supportive of Norstad's approach. However, he
was not able to push it through against both intra-governmental and
external opposition.

The second attempt at German co-ownership of the United States nuclear
weapon potential within NATO was the Multilateral Nuclear Forces (MLF).
According to the American proposal, 8 Polaris missiles each were to be
deployed on 25 ships. Joint ownership and joint control were to be reflected
in the mixed nationalities of the ship's crews. However, the British saw
their special nuclear status within NATO and *vis-à-vis* the United States
eroded by this proposal and went as far as making Moscow's concerns
about the "German finger on the trigger" their own. The French were
already building their own nuclear arsenal, the *"force de frappe,"* and in
the de Gaulle era they rejected any German access to nuclear weapons.
West German Defense Minister von Hassel was interested in that solution
because he believed that it would improve the credibility of deterrence,
the cohesion within the Alliance, and the German status in the Alliance.
However, it was not only the opposition party in Parliament that had
doubts about the value of MLF, there were second thoughts in the coalition
government and in the United States as well. Thus this effort also failed.

In between these two proposals, U.S. Secretary of Defense McNamara
presented a strategic concept which was to harmonize nuclear planning
and the military strategy of flexible response and to give NATO allies the
impression that the American nuclear weapons were part of NATO's po-

tential since they were only to be used in agreement with the Allies. In accordance with this American position, the 1962 NATO Council meeting in Athens established the Nuclear Committee, but it was unable to solve the problem of participation, which essentially came down to the right to require or to veto an American decision to employ nuclear weapons.

With both co-ownership and a final say in the decision to use nuclear weapons ruled out, the issue came down to one of German participation in the planning process. In 1966, NATO established the Nuclear Planning Group (NPG), which is responsible for devising all policy on the use of nuclear weapons and approving plans for this eventuality. The NPG adapted guidelines for consultation between the United States and the country or countries from which nuclear weapons are to be launched or against whose territory they are to be directed, matters of equal importance to the Federal Republic.

Partly because no workable system could be devised, partly because the U.S. and the USSR had agreed on measures to prevent the proliferation of nuclear weapons, West German co-ownership was not possible. Neither, given both the technical requirements for the release of nuclear weapons and the political problems associated with the decision to do so, was joint decision-making feasible. The way to joint nuclear planning involved recognition of these realities. Moreover, it was a way the Federal Republic could afford to go, involving active cooperation in a NATO with nuclear dimensions but not the actual possession of nuclear weapons.

A Summing Up

Even a cursory glance at the development of West German defense policy in the post-war world indicates that it followed a very different course from that of the United States. Whereas the latter, at least from 1953 onwards, centered around nuclear weapons and concepts for their employment, German defense policy emphasized conventional capabilities; when nuclear delivery systems were sought or accepted this was done in the name of equality, not of strategy.

While American concepts for the use of force varied widely over time, the operational doctrine outlined in the Himmerod Memorandum of 1950 is still in vogue today—though whether that is good or bad is another question. And while much of the U.S. defense effort was directed toward conflicts outside Europe (within Vietnam as the prime example) that of the Federal Republic was oriented almost entirely toward the defense of its borders. Furthermore, while the Atlantic Alliance was for the United States a marriage of convenience, in which the spouses sometimes nagged at one another, for the West Germans it was an absolute necessity; only through NATO could the Federal Republic justify rearmament to its people and its neighbors and only from NATO could it garner the support needed to make that rearmament meaningful—especially since West Germany had abjured nuclear weapons.

The reasons for these patterns in defense policy are almost self-evident. As a divided country in a divided Europe, West Germany had to focus all its attention on problems of regional security. Since it was, moreover, comparatively weak and highly vulnerable, it could cope with these problems only if all or some of its powerful neighbors would guarantee its frontiers; by necessity, as much as by choice, this required it to join NATO.

Even before it took sides in this East-West confrontation, Germany had been caught up in it and indeed was for some years the prize for which the U.S. and the USSR competed most vigorously. Both the choice itself and the way in which it took effect, through integration into the broader Western community, reinforced existing tendencies in political and economical fields and created domestic institutions and interests broadly supportive of German security policy—if not always happy about particular decisions, such as the arming of the *Bundeswehr* with nuclear weapons or the deployment on German soil of Pershing IIs and GLCMs.

It is significant that much of the dissatisfaction with West German defense policy centered around nuclear weapons. It did not take Khrushchev's brutal statement that eight 5 MT warheads could destroy the Federal Republic to remind its citizens of their terrifying vulnerability nor of their almost equally terrifying dependence on the United States to deter such an attack. The primary aim of West German policy was to insure that the U.S. nuclear guarantee remained valid and credible and, simultaneously, not to become the theater of a nuclear war. This ambiguous aim explains both West Germany's efforts to obtain a voice in decisions on the use of nuclear weapons and its emphasis on reductions in nuclear armaments. It also explains the desire to maintain strong conventional forces, since these could, according to the common wisdom, dissuade the Soviets from taking advantage of their numerical superiority in ground and air forces to launch an attack under the shield of *their* nuclear deterrent.

But this is a subject for the following chapter.

Notes

1. See "*Rede des Bundeskanzlers Konrad Adenauer auf einer Kundgehung der DEU in der Universität Bonn vom 28.3.1952*" in Klaus von Schubvert, ed., *Sicherheitspolitik der Bundesrepublik Deutschland, Dokumentation, 1945-1977*, 2 Vols. (Bonn: Schriftenreihe der Bundeszentrale für Politische Bildung, 1978), I, 172-175.

2. For surveys of post-war German history there are two representative editions available: (a) *Geschichte der Bundesrepublik Deutschland*, edited by Karl Dietrich Bracher, Theodor Eschenburg, Joachim C. Fest, Eberhard Jäckel (Wiesbaden: Deutsche Verlagsanstalt and Stuttgart: F. A. Brockhaus, 1983-1988), 6 Vols.; (b) *Die Bundesrepublik Deutschland: Geschichte in vier Bänden*, edited by Wolfgang Benz (Frankfurt: Fischer Verlag, 1989), 4 Vols.

Memoirs were written by Konrad Adenauer, Willy Brandt, Carlo Schmid and Helmut Schmidt.

A discussion of current West German foreign policy may be found in the yearly volumes "*Die Internationale Politik*" (München: Deutsche Gesellschaft für Auswärtige Politik, 1958-1988).

For even more topical coverage, see *Europa-Archiv* a journal of international relations from a German point of view, published since 1947 with 24 editions per year.

3. Fritz Erler, *"Sicherheit und deutsche Einheit II,"* SPD-Pressedienst, 4 April 1955, 2.

4. For a German perspective on the East-West conflict, see Werner Link, *Der Ost-West Konflikt* (Stuttgart: 1980).

5. For documentation of the Federal Republic's position in the conflict, see *"Deutschland in Ost-West Konflikt"*, in *Sicherheitspolitik der Bundesrepublik Deutschland*, I, 59-70.

6. For the history of German rearmament, see: Gerhard Wettig, *Entmilitarisierung und Wiederbewaffnung in Deutschland 1943-1955*, (München: 1967); Arnulf Baring, *Außenpolitik in Adenauers Kanzlerdemokratie*, (München: 1969); Klaus von Schubert, *Wiederbewaffnung und Westintegration* (Stuttgart: 1970).

7. Adenauer-Memorandum, in *Sicherheitspolitik der Bundesrepublik Deutschland*, I, 79-83.

8. Declaration of the French Prime Minister Pleven, 24.10. 1950, Ibid., I, 99-103.

9. See Paul Noack, *Das Scheitern der Europäischen Verteidigungsgemeinschaft*, (Düsseldorf: 1977).

10. For Adenauers' political goals, see Konrad Adenauer, *Erinnerungen 1945-1963* (Stuttgart: 1965-1969), 4 Vols.; *Geschichte der Bundesrepublik Deutschland*, Vols. II and III; and Baring, *Aussenpolitik in Adenauers Kanzlerdemokratie*.

11. Stalin Memorandum in *Sicherheitspolitik der Bundesrepublik Deutschland*, I, 167-170.

12. For the history of the German Democratic Republic (DDR), see Hermann Weber, *Geschichte der DDR*, (München: 1985).

13. For "Ostpolitik," see Richard Löwenthal, *"Vom Kalten Krieg zur Ostpolitik,"* in R. Löwenthal and H. P. Schwarz, *Die Zweite Republik* (Stuttgart: 1974); Helga Haftendorn, *Sicherheit und Entspannung. Zur Aussenpolitik der Bundesrepublik Deutschland, 1955-1982* (Baden-Baden: 1983); Hans-Adolf Jacobsen, *Von der Strategie der Gewalt zur Politik der Friedenssicherung* (Düsseldorf: 1977); Boris Meissner, ed., *Die Deutsche Ostpolitik 1961-1970, Dokumentation*, (Köln: 1975); Willy Brandt, *Begegnungen und Einsichten. Die Jahre 1960-1975*, (Brandt Memoirs) (München: 1978).

14. Erhard Peace Memorandum, in *Sicherheitspolitik der Bundesrepublik Deutschland*, I, 268-273.

15. Schmidt speech, in *Ibid.*, I, 273-286.

16. For decision-making in the Social Liberal Government, see Arnulf Baring, *Machtwechsel, Die ära Brandt-Scheel*, (Stuttgart: 1982);

William Griffith, *The Ostpolitik of the Federal Republic of Germany* (Cambridge/London: 1978);

Günther Schmid, *Entscheidung in Bonn, Die Entstehung der Ost und Deutschlandpolitik 1969-1970*, (Köln: 1979).

17. See Peter Bender, *Neue Ostpolitik, Vom Neuerbau zum Moskauer Vertrag*, (München: 1986).

18. See Dieter Mahncke, *Berlin im geteilten Deutschland* (München: 1973).

19. For CSCE see Hans-Adolf Jacobsen, ed., *Sicherheit und Zusammenarbeit in Europa (KSZE)*, (Köln: 1973 and 1977), 2 Vols.; Deutsche Gesellschaft für Friedens- und Konfliktforschung, DFG-Jahrbuch 1979-1980, *Zur Entspannungspolitik in Europa* (Baden-Baden: 1980); DGFK-Jahrbuch 1982-1983, *Zur Lage Europas im globalen Spannungsfeld* (Baden-Baden: 1983).

4

Deterrence and Defense

Joseph I. Coffey and Klaus von Schubert

If the preceding two chapters have proven nothing else, they have shown that the defense policies of the United States and (to a lesser extent) of the Federal Republic of Germany have fluctuated widely over time. These shifts have been influenced by transitory factors such as innovations in military technology, by improvements in the military posture of the Soviet Union and its allies, by developments in East-West relations and by changes in the "affairs of men;" had all external factors remained the same, it is likely that President Carter's policies would have differed from President Eisenhower's and those of Chancellor Schmidt from those of Chancellor Adenauer. Moreover, these policies have reflected the fundamental geographic, geo-economic and structural differences in the situations of the two countries and their differing perceptions of their positions and their interests.

Both permanent and transitory factors have impinged upon policies for the defense of Western Europe, which is *the* concern for the Federal Republic and one of the major problems facing the United States; hence, it is not surprising that the two countries have somewhat different ideas as to how this should be done. These extend not only to the political means of enhancing security, as through détente, but also to the military means, through defense. And they exist despite substantial agreement concerning the military capabilities of the Soviet Union and its allies and despite agreement in principle that the best means of inhibiting the exercise of these capabilities is through deterrence, i.e., through convincing the Soviet Union "that it has nothing to gain by using force of arms or threatening to use it, but that it runs the risk of having to accept serious setbacks in the event of a conflict . . . "[1] However, before looking at the ways in which each country has sought to enhance deterrence it might be useful to examine the concept itself, in order to see whether and to what extent differences in American and West German approaches derive from differing interpretations of that concept.

The Concept of Deterrence

At the start, it must be admitted that the concept of deterrence, i.e., of hindering or precluding action "by fear of consequences or by difficulty, risk, unpleasantness, etc.,"[2] lends itself to varied interpretations. For one thing, the definition itself suggests three ways of persuading Soviet leaders that they have "nothing to gain by using force of arms:" by denying them some or all of the gains anticipated from that use, by inflicting punishment that outweighs any gains, however large, or by increasing the risk that gains or losses will change to the detriment of the aggressor—as through Thomas Schelling's "threat that leaves something to chance." Each of these ways has its own strengths and weaknesses, which apply more largely under some circumstances than others.

One can, for example, practice denial through frustrating or rebuffing the attacks of an adversary. In the European theater, this would call for forces deemed capable of checking or repelling any Soviet/WTO conventional assault, whether this was launched without warning or preceded by (some form of) mobilization and whether it lasted only briefly or was continued for months; theoretically, the leaders of the Warsaw Pact countries would never attack because they knew that they would fail. It would also, however, call for forces which could frustrate any *nuclear* strike, whether by pre-emptive counterforce operations or by the installation of largely "leak-proof" air and missile defenses. Since the latter have not yet been developed, and since the former is not only difficult but dangerous, in that it may precipitate a nuclear counterblow, "deterrence through denial" in Europe can only be applied to conventional operations.

Here, however, two difficulties arise. The first is that the current balance of forces in Europe is such that this approach does not seem credible to many Western analysts, officers and officials—and hence may not be credible to their Soviet counterparts either. The second is that should deterrence fail, the costs of even a conventional conflict would be enormous, so that it may seem preferable to buttress deterrence by the threat of punishment should war ensue.

In its simplest form, deterrence through punishment calls for persuading adversaries "that they will suffer a net loss or lower net gain than would follow from . . . not attacking."[3] Although the calculation of gains and losses may present a problem, there is little doubt that punishment on an enormous scale can be inflicted through the use of nuclear weapons; indeed, this punishment could be so dire that *no* gain would be worth the cost. The difficulty is, of course, that even though the United States could "destroy the Soviet Union as a viable Twentieth Century society," the USSR could inflict similar levels of damage, even after absorbing an American first strike.[4] Since no "rational man" would order an attack deemed likely to precipitate such a response, many, in government or out, downgrade the credibility of the nuclear deterrent which, if useful at all, is deemed capable only of deterring the USSR from employing nuclear weapons against the United States.

If, therefore, deterrence through punishment is deemed incredible, and deterrence through denial is judged impossible, what is left? One answer is deterrence through risk, that is through changing the subjective probability that a given event will actually occur.[a] Thus, one need not threaten to launch a devastating nuclear strike, only that one will take actions which could increase the likelihood of such an outcome, thereby changing the circumstances under which aggression was presumably contemplated. Nor need one stop efforts to manipulate risk if deterrence fails; a limited response, such as the destruction of a small number of high-value targets, may both increase the costs of actions already taken and communicate the message that further aggression could conceivably lead to a massive nuclear exchange.

Risk is, of course, a two-edged sword, which may cut the deterrer as well as the "aggressor." More importantly, it (like the other approaches to deterrence described previously) involves a set of interacting decisions by two or more parties which will determine whether a conflict occurs and, if it does, its magnitude and its duration.

On this, virtually all theorists would agree; where they would differ is with respect to how those decisions would be made. One group of theorists would argue for a rational model, which in its purest form assumes the existence of a unitary actor (usually the mythical "national actor") with full and certain knowledge of all relevant factors, including the utility and the probability of all outcomes, the ability to determine the relative strength of policy preferences, etc. Under these circumstances, the "risk calculus" or "calculus of deterrence" is essentially mechanical: a "totting up" of factors whose weights and values are known to the last decimal place.

Other theorists maintain that the rational model is far removed from the realities of political life, where values not only differ but frequently conflict, where objectives are fuzzy, communications are not perfect and people make mistakes. Most deterrence theorists are, therefore, driven to accept a process model or prudential model, in which the decision maker "does his best to figure out what he wants to achieve, what his realistic capabilities and options are, and what the consequences of selecting one option rather than the other would be. . . . He does not make perfect decisions, and he is aware of the fact, but he does the best he can under the circumstances."[5]

This process model, though certainly more realistic, immediately gives rise to a number of questions, and creates a number of problems, all of which affect the requirements for deterrence. The prudent decision-maker must address not a "national actor" nor a "prototypical man," but particular leaders; to do this, he must know not only the personal characteristics of those leaders but also the system of government of their country, its decision making process, the role bureaucracy plays in that process, and a host of other factors which influence both inputs and outputs. Even so, this decision-maker will have less than complete knowledge of the values and interests of those whose actions he is seeking to influence and of the costs that enter into their "risk calculus." (For 30 years, American analysts have been debating the question whether the fact that the Soviet Union suffered twenty million fatalities in World War II meant that it would accept a similar number in World War III or that it would never again want to incur such losses.) In part because the values are different, in part because they are multiple, with every individual actor having a different value inventory, outcomes are indeed uncertain and can at best be assigned subjective probabilities. This means that the decision-maker seeking to deter action by another or others in a different state:

1. Cannot calculate with accuracy the force required to deter particular actions by an adversary, and may be tempted to hedge against uncertainties by increasing that force;

2. Cannot be sure that his interests are judged correctly and his intent clearly perceived, and hence may practice "overkill," rhetorically if not literally;[6]

3. Cannot be sure that he himself will act in the event deterrence fails, and hence will cast around for options that will enhance the credibility of the deterrent, in his own eyes if not in the eyes of the adversary.

There is, moreover, a fundamental difficulty with both of these models, in that they do assume a basically rational process, in which more or less detached decision-makers consider gains and losses before undertaking action. This may hold during the planning process, though it leads on the one hand to absurdities such as defining "victory" as recovering from a nuclear exchange in twenty years, compared to the USSR's twenty-one,[7] and on the other to statements that the consequences of nuclear war are so dire that nuclear weapons should never be used[8]—statements which, whatever their intent, may weaken the credibility of the nuclear guarantee. We do, however, know that decision-makers are not always rational, detached, and collected but are affected by grief, anger, pressures of time and even personal pique; thus John F. Kennedy's reported reaction on hearing about the installation of Soviet missiles in Cuba was not "This upsets the strategic balance" or "This threatens American interests" but "He [Khrushchev] can't do this to me!" Hence, one must always take into account non-rational factors, which make choices of outcomes in time of crisis largely unpredictable—and crises, therefore, things to be avoided.

A final point to note is that deterrence is a state of mind, which political leaders and military planners seek to create or to maintain. Since they cannot predict non-rational behavior, much less completely irrational behavior such as that manifested by Hitler in his last year, they try to operationalize deterrence in a way that will be convincing to a prudent or sensible person. This requires that military capabilities are adequate (and are perceived as such), that interests are clearly defined, that the intent to respond if those interests are jeopardized is stated, that all this is communicated to potential aggressors and that the will to carry out the actions threatened is made manifest.

Carrying through on some of these aims is simpler than implementing others. Capabilities to inflict heavy damage are relatively easy to develop;

McGeorge Bundy's "unthinkable" delivery of a hundred bombs on a hundred cities is well within the capacity of *any* of the five nuclear powers.[9] It is only as targeting becomes more selective, and/or numbers of targets increase, that requirements grow beyond the low hundreds of weapons. The total deemed necessary depends not only on (necessarily subjective) assessments of what will deter but also on the way in which deterrence is to be carried out, with punishment through "assured destruction," risk (through the execution of flexible options) and denial, through either damage limitation or destruction of non-nuclear forces, generating increasingly larger and more specialized requirements for SNF.[10]

As for defining interests that is, in the case of Western Europe, also comparatively simple: the rhetorical declarations about the geo-economic importance of the area, the political affinity between the United States and the European democracies, the contribution of the Alliance to American security and so on are, as indicated in Chapter 1, grounded in fact. There can be no doubt in Soviet minds that these interests are vital; the question is "How vital compared to the survival of the United States?" According to the common wisdom, though a state may risk nuclear war on behalf of another, it is not prepared to sacrifice its existence for this purpose. It is this belief which has raised doubts about the credibility of the U.S. nuclear guarantee, has led the French to create their own "national deterrent," and has inspired the United States to look for alternatives, such as "limited options" and "flexible response," which are viewed as less self-deterring.

This leads, of course, directly to the question of intent. Since it is easier to carry out actions short of all-out nuclear war than to precipitate one, lesser threats or contingent responses may be deemed credible when "massive retaliation" is not. Moreover, such responses may, by enhancing the risk of a full-scale nuclear exchange, affect calculations of costs and benefits and induce caution; to paraphrase the 18th Century English philosopher, Samuel Johnson, "The prospect of nuclear war clears a man's mind remarkably." At the same time, the proposed response cannot be either so small or so hedged that it can be discounted, which creates a dilemma for policy planners. And while some, like the French, have resolved this by moving in the direction of automaticity, this has not been true of American officials, who have increasingly "hedged their bets."

The problem of communicating capabilities is fairly easy: testing new weapons, publishing strength assessments and "leaking" the outcomes of war games are only some among dozens of means to this end. Nor is it difficult to make clear national interests, by speeches, statements, official visits, guarantees, alliances, and so on—though these admittedly cannot all be taken at face value. Communication of intent is also easy if one considers only declaratory policy but is extraordinarily difficult if one wants to persuade a potential aggressor that this policy will be implemented; i.e., if one looks to the will to take action. As indicated above, one way for decision-makers to finesse this question is by locking themselves into prescribed responses but these are easier to make if the homeland is attacked than if an ally is threatened; moreover, even in the former case, nothing short of a tamper-proof bomb-alert system linked directly to ready missiles is likely to be *wholly* persuasive. Other approaches, taken or suggested, have ranged from building weapons systems as an indication of "will" to engaging in rash or precipitate behavior to create an impression of irrationality. Ultimately, however, the issue of whether a state has the will to do what it has said it will do can only be resolved if deterrence fails—by which time it may be too late for either deterrer or deterree to worry about the matter.

Obviously, this brief synopsis touches only superficially on the issues involved in maintaining the credibility of deterrence, with all its assumptions about decision-processes, rational behavior and so on. It does, however, suggest that one individual or group can easily come to different conclusions about deterrence than another, since their values and interests will differ, their circumstances are not the same and the way in which the problems are perceived will vary accordingly. In subsequent sections, we will attempt to describe the views of American and West German officials with respect to the operationalization of deterrence, with particular reference to its application in Europe; however, before doing that, it may be helpful to examine the threats to security they are seeking to deter.

The Soviet Challenge

In addition to the ambiguities and uncertainties inherent in the concept of deterrence others arise from attempts at its application to particular situations. This is perhaps nowhere more true than in NATO, where one must take into account not only the enormous variations in the strength of the Allies but their different geographic positions, their degree of involvement in regional and global affairs, their socio-economic and political structures and a host of other factors. (As one illustration of this, a deterrent posture acceptable to France, which is sheltered by the West German *glacis* and free to acquire nuclear weapons, will not necessarily be acceptable to an exposed Federal Republic, which has voluntarily renounced any nuclear capability.)

These differences are intensified by varying interpretations of the Soviet threat to Western Europe. Although there *is* general agreement on the size and composition of Soviet/Warsaw Pact military forces, and at least some semblance of unity in defining potential threats to the security of Europe, there are sharp differences with respect to the real ability of the USSR to execute them, the likelihood that it will do so and the best means of deterring the use of force by the members of the Warsaw Treaty Organization. In this section, we will discuss briefly the military capabilities of the two alliances, describe the kinds of actions the Soviet Union and its allies could take and outline some of the reasons for disagreements concerning their imminence and their effectiveness, leaving to subsequent sections consideration of American and West German policies for the maintenance of "effective deterrence."

Soviet/WTO Military Capabilities

By all accounts, the Soviet Union (though not other members of the Warsaw Pact) has for over twenty years been engaged in a continuing modernization and strengthening of its armed forces. At the strategic level, this has involved the deployment of new and powerful ICBMs, some of which are armed with increasingly accurate MIRV-ed warheads; the construction of larger and better missile submarines, carrying longer-range SLBMs; the production of more modern bombers, armed with ALCMs; and the upgrading of air and missile defenses, accompanied by continued research on ground-and space-based lasers, particle beams and other exotic means of knocking out enemy aircraft and missiles. Although these measures have not achieved that strategic superiority which many in the West assume is their aim, they have eroded many of the advantages formerly enjoyed by the Alliance—and consequently the earlier confidence in the credibility of the U.S. nuclear guarantee.

Similar improvements have been made in theater nuclear forces, with the development of nuclear-capable artillery, the replacement of older missiles by newer, more reliable and more accurate ones (such as the SS-21, the SS-23 and the notorious SS-20) and marked increases in the range, payload, avionics and electronic countermeasures of strike aircraft.[11] Here again, the result has not been the attainment of a meaningful advantage in theater nuclear forces but the erosion of an earlier NATO advantage. And though this in itself may not be significant, given the number and variety of weapons on both sides, their dispersal over large areas, the ability to introduce additional forces from outside the theater and the possibility of employing SNF against targets in the European theater, it has also contributed to a loss of confidence in the nuclear guarantee—and in the feasibility of the doctrine of "flexible response." (So also, paradoxically, has the U.S.-Soviet agreement to scrap the medium-range and short-range missiles deployed both in Europe and outside it—in this instance because the redressal of the balance deriving from larger cut-backs in Soviet weapons is, to some, more than offset by the projected elimination of American GLCMs and P IIs, which will affect adversely the ability of SACEUR to execute certain strike options in the event of a clash of arms.)

A similar shift has taken place in the conventional balance, where the Soviets and their allies have always had a significant edge in numbers of divisions and in weapons such as artillery/mortars, tanks, armored personnel carriers and so on. Although advantages in numbers of weapons do not automatically translate into advantages in combat capabilities, and although simple displays may overstate even numerical advantages, it is apparent that the Warsaw Pact has deployed along its frontiers powerful and well-equipped forces, which can be augmented rapidly by the mobilization of additional elements and/or by the movement forward of ground and air units now stationed in the USSR. More importantly, it has also strengthened these conventional forces, improved their command, control and communication systems and augmented their logistic support; in fact, some analysts have suggested that the USSR has begun to overtake NATO in the application of technology to military problems and to surpass it in the speed with which newer weapons and more modern equipment are introduced into the field.[12]

In listing improvements in Soviet forces, those in the navy should not be overlooked. From a small, obsolescent establishment, whose main missions were coastal defense and protection of the flanks of army units, the Soviet Navy has evolved into one of first rank; today it has numerous modern ships of all types, including nuclear-powered missile and attack submarines, aircraft carriers (as well as "through-deck cruisers" for ASW operations), ocean-going surface combat ships, amphibious ships and logistic support vessels. It maintains squadrons on station in the Mediterranean, in the Indian Ocean and in the South China Sea and has sent units to maneuver with the Cuban Navy, to conduct exercises elsewhere and to visit ports throughout the world. Whether world-wide operations are sustainable even in peacetime is a debatable point but there can be little doubt that the Soviet Navy is a more formidable adversary now than ever before.

In sum, the Soviet Union has, at heavy cost, extensively improved all elements of its armed forces, offensive and defensive, strategic and tactical, land, sea and air. In the process, it has erased or eroded Allied superiority in strategic and theater nuclear forces, perhaps increased its relative advantage in conventional capabilities in the European theater and acquired a "global reach" through naval and air power. These improvements have significantly enhanced the ability of the USSR to utilize the military instrument of policy, should it choose to do so, but whether they have similarly enhanced the prospects for success in its employment is still debatable. In the next section, we will look at some of the ways in which the Soviets could threaten Western Europe militarily and in the following one some of the reasons for doubt as to either their ability or their willingness to translate threats into deeds.

Soviet/WTO Military Options

Theoretically, the options open to the Soviets in the utilization of their (and their allies') military capabilities are almost boundless, ranging from the clandestine attachment of limpet mines to a Western tanker by Soviet-supported terrorists to the initiation of all-out global war. Practically speaking, those options are narrowed by the costs, the uncertainties and the risks of military action, with the greatest risk, of course, being that of the destruction of the Soviet Union by American (and other Western) nuclear forces. They may be further narrowed if one applies to them the criteria of relevance and effectiveness: whatever the feasibility of torpedoing Japanese tankers in the Straits of Malacca this scenario seems so unlikely to further Soviet interests that it has dropped out of discussions in Western professional circles. The threats that are considered seriously are, however, ominous enough.

One set of these relates to operations outside Europe aimed at undermining Western influence in the Third World, denying or limiting Western access to resources and markets, creating client states whose activities could advance the Soviet cause (and perhaps affect the over-all "correlation of forces"), building bases for future operations (as at Cam Ranh Bay) and establishing a permanent Soviet presence in key areas as a counter to any efforts by members of the Alliance to reverse the process. Although these efforts to prevail through what General Beaufre called "an indirect strategy" may be more political and economic than military, they certainly have a military component, ranging from the sale of arms and the provision of cadres to the dispatch of either proxy forces (as in Angola and Ethiopia) or Soviet troops, as in Syria. The question of the form these operations may take, and the threats they may pose to Western security, will, however, be discussed in Chapter 6 on the "out of area" challenge rather than here.

Another set of options for the utilization of the military instrument derives from Soviet strategic and theater nuclear forces—with the latter being augmented slightly by delivery vehicles in the hands of other members of the Warsaw Pact. Certainly, the Soviets could, if they chose, destroy the United States, other members of the Alliance and, if necessary, potential rivals such as Brazil, China or Japan; barring the fruition of the Strategic Defense Initiative there is nothing to preclude their accomplishing this. There is, however, a major reason why they should not attempt it, this being that the Soviet Union could be—and undoubtedly would be—devastated in return. And as Khrushchev remarked feelingly some twenty-five years ago, one cannot build Communism out of radioactive rubble.

Another option open to the USSR is that of initiating a strategic disarming strike against the United States. In this scenario, which was popular some time ago, the Soviets would utilize their thousands of land-based missiles with accurate, high-yield warheads, perhaps supplemented by depressed-trajectory SLBMs, to knock out most of the American ICBMs[13], that portion of the missile submarine fleet then in port and the bulk of the U.S. bombers; if these strikes were accompanied by attacks on C³I systems, and perhaps by high altitude detonations of multi-megaton warheads which could "black out" communications and warning systems, U.S. SNF would be not only decimated but virtually incapable of a coordinated and effective response. Furthermore, according to the scenario, such a response (which could only be directed against "soft" targets in the USSR) could be deterred by the threat to obliterate American cities and the President of the United States would have no choice save to surrender.

Leaving aside the question whether the President *would* surrender (with Mr. Meese remarking at one stage that this scenario was no longer plausible because Ronald Reagan, and not Jimmy Carter, was in the White House!) there remain serious doubts about the technical possibilities of success. These stem from the fact that no ICBMs have ever been test flown over the North Pole, so that the consequences of magnetic flux for missile accuracy are unknown; from uncertainties about the effect of "fratricide" on the second incoming re-entry vehicle; from questions about the ability to coordinate an attack against the three components of the TRIAD; and so on.[14] Moreover, there is nothing in Soviet military doctrine to suggest that a strategic disarming strike unaccompanied by broader employment of nuclear weapons is a serious option and much in Soviet political thinking to indicate that it is not.

One further reason why a disarming strike against the United States may seem a less than optimal solution is that it would leave untouched American (and other) theater nuclear forces—including five Poseidon submarines, half of whose 800 re-entry vehicles are allocated to SACEUR. Thus military prudence, if not political realism, would suggest that nuclear delivery capabilities in Europe—including those of Britain and France—be attacked simultaneously, lest these be directed against Soviet troops, or even against the USSR itself.

A disarming strike against NATO nuclear forces would be easier than one against the United States, since the Soviets have more than enough weapons to knock out the 280 air and military bases, naval facilities, nuclear storage sites, and C^3I installations, used by Allied TNF; in fact, one analyst has estimated that this could be done either by the intermediate-range SS-20s and SS-5s or, once these have been dismantled, by the 180 SS-11 and SS-19 ICBMs that are believed to be peripherally-targeted, assisted if necessary by medium-range bombers and by SLBMs.[15] These forces could also direct barrage attacks against those American, British and French missile submarines at sea. If, however, strategic warning were received, the number of targets to be attacked would increase substantially, as more submarines put to sea, missiles and artillery moved from airfields and casernes to field positions and aircraft redeployed to auxiliary airstrips. And there is always the risk that preparations for such an attack, which would be hard to conceal, would induce a dispersion of U.S. SNF—or even the adoption of a "launch on warning" policy.

The same difficulties and the same risks would, of course, accompany a disarming strike aimed solely against Europe, with the added disadvantage that this would leave intact not only American tactical nuclear forces deployed outside Europe but also the full panoply of strategic nuclear forces. Short of a direct nuclear attack against the United States itself, nothing is so likely to prompt retaliation against the USSR as the kind of operation envisioned; whatever the theoretical desirability of confining a nuclear war to the continent of Europe, as suggested by Mr. Brezhnev in 1972, the destruction of NATO theater nuclear forces could well create a situation in which the exercise of "limited nuclear options" against the USSR would seem to American decision-makers to be not only a proportionate but indeed an essential response.

Perhaps for this reason, Western analysts have examined another Soviet option which would not cross the nuclear "firebreak:" that of a conventional disarming strike against the theater nuclear forces of the Alliance. Such an attempt would require a shift from missiles to aircraft as the principal instrument of attack and would enormously increase the number of vehicles required. Some analysts, noting that the Soviets have made strenuous efforts to increase their capabilities for air strikes against NATO C³I installations, early warning systems and operational forces, estimate that Soviet bombers and fighter-ground attack aircraft (FGAs) could significantly degrade NATO nuclear forces, especially if chemical munitions were employed.[16] In isolation, however, such an attack would make little sense, especially since airborne, air assault and mobile ground elements of the Soviet Army are also expected to play a role in the destruction of Allied nuclear forces. Thus a conventional disarming strike would seem more likely to be a part of a larger conventional operation, in which utilization of surviving NATO forces, such as nuclear submarines, is deterred by the threat of nuclear retaliation, than a separate effort to remove a particular threat or to create an exploitable political situation.

The real question facing Soviet leaders is not, however, whether they could successfully carry out a disarming strike (or "limited nuclear options" of their own, directed against Western Europe) but what purpose would be served by such operations. It is one thing to launch a pre-emptive attack if war seems certain; it is quite another to precipitate that war by initiatives of one's own. As analysts without number have pointed out, the Soviet military are operationally offensive but strategically defensive.[17] And whether one views that position as deriving from a judgment that the military balance is not yet favorable enough, from an estimate that Soviet objectives can be achieved without recourse to such drastic measures or from a preoccupation with avoiding nuclear war, the question of motivation for change still remains.

To a marked degree the same factors apply to Soviet conventional operations in Europe—though here Western analysts (if not Soviet ones) seem persuaded that the risks are less and the opportunities greater. One option open to the USSR is that of a full-scale conventional assault against NATO Europe, preceded by, or accompanied by, the mobilization of Soviet and Warsaw Pact reserves; in fact, that has been, for more than thirty years, the official NATO definition of the "threat." Depending on the weight of the initial assault, any attack on the Central Front could be launched after two to eight days of preparation (with 21 divisions), in eight to fifteen days(with 39 divisions) or in fifteen to forty days (with 59 divisions); to bring to bear the full potential weight of 120 divisions would require from sixty to ninety days.[18] Simultaneously, (smaller and slower) attacks could be launched against northern Norway, against Turkey and, should members of the "Southern Tier" (Hungary, Romania and Bulgaria) become involved, against Greece.

These attacks could be—and indeed for any assurance of success would almost have to be—preceded by massive air assaults against NATO air bases, air defense installations, command centers, and communications facilities; in the relatively circumscribed area of Western and Central Europe the side that strikes first can inflict heavy losses on the adversary's air force. Moreover, given the numbers of planes available to the USSR, concurrent attacks could also be launched against ground force barracks, depots, and headquarters; against the ports, airfields, and railroad junctions through which reinforcements would have to pass and against missile sites and storage igloos for nuclear warheads. At the same time, all these facilities could be hit by saboteurs, by airborne raiding parties and by mobile groups specially trained and equipped to penetrate enemy lines and knock out rear area installations, even before larger and more powerful armored spearheads reached these points.

From the Soviet perspective there are a number of disadvantages to an attack in strength, one being that it sacrifices the surprise so beloved of Soviet military planners. Given five to seven days warning time, NATO could not only flesh out its units with reservists but move them into forward positions and prepare minefields, tank traps, and field fortifications, thereby enhancing significantly its defensive capabilities. And with still more time NATO could deploy the units arriving by air from the United States, bring the West German territorial brigades into the combat zone and otherwise increase its operational reserves and improve its resiliency. The net result would be stauncher resistance to any assault by "first echelon" WTO forces, whose success in breaking NATO defenses would increasingly depend on the timely arrival of "second echelon" divisions from the USSR.[19]

One way of avoiding this "protracted war" would be for the Soviet Union to attack without warning, utilizing as many as possible of its 24 divisions in Czechoslovakia and East Germany, together with selected elements of the East German Army. In this way, Allied soldiers could, quite literally, be "caught in their beds," deep penetrations made before resistance could be organized and rear areas so disrupted that mobilization and redeployment of NATO forces would be virtually impossible. If this version of the *blitzkrieg* succeeded, the area east of the Rhine could be overrun almost before war was declared, setting the stage either for a further advance by WTO reinforcements or for a favorable peace. (In fact, it is conceivable that NATO nuclear forces in Germany could be cut off or destroyed before orders to launch could reach them, thereby ruling out any battlefield use of nuclear weapons.) And though this potential threat also has disadvantages, one of them being that the degree of surprise considered necessary may not be attainable and another that even if it were, success in battle may not come so easily, this Soviet option is being taken very seriously in both official and unofficial circles in the West.[20]

These are, of course, not the only options open to the Soviets, at least as Western analysts see them. Although the "Hamburg grab," a swift lunge by limited forces to seize a key locality for bargaining purposes, is no longer discussed in Western journals and at Western conferences, it remains conceivable. So do larger-scale but still limited operations against the flanks of NATO, such as a quick thrust into Turkish Thrace or an amphibious landing on Norway's North Cape, cutting off Norwegian troops in the

Finnmark and giving the Soviets air and naval bases which would be invaluable in the event of future operations in the Norwegian Sea. In all three of these illustrations the primary motivation would be political, not military, and the presumed results would be to discredit the American guarantee, disrupt the cohesion of the Alliance and create a favorable opportunity for its weakening, if not its dismantlement.

These scenarios, however unlikely they may be, reflect a Western concern with the *political* use of Soviet military power—which, in fact, is seen as the most likely threat by both West German officials and West German elites.[21] Most of those discussing this threat do not envision crude power plays of the type just described but rather foresee pointed reminders of Soviet capabilities and Allied vulnerabilities, jibes about the dangers the West Europeans face by virtue of association with the "American imperialist warmongers," vague but appealing proposals for dismantling the two alliances and establishing a European security régime, and so on. They do not rule out attempts at political blackmail such as Khrushchev's efforts in 1958-61 to force recognition of East German rights in West Berlin or Leonid Brezhnev's try in 1973, when the Egyptian Third Army was surrounded, to force an Israeli withdrawal by the threat of Soviet intervention. These are, however, all side effects of the steady growth of Soviet military power, which may ultimately pose to the Allies the question: who can afford to wage war and who cannot?[22] And though at the moment the answer to that question may be "nobody," there are those who envision that someday that answer will change.

Challenge and Response

If there is, as there seems to be, rather widespread agreement within the Alliance as to the nature of the actions the Soviets could take, why is there not a more uniform and cohesive response, a more determined effort to cope with dangerous increases in Soviet military power? Partly this is because such an effort would be costly and could be counter-productive, in terms of exacerbating relations with the East and stimulating the arms race. Partly, however, it is because it might be unnecessary: that the Soviets could undertake a particular military operation does not mean either that they would do so or that they would succeed if they tried. And though analysts, officers and officials can be found on both sides of these judgments, the very fact that they *do* differ contributes to the uncertainty about "What is to be done?"

These differences begin with the question why the USSR is building "an outrageously outsized force [of 180-190 divisions]—far beyond the requirements of Soviet security demands."[23] Dr. B. Huldt answers his own question by pointing out that the Soviets may deem these divisions essential to the maintenance of a balance with their (largely adversarial) neighbors, that the possession of these forces does not automatically imply aggressive intent and that even if the Soviets have an edge in continental capabilities, it is blunted by their inferiority in "global reach" and rendered largely useless by Soviet inability to create a strategic counterdeterrent which would rule out American nuclear retaliation.[24] Other analysts argue that the USSR does not accept the concept of "balance" but rather seeks a change in the "correlation of forces" which would lead to the undermining of the West[25] and still others that the Soviets seek a "war fighting capability" as a means of enhancing deterrence and as a hedge against its failure.[26]

This latter assessment does not lead to a judgement that the USSR is looking to start a war; in Gerhard Wettig's opinion the Soviet leaders would like to avoid an East-West conflict and deem strategic nuclear war "a formidable risk which is not to be engaged in deliberately."[27] Thus scenarios which open with a surprise attack upon American strategic nuclear installations (or even those in Western Europe) seem implausible to many; even if the "window of vulnerability" were open, those climbing through it would require iron nerves and an unlimited belief in the rationality of the very U.S. leaders whom the Kremlin criticizes for rashness and inconsistency.[28] How far the Soviets will go in *risking* a nuclear war may be another question but the only conditions under which they say they will start one is if an attack by the West appears inevitable and imminent.

Nor do the Soviets intend, if one can believe what they say, to initiate conventional operations against Western Europe. The Soviet view is that a war in Europe would be started by the West; indeed their "worst case scenario" is built around a coordinated NATO attack in Central Europe, a full-scale rebellion in Eastern Europe, and a Chinese invasion.[29] Furthermore, even if they should launch an offensive (or counter-offensive) against Western Europe it may not take the form envisioned by NATO. The Soviet Union has certainly trained its troops for non-nuclear as well as nuclear operations, has begun to organize and train "Operational Maneuver Groups" for rapid exploitation of success in a conventional battle and has even established "theaters of operations" for the better coordination of air and ground forces and for the better employment of operational and strategic reserves; there is even some reason to believe that Soviet analysts are beginning to draw distinctions between conventional and nuclear war, as their Western counterparts did long ago.[30] Such distinctions have, however, not yet hardened into differences and Soviet military doctrine still envisages the employment of nuclear weapons in offensive operations; under such conditions, to quote an unnamed Soviet author, "the concentration of superior conventional forces . . . will cease to be necessary and will even be dangerous."[31]

Finally, there are marked differences of opinion among Western analysts as to the ability of the USSR to carry out a successful conventional campaign against NATO. While some see the Soviets achieving strategic surprise, others view this as highly unlikely in a world of electronic surveillance. While some see the Group of Soviet Forces, Germany, benefitting from the ability to choose the time and place of any attack, others

FIGURE 4.1   Most Likely Axes of Advance in a Warsaw Pact Attack
Against NATO

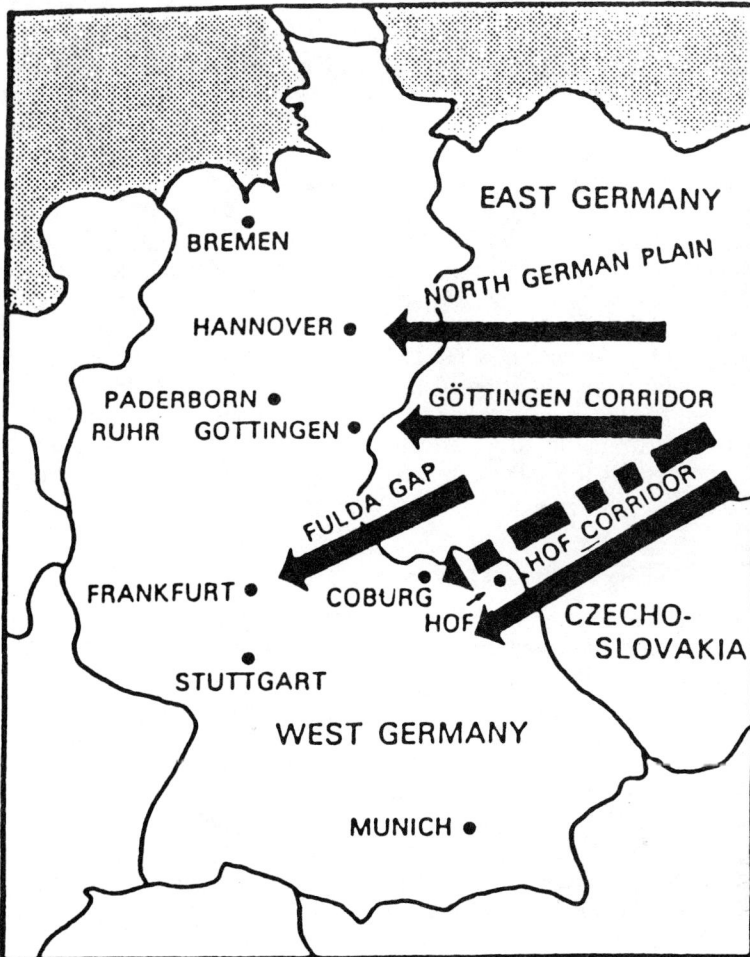

Source: John J. Mearsheimer, "Why the Soviets Can't Win Quickly in Central Europe," *International Security,* vol. 7, no. 1 (Summer 1982), p. 21. Reprinted by permission of The MIT Press, Cambridge, Massachusetts.

point out the relatively few avenues of approach into Western Europe and the difficulties in traversing them because of urban sprawl and other obstacles to movement. (See Figure 4.1) While some maintain that the availability of sizeable reserves in the Soviet Union gives the USSR the ability to mount successive attacks, employing "second echelon" forces, others point to the awkward gaps between units initially available and those coming in as reinforcements, and the time required to move them into position, even without opposition.[32] When to this are added considerations such as the doubtful reliability of Czechoslovak or Polish soldiers, the unsatisfactory state of readiness of even Soviet divisions in the GDR, (which are engaged for most of the year in training conscripts), the low level of logistical support and inadequate maintenance facilities for Soviet/WTO units, etc.,[33] it is obvious that sheer numbers may not be determining. And since there are disputes over numbers as well as over the other factors mentioned, it is obviously possible for reasonable men to disagree about the threat to Western Europe—as they do.

By far the most serious disagreements, however, arise over what is required to deter Soviet/WTO aggression, whatever its nature or whatever its motivation. Even among those who believe in the "official" threat of a massive conventional assault against Western Europe, differences exist over whether this can be best precluded by the current doctrine of flexible response, by the construction of a wholly conventional deterrent, the modernization and reconfiguration of theater nuclear forces, or both, or by the deployment of strategic defensive systems. In the next section, we will trace developments over time in American thinking about deterrence and defense in Europe and in the following section West German views on the same subject.

Coping with the Challenge: The American Approach

Whatever the likelihood that the Soviets might incur the costs and run the risks attendant upon any military moves against a member of the Alliance, the possibility does remain; one does not have to believe that intentions derive from capabilities to be concerned about the possible use of those capabilities. Of greatest concern is the threat that the Soviets may employ their powerful conventional forces to overrun Western Europe, relying on their strategic and theater nuclear forces to deter any use of nuclear weapons by NATO and/or on the speed of their advance to paralyze the decision processes within NATO. A related concern is that the Soviets may themselves decide to employ nuclear weapons, either on their own initiative or in response to a "first use" by NATO, and either against the Alliance as a whole or against the European members thereof. Hence, the members of the Western Alliance have decided that in order to neutralize these and other threats, military or political, they must both develop counter-vailing forces and assure the Soviets that these will not be utilized against a peaceful USSR, i.e., they have decided to pursue a policy of defense and détente. And they have concluded that this policy of defense can best be assured by deterring war rather than by waging it, a task to which both Americans and West Germans are committed—albeit in different ways.

The American Approach to Deterrence

To speak of an "American approach to deterrence" is in some sense misleading, since there is no single American view; different Presidents have looked at deterrence in different ways, not always consonant with the views of their own subordinates. Over time, this has resulted in bewildering conceptual shifts, from deterrence through punishment to deterrence through denial or risk, and back again. It has also resulted in fits and starts in weapons systems programs (which sometimes followed changes in concepts, sometimes preceded them and sometimes moved independently) and in pronouncements on targeting doctrine which sometimes ratified existing policy and sometimes set new directions, that might or might not be pursued.

The reasons for this are not hard to understand. For one thing, American nuclear forces, unlike those of France or Britain, must deter both a Soviet attack upon the homeland and aggression against Allies, requirements which pose very different problems, conceptually and operationally. For another, significant technological innovations have affected both capabilities and concepts; for instance, the feasibility of "deterrence through denial" at the strategic level is much more questionable in an age of MIRV-ed missiles, with maneuverable warheads, than it was when manned bombers were the principal means of delivering nuclear warheads across intercontinental distances. For a third, not all Presidents or Secretaries of Defense were careful students of deterrence—nor even as careful as they might have been about reading what some students of deterrence wrote in their names.[34] And finally, many factors other than the requirements of deterrence influenced official pronouncements on the subject; for example, Mr. McNamara's switch from "damage limitation" to "assured destruction" was motivated in part by a desire to hold down Air Force requests for additional missiles and President Johnson's decision to build a "light" ballistic missile defense was influenced less by concerns about the vulnerability of American cities to Chinese nuclear strikes then about his own political vulnerability on the issue.

There have, however, been a number of identifiable trends in American thinking which shed light on current policy. One is a downgrading of "deterrence through punishment," which was initially embodied in the doctrine of "massive retaliation" during the Eisenhower Administration and which was continued during the Kennedy and Johnson Administrations under the heading of "assured destruction." The concept of "deterrence through punishment" was acceptable as long as that punishment was essentially one-sided but once the Soviets began to develop significant retaliatory capabilities of their own, policies changed.

One change was that "assured destruction" became an ultimate option rather than a preferred one and was reserved largely for retaliation to an attack upon the United States rather than one upon the Allies.[35] A second was that "deterrence through risk" received increased emphasis. Although this concept was applied to extended deterrence as early as 1963, under the rubric of "flexible response," its full institutionalization occurred only in 1974, with the adoption of the Schlesinger Doctrine.[36] This called for deterrence of "limited" actions, such as a first strike on U.S. strategic nuclear forces or a Soviet assault against Western Europe, by limited reprisals against Soviet military installations. The exercise of these "limited nuclear options" was intended to demonstrate American resolve, to stress the risk that further escalation could spin out of control, with catastrophic consequences, and in this way to halt the war some place short of an all-out nuclear exchange. And this policy continued thereafter, perhaps the most notable expression being found in Presidential Directive 59, signed by Mr. Carter.

A third result of the enhanced Soviet ability to wreak destruction upon the United States was increased interest in "deterrence through denial," where denial essentially meant damage limitation. This was initially exemplified in Mr. McNamara's "counterforce doctrine," which called for the United States to destroy most of the Soviet strategic nuclear forces through attacks on air bases and missile sites. As Soviet SNF grew in numbers and decreased in vulnerability damage limitation through counterforce became less and less feasible, so that Mr. Nixon and Secretary of Defense Laird opted instead for ballistic missile defenses. When these proved technically infeasible and politically unacceptable they were bargained away in the SALT negotiations but Mr. Reagan, in his Strategic Defense Initiative, envisions a return to the concept of "deterrence through denial." Until the time that SDI can be implemented, however, the Reagan Administration, like its predecessors, proposes to exercise limited options while maintaining (very high) capabilities for assured destruction-with the added objective of being able to fight a "prolonged" nuclear war in which the United States will "prevail."[37]

Whatever concept of deterrence it espoused, every administration over the last thirty years has sought strategic nuclear forces at least equal to those of the USSR, partly in the hope of retaining an advantage in the event deterrence failed, partly to demonstrate its "will." (As Secretary of Defense Brown put it, "Our strategic nuclear forces should not be, or be seen to be, inferior to those of the USSR.")[38] Furthermore, technology (in the form of lighter, more accurate warheads and the development of MIRV-ed missiles) made possible force improvements which were also considered desirable, both for the exercise of limited options and for the conduct of extended deterrence. Only with increased concern about the stability of strategic deterrence (i.e., with the potential vulnerability of land-based systems to a Soviet disarming strike) did emphasis shift from building up the number of American warheads to limiting those of both countries, through arms control.

Interest was manifested largely by repeated references to the importance of Western Europe (and Japan), reminders of the indissoluble links between the United States and its allies and promises to shield those threatened by aggression—promises which, like old coins, grew thin with use. Aware of this, the United States sought to demonstrate its intent to honor its pledge by creating nuclear options which would increase the risk attendant on aggression (an approach already discussed) and by deploying nuclear weapons which would also increase that risk, either because they could be utilized to deliberately escalate a conflict or because efforts to destroy or capture them could prompt "inadvertent escalation."

Throughout this whole period, the American approach to deterrence was marked by a high degree of rationality; thus the doctrine of "limited nuclear options" assumed not only some calculus of costs and benefits but the continuation of this calculus throughout a series of nuclear exchanges, with no allowance for fear, human error, anger, or even a failure in communication.[39] It was also marked by an emphasis upon quantitative "indicators of effectiveness," such as U.S. and Soviet hard target kill-capabilities following a disarming strike or the speed with which one country or the other could rebuild its industrial base following a nuclear exchange. And it was, in this and other respects, very much ethnocentric, in that little account was taken of Soviet motives, intentions and conduct before war or during it. (It was not until 1980 that any senior official acknowledged that the Soviets had a concept of deterrence, based on war-fighting, which differed significantly from the American one and that the United States would have to take account of this in its plans and preparations.) And even now, the United States envisions the possibility of a limited war in Europe between the two superpowers, a possibility which the Soviets virtually rule out.

Indeed it is this possibility, which many regard as a virtual certainty, that has most strongly influenced American thinking on deterrence. Acting on the premise that the Soviets would eschew the use of nuclear weapons, save in retaliation to an American first use, U.S. planners and decision-makers have sought to avoid this retaliation while still preserving a credible deterrent to all forms of aggression. One approach taken has been to narrow the circumstances under which U.S. nuclear forces would be employed, so that their use becomes a last resort rather than an early option. (This turn away from "massive retaliation" reflects an understandable reluctance to commit suicide as well as a commendable desire to promise only what one might really do if forced to take action.) Another has been to emphasize risk rather than punishment as a means of maintaining deterrence; even though limited nuclear strikes were to be directed against targets of value to the Soviet Union, their purpose was primarily to remind Soviet leaders that still worse was to come should they continue the war. The third has been an effort to make extended deterrence more credible by emphasizing denial, in effect returning to the concept of the conventional "shield" for Western Europe promoted by General Lauris Norstad in the late 1950s. Taken together, they point clearly toward a marked shift in the relative emphasis placed on "deterrence and defense," a shift which will be further considered in the next section, on flexible response.

The American Interpretation of Flexible Response

All the trends described came together in the strategy of flexible response, which is really an operationalization of deterrence. This strategy is predicated on the ability to act effectively in a variety of ways across the "spectrum of conflict," leaving open the question of when, and under what circumstances, a particular response will be made. In this way, the defender keeps his options open, while the aggressor is left uncertain as to the risks he may run—and hence the costs he may incur.

Thirty years ago, there was neither a doctrine of flexible response nor any need for it; the first Eisenhower Administration relied heavily upon strategic nuclear forces for both deterrence and war-fighting, with conventional forces (and the still embryonic theater nuclear forces) serving primarily as trip-wires. By the late 1950s, however, then Secretary of State John Foster Dulles had signaled a change from "massive retaliation" in the event of aggression to a local defense employing theater nuclear weapons. This concept was carried a step further by General Lauris Norstad, SACEUR, who proposed to use theater nuclear and conventional forces as a "shield" against the WTO; moreover, as long as the shield served its purpose, SAC would not be ordered into action.[40] Thus, NATO came early to a doctrine of "flexible response", in which a stout defense was to bring any attack to a halt or, failing that, to give the Soviets time to think about the consequences of continuing their operations; should they persist, the United States would escalate to a strategic nuclear strike which, given the balance of forces at the time, would certainly bring the war to a close!

Mr. McNamara kept the bottle labeled "flexible response" but changed the contents: the defense was to be conducted primarily by conventional forces. Tactical nuclear forces were essentially trip-wires to a possible U.S. disarming strike, though they could also be used, once that occurred, to break up Soviet assaults and allow restoration of the conventional "shield." War termination was expected to result in one of three ways—through a successful conventional defense, if this could be developed; through the use of tactical nuclear weapons, which would remind the Soviets about possible escalation to the strategic level; or through a U.S. disarming strike against Soviet military and counterforce targets, forcing an end to the aggression. The deployment of powerful and less vulnerable Soviet SNF, which brought counterforce into question as a feasible doctrine, led Mr. McNamara to turn to "assured destruction" as the ultimate deterrent; otherwise, this doctrine remained unchanged through the Johnson Administration.

The Nixon Administration reverted in large measure to General Norstad's version of flexible response, in which deterrence was based on a combination of defense by conventional forces, theater nuclear forces which could, if necessary, play a role in that defense, and the threat of employing SAC should all else fail. The major difference from the policy approved by President Johnson was that TNF were given a more responsible role in both deterrence and defense, hopefully enhancing the prospects for terminating any war short of a U.S.-Soviet nuclear exchange.

The Ford Administration (or, to be more precise, Secretary of Defense Schlesinger, whom President Ford had inherited from his predecessor) initiated changes in the roles of both strategic and tactical nuclear forces, which were expected to exercise "limited, controllable options" at the theater level.[41] Moreover, TNF were given a war-fighting role: should conventional defenses fail, theater nuclear forces could either re-establish these defenses or escalate the conflict, or both.[42] And should escalation by TNF not persuade the Soviets of the risks they were running, strategic forces would be launched in a limited fashion over a period of time against pre-planned targets, in order to demonstrate U.S. (and NATO) resolve not to be defeated. If this should fail, presumably the full panoply of U.S. strategic power would be engaged—though it should be noted that Secretary of Defense Schlesinger never promised to do so.[43]

His successor, Mr. Donald Rumsfeld, repeated the missions assigned strategic and theater nuclear forces by Mr. Schlesinger; however, he placed on conventional forces "the primary burden of deterrence" and sought to maintain their ability to "conduct a successful, forward non-nuclear defense."[44] Theater nuclear forces were to back up the conventional defense by destroying breakthrough formations should that defense fail, though they also could launch attacks against targets deep in Pact territory, either before or in response to the first use of nuclear weapons by the Soviet Union.[45] Escalation was, of course, to be carried out in a controlled fashion, employing limited options as a means to that end and utilizing strategic nuclear forces as well as tactical ones. And though Mr. Rumsfeld was not explicit, it would appear that the Soviets were to be inhibited from launching an all-out nuclear war by the ability of the United States to overmatch them at this level, and presumably induced to negotiate a settlement before things reached this stage.

Essentially the same approach was taken by the Carter Administration. Strategic deterrence was to be insured by SNF which were not, and were not seen as, inferior to those of the Soviet Union, which were survivable and which possessed the ability to carry out selective attacks on "the things the Soviet leadership prizes most—political and military control, nuclear and conventional forces and the economic base needed to sustain war."[46] Deterrence within the theater was to be based primarily on conventional forces capable of a stout defense and secondarily on the controlled use of theater nuclear forces to escalate the conflict—apparently independently of and in advance of the employment of SNF. These latter were not, however, to respond to a continuing Soviet assault by initiating all-out war; instead according to General George S. Brown, USAF, at the time Chairman of the Joint Chiefs of Staff, "should deterrence fail, these [strategic nuclear] forces must be capable of flexible employment in order to allow conflict termination at the lowest level feasible. If such escalation control fails then the forces must permit conflict termination on the most favorable terms possible."[47]

The Reagan Administration sought to deter aggression in Europe primarily by building up conventional forces capable of deterring a conventional attack and of maintaining an effective defense should deterrence fail. As noted earlier, these strengthened conventional forces were to be capable of holding critical positions in Europe during a prolonged conventional war and ultimately of undertaking a counteroffensive, while other units engaged in "horizontal escalation," thereby "putting at risk Soviet interests, including the Soviet homeland"[48] and siphoning off reinforcements from other parts of the USSR.[b] And though less was said during the latter days of the administration about counteroffensives or counterpressures against Soviet client states, the emphasis on effective conventional defenses in Europe still held.

The principal mission assigned theater nuclear forces was that of linking conventional and strategic nuclear forces; in the words of Secretary of State George Schultz, "It is this crucial coupling which gives concrete form to the indivisibility of American and European security which [in turn] ensures that the Soviets could not attack Europe without risking strategic retaliation against their own territory."[49] If deterrence failed, theater nuclear forces were, together with other components of the TRIAD, to "respond effectively to any attack—including a theater nuclear attack."

As for strategic nuclear forces, their role was seemingly that of "escalation dominance," i.e., insuring that any use of nuclear weapons by the Soviets would be disadvantageous to them. There was no apparent eagerness to employ SNF unless and until the USSR forced the adminis tration's hand. And the buildup undertaken by President Reagan was intended to convince the Soviets that the use of nuclear weapons would never be in their interest, as well as to facilitate the conduct of sustained operations should a nuclear war break out.

As one looks at the roles assigned over time to various elements of the TRIAD, several things stand out. One is that the conventional component has for twenty-five years been tasked with contributing to deterrence through its ability to repel WTO assaults, an ability which was, under the Kennedy, late Ford and Reagan Administrations, expected to be virtually water-tight. A second thing to note is that while theater nuclear forces have had a variety of roles, enhancing deterrence through fear of escalation was always one of them. Generally this was to be accomplished by limited, controlled strikes at targets in the theater but it could also be brought about by one of the war-fighting missions assigned under Presidents Nixon and Ford: that of blunting a conventional breakthrough. Their third role, which was prominent in the Nixon-Ford period and again during Mr. Reagan's term of office, was to deter, or respond to, strikes by Soviet TNF but there is no indication that this latter mission has been reflected in force postures. Despite the clamors of some critics for this, a role for TNF which would enable them to fight and win a war on the continent of Europe did not seem to be considered seriously; indeed, the implementation of the agreement of 8 December 1987 on the elimination of short-and medium-range missiles will certainly "put period" to any such aspirations.[c]

Obviously, SNF played a major role in deterrence, through the threat of "limited nuclear options" more costly to the Soviets than any gains they could hope to make from operations in Europe, through the risk of escalation attendant on any such employment of SNF and through the ultimate sanction of an all-out nuclear attack—which was the second step, not the third, under the Johnson and Nixon Administrations. The leaders in most administrations obviously hoped—and perhaps prayed—that the Soviets would stand down before a major nuclear attack had to be initiated; at least none in recent history has unambiguously pledged to launch such an attack. War termination was to be achieved by maintaining forces capable of exacting greater relative costs, whether these were in terms of damage inflicted (Laird), rates of recovery (Donald Rumsfeld), surviving SNF (Brown) or some unspecified criterion (Weinberger) and virtually every official added, for good measure that the war was to be ended on terms favorable to the United States and its allies—without specifying what was meant by the word "favorable" or how this happy outcome was to be achieved.

The American interpretation of the concept of flexible response and the roles assigned to the three legs of the TRIAD must take into account the interests of the Allies as well as those of the United States—a point which will be discussed later in this chapter, when we examine West German approaches to deterrence and defense. However, even if one looks at the U.S. approach solely through American eyes, it is apparent that there are different views as to how to create a "robust" defense of Western Europe and how to devise a nuclear guarantee that will be credible without being suicidal. In the next two sections, we will review current thinking on these problems, beginning with conventional deterrence.

Conventional Deterrence

The Situation in American Eyes. For some thirty years successive American governments and successive generations of American analysts have worried about a massive Soviet conventional assault against the Western Alliance, with primary emphasis on its most important and most vulnerable sector: the Central Front. Although the intensity of concern has fluctuated with beliefs in the credibility of the nuclear guarantee, with changes in the balance of forces in Central Europe and with innovations in technology, a number of developments have combined to heighten this concern in recent years. One is that Americans have less faith in the credibility of the nuclear deterrent, in part because of the advent of strategic parity, in part because of the modernization of Soviet theater nuclear forces and in part because of the changes in U.S. policy and doctrine as it sought to accommodate to these. Another is that the cohesion of the Alliance has diminished, as it inevitably would over time, due to differences in the perception of threat, to disputes over doctrine (such as led to the formal withdrawal of France from the integrated military structure of NATO), to disagreements over activities in the Third World (with the heads of government of six members of the Alliance formally criticizing U.S. policy in the Middle East) and with deep fissures in the bodies politic of some member nations, both over specific issues like INF deployments and over more global ones such as the potential consequence of "an open-ended arms race and permanent confrontation with the Soviet Union."[50] A third is that the USSR has not only continued to strengthen its armed forces but has begun to overtake NATO in the application of technology to military problems and to surpass it in the speed with which newer weapons and more modern equipment are introduced into the field.[51] And a fourth is that these innovations and improvements have led to the formulation of a new doctrine which in the view of many, poses new threats to the conventional component of the NATO deterrent.

Prior to the mid-1960s Soviet doctrine viewed any major war with the U.S. as being "inevitably global and nuclear from the outset, with conventional forces merely supporting the blows delivered by strategic, operational and tactical missile troops."[52] In the late 1960s and the early 1970s the Soviets apparently began to realize that a change in the "objective conditions" had opened up the possibility of an extended period of conventional operations or, indeed, of a completely conventional war.[53] While they have not abandoned preparations to fight a nuclear war, and indeed have recently devoted increased attention to tactical nuclear support for theater operations,[54] they have seemingly begun the same process of differentiating between nuclear and non-nuclear war on which NATO has for so long been engaged. More specifically, the Soviets have planned and partly implemented a large-scale, systematic restructuring of the forces opposing NATO which could markedly increase their ability to mount conventional operations. Tank divisions have received more infantry and motorized rifle divisions have been allocated more tanks and armored personnel carriers, so that these units are more balanced and more flexible; supporting artillery has been upgraded and increased; anti-aircraft and anti-tank weapons have been modernized and augmented; logistic support has been improved; and, above all, command, control, communications and intelligence have been significantly enhanced. Frontal (tactical) Aviation and Air Defense forces have not only received more modern aircraft, with increased ranges, greater payloads, better all-weather capabilities and more effective electronic gear, but have been integrated at the theater level with army units, under a single commander.[55] And the Soviet Army has introduced (or rather, returned to) the concept of the Operational Maneuver Group, which is to penetrate gaps in NATO defenses, or smash through weakly held areas, with the mission of disrupting completely NATO rear echelons, hindering the advance of reinforcements and other-wise undermining the barrier against the main push from the East.[56]

If this reorganization and re-equipment is carried through, and not undercut by the much-discussed shift to "defensive defense." it will markedly increase the striking power, the mobility and the flexibility of Soviet forces. Whether these improvements will enable them to carry out a successful surprise attack is another matter, given the political and military warning NATO is likely to receive and the current and projected balance of forces in Central Europe.[57] They do, however, remind us that NATO has two problems: the old one of interdicting the arrival of second and third echelon Soviet forces, which could overwhelm the defenders on the Central Front and the newer one of insuring that those defenders can repel a surprise attack.

The Official American Position. As indicated in Chapter 2, every President and Secretary of Defense since 1961 has stressed the contribution to deterrence of strong conventional forces. Most of these, aware of the disparities in the military balance in Europe, have made strenuous efforts to improve these forces, in order to raise the "nuclear threshold." To this end, the United States has itself adopted a number of measures over the past twenty years, including the deployment to West Germany of two additional brigades, the stockpiling of heavy equipment for six divisions of reinforcements, annual tests of the feasibility of redeploying both ground and air units from the United States, training exercises which bring these units together with their companions in Germany, the provision of reserve supplies of food, fuel and munitions, and so on. Moreover, it has striven (sometimes more energetically and successfully than at others) to provide the forces in Europe with modern weapons, with advanced means of surveillance, with secure communications and with all the other equipment essential to effective operations. It has maintained naval forces capable of safeguarding the shipment by sea of reinforcements and supplies and has, more recently, sought to develop a mobilization base which could keep these ships filled once initial stocks of munitions and weapons were exhausted. And it has devoted to these ends one-third to one-half of its defense budget, with the current costs of meeting NATO commitments recently estimated at $122- $177 billion per year.[58]

The United States has also sought to energize the Allies, who provide some two-thirds of NATO's conventional forces, to increase and upgrade their contributions. This it has done in a variety of ways: through the NATO Annual Defense Review, through exhortations, through joint pledges (as to a 3% annual increase in defense budgets under the Long-Term Defense Improvement Plan) and through pressures—of which Senator Sam Nunn's move to reduce American troops in Europe unless the other members of NATO met that pledge was but one example.[59] The aim in all this is to provide within NATO forces which could, "defeat an attack or sustain a defensive line until reinforcements can be brought to bear or a decision made to employ other tactics."[60] And though no time has been specified for the duration of this defense, Mr. Weinberger stated elsewhere that the United States cannot prepare only for a "short war."

Moreover, this "defensive line" is to be drawn close to the borders between East and West. Although American planners have in the past decried the operational inflexibility imposed by the strategy of forward defense, and at an earlier period even considered using the Weser-Lech rivers as a "notional line of defense," despite the fact that this would have given up one-third of West German territory, this no longer seems to be an issue. One reason for this is, of course, the firm insistence of the Federal

Republic that such a "forward strategy" be implemented. A second is a growing recognition of the consequences of falling back from the frontiers, since this would uncover not only important West German cities and industrialized areas but also the forward air defense system on which NATO depends, as well as major military bases and facilities; moreover, as Phillip Karber points out, it could result in a more extended front whose maintenance would engage virtually all the reinforcing brigades, ruling out the possibility of forming an operational reserve.[61] A third is that NATO has adopted a concept of "active defense" which theoretically allows for the establishment and maintenance of a defensive line 20-30 km behind the frontier; though this concept has been criticized as excessively reactive, as difficult to carry out and as endorsing an attrition-oriented defense which the West could not maintain,[62] it at least provides a base on which to build.

If this line is to hold, however, it must be able to withstand an "unreinforced attack" by the Soviet forces now deployed on the Central Front, an attack which could, according to some sources, be launched following as little as 48 hours of preparation.[63] Since NATO units require 96 hours to move from peacetime to wartime positions, and still additional time to build hasty defenses, call-up reserve manpower, create an integrated logistic system and prepare to receive air-transported reinforcements, any attack with little or no warning, or any Soviet mobilization which is not matched by NATO, could place the West at an insurmountable disadvantage. Hence, U.S. planners are seeking earlier and unambiguous warning of Soviet moves, which could give NATO more time to decide on mobilization, and heightened readiness of both active and reserve units, which could cut down on response time. They would also like to see thicker covering forces, notably in the sector of the Northern Army Group, and the deployment farther forward of Dutch (and Belgian) units.[d] Of equal importance is the improvement of air defenses, particularly of those protecting airfields at which units of the American Army will land and air bases from which reinforcing USAF squadrons will operate; in fact, given the vulnerability of NATO bases, and the massive, preemptive air attacks apparently envisaged by Soviet planners, better air defenses might be of the highest priority.[64]

Once battle was joined, U.S. (and other NATO) forces would conduct a mobile defense, in three stages.[65] In the first stage, heavily-armed mechanized covering forces would slow the initial WTO assault, allowing time for units in Europe to complete their redeployment and prepare defensive positions for the mobilization and movement of German and other Allied reservists and, hopefully, for the arrival of personnel to operate the U.S. equipment stored in Europe, increasing to ten the number of American divisions available for combat. With or without the arrival of reinforcements, the U.S. Seventh Army would maintain the integrity of the battle zone in its assigned sectors by holding hastily-fortified positions and counterattacking such WTO elements as penetrated into the zone. In the third phase, fresh troops from the United States would initiate counter-attacks against weakened WTO first echelon forces, with the aim of destroying these or forcing them to retreat. And throughout all phases, but especially the first, tactical air forces would attempt to gain air superiority by strikes against enemy air fields, dispersal bases, and air-defense missile sites; if these were successful, U.S. squadrons would then be used to support operations on the ground and to interdict the advance of Soviet/WTO reinforcements.

Since, however, tactical airpower alone may not suffice to accomplish this latter task, U.S. planners have developed (and NATO has approved in principle) a concept called the Follow-on Forces Attack (FOFA). Under this approach, the long-planned interdictory attacks on key rail and road centers, bridges over the Vistula and the Oder and other line of communication targets in Eastern Europe would be supplemented by strikes against units on the march all the way back to the Soviet frontier, employing not only strike aircraft but also short- and medium-range missiles carrying clusters of homing anti-tank rockets, anti-personnel mines and other sub-munitions. As a means to this latter end, the Allies would be asked to develop and procure not only new missiles but also real time intelligence and communication systems which could enable commanders to speedily and flexibly direct attacks against fleeting targets. The aim is to disrupt advancing units and to inflict on them such heavy casualties that they could not significantly increase the weight of an initial assault against NATO forces attempting to hold forward defenses, thereby enabling these forces to repel—and possibly defeat—those WTO troops carrying out the initial assault on the Central Front. This dual capability, to check an initial attack and to preclude the entry of reinforcements into the battle, would deny the Soviets victory, even if it did not enable the Allies to prevail in a conventional war, and would therefore enhance conventional deterrence.[66]

Alternative Approaches to Conventional Deterrence. One variation on the official doctrine originated within, and is found principally within, the United States Army, the sponsors of AirLand Battle. This innovative approach, like the official one, relies on "high tech" to offset WTO advantages in numbers of men and weight of equipment but it differs in three significant respects. The first is that it would substitute for a largely positional defense, in which operations are restricted by the necessity to maintain the integrity of the main battle area, maneuvers by highly mobile tactical units against the flanks and rear of advancing Warsaw Pact formations—culminating, in the view of some proponents, in counteroffensives against key cities such as Dresden and Leipzig.[67] Another is that it would delay the full weight of the attack against WTO reserves and reinforcements until these had moved into a zone within 50-150 km of the front line, where airpower could deliver heavier blows and where Pact units would be subjected to attacks by long-range artillery and short-range rockets, tied together by an integrated intelligence and communications net. And a third is that it envisions (and seeks to prepare for) operations in which chemical and/or nuclear weapons are employed, whereas other concepts, including the German, focus almost entirely on conventional war.

Save for this, the differences between Deep Strike and AirLand Battle relate more largely to means than to ends, but these means have both programmatic and service implications. For one thing, AirLand Battle would require smaller, more flexible and more mobile ground force units than are now extant and would therefore require a substantial restructuring and re-equipping of the Army—at considerable cost. For another, the command, control and communications systems for AirLand Battle may be more demanding than those for Deep Strike and the weaponry different, so that one cannot readily develop dual-purpose equipment. For a third, AirLand Battle would require the Tactical Air Force to operate in close coordination with the Army, rather than quasi-independently, as Deep Strike would allow.[68] Perhaps for these reasons, former Secretary of Defense Weinberger, who initially seemed to favor AirLand Battle, subsequently distanced himself somewhat from this approach.

Others, outside the Pentagon, have distanced themselves from both approaches, noting that their effectiveness may depend on equipment not yet developed and programs not yet funded. Moreover, they point out that the cost of this equipment may drain off resources badly needed for other purposes, such as sustainability, and that the concepts might not be implemented even if funded, since they place major demands on both troops and equipment. Accordingly, the so-called "Military Reformers" prefer the development of "brilliantly simple" weapons, which would be quicker and cheaper to produce, easier to maintain and yet highly effective, even if not at "the cutting edge of technology."[69] Assuming that their approach were followed, one might expect to find, five to ten years hence, important differences in the forces assigned to the defense of Western Europe. Presumably, the numbers of aircraft, tanks, armored personnel carriers and other weapons would increase, as would, to some extent, the number of men manning these. Conceivably, the introduction of simpler weapons could lead to a reduction in maintenance requirements, despite the greater number of weapons to be maintained, to an improvement in the "teeth-to-tail" ratio and to an increase in combat capacity and sustainability. With larger numbers of combat units, commanders should be able to fill gaps in the line, to thicken defenses and to increase the all-too-scant operational reserves. The result, especially if accompanied by changes in concepts emphasizing maneuver rather than attrition, would be to improve NATO's ability to repel attack and hence to enhance deterrence—again, as with "high tech," through denial.

The "Military Reformers" are only the most prominent of a number of groups arguing that the primary need is to bolster forward defenses so that these could outlast "the conventional Center Region blitzkrieg for which Warsaw Pact forces are so obviously configured"—which, according to Ambassador Robert Komer, means holding the line for some 30 days, without significant loss of territory.[70] Although modernization as such is not opposed, the emphasis is on the allocation of resources to *this* task, as opposed to others, with resultant increases in the manning levels of units, their readiness for combat and their sustainability, which requires large stocks of weapons and equipment, spare parts and ammunition. Some, like John Mearsheimer and Barry Posen, argue that the existing doctrine is sound and that current conventional capabilities are robust, so that this increased effort should suffice to maintain an acceptable military balance in Europe.[71] Others would opt for increased reliance upon proven defensive measures such as barriers across roads, pre-arranged demolition sites and modest field fortifications. And some would go further, arguing that the U.S. forces in Europe should be restructured to provide greater combat capabilities (Steven Canby), should be supplemented by a territorial militia (James Garrett) or should be organized into more specialized units, to include "area combat troops" whose purpose would be to disorganize and cripple an invader as he tried to traverse the forward defense zone (Corcoran).[72] What these analysts have in common, however, is the belief that marginal and supportable force improvements, rather than drastic changes in weaponry or in operational concepts, will suffice for conventional deterrence.

Although they have significant implications, these intra-American differences over doctrinal and operational issues all fit within the framework of a "continental strategy," in which massive enforcements would be directed to the point of attack.[73] This represents a switch from an earlier policy calling for "counteroffensives directed at places where we can affect the outcome of the war" and against territory or assets that are of comparable importance to the ones being attacked,[74] and not all have made the switch. The Navy, for obvious reasons, remains a strong proponent of the maritime strategy envisioned earlier, which it would implement by sweeping the Soviet Navy from the oceans, penetrating "narrow waters" such as the Baltic and the Norwegian Seas, attacking major bases on the Kola Peninsula and in the Maritime Provinces of the Far East and projecting military power against hostile shores.[75] At a minimum such a strategy would, it is argued, cripple Soviet efforts to disrupt the flow of men and supplies across the Atlantic and frustrate amphibious operations directed against the North Cape in Norway or the Jutland Peninsula, thereby enhancing deterrence and strengthening the defense of Europe. (According to the then Chief of Naval Operations, Admiral Watkins, it could also attrit Soviet ballistic missile submarines, thus reducing both the ability of the USSR to wage nuclear war and the incentive to do so.[76]) If maximally successful, it would force the Soviet Union to hold in distant regions air and ground forces which could otherwise be dispatched to Central Europe. And should the defenses there fail a maritime strategy would insure that the USSR would still have to fight a long war against an island power which would, like Britain in 1940-41, find safety in its navy.[77]

Variants of this maritime strategy are upheld vigorously by a number of analysts and former officials, some of whom maintain (as did former

Secretary of State Kissinger) that the United States should leave the defense of Europe to the Europeans.[78] It has been equally vigorously attacked by others, who point out the difficulty of finding "territory and assets" as valuable to the Soviets as those in Western Europe, deny the effectiveness of naval and air power in putting these assets at risk with conventional weapons and maintain that the resources required for the maritime strategy would better be devoted to the direct defense of Western Europe.[79] And, as noted in Chapter 5, the choice between strategies is likely to be made more on the basis of their implications for service budgets than on their intrinsic merit.

Perhaps more important than any of these differences over how to buttress defenses is the question of purpose. If conventional defenses are to be stiffened in order to create uncertainties for Soviet planners and/or to give NATO decision-makers more time to consider their responses to any aggression, some Allied support may be forth-coming—though not nearly as much as either General Galvin (the current SACEUR) or Senator Nunn would like. If the aim is to weather the first phase of a Soviet attack, in the hope that this will induce the Soviets to reconsider their initial decision, few among the Allies will be willing to bear the costs and the consequences—especially since the Warsaw Pact is better prepared than the Western Alliance to conduct large-scale operations in the second or third month of a war. (Furthermore, such an approach flies in the face of Soviet assertions that Europe is so important that no conflict there can be contained at the conventional level.[80]) And if the purpose is to "prevail" through conventional counterattacks or through a campaign of attrition, not only Germans will say "Ohne mich." For most of the Allies, as for many Americans, the aim is deterrence, not defense. And to them, that means keeping the strategic deterrent linked firmly to the security of Western Europe.

Deterrence and the Nuclear Guarantee

The Situation in American Eyes. As has been repeated *ad nauseam*, most American political elites believe that the credibility of the strategic deterrent has diminished—if not vanished—with the growth of Soviet counter capabilities. Thus, former Secretary of Defense McNamara asserted that the nuclear deterrent lacked all credibility because "the launch of strategic nuclear weapons against the Soviet homeland . . . would be an act of suicide . . . " and indicated that he himself had advised Presidents Kennedy and Johnson never to initiate nuclear war.[81] His statement was paralleled by that of former Secretary of State Kissinger to the effect that the United States would never respond to an attack on Europe by employing strategic nuclear forces and that those Europeans who believed this were somewhat credulous.[82] And many American analysts, officers and officials would agree with Chancellor Helmut Kohl that "the loss of strategic nuclear superiority on the part of the United States is one of the gravest developments in the last two decades. In Europe, there is no longer anything to counterbalance the Warsaw Pact's conventional superiority and the Soviet Union's Eurostrategic threat."[83]

Whether these implications are valid is perhaps another question; capabilities are not the only factor affecting deterrence, which also depends on interest, commitment and intent. Certainly the United States has a vital interest in preserving Europe from domination by a single power, an interest which has existed since the early days of the Republic. It also has a commitment to resist aggression in Europe, epitomized in Article 5 of the North Atlantic Treaty, which states that an armed attack against one should be considered an attack against all, to be dealt with, if necessary, by the use of armed force. And successive Presidents and Secretaries of Defense have repeatedly pledged that this use of armed force will, if necessary, include the employment of U.S. strategic nuclear forces, though they have sometimes been either ambiguous or conditional as to the circumstances which would trigger that employment and the scale and nature of any response.

Many analysts and officials, while acknowledging that these are factors tending to push an American president in the direction of engaging strategic nuclear forces, should this be the only means left at his disposal, will nevertheless maintain that none of these "hostages to fortune" are as important as maintaining the integrity and the viability of the United States, neither of which could easily survive a large-scale nuclear strike by the USSR. And even those who go a step further and acknowledge that refraining from action while the Soviets overrun Western Europe would mean the end of United States as a great power, and the end of the world which it aspires to create, would still argue that life is preferable to death, even death with honor. Since, moreover, these same analysts and officials tend to believe in the "rational model" of deterrence, they make no allowance for fear, anger and shock as incentives to action, or for irrational behavior—though that has not been uncommon in history.

If these considerations do not move some Americans to place much confidence in the willingness of an American president to engage strategic nuclear forces in the event of dire threats to the security of Western Europe, it is understandable that the Europeans should have even less confidence and that they should seek a firm and unambiguous commitment on the part of the United States to employ nuclear weapons under some circumstances, thereby enhancing deterrence. The issue is how to insure that the threat of such use remains palatable to Americans, reassuring to West Germans and credible to the Soviets.

The Official American Approach. In essence, the United States has sought to reassure the Allies and to deter the Soviets not only by repeated pledges but by programmatic and operational decisions. For one, it has provided to both Allied and American forces tactical nuclear weapons which could be used to blunt a Soviet breakthrough. For another it has, as former Secretary of Defense Weinberger said, provided "nuclear capabilities at the lower end of the spectrum, firmly linking strategic forces to our [U.S.]

conventional capabilities"[84]—though whether these capabilities will be as evident or as suitable in the future as they were when Mr. Weinberger referred to them is perhaps questionable.[85] For a third it has developed weapons, such as the MX, which give it "the ability to respond promptly and controllably against hardened military targets," thereby supposedly deterring massive conventional or limited nuclear attacks.[86] For a fourth, it has maintained strategic nuclear forces so strong and so diverse as to virtually guarantee that it can destroy the Soviet Union, even under the worst of circumstances. And finally, it has (as discussed in Chapter 7) proposed establishing a multi-layered defense system which could, if carried out successfully, ultimately afford protection not only to missile silos but also to cities—thereby altering the calculus of costs and gains attendant upon any use of nuclear weapons.

Each of these programs has its own impact on the credibility of deterrence. Thus, the provision of relatively short-range tactical nuclear delivery vehicles forces Soviet planners to thin out attacking troops, lest these become too vulnerable, and consequently reduces the weight of any assault against a given sector of the Central Front. Moreover, these short-range weapons can, if the decision to employ them is made, not only wreak considerable damage on Soviet breakthrough units and armored spearheads but can, at the same time, serve notice of American and Allied determination to take any measures necessary to avoid defeat, whatever the risk. While no one can guarantee that such a response would either check a Soviet assault or cause Soviet leaders to call off their troops, these are possibilities—as is, of course, a Soviet nuclear response on the same or a larger scale. Furthermore, the fact that many tactical nuclear weapons are short range may even enhance their deterrent effect, as Soviet decision-makers can never be certain that United States will choose to "lose them" rather than "use them."

The longer range theater nuclear weapons, such as F-16s, make their own contribution to deterrence. For one thing, their range enables them to strike at a variety of targets deep in Eastern Europe and in the western part of the USSR, thereby bringing the war home to the Soviet Union. For another, that same range and dispersability (with aircraft stationed in Britain and in Spain, as well as in the Low Countries and Germany) means that it is more difficult to knock them out, whether by nuclear strikes or by conventional munitions. For a third, though no one can say that it will be easier for any president to authorize the use of TNF than the launching of ICBMs, it well may be; to those engaged in searching for a way to bring a regional conflict to a halt, without escalating to a global one, this may seem at least a conceivable option.

As for strategic nuclear forces, their ultimate purpose is, as already noted, to "prevail" in a "protracted" nuclear exchange with the USSR, by weathering Soviet counterforce attacks, by inflicting such losses on Soviet SNF that the nuclear balance tips in favor of the United States and by preserving "assured destruction forces" that would dissuade the USSR from directing its weapons against American politico-economic targets. Since, however, success in these endeavors is uncertain, and failure could be catastrophic, American planners have also promoted concepts such as "limited nuclear options" whose implementation would be easier than ordering out SAC and whose actual damage to, and potential risk to, an adversary might give that adversary pause. Thus to the possibility that any remaining short or medium range nuclear weapons may be used in the defense of Western Europe must be added the possibility of small-scale strategic nuclear strikes.

Criticisms of the Official Policy. All these assessments of the American approach to the maintenance of the "nuclear guarantee" are, of course, subject to criticism. One such criticism is that the Soviets may, as their doctrine and their policy statements suggest, respond to any limited use of nuclear weapons with an all-out nuclear strike of their own, the prospect of which may deter the United States from taking action in the first place. This is, of course, possible, although there are doubts as to whether Soviet political leaders are quite as inclined as Soviet commanders to take lightly the idea of waging nuclear war and there is some question as to the credibility of Soviet pledges to execute their own version of the SIOP should the West initiate the use of nuclear weapons. And in any event, as former U.S. Secretary of Defense Schlesinger said, decision-makers owe it to their citizens not to foreclose the possibility that a nuclear war could be kept limited.[87]

A more wide-spread and trenchant criticism is that the emphasis placed upon counterforce attacks by American planners may (like the similar emphasis given "war-fighting" by Soviet planners) trigger large-scale disarming strikes which would almost inevitably lead to an all-out nuclear war. (Indeed the Strategic Defense Initiative is deemed provocative by some Americans because it could lead Soviet decision-makers to believe that they had to strike first in order to inflict any significant damage upon the United States.) And the 29.9 billion dollars spent annually on strategic nuclear forces (a sum which has more than doubled since the advent of the Reagan Administration, and now accounts for 9.5% of the defense budget as compared with the previous 7.2%) is criticized both as insufficient to achieve the desired ends, particularly with respect to command, control and communications, and as diverting resources which could be better spent on conventional capabilities.[88]

A third criticism is that theater nuclear weapons in Europe are so vulnerable that the Soviets could knock out all or most of them at a single blow, thereby breaking the "nuclear link." Here again, this is possible, although extremely difficult, especially since some available weapons are submarine based and more may be, if and as nuclear-armed SLCMs are deployed. Moreover, any attempt at this would require attacks so widespread and so massive as to virtually require an American response—especially if, as seems likely, such an attempt could only be effective if nuclear weapons were employed.[e] And further diminishing the vulnerability of U.S. (and Allied) TNF is an operational problem, not a political-military one.

Other criticisms focus on the whole concept of "nuclear links," which many see as making war more likely, because of the sense of threat that accompanies their introduction into Europe, because of the fact that their deployment may tempt or force the Soviets to preempt in time of crisis and because of the possibility of inadvertent use. Some would go still further and say that nuclear links are unnecessary, in that the Soviets have no intention of attacking Western Europe; even if they had, the potential risk that such action might trigger a limited strategic strike, and the incalculable consequences thereof, should suffice for deterrence.[89] (In fact, the strongest opposition to official U.S. policy comes not from those who would tighten the "nuclear link" but from those who would loosen it still further, by removing all or most of the American nuclear weapons in Europe, by eliminating or drastically reducing the capacity for executing counterforce strikes and other limited nuclear attacks and by adopting a policy of "no first use" of nuclear weapons.[90]) And still others will argue that, whatever their contribution to deterrence, "nuclear links" are the cause of increasing fissures within the members of the European Alliance, and especially West Germany. But this is, of course, a point better made by Germans than by Americans.

Coping with the Challenge: The West German Approach

The official West German estimate of the Soviet military posture does not differ significantly from that of the United States, and where it does, the figures it gives are even higher than those provided by the Pentagon. Nor do assessments of Soviet capabilities differ; German officials and officers recognize a broad range of potential Soviet threats, from that of a disarming nuclear strike to that of political blackmail. When, however, it comes to identifying the threats that seem most probable, and hence are of greatest concern to those formulating defense policy, Germans would make a somewhat different list than would Americans.

Since West Germans tend to believe (and believe that the Soviets believe) that nuclear weapons deter the use of nuclear weapons, they are less concerned than are many Americans about nuclear disarming strikes or other nuclear options which would heighten markedly the likelihood of a nuclear *riposte.* Moreover, they are less concerned than are many Americans about a deliberate Soviet decision to launch a conventional attack against NATO Europe, whether "out of the blue" or following a partial buildup. This is partly because they see the Soviet Union as "strategically defensive, operationally offensive," i.e., not desirous of starting World War III, but it is also a result of their thinking about deterrence and their assessment of the conventional capabilities of the Atlantic Alliance. West Germans are, however, worried about the possibility that a crisis could lead into war, either because the Soviets fear a preemptive strike by NATO and hence try to knock out offensive weapons systems, conventional and/or nuclear, or because they see an opportunity to obtain a local military advantage which could be converted into territorial gains or political rewards. Thus, there are differences between American and West German interpretations of the challenge which, other things aside, will inevitably lead to differences in their responses.

The West German Approach to Deterrence

As is true of the United States, there are many German approaches to deterrence, most of which derive from, or are variants on, U.S. thinking; the West Germans came late to the game and have preferred, as Bismarck once advised, to "draw on the experiences of others." Partly for this reason, partly because of a desire to keep in line with its principal partner in the Atlantic Alliance, official West German thinking closely follows that of the United States, at least at the declaratory level. There are, however, enough nuanced differences so that it may be useful to recite both those and the similarities, in order to gain a better understanding of the German approach.

One difference, which should be noted at the outset, is that the entire body of strategic literature links deterrence with nuclear weapons. The West Germans have no counterpart to American's Glenn Snyder, who attempted to develop a general theory of deterrence, or to John Mearsheimer, who wrote the book *Conventional Deterrence*. Instead, they have largely concerned themselves with developing concepts for non-provocative defense, of which one of the earliest and most influential was Horst Afheldt's proposal for "defensive defense," involving lightly armed "technocommandos" rather than regular troops.

As far as nuclear deterrence goes, the West Germans agree with virtually every American theorist that "deterrence through punishment" requires an overwhelming nuclear superiority. While the Americans had a nuclear monopoly, and for a further period when they had meaningful superiority, they were able to think of "massive retaliation" or of "assured destruction." With the coming into being, around the beginning of the 1970s, of strategic nuclear parity, deterrence based on punishment had to be ruled out and other forms of deterrence came forward in its place.

In the German view, this change required thinking in terms of "deterrence through risk"—though that term is not commonly employed in German literature—either by responding proportionately to any employment of nuclear weapons by the Soviet Union or by escalating a conflict if—and only if—conventional defense should fail. The Germans acknowledge that the nuclear stalemate, which rules out any possibility of "victory" in an all-out nuclear war, enhances strategic stability at the expense of instability at lower levels of conflict. They also acknowledge that attempts to extend deterrence to these lower levels of conflict by nuclear escalation risks destruction, and hence is self-deterring. They do, however, tend to think that pressures of time and the urgency of events may make a decision to escalate conceivable—and that even that small possibility can serve to deter aggression. This uncertainty as to the nature of a Western response means that the aggressor cannot calculate his chances of success—or rather, as Count von Baudissin phrased it, the risk is "calculated to be intolerable."[91]

As applied to Europe, this means that an aggressor would have to be completely convinced of self-deterrence on the other side before he would dare launch an attack and under present circumstances this is inconceivable. This is why even critical analysts of the strategic situation in Europe draw the conclusion that, for the time being, extended deterrence may work.

This does not, however, mean that the West Germans rely wholly on the nuclear deterrent; far from it. As was noted in Chapter 3, the *Bundeswehr* is assigned the primary mission of defending the homeland, by conventional means against a conventional attack. Furthermore, robust conventional capabilities are viewed as contributing to deterrence, in that they create greater uncertainty about the outcome of any (conventional) attacks, raise "the nuclear threshold" and give time for political maneuvers aimed at ending the conflict. This is, indeed, one of the bases of the German version of "flexible response," of which more later.

In a larger sense, however, deterrence or, as the Germans prefer to call it, "war forestalling," is only the means to a longer term end: the attainment of true security. This points up several of the basic problems of deterrence, one of which is that war may result not only from attacks with a strategic aim, such as Hitler's invasion of the Soviet Union in 1941, but also from unexpected crises similar to that which led to the outbreak of World War I. Another is that the basic contradiction in deterrence strategy, i.e., wanting to achieve de-escalation by threatening escalation can be a disadvantage in time of crisis. A third is that decisions must be made under pressure of time and uncertainty, particularly when one is trying to anticipate the measures or counter-measures of an opponent.

Self-imposed deadlines for action can result in a series of erroneous decisions which can exacerbate a crisis. Self-declared dependence on measures such as an early use of nuclear weapons can be exploited by a determined opponent, either through military operations, as discussed earlier in this chapter, or through threats of counter-actions which can undermine that dependence. And finally, innovations in technology such as the increased accuracy of nuclear delivery systems can both facilitate and require a preemptive use of weapons in a crisis; the American axiom "use them or lose them" has its counter-part in German thinking. Thus there are a number of ways in which crises, and even more, policies for coping with crises, can lead to an undesired war.

This means that the effectiveness of a military strategy aimed at preventing wars must above all be assessed by its viability in crisis situations. The operative instruments must not serve to escalate a crisis into actual conflict but rather to make it more difficult. This means first and foremost that such a strategy should make any attack by an adversary seem unreasonable, without creating the impression that it might be necessary to undertake an offensive action, i.e., without encouraging preemption. Those who propose alternative strategies, as does Horst Afheldt, who wants area defenses, or some high-ranking German officers like the former Inspector-General of the *Bundeswehr*, General Wolfgang Altenburg, who wants to further develop NATO strategy, agree that the declared military doctrine and the actual level of arms must convey an impression of the Federal Republic as being capable of successful defense but incapable of strategic offensives.

More importantly, one must recognize that in the debate on strategy now underway in the Alliance, nuclear weapons are discussed as means and deterrence as the desired end. But deterrence is not an end in itself; it is a way of achieving the higher goal of security. Peaceful change from confrontation and a high level of armaments to cooperation reducing both arms and the likelihood of conflict within the East-West security system are, therefore, the preferred means.

It will, however, not be easy to think of East-West relations in terms other than those of deterrence, because this way of thinking has become customary in political as well as in military circles, because technology provides us with the instruments of deterrence and because force is a component of, as well as a contributor to, the East-West confrontation. It is the task of Germans and Americans alike to develop strategies which relate the instruments to the ends and do not allow the instruments to determine the ends. The problems of nuclear weapons, deterrence and military strategy must be put in a framework that clearly acknowledges the primacy of politics over technology. In the short run, that may require keeping alive consciousness of the destruction which could result from a nuclear war. In the long run, it may require diminishing, if not abolishing, dependence on the threat to use nuclear weapons, an outcome toward which many in Germany are tending, and an expectation encouraged by the INF agreement.

The West German Interpretation of Flexible Response

There is widespread agreement in the Federal Republic of Germany with the American (and NATO) definition of flexible response as the ability to act effectively in a variety of ways across the "spectrum of conflict," leaving open the question of when, and under what circumstances, a particular response will be made. Germans, like Americans, see flexible response basically as a deterrence strategy, since, even if the first reaction to an attack is to consist of classical, i.e., conventional, defense the aggressor is threatened with the use of nuclear weapons should he be successful or be expected to be successful.[92]

According to that strategy and the associated military planning, such use can begin with so-called theater nuclear weapons, i.e., short- range or medium-range delivery systems in the European theater, and be ultimately pushed up all the way to the use of strategic (intercontinental) nuclear weapons. The carefully prescribed and preplanned increase in the use of nuclear weapons is intended to make the aggressor abandon his offensive.

Since the threat of further escalation up to an all-out nuclear war exists throughout the conflict, a potential aggressor can fix no exact point at which he can stop the war on terms favorable to himself.[93]

This congruence of thinking did not always exist. In 1955, when the *Bundeswehr* was first formed, its self-assigned mission was that of conventional defense, alongside the forces of the Western allies. The Lisbon Conference of 1952 had even decided that 90 divisions were necessary to conduct such a defense, under the shield of a (very ragged) nuclear umbrella. However, by this time American strategic thinking had developed in a totally different direction. As described in 1954 by Secretary of State Dulles, the United States proposed to deter Soviet aggression by the threat of "massive retaliation with nuclear weapons," a threat which should also serve as a deterrent against smaller wars and limited infringements on U.S. interests. Thus, at the very moment that the first divisions of the *Bundeswehr* were being formed, the United States had changed the rationale underlying their formation. The American ideas led to confusion in Bonn but did not result in any basic changes in the structure or mission of the *Bundeswehr* as it was built up.

By 1958 Mr. Dulles had modified the conditions and circumstances under which nuclear weapons would be used. And the Supreme Allied Commander, Europe, General Norstad, had put forward the idea that a shield of conventional forces should hold off the Soviet Army while the U.S. Strategic Air Command destroyed the Soviet Union—something which the United States Army estimated would take six months, the U.S. Air Force believed would require thirty days and some analysts estimated would take only two hours! Be that as it may, General Norstad's proposal gave conventional forces a larger role than that of a tripwire, whose crossing would trigger off a massive retaliatory strike. This change enabled Inspector General Heusinger, in 1958, to express the widely held view that the *Bundeswehr* did have an important function in West European defense, which corresponded with its original mission, thus preparing the way for the reversal of "shield" and "sword."

Two years later General Speidel, the first German Commander of NATO ground forces on the Central Front, explained the increased importance and the function of the shield-forces. "With the accession of the Federal Republic to NATO and with the formation of the *Bundeswehr*, as well as the introduction of tactical nuclear weapons, our shield-forces have gained in strength. In fact it has increased so much that we are able to defend Europe-Center not at the Rhine but at the Eastern border—the Iron Curtain." In the first phase of the "battle for Europe" the ground forces would pretty much have to *defend* Europe without support from the air forces, which would be tied up by other operations, in order to *defeat* the intruding enemy forces in a second phase in which the air force and the navy would join. There should not be an automatic escalation to the use of strategic nuclear weapons. On the other hand, the operations of the shield-forces should not be detached from the strategic nuclear potential of the air force which, should these weapons be used, would bear the main burden of the battle. NATO's development had transformed the mission of the shield-forces from that of making a vague contribution to defense to one of crucial importance.[94]

Speidel's comment that it should be possible to stop an initial attack without the immediate intervention of the Strategic Air Force showed that NATO was turning away from the doctrine of massive retaliation. After the initial phase, fought out by the shield-forces only, a "pause" should be forced upon the enemy before the decisive escalation in order to enable political negotiations. But it would be essential to make sure that the enemy did not have the slightest reason to suspect that in reality defense by all means was not envisaged. Accordingly, the strategic purpose of the shield-forces was defined as follows: "In all such cases, we must have the means to stop the enemy, to strike him hard and to make him understand that we are serious. Once he is stopped, the enemy must clearly realize that he would cause a great war by continuing the battle—and that he would have to bear the consequences. That is the moment when the politicians have to speak up, before the so-called absolute weapons speak."[95]

If one compares these comments by Speidel from 1960 with his memorandum of 1949/50, two basic ideas appear throughout both texts: the principle of flexible warfare and the requirement—now formulated as an intention by NATO—to defend as far east as possible, i.e., to take up defense directly at the border of the Eastern Bloc. If compared with the NATO defense plan of five years earlier, when the *Bundeswehr* was founded, a fundamental change in the role of conventional forces is noticeable. This meant the introduction of important German security interests, via NATO's military strategy, into the still valid doctrine of massive retaliation.

The process of change did not, however, stop there. Criticisms of massive retaliation by American military experts (for which see Chapter 2) led in the Kennedy Administration to a new strategy of deterrence under the heading of "flexible response," a strategy which, as noted previously, further emphasized the importance of conventional forces.

At first the new U.S. strategy led to considerable uncertainty in Bonn. As opposed to the so-called Radford Plan, which had envisioned the early use of nuclear weapons, the flexible response concept aroused some doubts as to whether conventional defense was still linked to the strategic nuclear potential of the United States and generated fears that deterrence would be weakened. In the summer of 1961, Federal Minister of Defense Strauss expressed the concern that a potential enemy could regard conventional aggression without the risk of a nuclear response as calculable again.

In this context, Strauss also brought forward arguments against the concept of the "pause" before nuclear escalation. In his opinion, this should only be one of many possible developments in the case of aggression, because, "There must not be a calculable risk for the enemy with a reasonable price quoted beforehand, otherwise there would be no more deterrence."[96] The use of all possible means should be reserved, though, of course, adequate means would be used in each case. The adversary should always have to include in his calculations the use of nuclear weapons by NATO at any given time.

This was only part of the dissent from American ideas on flexible response; however, it showed the dilemma between the upholding of German interests and the formulation of NATO strategy, a dilemma which is still characteristics of the discussion today. Demanding the most massive use of weapons by NATO increases the risk of one's own devastation through an (almost) inevitable counter-blow. It also introduces an element of self-deterrence into the strategy designed to deter a potential adversary. On the other hand, demanding restricted uses of weapons, that can only just be envisioned as possible, does reduce self-deterrence but at the same time reduces the deterrent effect on the adversary, unless it is believed that this reduction in levels of damage is offset by the greater likelihood that this threat will actually be carried out.

The Social Democratic opposition showed a different reaction to the American change in strategy at the beginning of the 1960's than did the Federal Government, which at that time was dominated by a Christian-Liberal coalition. The new strategy contained a number of elements which had already played an important role in the discussions within the party, and which Helmut Schmidt, for example, had expressed in his book *Verteidigung oder Vergeltung (Defense or Retaliation),* published in 1961. Fritz Erler, Carlo Schmid and Helmut Schmidt himself had earlier talked about a necessary strengthening of conventional defense after a visit to the new Kennedy Administration. Thus high-ranking Social Democratic politicians not only held the same view of the new U.S. strategy as did its American progenitors but may possibly have influenced its development.

Two fairly long articles by Schmidt, then Hamburg Senator for the Interior, tried to put into context the largely incomprehensible Bonn discussion on the change in strategy. He explained the strategic consequences of a "nuclear stalemate:" it would be impossible to off-set numerical inferiority in conventional forces by nuclear superiority, since the nuclear arsenals would neutralize each other; therefore a sufficient amount of conventional weapons would be needed to deter conventional attacks. One must not take the chance of turning the nuclear poker game into a game of chicken where, as the Senator said, two cars race head on towards each other and the driver who has the least nerve and swerves first is the loser. What was decisive at the stage that had been reached in nuclear armaments with their indestructible delivery systems, such as underground silos, was the ability of both sides to strike back devastatingly with the same weapons after a full-fledged nuclear attack, i.e., to retain a second strike capability. "The threat of thermo-nuclear destruction against a world power of strategic nuclear capacity is not an effective deterrent against any aggression except a total one, because of the risk to the defender's very existence which is bound up with realization of the threat. The actual use of thermo-nuclear retaliation in reply to limited or even non-nuclear aggression proves itself to be irresponsible; the threat of it therefore loses credibility and leads to self-deception by the defender as to his own security against such aggression."[97] In Schmidt's view, the planned first strike, as well as the preemptive strike against the nuclear power of the adversary with the aim of disarming him, had equally lost their significance—an insight which U.S. Secretary of Defense McNamara had not quite gained at that time. A temporary and partial superiority in nuclear weapons and delivery systems had proven to be of no political value. The Soviet Union had found that out in 1958 during the Berlin Crisis and had had it confirmed in 1962 in Cuba; the United States had to learn a similar lesson in Vietnam.

In the German debate on flexible response, after Franz Josef Strauss had left the cabinet, views of the opposition and the parties represented in the government, with von Hassel as Minister of Defense, regarding military strategies soon converged. After the concept of flexible response had become the official NATO strategy in 1967, Gerhard Schröder—Minister of Defense in the Grand Coalition—explained the new doctrine, including the consequences for the mission of the *Bundeswehr*. However, the first comprehensive and official presentation of the basic military strategies of NATO and the *Bundeswehr* on the basis of flexible response was given in the White Paper of 1970, which was drawn up during Helmut Schmidt's term of office as Minister of Defense and under the supervision of Theo Sommer. In this White Paper the principles of the NATO strategy were listed: (1) balancing of means and aims; (2) sufficiency of forces; (3) limitation of goals. This strategy of flexible response, so it said, "deters without losing defense credibility in the case of a failure to deter."

All three Ministers of Defense under the Social-Liberal coalition, Helmut Schmidt, Georg Leber and Hans Apel, were committed to these principles. It was their goal, regardless of fluctuations in American strategic thinking, to apply the aims of the agreed NATO strategy of flexible response to the working procedures and programs of the Alliance in Europe. The modernization of the *Bundeswehr* and the second generation of arms, produced in the 1970s, were to comply with the requirements of the Alliance strategy. And this too was the mission of Manfred Wörner, who as a CDU expert on defense questions had presided over the Committee for Defense of the *Bundestag*, when he became the first Minister of Defense of the Conservative-Liberal coalition in 1982.

When comparing the White Papers on defense of the Social-Liberal Coalition with that Minister of Defense Wörner, it becomes clear that there is a continuity in strategic thinking in the Federal Republic and with respect to the Federal Republic's contribution to NATO. In the *White Paper 1985* the strategy of flexible response, including the concepts of direct defense, deliberate escalation and a general nuclear engagement, is still regarded as determining the German NATO contribution, regardless of the renewed debate on strategy. Still valid also are the principles of securing peace as the aim of deterrence, the balancing of means and aims, the sufficiency of forces and the limitation of goals, i.e. the orientation of all military options towards the defensive rather than preemptive, preventive or offensive operations. "It is the aim of the Alliance to prevent any war. As long as there are not better possibilities of preventing war than the strategy of flexible response, this strategy has to keep its unmodified validity."[98]

Continuity and Change

At the moment, the West Germans seem confident of their ability, together with their allies, to check any thrust by the Soviet troops in Central Europe, even if these are supported by hand-picked units of the East German and other East European armies. This does not mean that the Germans are unmindful of all the difficulties of conducting a successful defense: mal-deployment of some Allied units, lack of staying power, problems in the interoperability of equipment and, above all, the vulnerability to an attack of key installations in Western Europe; rather, they believe that these will not, on balance, so degrade NATO capabilities as to enable a quick victory by the Warsaw Pact. Nor do they believe that enough Soviet units from the Western Military Districts can "run the gauntlet" of attacks on bridges, marshalling yards and communication centers in Eastern Europe to tilt the balance in the later stages of a conventional war—if there are any later stages.

What is true at present is not, however, certain for the future, in that the continuing modernization of Soviet forces (and to a lesser extent those of other members of the WTO), the introduction of new weapons and potential improvements in the organization and training of Pact units may change the military balance in their favor. In this case, as K. Peter Stratmann, a senior German analyst, observed, NATO's lack of operational reserves could result in inflexibility. This, in turn, could mean falling back on tactical nuclear weapons to avoid defeat, and perhaps taking risky escalatory steps that would jeopardize controllability of the war and bring an all-out nuclear exchange dangerously close.[99]

While this judgment is not shared by everyone, concern over possible instability has spawned a vigorous debate over the doctrine of flexible response. One group, following the lead of American experts, has called for bolstering conventional defenses, thereby decreasing dependency on the early use of nuclear weapons and perhaps ultimately arriving at a policy of "no first use."[100] Indeed, the government of the Federal Republic, though not espousing that objective, has already embarked on measures to strengthen conventional forces. One way of doing this is through enlarging the role of reserve forces and the Federal Republic is already upgrading the status of its twelve reserve territorial brigades, altering their mission to that of manning strong points in the battle zone and providing operational reserves and replacing them by new units which are to insure the security of the rear areas. There are, unfortunately, severe limits to the process of strengthening the *Bundeswehr*, both in terms of available manpower and in terms of allocatable resources (See Chapter 5). And while some may argue that the limits on resources are political rather than economic, they are none the less real.

A second way can be through more rapid modernization of the existing army and air force, particularly through the introduction of very advanced weapons and equipment: short-range missiles carrying cluster munitions, "real time" command, control and communications systems, perhaps even an anti-tactical ballistic missile defense, as recommended by the European Study Group.[101] All these proposals and more have been the subject of discussions within the German government and with NATO and of inter-actions with elements of the U.S. Department of Defense which are engaged in developing similar weaponry. Here, however, the scarcity of resources also has an impact: though "high tech" may be a less expensive means of improving capabilities than force augmentation, it is by no means cheap. Moreover, there are considerable doubts as to whether new weapons (par-ticularly if these are linked with complicated C^3I systems requiring inter-faces at many points) will be as effective as their proponents make them out to be. Thus in the Federal Republic, as in NATO, there has been a willingness to endorse in principle weapons systems and concepts for their employment which could attrit WTO units before they reached the main battle area, but a reluctance to commit substantial funds to their devel-opment and implementation.

More promising, from both German and NATO perspectives, have been efforts to arrange for a French contribution to the defense of the Central Front should war break out. In part, such a contribution has long been envisioned, in that military planners have discussed the movement forward of the French First Army, some elements of which are stationed in the Black Forest area, to replace the United States V Corps when that unit advances to its positions on the forward line of defense; in this way the Central Army Group could acquire the operational reserves it badly needs. More importantly, Franco-German talks have led to arrangements for the deployment of elements of the FAR (*Force d'Action Rapide*) to northwest Germany in the event of a Soviet breakthrough in that region and these helicopter-borne units are designed and equipped for an anti-armor role. While this movement, like that of the French First Army, is contingent on a political decision, France has repeatedly proclaimed that it will honor its obligations as a member of the Alliance. (Thus, President François Mit-terand, while attending the fall 1987 FAR and *Bundeswehr* maneuvers along with Chancellor Kohl, underlined the French commitment even though he simultaneously confirmed the French intention to take an in-dependent decision on the use of French troops.)

Increasing attention has also been paid to "alternative strategies," i.e., force postures and operational doctrines which could provide an effective defense at lower cost—perhaps in a manner that would be deemed less provocative than one based on mobile operations by armored and mech-anized divisions or one relying on new weapons capable of striking deep into Eastern Europe.[102] In 1985 the Defense Committee of the *Bundestag* reviewed 26 different proposals for a re-shaping of current military doctrine, most of which suggested some form of area defense.[103] None of these was given the "green light," but individuals and groups outside the government have continued to call for re-shaping defense concepts. Thus, one spokesman for the SPD, Andreas von Bülow, has suggested that the multi-national covering force on the border be stiffened by a static defense network, manned by German reservists, with highly mechanized mobile forces stationed in and behind the network to block Soviet attempts to penetrate the forward defenses.[104] And others, in and out of Germany, have gone still further in proposing a restructuring of military forces and a re-deployment of troops and weapons which would clearly eliminate offensive options, while simultaneously strengthening defensive capabilities.[105]

Finally, it is conceivable that the Federal Republic could again turn to arms control as a way of reducing the threat of, and the weight of, a conventional attack. As indicated in Chapter 7, the CSCE and its offspring, the CDE, have been fairly successful in agreeing on measures to give warning of surprise attack and to inhibit the use of troops for the exercise of political pressures; in theory, at least, no such mobilization of Soviet forces as took place in 1981 along the Polish frontier could be repeated. What is less certain is whether the Conventional Forces Talks, scheduled to start before the end of 1988, will be any more successful than their predecessor, the MBFR negotiations, in bringing about actual reductions in forces—although the announcement by General Secretary Mikhail Gorbachev of unilateral reductions in Soviet forces (an example followed by Czechoslovakian, East German, and Polish leaders) has markedly enhanced the prospects for still further drawdowns by both sides. What *is* certain is that the approach to arms control is changing, from the quantitative one of counting guns, tanks and troops to the qualitative one of constraining military options—and this, while more difficult, may be more productive.[106]

More significantly, there is a strong currnet of opinion within the Federal Republic which looks beyond unilateral measures to enhance security, and even beyond efforts to do so through bilateral or multilateral negotiations on arms control, to establishing "common security," i.e., a framework of relationships which would, so far as humanly possible, guarantee the safety, the independence and the well-being of all member states. This concept, formulated in the late 1970s,[107] was further developed by the Palme Commission[108] (whose members included Cyrus Vance, former U.S. Secretary of State, and Georgi Arbatov, Director of the Institute for the Study of the U.S.A. and Canada) and became a paradigm for multilateral solutions to East-West security problems. In some sense, therefore, both deterrence and defense are to be replaced by détente.

Ironically, these efforts to find an alternative to deterrence seem to be spurred not by doubts about the nuclear guarantee but by concern that in case of defeat the West *would* employ nuclear weapons; in fact, the West Germans seem to have more confidence that the United States would "go nuclear" than do many Americans. In part this may derive from their view of the process whereby such a move could be ordered, which takes more account of the non-rational factors in decision-making than do the views of many U.S. officials and analysts. In part it may stem from the conviction that Ronald Reagan is different from Jimmy Carter, and while this can be a source of anxiety it can also, in the circumstances envisaged, be reassuring. In some sense, however, it reflects the closeness of German-American relations; despite doubts about the wisdom of some U.S. actions, such as the recent raid on Libya, and continuing differences over issues such as burden-sharing, there are currently no major difficulties with the United States.

Whatever the reasons, the result is that the Federal Republic is not demanding new pledges of U.S. solidarity or new evidence of U.S. preparedness to initiate nuclear war, should this possibility ever have to be faced. To the contrary, as noted in Chapter 7, the West Germans have been in the forefront of efforts to promote détente in general and "military détente," i.e., arms control, in particular. Though there were come complaints that the INF Treaty would remove weapons previously deemed necessary for linkage with the U.S. strategic deterrent the Germans not only supported the treaty but, after some hesitation, offered to remove also the Pershing IA missiles manned by the *Bundeswehr*. West Germany has also expressed interest in the "third zero," the removal of short-range nuclear weapons from Europe. In sum, the Germans are seemingly prepared to endorse reductions in nuclear armaments at all levels, despite the role these play in implementing the concept of flexible response. (For a further discussion of this point, see Chapter 7.)

A Final Word

To attempt to summarize here what has been written earlier about deterrence and defense would be both difficult, in view of the range of issues discussed, and redundant, in that a comparative analysis of American and German perspectives on these subjects will be part of the conclusions. It might, nevertheless, be useful to highlight similarities or differences on several significant issues, for fuller discussion later.

One point worth noting is that both the official American concept of deterrence, as a *rational* calculus of costs and benefits, and the operationalization of that concept in the form of capabilities for fighting a protracted nuclear war, are not widely held in the Federal Republic—or, for that matter, in many circles in the United States. Both because they deem such an approach unnecessary, and because they consider it destablilising, many West Germans oppose the development of war-fighting capabilities (by both of the superpowers) and seek instead both limitations on the development of missiles such as the MX and the SS-24 and reductions in numbers of weapons which would leave each side with smaller but less vulnerable strategic nuclear forces. Although the United States is seemingly prepared to move in this direction, as evidenced by support in some quarters for the Midgetman (a small, mobile missile equipped with a single warhead) and by official proposals for cuts in strategic armaments, there is some question whether the U.S. Government will go as far toward reliance on "assured destruction" capabilities as the Government (and people) of the Federal Republic might like.

A second point, where agreement seems closer, is with respect to theater nuclear forces. Here both American and West German policies (like those of the Atlantic Alliance as a whole) aim at reductions in the number of nuclear warheads in Europe, at the substitution, to the extent possible, of rear area missiles for forward area artillery pieces and at generally smaller and more secure tactical nuclear forces. Although the INF Treaty, which will eliminate all missiles with ranges over 500 km, actually runs counter to this trend, it was accepted despite German concerns that the bulk of the remaining landbased systems could only be used against targets in the FRG and the GDR. At this point, however, Americans and Germans parted company, with the former seeking to modernize Lance and to increase its range and the latter seeking instead to reduce the number of all short-range missiles, and perhaps of artillery pieces as well. In brief, a success in arms control has created new difficulties with respect to the implementation of the nuclear guarantee.

The third point to note is that the governments of both countries are in agreement on the need to strengthen *conventional forces* in Europe—a statement which could not have been made with such certainty three or four years ago. The differences that exist—and will undoubtedly persist—have more to do with means than with ends. For one, the Americans are pushing a "high tech" solution which has not yet achieved acceptance in the Federal Republic. For another, the Americans are clinging to an operational doctrine that emphasizes the employment of highly mobile, heavily-armored units against the flanks and rear of WTO forces; while such a doctrine is still popular within the German Army it is questioned elsewhere, both because of its potential costs and because of what many regard as its provocative aspects, which closely parallel those of the Soviet Group of Forces, Germany.

The fourth point to note is that differences over "deterrence and defense" not only remain but may well increase. Although the "forces of change" in the Federal Republic are a minority, they are an influential minority, with sympathizers in the Kohl government and spokesmen in the *Bundestag*; moreover, some of those who vigorously oppose current concepts of deterrence and current programs for defense have already demonstrated their ability to sway public opinion, especially on emotional issues like the deployment of new weapons. Although people holding similar views can be found in the United States (where, indeed, some of the ideas for alterations in defense policy originated), they are, by and large, somewhat isolated from the main stream of thinking, which indorses strengthening conventional forces, preferably at European expense. Unless the deep suspicion of Soviet motives which is held in the United States can be overcome, and the latent support for improvements in East-West relations can be developed, Americans are likely to lag behind their German allies in their willingness to adjust defense postures, much less to accept "deep cuts" in armaments or to support the establishment of a "security régime" in Europe. Hopefully, these differences will not become divisive but they do suggest that the debate over the policies to be adopted will be long and difficult—even before the members of the WTO are invited to participate in it.

Notes

1. The Federal Minister of Defence, *White Paper 1983, The Security of the Federal Republic of Germany* (Bonn: 1983), Hereafter cited as *White Paper, 1983*.

2. *Webster's Third New International Dictionary of the English Language*, 2nd Ed., Unabridged, 711.

3. Glenn Snyder, *Deterrence and Defense* (Princeton, NJ: Princeton University Press, 1961), 12.

4. For example, five Soviet submarines, each carrying sixteen (16) SLBMs with 1 MT warheads, could inflict something like 80 million casualties upon the United States.

5. Patrick M. Morgan, *Deterrence: A Conceptual Analysis* (Beverly Hills, CA: Sage Publications, 1977), 82.

6. Thus President John F. Kennedy, during the Cuban Missile Crisis of October 1962, threatened to "initiate a full retaliatory resonse upon the Soviet Union" if a single nuclear warhead were delivered from Cuba against any point in the Western Hemisphere. Address of 22 October 1962, reprinted in David L. Larson, ed., *The "Cuban Crisis" of 1962: Selected Documents and Chronology* (Boston: Houghton-Mifflin, 1967), 43-44.

7. *Report of Secretary of Defense Donald H. Rumsfeld to the Congress on the FY 1978 Budget, FY 1979 Authorization Request and FY 1978-1982 Defense Programs*, (Washington, D.C.: Department of Defense, 1977).

8. Robert S. McNamara, "The Military Role of Nuclear Weapons: Perceptions and Misperceptions," *Foreign Affairs*, 62, 1 (Fall 1983), 79.

9. McGeorge Bundy, "To Cap the Volcano," *Foreign Affairs*, 48, 1 (October 1969), 10.

10. For a discussion of how this has occurred in practice, see David Alan Rosenberg, "U.S. Nuclear War Planning, 1945-1960," 49-56 and Desmond Ball, "The Development of the SIOP, 1960-1983," 80-83, in Desmond Ball and Jeffrey Richelson, eds., *Strategic Nuclear Targeting*, (Ithaca, New York: Cornell University Press, 1986).

11. Robert Kennedy, "Soviet Theater Nuclear Capabilities: the European Nuclear Balance in Transition," in Robert Kennedy and John M. Weinstein, eds., *The Defense of the West*, (Boulder, CO: Westview Press, 1984), 230-236.

12. For a succinct account of the Soviet build-up see Maj. Gen. William E. Odom, "Trends in the Balance of Military Power Between East and West," *The Conduct of East-West Relations in the 1980's, Part III*, Adelphi Paper No. 191 (London: The International Institute for Strategic Studies, Summer 1984), 14-25.

13. See "Remarks of Secretary of Defense Harold Brown at the U.S. Naval Academy given May 30, 1979." Reprinted in the Department of Defense *Selected Statements* 79-4 (1 July 1979), 51.

14. For an excellent discussion of the technical difficulties that can possibly affect nuclear weapons once the launch order is given, see Stanley Sienkiewicz, "Observations on the Impact of Uncertainty in Strategic Analysis," in John F. Reichart and Steven R. Sturm, eds., *American Defense Policy*, Fifth ed., (Baltimore, MD: The Johns Hopkins University Press, 1982), 217-27.

15. Stehen M. Meyer, *Soviet Theater Nuclear Forces: Part II: Capabilities and Implications*, Adelphi Paper No. 188 (London: The International Institute for Strategic Studies, Winter 1983/4), 24-25.

16. *Ibid.*

17. Richard Ned Lebow, "The Soviet Offensive in Europe: The Schlieffen Plan Revisited?," *International Security*, 9, 4 (Spring 1985), 52.

18. William Mako, *U.S. Ground Forces and the Defense of Central Europe*, Studies in Defense Policy (Washington: The Brookings Institution, 1983), 45-48.

19. *Ibid*, 101-104.

20. James M. Garret, "Conventional Force Deterrence in the Presence of Theater Nuclear Weapons," *Armed Forces and Society* 11, 1 (Fall 1984) 66-67. See also, The Federal Minister of Defence, *White Paper, 1985, The Situation and Development of the Federal Armed Forces* (Bonn: 1985), 62-63.

21. For the official view, see the *White Paper, 1983*, 113; for elite perceptions see Peter Schmidt, "Public Opinion and Security Policy in the Federal Republic of Germany," *Orbis*, 28, 4, (Winter 1985), 722 and 724.

22. Gerhard Wettig, "The Garthoff-Pipes Debate on Soviet Strategic Doctrine: A European Perspective," *Strategic Review*, XI, 2 (Spring 1983), 76.

23. Bo Huldt, "Considering the East-West Military Balance," in *The Conduct of East-West Relations in the 1980s, Part III*, 1984, 5.

24. *Ibid*, 5-6.

25. Odom, "Trends in the Balance," 21, citing V.G. Kulikov, "Army of a Developed Socialist Society," *Red Star*, (23 February 1977).

26. Wettig, "The Garthoff-Pipes Debate," 72.

27. *Ibid.*

28. Huldt, "Considering the East-West Military Balance," 6.

29. Jerry Hough, "The World as Viewed from Moscow," *International Journal*, (Spring 1982), cited in Huldt, "Considering the East-West Military Balance," 5.

30. Christopher Donnelly, "Development of the Soviet Concept of Echeloning," *NATO Review*, 32 (December 1984), 9-17

31. William F. Scott, "Soviet Concepts of War" *Air Force Journal*, March 1985, reprinted in *Current News, Special Edition*, 1276 (March 1985), 5.

32. Christian Krause, "Do the Russians Threaten Us?" *Paper No. 10, Study Group on Security and Disarmament*, Friedrich Ebert Stiftung, (Bonn: March 1985) 9.

33. *Ibid*, 6-8; Mako, *U.S. Ground Forces*, 59-64.

34. See Robert Jervis, *The Illogic of American Strategic Doctrine*, (Ithaca, New York: Cornell University Press, 1984) p 72-85.

35. For example, Fred Iklé, at that time Director of the Arms Control and Disarmament Agency, described Nixonian thinking on deterrence as follows, "One, our nuclear forces must be designed almost exclusively for retaliation in response to a Soviet attack; two, retaliation must be simple and inflicted by means of a massive and prompt strike; three, threatened retaliation must be the killing of a major fraction of the Soviet population." Quoted in Donald M. Snow, *Nuclear Strategy in a Dynamic World*, (University, Alabama: The University of Alabama Press, 1981), 77.

36. *Report of Secretary of Defense James R. Schlesinger to the Congress on the FY 1976 and Transition Budgets, FY 1977 Authorization Request and FY 1976-1980 Defense Programs, 5 February 1975*, (Washington, D. C.: Department of Defense, 1975), I-13. Hereafter cited as Schlesinger, *Annual Report, FY 1975*.

37. Discussed in Chapter 2.

38. *"United States Military Posture FY 1981"*, prepared by the Organization of the Joint Chiefs of Staff, (Washington, D.C.: GPO, 1981), 1.

39. To be fair, Secretary of Defense Brown did refer to the unlikelihood that limited nuclear wars would in fact stay limited. Harold Brown, *Thinking About National Security: Defense and Foreign Policy in a Dangerous World* (Boulder, CO: Westview Press, 1983), 81. This recognition of reality was not, however, acknowledged by others holding his post.

40. Mutual Security Act of 1958, Senate Hearings, 187, 200-201, and "Text of General Norstad's Cincinnati Speech," 27, as referred to in David N. Schwartz, *NATO's Nuclear Dilemmas* (Washington, D. C.: The Brookings Institution, 1983), 58-59.

41. Schlesinger, *Annual Report, FY 1975*, I-13.

42. *Ibid.*

43. The remaining U.S. SNF were to be withheld and targeted against the Soviet economic base "so as to deter coercive or desperation attacks on the economic and population targets of the United States and its allies." *Ibid.*

44. Rumsfeld, *Annual Report, FY 1978*, 22, 100 & 109.

45. *Ibid.*, 82-83 and 22.

46. *Report of Secretary of Defense Harold Brown to the Congress on the FY 1981 Budget, the FY 1982 Authorization Request and FY 1983-1988 Defense Programs*, (Washington, D. C.: 1980), 40. Hereafter cited as Brown, *Annual Report, FY 1981*.

47. *Statement by General George S. Brown, USAF, Chairman, Joint Chiefs of Staff to the Congress on the Defense Posture of the United States for 1978*, 20 January 1977 (Washington, D.C.: The Organization of the Joints Chiefs of Staff, 1977), 6.

48. *Report of the Secretary of Defense Caspar W. Weinberger to the Congress on the FY 1985 Budget, FY 1986 Authorization Request and FY 1985-89 Defense Programs*, 1 February 1984 (Washington, D.C.: GPO, 1984), 39.

49. George Schultz, "Security and Arms Control: The Search for a More Stable Peace," *Department of State Bulletin* (June 1983), 10.

50. Gregory Flynn, "Public Opinion and Atlantic Defense," in *Occidente*, (1 January 1984), 41.

51. Benjamin F. Schlemmer, "Soviet Technological Parity in Europe Undermines NATO's Flexible Response Strategy," *Armed Forces Journal International*, 121, 10 (May 1984), 80-94.

52. C. J. Dick, "Soviet Doctrine, Equipment, Design and Organization: An Integrated Approach to War," *International Defense Review*, 16, 12 (December 1983), 1715-1722.

53. For further details see the excellent piece, "The Conventional Offensive in Soviet Theatre Strategy" by Philip A. Peterson and John G. Hines, in *Orbis*, 27, 3, (Fall 1983) 695-740.

54. Ilanna Kass and Michael J. Deane, "The Role of Nuclear Weapons in the Modern Theater Battlefield: The Current Soviet View," *Comparative Strategy*, 3 (1984), 193-213.

55. Mark L. Urban, "Major Reorganization of Soviet Air Forces," *International Defense Review*, 16, 6 (June 1983) 765.

56. Petersen and Hines, "The Conventional Offensive in Soviet Theater Strategy;" C. J. Dick, "Soviet Operational Maneuver Groups: A Closer Look," *International Defense Review*, 16, 6 (June 1983) 719-721.

57. As will be seen later, success in such an attack is highly dependent on the scenario envisaged, as well as on assessments of NATO and WTO capabilities—for which see Barry R. Posen and Stephen van Evera, "Defense Policy and the Reagan Administration: Departure from Containment," *International Security*, 8, 1 (Summer 1983), 15-19.

58. The lower assessment is by the General Accounting Office, the higher by the Department of Defense. Richard Halloran "Two Studies Say Defense of Western Europe Is Biggest U.S. Military Cost," *The New York Times*, 20 July 1984, 4.

59. Senator Sam Numm, *The New York Times*, 21 June 1984, 6.

60. *Report of Secretary of Defense Caspar W. Weinberger to the Congress on the FY 1986 Budget, FY 1987 Authorization Request qust and FY 1986-90 Defense Programs, February 4, 1985* (Washington: GPO, 1985), 28. Hereafter cited as Weinberger, *Annual Report, FY 86*).

61. Phillip A. Karber, "In Defense of Forward Defense," *Armed Forces Journal International*, 121, 10 (May 1984), 34-36 & 47. Mr. Karber presumably knows whereof he speaks, since he at one time headed the Secretary of Defense's Strategic Concepts Development Center.

62. Boyd D. Sutton, *et al..*, "Deep Attack Concepts and the Defense of Central Europe," *.Survival*, 16, 2 (March-April 1984), 52.

63. The *Washington Times*, 21 October 1982, 7, cited in Daniel Gouré and Jeffrey R. Cooper, "Conventional Deep Strike: A Critical Look," *Comparative Strategy*, 3 (1984), 233. See also Benjamin F. Schlemmer, "Successful Blitzkrieg Possible in 15 years if NATO Doesn't Produce Better," *Armed Forces Journal International*, 122, 12 (July 1985), 64, where he reports an assessment by the NATO Military Committee that the Soviets might, over time, achieve an advantage so great that there "might not even be enough *time* for NATO to mobilize, or reinforce, *or* for SACEUR to obtain nuclear release from NATO political authorities. . . . " (Italics in original)

64. Karber, "In Defense of Forward Defense," 40-41.

65. *Ibid.,* 46.

66. John R. Landry *et al.*, "Deep Attack in Defense of Central Europe: Implications for Strategy and Doctrine," *Essays on Strategy: Selections From the 1983 Joint Chiefs of Staff Essay Competition* (Washington, D.C.: National Defense University Press, 1984), Appendix A, 70-74.

67. *Report of Secretary of Defense Caspar W. Weinberger to the Congress on the FY 1983 Budget, FY 1984 Authorization Request and FY 1983-1987 Defense Programs, February 8, 1982.* (Washington: GPO, 1982), I-16. Hereafter cited as Weinberger, *Annual Report, FY 1983*. See also Samuel Huntington, "Conventional Deterrence and Conventional Retaliation in Europe," *International Security*, 8,3 (Winter 1983-84), 46-54.

68. Sutton, *et al..*, "Deep Attack Concepts and the Defense of Central Europe," 52.

69. Walter Kross, *Military Reform: The High-Tech Debate in Tactical Air Forces,* (Washington, D.C.: National Defense University Press, 1985), 15-18.

70. One of the more articulate and more authoritative exponents of this point of view is Robert W. Komer, author of *Maritime Strategy or Coalition Defense?*, (Cambridge, MA: Abt Books, 1984).

71. John J. Mearsheimer, "Nuclear Weapons and Deterrence in Europe," *International Security* 9, 3, (Winter 1984-85) 45. See also Barry R. Posen, "Measuring the European Conventional Balance," *Ibid*, 87-88.

72. Huntington, "Conventional Deterrence and Conventional Retaliation in Europe," 46-54: Richard Hart Sinnreich, "Strategic Implications of Doctrinal Change: A Case Analysis," in Keith A. Dunn and William O. Staudenmeier, eds., *Military Strategy in Transition: Defense and Deterrence in the 1980s*, (Carlisle Barracks, PA.: Strategic Studies Institute, 1984), 53-54. For details see *The Airland Battle and Corps 86*, Pamphlet 525-6, U.S. Army Operational Concepts and Doctrine Command, 21 March 1981; and *FM-105, Operations*; Headquarters Department of the Army (Washington, D. C.: 1982).

73. For a critical discussion of FOFA and Airland Battle see Jeffrey Record, "NATO in 1984—An Update," in Barry M. Blechman and Edward N. Luttwak, eds., *International Security Yearbook 1984/85*, (Boulder, CO: Westview Press, 1985), 96-97. Record notes that not only intra-alliance controversies but inter-service rivalries within the U.S. make the adoption of a Deep Strike strategy very unlikely.

74. Komer, *Maritime Strategy or Coalition Defense?*, 67-75.

75. Keith A. Dunn and William O. Staudenmaier, "Competing Strategic Concepts: The Need for a Unified Military Strategy," in Stephen J. Cimbala, ed., *National Security Strategy: Choices and Limits*, (New York: Praeger Publishers, 1984), 17.

76. Excerpts from article written by Admiral James D. Watkins, "The Maritime Strategy," in *Naval Institute Proceedings* reprinted in "From the Pentagon, An Ultimate Battle Plan," *The New York Times*, 12 January 1986, Section 4, 1.

77. F. J. West, Jr., "Maritime Strategy and NATO Deterrence," *Naval War College Review*, 28, 5, (September-October, 1985), 11, 16-19.

78. Henry Kissinger, "A Plan to Reshape NATO," *Time* (5 March 1984), 26.

79. See Komer, *Maritime Strategy or Coalition Defense?*, 67-75.

80. See Joseph D. Douglass, Jr., *Soviet Military Strategy in Europe*, (New York: Pergamon Press, 1980), especially 55-116 and 181-183.

81. Robert S. McNamara, "The Military Role of Nuclear Weapons," 73 & 79.

82. Henry Kissinger, "NATO's Future," Reprint of a speech given in Brussels, Belgium, *The Washington Quarterly*, 2, 4, (Autumn, 1979), 123.

83. "Freedom Is the Prerequisite for Peace," policy statement to the *Bundestag*, 21 Nov. 1983 translated and reprinted in the *Bulletin*, (20 Dec. 1983) 2.

84. Weinberger, *Annual Report, FY 1982*, III-11.

85. Excerpts from the Report of the Commission on Strategic Forces, *The New York Times* 12 April 1983) 18. (As noted earlier, Mr. Reagan endorsed and adopted this report.)

86. Schlesinger, *Annual Report, FY 1976*, 1-13.

87. Weinberger, *Annual Report, FY 1983*, III-11.

88. George Hudson and Joseph Kruzel eds., *American Defense Annual, 1985-1986*, (Lexington, MA: D. C. Heath and Company, 1985), 56.

89. George Schultz, "Security and Arms Control: The Search for a Stable Peace," *op. cit.*.

90. McGeorge Bundy, George F. Kennan, *et al.* "Nuclear Weapons and the Atlantic Alliance," *Foreign Affairs* 60, 4 (Spring 1982), 753-768.

91. Wolf Graf von Baudissin, "*Kernwaffe und das Atlantische Bundnis,*" in *Sicherheitspolitik am Scheideweg?* Dieter S. Lutz, ed. (Bonn: Schriftenreihe der Bundeszentrale für Politische Bildung, 1982), 191, 627.

92. Helmut Schmidt, *Defense or Retaliation* (New York: Praeger, 1962), 16-19.

93. *Ibid.*, 36-39.

94. *"Rede des Befehlshabers der NATO-Landstreitkrafte in Mittleuropa,* General Hans Speidel, vor der Association of the United States Army in Washington am 8.8. 1960," in *Sicherheitspolitik der Bundesrepublik Deutschland, Dokumentation 1945-1977,* 2 Vols., Klaus von Schubert, ed. (Bonn: Schriftenreihe der Bundeszentrale für politische Bildung, 1978), II, 119.

95. *Ibid.,* 121.

96. *"Artikel des Bundesministers der Verteidigung Franz Joseph Strauss zu Fragen der Westlichen Strategie vom August 1961,"* in *Sicherheitspolitik der Bundesrepublik Deutschland,* II, 132.

97. Schmidt, *Defense or Retaliation,* 210.

98. *White Paper, 1985* 29-30.

99. Peter K. Stratmann, "Prospective Tasks and Capabilities Required for NATO's Conventional Forces," European Security Study, *Strengthening Conventional Deterrence in Europe: Proposals for the 1980s* (New York: St. Martin's, 1983), 163-165.

100. Mc George Bundy, George F. Kennan, *et al.,* "Nuclear Weapons and the Atlantic Alliance," 763-768.

101. European Study Group, *Strengthening Conventional Deterrence in Europe.*

102. This search for ways of safeguarding the Federal Republic without relying on nuclear deterrence began in the 1970s when Carl Friedrich von Weizsächer analyzed the devastation resulting from even a limited nuclear war in Europe. One approach was that of "area defense" carried out by a network of small units which would present no targets for nuclear attacks, suggested by Horst Afheldt in his book *Defense and Peace* (Munich: 1976). This was later developed by Afheldt and others into the concept of "defensive defense."

103. *White Paper, 1985,* 79.

104. Andreas Von Bülow, "Defensive Entanglement: An Alternative Strategy for NATO," *The Conventional Defense of Europe: New Technologies and New Strategies,* Andrew J. Pierre, ed., (New York: New York University Press, 1986), 148-149.

105. See Klaus von Schubert, "Conditions of Survival," *Aus Politik und Zeitgeschichte: Das Parlament* (Bonn: 10 March 1980); Horst Afheldt, *Defensive Defense* (Starnberg: 1983).

106. See, in this connection, Jonathan Dean, *Watershed in Europe: Dismantling the East-West Military Confrontation,* Union of Concerned Scientists (Lexington, KY: Lexington Books, 1987).

107. First mentioned by Klaus von Schubert, "Conditions of Survival," *loc. cit.*

108. *"Common Security,* The Palme Report (London: 1982).

Comments

a. Technically speaking, risk is the probability that a given event will take place when the probabilities of that happening or not happening are known, as in the "risk" that a tossed coin will land heads up. The proper term for what is described here is "uncertainty;" however, in deference both to Webster's Dictionary and to common usage, the word "risk" has been used.

b. As some West Europeans have noted, the concept of "horizontal escalation" applies equally in the event of conflicts outside Europe, which raises at least a possibility that NATO may become involved in a war started elsewhere.

c. It may also "put period" to the notion that theater nuclear forces alone can carry out limited, controlled strikes at missile sites, command-control centers and other high value targets, thereby establishing a new "firebreak" between theater and strategic nuclear forces. Whatever the validity of this notion, it is one which has found some acceptance in the United States and perhaps even some importance in American strategic planning. (In an interview in *The New York Times*, 6 December 1987, General John P. Chain, Jr., Commander-in-Chief of the Strategic Air Command, noted that NATO strategy for defending Europe against Soviet invasion "was to fight with conventional arms as long as possible, then to resort to intermediate-range nuclear weapons in a second stage if Soviet conventional strength proved to be superior.")

d. In the best of all worlds, they would also like an early commitment to battle of the French Quick Reaction Force, with its 2-1/3 air-transportable divisions, and of the three small armored divisions stationed in southwestern Germany; indeed, according to some sources, the deployment of U.S. and German units in time of crisis is planned on the basis that these three French divisions will be available to back up the "forward defenses."

e. Aside from the fact that the use of long-range aircraft would strain Soviet resources, these could not reach many bases in Western Europe before the planes stationed there could take off or the missiles deployed there could be launched; hence missiles would almost certainly have to be directed against GLCMs in Italy and Great Britain as long as these remain and against F-16s in Spain and F-111Es in England. Given the projected elimination of short- and medium-range Soviet missiles (the only ones for which conventional warheads are even conjectured) this task would have to be carried out either by SLCMs—which are as yet neither as accurate nor as suitable for disarming strikes as are ballistic missiles—or by ICBMs. Moreover, destruction of U.S. missile submarines in the Mediterranean, and British and French ones in the Atlantic, would probably require nuclear barrages saturating the area(s) in which these submarines were (presumably) located, as precise fixes are not known to be possible and surveillance by Soviet ASW forces would give warning of their intention. Thus, the ability of the USSR to mount a conventional disarming strike would seem to be diminishing, rather than increasing.

5

Burden-Bearing and Burden-Sharing

*James R. Golden**

The NATO Alliance has historically drawn strength from the convergence
of economic and security interests among the member states. There have
been points of disagreement to be sure, but there was always fundamental
agreement that the emergence of free, integrated economic markets would
increase common living standards just as cooperation on security matters
would strengthen the common defense. Economic strength would provide
the basis for sustaining an adequate military deterrent, and it would also
contribute to a social compact under which current sacrifices contributed
to a stronger social fabric. Military strength was justified not only by a
near and present military threat, but also by a set of economic and social
values that were worth defending. Those values, moreover, were not unique
to individual states but were held in common by all members of the
Alliance.

The task of providing an adequate military deterrent on the one hand,
and an open international economic system on the other, was made vastly
easier by the dominant position of the United States. The U.S strategic
nuclear deterrent made defense at acceptable economic cost feasible, just
as U.S. economic dominance, and hence leadership, made the emergence
of a liberal economic order possible. In particular, the U.S position made
it possible for the Federal Republic of Germany to assume a major role
in the world economy and in the NATO Alliance without posing an
unacceptable threat to the rest of Europe.

By the 1970s the economic and military landscapes were quite different.
The United States was still the world's leading economic power, but it was
no longer a dominant power capable of unilateral leadership. Massive
retaliation had given way to a potentially more expensive strategy of flexible
response, and the old standards of deterrence and defense were joined by
the new more subtle idea of détente. Moreover, the Western economies,

---

* The views expressed in this chapter are those of the author and do not reflect the official
position of the U.S. Army or any other government agency.

which had been relatively isolated from external shocks, were now clearly vulnerable to resource supply shocks from the South as well as potential disagreements over trade policy with the East. At the same time, the role of governments had dramatically expanded with an explosion of social welfare expenditures, an expansion that was financed without reductions in defense outlays thanks to the additional revenues generated from rapid economic growth. But as overall economic growth slowed, the tension between social and defense programs intensified. Economic and security issues remained intertwined, but the strands were now more complicated and they occasionally threatened to unravel.

In the mid-1980s the dual economic and security strands of the NATO Alliance may actually pull in opposite directions. The international economic order faces severe threats from protectionism, third world debt, and the loss of confidence in the floating exchange rate regime. The NATO Alliance is challenged by slower economic growth, potential reductions in real defense spending, apparent adverse shifts in the balance of conventional forces in Europe, and the need to adjust to threats from outside the traditional NATO area that the United States, at least, perceives as vitally important. Cooperation on the economic and security fronts could well be synergistic and produce a strengthened Alliance structure more attuned to the challenges of the rest of the century, but there is also a risk, perhaps even an equal risk, that disagreements on both fronts will substantially weaken the traditional Alliance structure.

At the same time that economic factors have become potentially more divisive, public opinion toward the NATO Alliance and willingness to fund defense programs has also been drawn into question. In Europe the challenge has often taken the form of opposition to Alliance deterrence strategy in general and nuclear deterrence in particular. The Alliance succeeded in proceeding with the deployment of the Pershing II and ground-launched cruise missiles (GLCM's), in response to Soviet SS-20 deployments, despite the opposition of a vocal minority. Nonetheless, the opposition to deployments raised public attention to defense outlays and worked to legitimize public opposition to the Alliance itself. Thus while the Green Party has not been able to build enough strength to alter German defense policy, and is unlikely to do so, it has had an impact on the consensus toward NATO in the much larger and more influential Social Democratic Party. Shifting attitudes toward the Alliance among younger groups have prompted wide interest in the "successor generation" that has not had first hand experience with the problems in the aftermath of World War II that forged the Alliance. The concern is that, while current opinion polls continue to show strong support for the Alliance, a more neutral national policy, with less emphasis on military deterrence, will become more attractive over time.

In the United States, the public opinion challenge lies more in questions about the extent of contributions by European allies to the common defense, particularly contributions to managing potential threats outside of the

traditional NATO region. As concern for public deficits rises, defense outlays
are more constrained, and global challenges mount, the United States will
inevitably look to Europe and Japan to help take up the slack. The U.S.
Congress has led the attack on European and Japanese defense contributions, and there is a very real danger that perceived inequities in relative
outlays could lead to a fundamental re-evaluation of the Alliance itself.
The "burden sharing" debate threatens to move from relatively dry statistical reports to Congress to the center of the political stage.

Economic and public opinion constraints will soon be joined by growing
manpower limitations. The *Bundeswehr* has relied heavily on conscripts to
man the defense force with mandatory service for all males, but the pool
of available manpower will drop below annual requirements to sustain the
current force structure in 1987. This will force consideration of changes in
pay, length of required service, female service, and force structure, and it
will make it more difficult for the Federal Republic to respond to U.S.
calls for greater contributions on the Central Front. The same problem
will occur a bit later in the United States, as the manpower pool drops in
the early 1990s. The decline will put greater pressure on the volunteer
force approach and, as in Germany, produce a painful re-evaluation of
compensation, quality of recruits, and force structure. In both countries,
manpower constraints will force greater emphasis on technology to provide
what technicians often call "force multipliers," equipment and organizational changes that will make limited active forces more effective in wartime
and hence enhance deterrence.

Economic, social and demographic factors will have increasingly important impacts on the search for common security within the Alliance. There
are clear indications that those factors will become more divisive over the
next decade. The challenge will be to find new approaches to our common
interests that exploit the enormous potential strengths of the Alliance,
approaches that are consistent with the economic, social, and demographic
realities.

The Socio-Economic Context
for the Definition of Security Policy

Interrelationships of Socio-Economic Factors
and National Security

The goal of national security policy is to protect and promote national
values, values which are translated into more specific national interests in
the context of the domestic and international environments. For example,
the value of preserving the state is translated into the national interest of
defense against external attack in the context of current military threats
and national military capabilities. Social and economic factors are therefore
a vital component of national security policy. In the first instance, they
are part of the national values that national security policy is designed to

protect. They also form a crucial part of the environment within which national values are translated into the more specific national interests. In addition, they define and constrain some of the means by which interests can be pursued. Economic policy, along with military and diplomatic policies, constitutes a major dimension of overall national security policy.[1]

As economic interdependence with other states expands, the importance of the economic component of national security also increases. First, economic values are at greater risk in the international arena because of the domestic implications of international economic actions. Second, economic policy becomes a more important element of security policy because of the expanded potential impacts in influencing the behavior of other states. Third, military and diplomatic capabilities become potentially more important, because of the greater potential risks to economic values, but the use of those capabilities also becomes more constrained, because of the possible economic feedbacks from military or diplomatic action. The sharp expansion of economic interdependence has therefore worked to change the focus and structure of national security policies, although national and Alliance policy-making institutions have typically been slow to adjust to this important shift in the international environment.

Economic capacity also constrains force structure and hence the military policy that can be pursued. This relationship dominates national budgeting processes. As economic growth rates have declined, the trade-off between defense and social programs, which is always difficult, has become even more painful. German analysts have been quick to note that social spending cuts would weaken the social compact upon which defense outlays have been based, and hence actually weaken national security in the long run. One does not need to be German to understand the point, as the U.S. Congress has made abundantly clear. The tighter budgetary environment forces greater attention on force structure issues in general, and the trade-off between manpower and equipment, especially high-technology equipment, in particular. It also forces greater attention on the efficacy of various social welfare programs and their impact on economic performance. Different opinions on these trade-offs have increasingly become the focus of national and international debate.

Changes in the military environment have not made the dilemma of choosing between social and defense expenditures any easier. The actual pace of Soviet military outlays and the actual balance of military capabilities between NATO and the Warsaw Pact provides ample room for endless speculation. Some trends do, however, seem clear. The nuclear stalemate at the strategic level has now been extended to the intermediate level, increasing the potential importance of conventional deterrence. Despite improvements in NATO conventional forces, there have also been substantial improvements in Warsaw Pact forces, particularly in the quality of individual weapon systems. Thus at a time when the conventional balance may be increasingly important, there is little reason for complacency. These trends have heightened concern for negotiations in force reductions as one way out of the budgetary dilemma. They have also reinforced the importance of economic constraints on achievable force structure.[2]

Economic well-being is an important national value, economic policy is a vital dimension of security policy, and economic capacity is a key constraint on sustainable military force structure. Coordination of economic policy is also a conduit for coordination on security matters. The heads of state who meet at annual economic summits are the same individuals who meet to consult on NATO policy. The spillovers from one set of consultations to the next are obvious. A framework of compromise and cooperation in one area creates a positive environment for joint action in the other. In the Soviet context, such activities are termed "confidence-building measures." They are no less important in the Alliance context.

The Shifting Economic Balance

The stability of the NATO Alliance was originally reinforced by the post-war conviction that there was a common interest in rebuilding the wartorn economies of both the victors and the vanquished, that the NATO allies would all benefit from a liberal economic order that encouraged free trade and free capital flows, that the North would be the engine for world growth through the consumption of resources from the South, and that East and West would remain economically isolated. Thus economic interests paralleled security interests. The costs of the common defense were funded from the fruits of common economic success. Economic and security priorities focused on Europe. As colonial empires faded, economic self-interest would continue to bind the developing world to the West. Common Alliance restrictions on trade with the East would delay economic recovery there, slow the development of military capabilities in the East, and ease the burden of defense in the West.

In the last two decades each of these economic factors has changed. The economic recovery of Europe and Japan produced economic parity with the United States, shifting relative economic strength in favor of the Alliance, but that very economic success made the obstacles to further economic growth more complex, as national economic interests diverged and defense of the liberal economic order became more difficult. Resource constraints threatened to shift the terms of international trade in favor of the South in the 1970s, but those fears were quickly replaced in the 1980s by the realization that resource prices would not grow quickly enough to finance mounting debt in the developing countries. In both decades, economic events in the South were no longer peripheral to economic performance in the North. Economic and security interests had important new global dimensions. At the same time, the perceived role of trade with the East took a new twist with détente and *Ostpolitik,* but the Alliance was not able to settle on a consistent, integrated approach to such trade as divergent national economic and political interests took hold. The economic challenges facing the Alliance remain substantial. While aggregate economic performance has been acceptable, particularly in comparison with slowing growth rates in the East, structural problems have emerged that could well cause continuing friction and hamper cooperation on pressing defense issues. A brief geographic survey will serve to highlight some of the central economic issues.

The oil shock of the 1970s was accommodated with expansionary monetary policy in the United States that generated high inflation and accelerated the devaluation of the dollar. Europe, which potentially was more vulnerable to higher priced crude oil, was more successful in holding down inflation with restrictive monetary policies. As shown in Table 5.1, throughout the decade the developed countries managed to sustain real growth rates averaging around three percent per year, with somewhat higher growth in Japan and lower growth in the United Kingdom. The United States and Germany had similar growth patterns, with real growth in the 2 to 2.5 percent range from 1971 to 1975 and in the 3.5 to 4 percent range from 1976 to 1980. In the latter period, the United States pressed the Federal Republic, which enjoyed lower inflation and an appreciating mark, to provide more economic stimulus and serve as a "locomotive" for the other developing countries. The stimulus Germany did provide generated more inflation than growth and discredited, at least in the Federal Republic, the locomotive concept.

The early 1980s brought a reversal of monetary and fiscal policy in the United States. The Reagan Administration was committed to tax cuts designed to stimulate more saving and more effort, to reductions in social spending, and to rapid increases in real defense outlays. At the same time, the Federal Reserve Board, in a successful effort to reduce inflation, lowered growth in the money supply, apparently with the administration's blessing, and drove real interest rates to new heights. The tax cut was achieved, but with larger, more broadly targeted reductions than the President had requested. There were some cuts in social outlays, but few real reductions in entitlement programs such as social security. Real increases in defense outlays were obtained, although the levels were consistently below Administration requests. The net result was a rising federal deficit, which crowded out some private investment and fueled the rising interest rates. Capital flows from overseas to take advantage of high yields in the United States drove up the value of the dollar, stimulated U.S. imports, and held down U.S. exports. The huge surplus in the capital account produced a rising deficit in the trade account.

The impact of these policies on real growth in the United States is shown in Table 5.1. By 1982, the United States was in its deepest postwar recession with a decline in real output of over two percent. The medicine did have the desired impact on inflation, however, and the large fiscal stimulus took hold in 1983 and 1984, lowering unemployment without rekindling high inflation. The recovery was unfortunately unbalanced with large trade and budget deficits. The trade deficits, driven by the rising dollar, heightened domestic pressure for protection against imports.

In Germany lower growth reduced tax receipts below expected levels and made it impossible to sustain the rate of increase in social spending

TABLE 5.1 Growth Rates in Real Gross National Product by Region, 1971-1986 (percent change)

Area and Country	1971-75 Annual Average	1976-80 Annual Average	1981	1982	1983	1984	1985	1986[a]
Developed countries	3.7	3.2	1.9	-0.5	2.8	5.0	3.0	2.8
United States	2.2	3.4	1.9	-2.5	3.5	6.5	2.7	2.5
Canada	5.0	3.1	3.3	-4.4	3.3	4.7	4.0	3.3
Japan	4.7	5.0	3.7	3.1	3.2	5.1	4.7	2.7
European Community	2.8	3.0	-0.2	0.3	1.3	2.3	2.2	2.5
France	4.0	3.3	0.5	1.8	.7	1.6	1.4	2.2
West Germany	2.1	3.4	0.0	-1.0	1.5	3.0	2.5	3.0
Italy	2.5	3.9	0.2	-0.5	-0.4	2.6	2.3	3.1
United Kingdom	2.2	1.7	-1.4	1.4	3.5	1.8	3.4	2.5
Developing Countries	7.0	5.5	1.4	0.9	0.4	3.0	3.2	2.7
Communist Countries	4.2	2.8	2.0	2.6	3.6	3.2	3.6	_[b]
USSR	3.0	2.3	1.5	2.5	3.4	1.4	1.2	3.5
Eastern Europe	4.9	1.9	-1.0	.9	1.8	3.3	1.4	2.5
China	5.5	6.1	4.9	8.3	9.1	12.0	12.0	7.0

[a]Preliminary estimates.
[b]Not available.
Source: Council of Economic Advisers, *Economic Report of the President, 1987* (Washington, D.C.: U.S. Government Printing Office, 1987), p. 368.

that had been set in the 1970s. The Kohl Government resolved to limit increases in government outlays in order to combat the growing deficit, and real growth actually fell by one percent in the recession of 1982. The recession produced a rapid increase in unemployment, as shown in Table 5.2, from 2.9 percent in 1980 to 7.3 percent of the labor force by 1983. The social welfare net, which had been strengthened in the 1970s, reduced the social cost of the unprecedented unemployment, and made it possible for the government to resist pressure for greater monetary and fiscal stimulus.

Although Germany benefitted from the high value of the dollar through increased exports to the United States, the Kohl Government remained concerned that the dollar was overvalued and that a rapid decline of the dollar would cause large economic shocks. In order to prevent greater appreciation of the dollar, German monetary policy remained restrictive to hold interest rates in Germany high enough to limit further capital flows

TABLE 5.2 Civilian Unemployment Rates in Selected Countries, 1980-1985 (percent based on U.S. unemployment concepts)

Year	United States	Canada	Japan	France	West Germany	Italy[a]	United Kingdom
1980	7.1	7.5	2.0	6.4	2.9	4.3	7.1
1981	7.6	7.5	2.2	7.5	4.1	4.8	10.5
1982	9.7	11.0	2.4	8.3	5.9	5.4	11.4
1983	9.6	11.9	2.7	8.5	7.3	5.9	11.9
1984	7.5	11.3	2.8	9.9	7.8	5.9	11.7
1985	7.2	10.5	2.6	10.4	7.9	6.0	11.3

[a]This number excludes those unemployed who have not actively sought employment in the last 30 days. Their inclusion would more than double the rates shown here for Italy.
Source: Council of Economic Advisers, *Economic Report of the President, 1987* (Washington, D.C.: Government Printing Office, 1986), p. 367.

to the United States. Thus the German government argued that high interest rates in the United States, caused in part by the U.S. budget deficit, were causing high interest rates and lower real growth in Germany.

The United States saw the answer to this dilemma in more expansionary monetary and fiscal policies in Germany, which would raise German income and increase the demand for U.S. exports. Germans viewed this as a new version of the old, rejected locomotive theory. Instead they argued that the solution lay in more fiscal restraint in the United States, and more cooperative intervention to stabilize exchange rates.

M.I.T. economist Lester Thurow, in a recent article in *The Economist*, suggests that these problems of coordinating monetary and fiscal policies to limit movements in exchange rates are manageable, but their management is not within the realm of political feasibility.[3] He argues that the long-term problem in the United States is low growth in productivity, output per worker, that results from lower quality capital and labor inputs. The low quality, in turn, results from very low rates of saving, and hence investment, and a poor educational system. In his view, both problems could be solved, but they would require government efforts that are unlikely to occur. The long-term European problem, on the other hand, has been a failure to generate new jobs, a problem he attributes to the high cost of labor compared to capital. High labor costs, in turn, are the result of wage rigidities, high minimum wages, and restrictions on firing. Thurow's pessimistic conclusion is that the United States and Europe will turn inward, with protectionist measures designed to provide more freedom in handling their unique domestic problems with less pressure from international com-

petition. There is ample evidence that Thurow's forecast of greater protectionism may be all too accurate. More than 300 protectionist trade measures
were introduced in the last session of Congress.

The changing balance among the economies of the United States, Europe,
and Japan has produced structural changes that will make the coordination
of economic policies more difficult. The search for a new Bretton Woods
structure that would narrow the zone of exchange rate fluctuation ultimately
depends on agreement to coordinate domestic economic policies, but there
is little evidence that governments will be any more willing to submit to
such coordination in the future than they have been in the past. Even the
meeting of finance ministers in New York in September of 1985, at which
they agreed to a U.S. plan to lower the value of the dollar through
cooperative intervention in currency markets, did not produce a fundamental shift in the landscape. Cooperative intervention is one thing. Following through with the requisite coordination of monetary and fiscal
policies is quite another. At the moment, it does appear that the U.S. will
be able to pursue an expansionary monetary policy to bring the dollar
down without rekindling new inflation.[4] The problem will come when
domestic objectives again conflict with the targeted value of the dollar.

National Economic Policies and Defense Spending

Defense outlays are constrained not by the economic capacity of a nation,
but by political decisions on the share of national output that will be
committed to defense. Thus the Soviet Union, whose gross national product
is somewhere between 50 and 75 percent of U.S. output, depending on the
statistical method used for comparison, commits roughly the same amount
of resources as the United States to military outlays each year. Although
the share of resources allocated to defense varies substantially from country
to country, the share of national output that one country commits to
defense tends to be very stable from year to year. One reason for this is
that, in the short run, the capacity of the defense industry places an upper
limit on the level of potential defense spending, and the need to keep
defense production lines in operation and to sustain an adequate long-run
man-power structure places a lower limit on outlays. Another explanation
is that the political consensus on the appropriate level of defense outlays
and the military threat being faced also tend to change slowly over time.
European parliamentary governments tend to reach long-term decisions on
the appropriate share of resources to commit to defense, and those decisions
frequently endure even when the party or coalition in power shifts. The
share of resources for defense is typically defined as a share of gross
national output or as a share of total government outlays, rather than as
a target level of increases in real defense outlays. The U.S. government's
approach to defense budgeting is quite different. Defense outlays are typically justified based on changes in the nature of the perceived threat.

Those perceptions are linked to objective changes in the military capabilities of other countries, but they are also the result of evaluations of national priorities, the relative emphasis given to different regions, and to an assessment of U.S. capabilities for influencing world events. As a result the level of defense outlays is perceived as a major policy issue for each new administration, and shifts in administrations typically produce substantial adjustments in the level of defense outlays.

The defense share of U.S. gross domestic product has varied over the past 25 years from peaks of over nine percent in the early 1960s, to a trough in the late 1970s of just over five percent, and back up to seven percent by 1985. Even if one removes the Vietnam War buildup from the calculations the shifts in defense shares of national output are substantial. In comparison, the rest of NATO committed an average of about four percent of national output to defense in the 1960s, and a virtually constant three and one-half percent in the 1970s and early 1980s.[5]

In Europe, rapid economic growth made it possible over much of this period to finance both substantial increases in social welfare programs and increases in real defense outlays. In the United States expansion in social programs came largely at the expense of a declining share of resources committed to defense. The decline in real defense resources, in turn, was justified by a narrower view of U.S. global defense responsibilities in the aftermath of the unpopular war in Vietnam. President Carter initially justified reduced defense outlays on the grounds that the U.S. could withdraw some forces from the Pacific, that NATO was the U.S. top priority and resources should be focused there and used more efficiently, that some weapon systems such as the B-1 bomber were not needed, and that a SALT II agreement would reduce future outlays for strategic offensive systems. In other words, the decision on the appropriate level of defense expenditure in the United States was the result of clear decisions on national priorities between social and defense spending, on regional defense priorities, and on the prospects for arms control negotiations with the Soviet Union. In Europe in the 1970s defense outlays proceeded at a constant rate of real increase without any such fundamental review of national priorities.

One might argue that in Europe, the role of defense in the budgetary process has been relatively passive, with defense shares set by long term political compromise and defense outlays driven by the actual performance of the economy. In contrast, defense plays a very active role in the U.S. budgetary process, with more frequent adjustments based on shifts in assessments of global threats to national interests, judgments on the trade-offs between defense and other government programs, and evaluations of the impact that defense outlays are having on the performance of the national economy. A brief assessment of the national economic and defense strategies in West Germany and the United States will serve to clarify this fundamental difference.

The Interaction of Economic and Defense Policies in West Germany

The pattern of fiscal restraint through the early 1980s had a profound effect on defense outlays. In the late 1970s the agreed framework was that defense should receive roughly three to four percent of the gross national product. Long term defense plans, based on that fiscal framework, were developed to achieve the most efficient patterns of procurement based on the capacity of defense industries and replacement requirements. Departures from the long term plan in any one year would be compensated for by offsetting changes in future years.

This long term planning approach was made possible by the perception of an agreed social balance. Defense debates were limited to elite judgments within the government and rarely reached the broader public. Even within the government, defense issues came under the purview of the Chancellor, the Minister of Defense, and the Foreign Office. Without an executive equivalent of the Office of Management and Budget and in the absence of a tradition of strong parliamentary oversight of defense outlays, there was a limited framework for interagency bargaining. Thus the Minister of Defense was traditionally allocated a fair share of total government outlays and was left relatively free to determine the appropriate uses for those funds.[6]

As long as government outlays remained a constant or rising share of national output, and national output continued to rise rapidly in real terms, this formula meant that defense outlays could expand in real terms. As shown in Table 5.3, West German real defense expenditures grew at an average annual rate of 2.9 percent from 1971 through 1978, and then expanded at rates of 2.0 percent in 1979, 1.8 percent in 1980, 1.9 percent in 1981, and 3.2 percent in 1982. The lower rates after 1979 reflected lower overall economic growth, which was partially offset by a rising share of national output allocated to the government through 1982.[7]

Chancellor Kohl's 1982 decision to stop the growth in government's share of national output as part of the policy of fiscal restraint forced a difficult decision about defense spending. If all government programs were cut proportionately, defense outlays would be held virtually constant in real terms, despite commitments to NATO to expand real outlays at about three percent per year. On the other hand, an exception which permitted more rapid increases in defense outlays would threaten the traditional social balance and weaken, if not destroy, the consensus for fiscal restraint. Faced with the alternatives of abandoning fiscal restraint, losing the consensus for cuts in social welfare programs, or cutting defense along with other programs, the Kohl Government, despite a strong commitment to NATO, chose to cut defense. The consequences of that decision are shown in Table 5.3, as real defense outlays actually fell by .7 percent in 1983, rose gradually by .8 percent in 1984, and dropped by .4 percent in 1985. But, as Table 5.4 shows, defense outlays were maintained at a roughly constant percentage of GDP and of total government spending.

TABLE 5.3 Percentage Changes in NATO Defense Spending in Constant
Prices, 1971-1987

Country	Period Average			Annual Rate				
	1971-78	1978-82	1982-86	1982-83	1983-84	1984-85	1985-86	1986-87
Belgium	4.8	2.4	-0.9	-0.1	-0.4	-1.3	-1.7	7.7
Canada	2.7	2.1	5.5	4.5	8.0	7.2	2.4	3.7
Denmark	2.8	0.4	0.1	-0.3	0.8	-1.1	0.9	1.6
France	3.2	3.3	0.7	1.3	1.8	-0.2	-0.2	2.6
Germany	2.9	2.2	--	-0.7	0.8	-0.4	0.3	0.1
Greece	5.5	2.9	2.2	-1.1	-7.9	17.1	0.7	-3.9
Italy	3.1	2.0	2.9	3.1	2.5	2.8	3.0	1.8
Luxembourg	6.3	6.5	0.7	0.2	3.4	0.5	-1.5	9.5
Netherlands	3.3	2.5	1.5	2.2	0.5	3.2	0.2	3.4
Norway	3.0	2.3	4.7	4.1	4.0	-4.6	15.2	-0.4
Portugal	-6.0	6.7	-1.9	0.6	-3.1	-4.6	-0.3	5.2
Spain	--	--	2.7	3.5	2.1	2.6	2.5	-4.7
Turkey	7.8	2.1	1.8	4.6	-4.4	-1.3	8.5	13.0
U.K.	1.6	2.8	2.6	6.0	0.4	4.0	-0.2	0.2
U.S.	-2.7	4.1	6.9	7.0	7.9	4.7	7.8	6.0
Non-US NATO	--	--	1.7	2.4	1.3	2.0	1.0	1.4
NATO Total	--	--	5.3	5.5	5.8	3.9	5.8	4.7

Notes: Based on NATO definitions. Period averages are computed as simple
averages of annual growth rates during that period. Annual figures are for fiscal
years ending in the second year given. Fiscal years correspond to calendar years
except for the United States, Canada, the United Kingdom, and Turkey. Data shown
for 1986-1987 are preliminary estimates and should be used with extreme caution.
Subsequent revisions of preliminary estimates are often substantial. The figures
shown for 1986-1987 for Belgium, Greece, Norway, the Non-US NATO total, and the
NATO total are averages of the range of estimates given in the source. All data for
France are estimates from the U.S. Department of Defense.
Source: Congressional Research Service, *NATO After Afghanistan,* a report prepared
for the Subcommittee on Europe and the Middle East of the Committee on Foreign
Affairs, U.S. House of Representatives (Washington, D.C.: U.S. Government Printing
Office, 1980), p. 46; Caspar W. Weinberger, *Report on Allied Contributions to the
Common Defense* (Washington, D.C.: Department of Defense, March 1982 and April
1987), pp. 77 and 38, respectively.

TABLE 5.4 Percentage Size and Composition of West German Defense
Spending, 1981-1985

Category	1981	1982	1983	1984	1985
Defense Share of GDP[a]	2.8	2.8	2.8	2.7	2.8
Defense Share of Outlays by All Levels of Government[b]	23.2	23.5	24.0	24.0	23.8
Share of Personnel and Operations Expenses in Defense Outlays[c]	67.4	66.4	65.6	65.1	64.7
Share of Investment in Defense Outlays[d]	32.6	33.6	34.4	34.9	35.3

[a]Based on annual outlays. NATO definitions for outlays are broader than the data
reported by the Federal Republic in the *White Paper*. For example, by NATO
definition in 1983 the Federal Republic allocated 3.4 percent of GDP to defense.
Regardless of the definition used, however, the defense share of GDP remained
roughly constant in this period.

[b]The level of the percentage reported here will vary widely with the precise definition
of government outlays used. The data used here from the OECD *Economic Survey*
include social security, central government, and local outlays. Again, the precise
percentage is far less important here than the trend, which shows defense maintaining
a roughly constant share of government outlays.

[c]This includes outlays for personnel (active and retired), maintenance, and
operations. Roughly two thirds of this category goes to personnel outlays (20.3
billion marks in 1985 out of 31.7 billion marks).

[d]This includes procurement, installation construction, research, development, and
testing.
Source: OECD *West Germany, Economic Survey, 84/85* (Paris: OECD, June 1985),
p. 70. Ministry of Defense, *White Paper, 1985* (Bonn: Ministry of Defense, June 19,
1985), p. 124.

The Interaction of Economic and Defense Policies
in the United States

The Reagan Administration's economic blueprint provided for an expansion in defense outlays to compensate for the preceding decade of erosion in defense capabilities. The Carter Administration, reacting to the steady expansion in Soviet military capabilities and Soviet willingness to use those capabilities in a series of interventions culminating in the invasion of Afghanistan, reversed its position on defense spending and adopted budget proposals that would have produced real increases in defense outlays of five percent per year. That increase followed from a new sense of global strategic priorities illustrated by the Carter Doctrine, declaring that the Persian Gulf was an area of vital U.S. interest. The Carter budget plans submitted by what became a lame duck administration had little binding impact on subsequent outlays, but they did form a lower bound of defense expenditures to which the Democratic Party was committed. The Reagan Administration's calls for a more rapid buildup were aided by the bipartisan consensus that real increases were needed, and as Table 5.5 shows the defense share of the U.S. gross national product rose sharply from 1981 to 1983. At the same time the share of the defense budget allocated to investment surged, so the increase in procurement proceeded even faster than the overall increase in defense budget authority.

The budgets obligated funds for improvements in strategic offensive forces (the MX missile, the Trident submarine, and the reinstated B-1 bomber), for the deployment of the Pershing-II and GLCM intermediate-range nuclear forces, for an expansion to a 600-ship navy with enhanced two-ocean capabilities, for improved fighter aircraft, for the procurement of new, higher technology ground force systems, and for general improvements in military pay. In addition, funding for further research and development was approved for the Strategic Defense Initiative.

By 1985, however, it was apparent that the pace of the defense buildup could not be sustained in the face of a growing budget deficit. Debate in the Congress focused only on the size of the desired cut from the President's request, with the Senate favoring an increase in obligational authority equal to expected inflation (a freeze in real terms) and the House advocating a budget for fiscal 1986 equal to fiscal 1985 (a cut in real terms). The ultimate compromise held budget authority constant in real terms for fiscal year 1986. Similar restrictions were applied in fiscal year 1987. The momentum of budget authority granted in earlier years will, in either case, sustain real increases in actual defense outlays through 1986. Some $280 billion in government outlays was authorized as of October 1985, but not yet spent, including some $75 billion for defense.[8] Only thirty to forty percent of the new authorizations for fiscal 1986 will actually be spent in that year. Reductions in new authority will, however, reduce outlays in future years. Thus real defense expenditures should continue to increase by some three to four percent in 1986, but real growth will decline substantially in 1987.

TABLE 5.5 Percentage Size of U.S. Defense Spending and Composition of Budget
Authority, 1981-1986

Category	1981	1982	1983	1984	1985	1986
Defense Share of GNP[a]	5.2	5.8	6.2	6.0	6.2	6.2
Share of Personnel and Operations Expenses in Defense Budget Authority[b]	59.6	56.3	53.6	52.6	50.8	50.7
Share of Investment in Defense Budget Authority[c]	38.1	41.9	45.0	45.6	46.6	47.8

[a]Based on annual outlays. NATO definitions for outlays are broader than the
definition used here. For example, by NATO definition in 1983 the United States
allocated 7.0 percent of GNP to defense.

[b]This includes funds obligated for personnel (active and retired), maintenance, and
operations. Roughly forty-seven percent of this category goes to personnel outlays
(67.8 billion dollars in 1985 out of 145.6 billion dollars).

[c]This includes procurement, installation construction, research, development, and
testing.
Source: Caspar W. Weinberger, *Annual Report to the Congress, Fiscal Year 1987*
(Washington, D.C.: U.S. Government Printing Office, 1986), pp. 313, 315.

The size of the defense cuts in the projected five year program are
staggering. The $300 billion in cuts from earlier plans imposed in 1985 is
the equivalent of the loss of a full year of defense spending. Although there
is considerable debate over the ultimate impact of the Gramm-Rudman
reforms on future defense outlays, it is increasingly clear that even the
current levels of lower projected defense outlays will be difficult to sustain.
Without a tax increase, further cuts seem inevitable, and thus far the
Reagan Administration has remained firmly opposed to any such increases.

The shift in economic strategy to eliminate the deficit will place the
United States in a position somewhat similar to the situation West Germany
faced in the early 1980s. West Germany chose to protect its perceived
social balance by cutting defense proportionally with other programs. That
decision clearly imposed costs in reduced defense capabilities, but it did
not force a fundamental review of strategic priorities. If the United States
chooses to reduce the pace of military spending, and it seems inevitable
now that it will do so, it will face serious questions on the strategic

implications of the level and composition of defense outlays. In that climate of fundamental review of strategic priorities, perceptions of Alliance burden-bearing and burden-sharing will take on new importance.

Burden-Sharing

The preceding sections have suggested that economic disputes are apt to pose larger problems for the Alliance in the future. In addition, the nature of current economic problems will impose fiscal constraints in the near term that will inevitably constrain the growth in real defense outlays below the levels achieved in the early 1980s. Thus the Alliance in general, and the United States in particular, will face difficult strategic choices in an atmosphere that could become highly confrontational. In this climate, arguments about relative contributions to common Alliance objectives could become even more divisive and might even lead to fundamental reconsiderations of national roles in NATO. The question of how these trends can best be managed is discussed in the last two sections of this paper. First, this section will examine the difficulties of applying the burden-sharing concept to the Alliance, review the shortcomings of many burden-sharing measures, and suggest areas where the burden-sharing approach may be useful.

Difficulties in Applying the Burden-Sharing Concept

The pursuit of national interests imposes economic, social, political, and military burdens on a state. Consideration of the constraints imposed by those burdens contributes to the definition of the specific objectives that are ultimately pursued. Cooperation with other states in an alliance system makes some objectives more attainable and changes both the level and the composition of national burdens.

These interactions make a clear definition of national burdens very difficult. For example, NATO clearly permits both the United States and the Federal Republic of Germany to achieve jointly goals that neither could achieve alone. The Alliance may or may not increase the burden of defense spending, depending on what one assumes about national objectives and policies in the absence of the Alliance, but it clearly changes the structure of defense outlays. It also changes the distribution of political, economic, and social burdens. Cooperation with other Alliance members helps to achieve some national objectives, but it also risks the subordination of other unique national interests.

Estimates of relevant burdens quite naturally depend on the perspective taken in the evaluation. Each member of NATO feels its own set of burdens, some imposed or redistributed by membership in the Alliance, and some that would still exist without the Alliance. The Federal Republic is "burdened" by its location, its history, and the perceived fragility of its social and political cohesion, for example, as well as its defense outlays, just as the United States is burdened by global economic, political, and military interests that flowed from the course of post-war events, as well as its military budget.

If one seeks to understand national defense policies, all of these burdens are relevant. But this perspective is not very useful in assessing the equitable distribution of burdens in meeting common objectives from an Alliance viewpoint. Contributions to these Alliance objectives are most appropriately measured not by the domestic economic, political and social burdens of national defense spending, but by outputs of integrated military, economic, and political capabilities that contribute to deterrence and Alliance influence. The correct measure of the burden of Alliance membership is not the level of all burdens imposed by the pursuit of national interests, but changes in the level and composition of those burdens based on differences between Alliance and national priorities and requirements.

This precise concept of Alliance burden sharing is, unfortunately, virtually impossible to evaluate in practice, because it is inherently counterfactual. The baseline for evaluation would be an estimate of what Allies would do in the absense of the Alliance, and that baseline could never be established. As a result, the analyst is forced back on a series of proxy measures of Alliance burdens that are very unsatisfying.

The first line of retreat is to accept estimates of total national efforts as measures of contribution. This is misleading not only because the change in effort caused by the Alliance is more relevant, but also because measures of effort routinely focus on inputs of narrowly defined defense outlays. Contributions to Alliance objectives are more appropriately measured by outputs of integrated military, economic, and political capabilities that contribute to deterrence and Alliance influence. As the next section indicates, even those who understand these points frequently find it expedient to embroider political debate with narrow measures of burden sharing that are only indirectly related to broader Alliance objectives.

Measurement

The most widely cited measures of Alliance contributions are, understandably, based on ease of measurement rather than relevance. Economic contributions, in aid to less prosperous countries on NATO's southern tier for example, or political contributions, such as making and following through on commitments to deploy intermediate range nuclear forces, can be enumerated, but they are often impossible to measure in quantitative terms. Similarly, outputs such as integrated capabilities to communicate and resupply forces in the event of hostilities, are harder to measure than numbers of soldiers or tanks, and hence they receive little attention from many analysts. The inputs of defense outlays are far easier to measure and aggregate, even though they are often poor measures of the ultimate output of integrated defense capability. The unfortunate result is that burden-sharing debates often center on one of the least relevant measures of national contribution.

Of course one would hope that over time there would be some correlation between defense outlays and defense capabilities. It is certainly true that this should be the case in the long run, if reports of "defense" outlays are limited to appropriate categories of expenditure, if actual outlays are adjusted to take into account the changing prices of defense inputs, and if the efficiency of converting defense inputs to outputs remains relatively constant. Even then, however, the figures would only provide a sense of the rate of change in defense capability, not a measure of the level of capability. Moreover, if the financial data of different countries were aggregated we would have even less confidence that changes in the totals were closely correlated with changes in defense capabilities. These problems are widely understood by NATO planners who rely more heavily on the force goals process in gauging changes in capabilities than on levels of aggregate defense spending. The reality is, however, that political actors frequently do place a great deal of emphasis on short-term changes in the financial data.

Asymmetries

Measurements of relative contributions are easier when national forces are similar and more difficult when force structures diverge. Different capabilities must be weighted, based on assessments of their relative importance, to produce estimates of total contributions. Those assessments of the relative importance of nuclear and conventional ground, air, and naval forces depend, in turn, on complex judgments on appropriate Alliance strategies and operational doctrines. If two countries have similar force structures, such as the United Kingdom and France with a full range of nuclear and conventional forces, comparisons of defense effort will be less sensitive to the weights assigned to different capabilities. Comparisons of the United Kingdom and West Germany, with no national nuclear forces and much smaller relative naval strength, will depend heavily on the perceived importance of different capabilities. To the extent that financial outlays may be used as a measure of changes in defense capability, the aggregation problem is solved by using the relative costs of different systems. As we have seen, however, there are numerous problems in using the available financial data, and realistic assessments of relative contributions do depend on a far more complex process of evaluating progress toward common force goals.

Conflicting Assessments of West German Contributions: An Illustration

At the highest level, estimates of West German burden-sharing must assess the pattern of European defense policy that might have developed if the Federal Republic had not played such a vital role in NATO. The alternative baseline for comparison is open, of course, to wide speculation, but it is clear that West German participation was and remains the political and military foundation of the Alliance. As discussed in earlier chapters, to meet the threat from the East effectively, the European Allies had to find a way to permit the rearmament of West Germany without posing an unacceptable threat to its neighbors, and to provide a credible link between potential hostilities in Europe and the U.S. strategic deterrent. The United States needed to insure that there would be sufficient military strength in Europe to make the threat of a strategic response credible to the East and politically acceptable at home. The forward deployment of U.S. forces in Germany, coupled with a strong West German conventional force contribution, made it possible to manage these complex military and political problems. By deploying forces forward along the inter-German boundary, the domestic political costs in Germany of rearmament were held at acceptable levels. The eventual development of the strategy of flexible response, deterring the outbreak of hostilities in any form by maintaining the capability to respond at any level, was sufficiently vague and sensible to seal the trans-Atlantic bargain.

Retreating to the second level of burden-sharing, evaluation from the perspective of total effort, it is clear that national contributions to the Alliance obviously cannot be evaluated solely in terms of military outlays or even military capabilities. The German penchant for European approaches to economic, political, and military policy has provided further cement for binding the Alliance together. German support for the European Economic Community, its leadership in northern Europe, its special relationship with France, and its preference for the coproduction of military systems, have made it a positive force for military as well as political and economic integration. Special West German interests in Eastern Europe and in trade with the Soviet Union have added a more controversial dimension to its role in the Alliance, but have, arguably, on balance added to the available policy options for dealing with the East.

Even in the more limited terms of defense inputs the German contribution to NATO has been impressive. The Federal Republic has already, in peacetime, assigned all of its combat forces, except for its twelve home defense brigades in the Territorial Army, to NATO. The *Bundeswehr* provides roughly fifty percent of NATO's Central European ground forces, fifty percent of its ground air defense, and thirty percent of its combat aircraft. The West German conscription system, requiring that virtually all men serve in the armed forces, has held down manpower costs and provided a pool of roughly 700,000 reservists who can be activated on short notice. This conscript system provides a pool of highly qualified soldiers and also serves as a highly visible, and socially costly, symbol of the depth of German commitment to its own and NATO's defense. The West German government also considers the allocation of over one million acres of land for military bases and the impact of military maneuvers and airspace use as major contributions to the Alliance.[9]

Contributions, however, are difficult to assess in absolute terms. The German contribution is impressive and obviously important, but how does it compare with the contributions of other Allies? Comparisons typically rely on standardization based on measures of size, such as population, on measures of ability to contribute, such as gross output or per capita income, or on measures of change over time, such as real increases in defense outlays. These statistics produce a more complicated assessment of Germany's contribution, and the way in which that contribution has changed over time.

The relevant data are assembled each spring in the U.S. Secretary of Defense's *Report on Allied Contributions to the Common Defense*, which is required by the Congress. Standardization based on measures of size places German contributions in the top half of the Alliance. West German per capita defense outlays of $360 in 1983 were the fifth highest in NATO, behind the United States, the United Kingdom, Norway and France, rankings which were the same as in 1971.[10] Germany's 1983 active duty military and civilian manpower total of 671,100 placed it fourth in absolute numbers, but seventh as a share of total population.[11] Measures of ability to pay place Germany a bit lower. It ranked third in armored division equivalents provided and third in combat aircraft, but twelfth in both categories based on one measure of ability to contribute.[12] With 3.4 percent of national output allocated to defense in 1983, the same percentage as in 1971, Germany ranked sixth in the Alliance, with Greece and Turkey moving ahead in the rankings compared with per capita spending and Norway dropping behind.[13] The final criterion, changes in real defense outlays over time, suggests a mixed pattern, as shown in Table 5.3. From 1971 to 1978 real defense outlays grew at an average rate of 2.9 percent per year (eighth highest in NATO), as U.S. outlays fell by 2.7 percent per year, and as a result the German share of total NATO outlays grew from just over six percent in 1970 to over 10 percent in 1980. From 1982 to 1986, however, West German outlays remained virtually constant, as U.S. outlays rose by an average of 6.9 percent per year, and the German share of NATO outlays dropped to under six percent of NATO outlays.

The statistical errors involved in producing such measures of contribution make specific rankings and annual variations suspect. The numbers do, however, suggest some broad conclusions concerning trends in West Germany's military contribution. In total terms, Germany clearly provides a vital share of Alliance military capabilities, particularly armored and air forces dedicated to the Central Region. Those contributions have been roughly proportionate to measures of Germany's ability to pay, although several measures of total contribution place the Federal Republic behind the United States, the United Kingdom and France, all of whom have nuclear forces and larger naval forces. More recent patterns in real defense outlays, however, suggest that the share of Alliance spending and defense capabilities contributed by the Federal Republic have been declining.

Emphasis on Alliance Capabilities

Measures of national inputs to the Alliance, whether financial outlays, personnel, weapons systems, or even maneuver units, are not very satisfying standards for gauging contributions to overall deterrence and defense capabilities. Military planners prefer to think in terms of efforts to meet identified Alliance shortcomings. Unfortunately, one of the Alliance's major problems has been in this critical area of modifying domestic defense priorities to meet common requirements.

NATO Force Planning

NATO force planning proceeds in a two year cycle of first establishing broad Ministerial Guidance to set defense priorities, and then setting specific force goals for each country based on agreed requirements and assessments of the country's current economic situation. Force goals are given priorities based on the time required for completion, rather than relative importance. The goals are established through a series of "Trilateral" reviews, conducted with each country by the international staff, the international military staff, and representatives of the major NATO commanders, and "Multilateral Reviews," which involve representatives of all the NATO countries. The goals are typically set to include a "challenge," somewhat above the country's expected level of defense outlays.

The force goals process correctly focuses on Alliance needs and provides a useful emphasis on integrated requirements, but the process has been criticized in its ability to really influence national plans. Unfortunately, the Trilateral and Multilateral Reviews have no binding authority, and ultimate force goals are only voluntary targets for the members. As a result, force goals in practice place heavy emphasis on national force plans and expected defense outlays. In addition, military commanders have consistently opposed setting force goal priorities that reflect relative importance, because they feel that all of the goals are essential. In their view, setting priorities might simply provide national political authorities with an excuse for focusing only on the highest priority goals. Finally, the force goals process is limited to budget plans for the next five years, while national plans typically encompass much longer planning periods. Thus the force goals are imposed on longer term plans that have already been made and are difficult to change.

Joint Programs

Joint programs, where countries actually pool their funds to procure or operate agreed systems or facilities, come the closest to the efficient allocation of funds to meet established NATO priorities. If NATO had the ability to tax its members and allocate funds as it saw fit, joint programs would play a far more prominent role in Alliance planning. Unfortunately, the sacrifice of national control inherent in these programs guarantees that they will remain a small part of total NATO outlays.

The NATO infrastructure program, designed to provide common funding for operating facilities that would become available to all Alliance members during hostilities, provides, for example, airfields, naval bases, storage and communications facilities, and wartime headquarters. Such projects provide enormous benefits to NATO by targeting funds on agreed priorities based on perceived wartime requirements, but unfortunately they constitute less than .3 percent of NATO defense spending. The requirement for unanimity, the strict limitation to projects which would be available to all members in wartime, and the trade-off with nationally sponsored construction projects in domestic budgets, currently limit the scope for expansion in infrastructure programs.

NATO infrastructure expenditures have not kept pace with the growing complexity of command, control, and communications, with the needs for sheltering combat aircraft, or with the requirements for storage facilities to replace potential combat losses. The 1984 Nunn Amendment called for the withdrawal of some U.S. forces if these problems were not addressed. The infrastructure program received a large boost in December of 1984, when the NATO ministers agreed to an increased ceiling of eight billion dollars over six years to facilitate the deployment of new units, provide better support facilities, and provide more shelters for combat aircraft.[14] Nonetheless, the infrastructure program provides only marginal adjustments in Alliance outlays, and national priorities continue to dominate the allocation of available resources.

Initiatives to Increase Alliance Efficiency

Frustration with the shortcomings of the normal force goals planning process has produced a series of "out-of-cycle" initiatives, typically with strong U.S. sponsorship, aimed at focusing resources on the most urgent priorities. The Long Term Defense Program (LTDP), adopted in May of 1978 at the urging of the Carter Administration, established ten specific action programs focused on mid-term planning through 1984 and longer-term targets through 1995. The programs dealt with readiness, air defense, electronic warfare, maritime posture, command-control-communications, reinforcement, reserve mobilization, consumer logistics, rationalization, and medium- and long-term theater nuclear-force programs. The initiative did lead to a number of new committees with reports that addressed problems beyond the normal force goals process, but in the final analysis it did not generate additional funding for those programs or change the way the normal planning cycle worked. In retrospect, the LTDP's legacy was primarily frustration with out-of-cycle initiatives that created committees and reports, but little help in generating or focusing defense spending.

More recently a special initiative attempted to identify emerging technologies that would be most useful in implementing the flexible response strategy, so that national budgets and research efforts could be focused on the most promising technology areas. This effort produced a requirement for a Conceptual Military Framework that would be useful in identifying, among other things, resource priorities for different phases of potential conflict. In particular, calls for capabilities to attack second echelon follow-on forces with sophisticated conventional weapons had to be compared with needs to repel first echelon forces. In December of 1984 Defense

Ministers called on the Secretary General and the Defense Planning Committee (DPC) to make a coherent effort to improve conventional forces, and the NATO military authorities were directed to develop a Conceptual Military Framework. In May of 1985 the DPC approved a Conventional Defense Initiative, and directed a review of force goals to establish priorities in specified areas.[15] The new initiative has the advantage of working through the normal force goals process and establishing clearer priorities based on an accepted military framework. It has the disadvantage, however, of emphasizing priorities for procurement at a time when funds will be limited. In addition, many of the most pressing problems require not simply additional funding but fundamental changes in the interaction of NATO and national budget planning and better coordination of logistical and communications systems. If the Conventional Defense Initiative can develop more innovative approaches to those problems, it may make a long term contribution to the primary problem of coordinating largely independent national planning systems.

Bilateral Cooperation

The members of NATO interact with each other in a complex set of bilateral relationships that can often be used to reinforce Alliance objectives. For example, from 1961 to 1975 West Germany offset the balance of payments impact of the forward deployment of U.S. forces through the purchase of U.S. military equipment and treasury securities, and in 1976 the Federal Republic paid for the construction of facilities for a U.S. brigade newly deployed in northern Germany. In 1982, the West German and U.S. governments reached an important agreement for the Wartime Host Nation Support of U.S. forces. The United States agreed, in the event of hostilities, to reinforce its troops in Germany with six divisions and proportionate air forces within ten days. The Federal Republic agreed, in turn, to provide specified civilian resources in the event of war, and to establish by 1987 a support organization, which in peacetime would be manned by a cadre of some 1,500 personnel and in wartime would be augmented by some 90,000 reservists. The initial combat support and combat service support units have been formed, and the rest of the reserve structure should be in place by 1989.[16] This concept, allocating reserve forces to assume specific Alliance responsibilities in the event of hostilities, shows enormous promise as a technique for developing a more efficient division of labor over different Alliance tasks.

Issues in the Composition of Defense Spending

The strategy of flexible response demands a wide range of capabilities at the strategic nuclear, intermediate nuclear, tactical nuclear, and conventional levels. The strategy seeks not controlled escalation, or even a raised nuclear threshold, but rather a range of capabilities designed to create such uncertainty as to the form of possible response, that any threat or actual outbreak of hostilities will be deterred. The challenge at the strategic nuclear level has been to insure sufficient survivability of ground and sea-based ICBM's and manned bombers through force modernization, while pressing negotiations for verifiable reductions in nuclear arsenals. At the intermediate nuclear force (INF) level, negotiations in Geneva failed to reduce Soviet deployment of the SS-20 missile, and the Alliance, following its 1979 dual-track decision, proceeded with partially offsetting deployments of Pershing II and ground-launched cruise missiles. By early 1985 the Soviet Union had deployed a total of 414 SS-20's, and the Alliance had countered with 134 Pershing II and cruise missiles, including 54 Pershing II's in the Federal Republic of Germany.[17] The ability of the Alliance to proceed with those deployments, despite strong opposition from small but vocal minorities, was a major test for the strategy of flexible response. As discussed in Chapter 7, these NATO deployments contributed to the successful negotiation of a "zero-zero" INF agreement.

The INF debate focused attention on the relative roles of nuclear and conventional forces in Alliance strategy, at the same time that General Bernard Rogers, former SACEUR, was arguing that, in the face of a major Warsaw Pact offensive, he would only be able to sustain a purely conventional defense for a matter of "days," while the Soviet Union could sustain a conventional attack for "weeks or months."[18] This discussion produced a series of studies on how conventional capabilities might be improved. General Roger's own prescription was to increase the target rate of growth for real defense outlays from three to four percent per year, and to focus the increment on new technologies that could identify, attack, and disrupt the second-echelon of Pact follow-on forces with sophisticated conventional weapon systems.[19] Such an approach would make forward defense more practical by containing first-echelon forces, limiting Pact reinforcement, and providing time for U.S. reinforcements to arrive. A collaborative effort of Europeans and Americans published under the title *Strengthening Conventional Deterrence in Europe: Proposals for the 1980s* generally supported SACEUR's position and called for the procurement of a series of advanced systems at an estimated cost of some $10 to $30 billion over ten years.[20]

Other studies focused on ways of containing first echelon forces with improved barrier planning, more emphasis on mobile armored reserves, improved peacetime dispositions of forces, the innovative use of counter-attacks on a highly fluid battlefield, revised missions for reserve forces, better use of light anti-tank systems, improved ground-air coordination, or various combinations of those elements. As an illustration of this flurry of reform advice, the Defense Committee of the Bundestag sorted through the testimony of 26 experts in the winter of 1983/1984, who apparently advocated everything from the renunciation of nuclear weapons to the abandonment of the principle of forward defense.[21]

Constraints on Improvements in Defense

In the midst of this renewed debate over operational doctrine it is important to review the substantial constraints that will limit any procurement, and manpower constraints faced by both the Federal Republic and the United States will clearly limit the range of feasible options.

West German Constraints

Issues of operational doctrine are typically subordinate to the political and economic factors that determine the constraints on available tactics and resources. Proposals for operational reform rarely provide options for more effectiveness given current constraints, but instead provide arguments for the removal of a current constraint. The political and economic constraints facing West Germany provide virtually no strategic alternatives to its current defense posture, and very little flexibility at the level of operational doctrine.

Economic and Political Constraints

West Germany is prevented by the Basic Law from deploying its forces outside of Europe. The constitution could, of course, be amended, but the legal limitation reflects a broader political consensus that Germany's history effectively rules out such deployments. Similarly, national inclination and Germany's unique position in the Alliance argue against the development of nationally-controlled nuclear forces. Indeed the Paris agreements of 1954 made German entry into NATO contingent on its renunciation of the manufacture or possession of chemical, nuclear, or biological weapons, and on its placing all military units under NATO command. Political factors as well as military realities constrain West Germany to its role as a non-nuclear, European power.

Geography further constrains strategic options within Europe. With major population centers so close to the inter-German border, a strategy of forward defense has been a political necessity. That posture requires a large number of active ground forces deployed in reasonable proximity to initial battle positions, a force structure which inevitably leads to a relatively large army equipped to withstand initial assaults by armored-heavy Warsaw Pact forces. Forward defense also requires emphasis on the early air battle, both with fighter aircraft and ground air defense systems. In addition, with little expected time for mobilization, forward defense requires reserve forces that are trained and equipped for early commitment. With limited resources, and priorities so clearly tied to the ground and air battle on the Central Front, naval forces have assumed a role limited to Baltic defense and North Sea security. Departures from the traditional allocation of roughly 70 percent to the Army, 20 percent to the Air Force, and 10 percent to the Navy, would be difficult to achieve.

More flexibility could be achieved through greater resource allocations to defense, particularly in the substitution of new high-technology systems for scarce manpower. As mentioned early, however, the Federal Republic will be fortunate to maintain its real defense expenditures at current levels in the near term, and may even face real defense cuts. Substitutions of sophisticated systems for manpower are unlikely, even though manpower costs are expected to rise substantially.

Production Constraints

Even if funds were available, shifts in procurement patterns are difficult to achieve. The 15 year *Bundeswehr* Plan integrates requirements for replacement capacity, and projections for new technologies into an integrated procurement plan.[22] Given the scale of defense outlays, procurement is typically dominated by a few major weapon systems such as the Leopard-2 main battle tank and the Tornado fighter aircraft. Other systems vie for priorities based on estimates of major deficiencies. By 1987, for example, Leopard procurement should be complete and army emphasis will shift to the artillery, before focusing on anti-armor weapons in 1994.[23] Such plans obviously require sensitive balancing among different services, and within services among different branches, and procurement patterns are therefore very difficult to change based on revised assessments of operational doctrine.

The dominance of major weapon systems in procurement planning makes current negotiations for the production of a new European Fighter Aircraft (EFA) for the 1990s extremely important. The EFA is expected to replace the F-4 and the F-104 as the front line air defense into the next century. The aircraft will be built by the Panavia consortium for the mainframe (British Aerospace, German MBB, and Aeritalia) and the Turbo-Union consortium for the engines (British Rolls-Royce, German MTU, and Italian Fiat Aviazionc), apparently with some Spanish and French participation as well. The total bill for the EFA is expected to be roughly fourteen billion dollars.[24] The relevant point here is that decisions are being made now that will determine budget structures through the end of the century. Given the complexity of international production and purchase agreements, there will be little flexibility in the future for short-term deviations from those plans.

Manpower Constraints

As shown in Table 5.6, the Federal Republic currently plans to mobilize a wartime force of roughly 1,250,000 military personnel, which would be drawn from an active force of some 495,000 and a reserve force of about 755,000. Over 40 percent of the active force is composed of conscripts completing the mandatory 15 months of service, another 40 percent includes temporary career volunteers who enlist for longer periods of service, and the remaining 20 percent form the core of regular officers and non-commissioned officers. This structure insures that a large pool of conscripts will be reverting to reserve status each year, sustaining a very large reserve structure. Roughly 6,000 reservists are on active duty for training at any

TABLE 5.6 Authorized Peacetime Strength and Anticipated Wartime Strength of the Armed Forces of the Federal Republic of Germany, 1984 and the 1990s

	1984	1990s
Bundeswehr Active Strength		
Conscripts	219,000[a]	206,000[b]
Temporary Career Volunteers	206,133	160,000
Regulars	<u>63,867</u>	<u>90,000</u>
Subtotal Active Force	489,000	456,000
Reserves on Active Duty	6,000[c]	15,000[d]
Men in Standby Readiness Counted in Active Strength	--	--
Total Reserves Counted in the Active Force	6,000	39,000
Total Active Force	495,000	495,000
Reserves in Mobilization Plans (Not on Active Duty)	756,000[e]	813,000[e]
Wartime Strength	1,251,000[f]	1,308,000[f]

[a]Conscripts required to serve for 15 months.
[b]Conscripts required to serve for 18 months beginning in 1989.
[c]Permits annual training in 2-4 week increments of 180,000 reservists.
[d]Permits annual training of an estimated 400,000 reservists.
[e]Based on mobilization planning for 762,000 less 6,000 on active duty in 1984. The estimate for the 1990s adds 90,000 for the Wartime Host Nation Support increment that will be in place by 1987 and subtracts those reserves moved to the active force.
[f]The *White Paper* estimate is 1,270,000 for 1984 and 1,340,000 in the 1990s, apparently based on individual reserves not counted in "plans for assignment that must be filled by mobilization."
Source: White Paper 1985: The Situation and the Development of the Federal Armed Forces (Bonn: Federal Minister of Defense, 1985), pp. 236-238, 255, 399.

time (permitting the training of some 180,000 reservists each year in two to four-week increments), and they are counted in the active force figures.

Unfortunately, the number of conscripts required to sustain the current force structure, 225,000 each year, will exceed the available pool in 1987, and by the late 1990's there would be an annual deficit of 100,000 per year. This decline in the manpower pool will also make it difficult to attract the current number of temporary career volunteers at current pay levels. The alternatives to compensate for the shortfall would be to reduce the force structure, to increase the length of conscript service, to expand the pool by limiting conscientious objectors or accepting women, to increase the percentage of temporary career volunteers and regulars through wage incentives, or to increase the readiness level of reserve forces. As indicated in Table 5.6, the planned solution includes most of these elements, except for permitting women to serve in the armed forces or increasing the number of temporary career volunteers.

Beginning in 1989, conscripts are now required to serve for 18 months instead of 15 months. Despite a six percent reduction in the number of conscripts in the 1990s, the increased period of service will actually increase the conscript force by almost 13 percent. That increase, and a 40 percent expansion in the regular force, will compensate for an expected 22 percent reduction in the number of temporary career volunteers. The current balanced structure of a small regular force, a fairly large group of volunteers on extended duty, and an equal group of new recruits, will slowly give way to a structure with a larger core of experienced leaders and a larger share of recruits. Even with these adjustments, the active force would drop from 489,000 to 456,000. To offset that reduction, the number of reserves on active duty will be expanded by 9,000 (permitting the training of some 400,000 reservists each year), and 24,000 reserves will be placed in a heightened readiness status.

Although the active force of the 1990s will still claim 495,000 men, it will be a much different force from the one that exists today. Far more emphasis will be placed on the ability of an expanded core of regulars to mold conscripts quickly into effective units, and reserves will play a more vital role in the overall force structure. Under these constraints, the Federal Republic will be hard-pressed to sustain its current active force structure, much less expand to meet new NATO missions.

Current West German Defense Options

Current West German defense options are clearly limited by these severe constraints. At the strategic level, there are no viable alternatives to the commitment of military forces to NATO control in support of the strategy of flexible response implemented through a forward defense posture. At the level of operational doctrine, Germany faces the problem of developing doctrine to match current constraints. The prospects for generating additional resources to support new operational doctrine, no matter how brilliantly conceived, are remote. One would expect that future debates over operational doctrine will concern the best ways of reacting to resource and manpower limitations, particularly innovative ways of training and employing reserve forces.

The expected shortages may partly explain heightened interest in new technologies that will permit the flexible emplacement of obstacles, conserve on front line forces, and support the formation of mobile reserves.[25] The key point in this line of thought is that barriers should not be erected prior to hostilities as part of a "Maginot" concept to channel attacks into planned defensive positions, but to react to changes on the battlefield as they occur in order to mass forces for effective counter-attacks.[26] Such new approaches interpret forward defense as a broad principle that still permits corps commanders to organize a mobile defense within their designated areas.[27]

The prospects of gaining additional defense capabilities from available resources are remote. West Germany will undoubtedly continue to support co-production arrangements to sustain its defense industrial base, but the prospects for lowering unit costs through such arrangements are remote. Participation with the United States and others in the development of the Strategic Defense Initiative does hold out the promise of access to emerging technologies with potential applications in a variety of defense and commercial ventures, but such prospects are clearly for the long term. In the near term, the real options appear to be limited to developing a closer convergence of operational doctrine with pressing resource constraints.

United States Constraints

The United States is also constrained by political, economic, procurement, and manpower constraints, but the nature of the constraints is different and the range of available options is much broader. At the strategic level, the United States will face difficult choices on the relative priorities to be accorded to strategic and conventional modernization and to different regions, particularly as those priorities influence the allocation of forces in the United States to potential sequences of reinforcement. At the level of NATO operational doctrine, the central issue is how to balance the desire to employ emerged and emerging technology against second echelon forces with the need to contain first echelon forces.

Economic and Political Constraints

In contrast to Germany, the United States faces a series of strategic options. As a superpower, first priority must go to the deterrence of any nuclear exchange, and this priority has been reflected in the development of the triad of ground-launched ICBM's, submarine-launched ballistic missiles, and manned bombers. Second priority has consistently gone to support of the strategy of flexible response implemented through forward defense in Europe. Lower priority has been given to the possibility of conflict in other regions, despite the fact that hostilities in other regions are more probable, or to the possibility of opening second fronts in support of potential conflict in Europe. Over the past decade, however, more attention has been focused on the possibility that the United States might be forced to face a sophisticated opponent outside of Europe. The development of a Central Command and a Rapid Deployment Force grew first out of concern for possible Persian Gulf contingencies, but the spread of modern weapons systems throughout the world, illustrated by the conflict over the Faulkland Islands, suggests that substantial forces may be needed for other contingencies as well. The development of lighter, more strategically mobile forces, does mean that U.S. forces will be more capable of rapid reinforcement in Europe, but it also suggests that those forces can be used for contingencies in other regions as well.[28]

Choices among those strategic options, however, are highly constrained. The forward deployment of U.S. forces in Europe has been the cornerstone of NATO strategy by making forward defense feasible, and the risk of nuclear confrontation remote enough to be politically acceptable. Unilateral reductions in U.S. force levels, particularly in the face of clear improvements in Warsaw Pact capabilities, could lead to fundamental military, political, and economic realignments in Europe. There are always optimists available to argue that the European Allies would be forced to make up for any U.S. force withdrawals, but the risks in such arguments are enormous. Similarly, efforts to negotiate with the European Allies to compensate for U.S initiatives elsewhere through expanded European efforts, for example, on the Central Front, assume first that there are available European resources for such an effort, and second that the potential adjustments in resources would be desirable. It is very likely, however, that such arguments would encourage shifts in European resources away from ground forces on the Central Front by raising the importance of global missions in the United Kingdom and France, and encouraging, for example, an expansion of West German naval forces to take up the slack in the North Sea.[29] In short, the United States has strong political, economic, and military ties to Europe, and any realignment of strategic priorities would produce great uncertainty as to the future of those relationships.

In West Germany, economic constraints reinforce political constraints in narrowing the range of defense options. In the United States, economic constraints may actually force difficult strategic choices, despite a political reluctance to face the uncertainties involved. As noted above, after 1986 it will be difficult to even sustain the current level of real defense outlays, and real cuts are not out of the question. The Gramm-Rudman proposals may well confront President Reagan with a very difficult choice between tax increases and real defense cuts, and it is not at all clear how such a dilemma would be resolved. The pace of real increases in the first half of the decade has done a great deal to improve U.S. defense capabilities that had eroded in the preceding decade, but those increases also permitted a number of new initiatives without forcing a review of strategic priorities. In the face of real defense cuts, difficult strategic judgments will clearly be required.

Procurement Constraints

Several long-term procurement decisions, made during the defense buildup of the early 1980s, will now limit U.S. flexibility in adjusting resources to match strategic priorities in the face of new resource constraints. At the strategic offensive level, funds have been committed for the MX missile, the development of a small, mobile ICBM, the deployment of the B-1B bomber late in the 1980s, development of the Stealth bomber for deployment in the 1990s, and deployment of the Trident II submarine. In addition, the Strategic Defense Initiative combines development of known technologies for intercepting and destroying ballistic missile reentry vehicles with research into new directed energy devices that may be capable of engaging the missiles soon after launch. The modernization and expansion of strategic forces, by one estimate, cost some $40 billion from fiscal 1981 to 1984, and is expected to cost an additional $80 billion from 1985 to 1989.[30]

At the conventional force level there has been an impressive effort to modernize and expand the fleet to "600 deployable battle force ships, including 15 deployable carriers, 100 nuclear-powered attack submarines, a one-third increase in amphibious lift capacity, and expanded support forces."[31] At the end of fiscal year 1985, 541 deployable battle force ships were in place and authorized expansion, including three aircraft carriers and fourteen cruisers, were expected to bring the force to slightly over 600 ships by 1989;[32] however, the projected retirement in FY 1989 of 16 older ships will delay the attainment of that objective.

The Air Force program for fiscal years 1986-1990 emphasizes improvements in combat readiness and modernization of active and reserve components with the purchase of some 1,284 F-14, F-15, F-16, F/A-18 and AV-88 aircraft.[33] The Army program calls for a wide range of modernization programs including the procurement of some 70 M1 Abrams tanks per month through the early 1990's and the acquisition of some 6,882 Bradley Fighting Vehicles in the same period.[34] Such production schedules can, of course, always be adjusted for new priorities, but such adjustments invariably increase the unit costs and ultimately the total program costs of the weapon systems.

The pace and structure of the defense buildup of the early 1980s produced obligated patterns of future procurement that stretch well into the 1990's. In this sense, prior procurement decisions reduce the flexibility that is available to react to future budget constraints. The longest-term commitments have been made for naval and strategic nuclear forces. Hence future budget constraints are apt to fall most heavily on the types of forces that have traditionally been allocated to the Central Front in Europe.

Manpower Constraints

The military services recruit roughly 330,000 enlisted men and women per year (Army 142,000, Navy 83,000, Air Force 61,000, Marine Corps 42,000) based on a current authorized active strength of just over 2.1 million and recent retention rates.[35] The number of required recruits might rise by some 25,000 per year through 1990, although projected increases in the total strengths of the Air Force and Navy must still survive Congressional review. In 1985 the 310,000 recruits came primarily from a population pool of 7.2 million men between the ages of sixteen and nineteen.[36] Thus the U.S. manpower problem is one of attracting sufficient quality recruits from a relatively large pool at acceptable levels of compensation.

Note that the Federal Republic of Germany currently requires 225,000 conscripts each year to fill an active force of 489,000, or roughly 46 percent of the force. The United States volunteer force, with longer terms for initial enlistments, requires only 330,000 recruits for an active force of 2.1 million, or roughly 16 percent of the force. As discussed earlier, German requirements will actually exceed the total available manpower pool in the near future, but U.S requirements are far below the available pool. The nature of the manpower problems facing the two countries are therefore very different.

The United States has already absorbed a substantial decline in the recruiting pool, from 8.2 million in 1981 to 7.2 million in 1985. The pool will remain relatively constant through 1989 (7.0 million), and then will decline to about 6.4 million 1992, before expanding back to the 1985 level by 1997.[37] These numbers obviously do not pose any absolute limits on the size of the military force, but they do suggest that the recruitment of quality volunteers may become more difficult.

The two most widely used measures of the quality of recruits, scores on the standardized Armed Forces Qualification Test (AFQT) and numbers of high school graduates, are clearly very indirect measures of ability to learn and apply military skills as part of a disciplined military team. Comparisons of the AFQT scores of recruits with the broader population pool do, however, provide some evidence of training potential. The possession of a high school diploma does not necessarily indicate anything about relative scholastic accomplishments, but it does seem to be a useful measure of perseverance and willingness to conform to group norms, traits that tend to correlate with performance in military units and ultimate retention. These measures of quality indicate a significant improvement in recruits between 1980 and 1984, despite a substantial decline in the recruiting pool.[38] More direct, although largely anecdotal, evidence of the performance of troops in the field tends to confirm this statistical record.

Quality variations have the most severe impact on the Army, since the Air Force and Navy have traditionally attracted a high quality enlisted force with relatively modest recruiting efforts. The sharp improvement in the composition of Army recruits from 1980 to 1984 may be attributed to a wide range of factors such as increases in relative military pay compared to the private sector, changes in national perceptions about military service, better targeting of pay incentives— the new GI bill and the Army College Fund are examples—on high-quality groups, and better allocation of recruiting resources. Whether or not these factors will continue to operate in the future is clearly open to question.

The Army's decision to hold its active strength at 781,000 will clearly limit pressure on future manpower pools, although the planned expansion in the Air Force and Navy could pose some problems. Backlogs of current recruits for the near term suggest that there will be no immediate quality problems. For the longer term, it will clearly become more difficult to sustain real compensation relative to civilian pay at current levels in the face of general budget austerity.

U.S. Defense Options

Although clear priorities are useful in making intelligent decisions on resource allocation, clear priorities also antagonize the losers. It is not at all surprising, therefore, that strategic priorities are typically only vaguely defined. In the face of the constraints outlined above, however, strategic choices will have to be faced, and the outcome of those choices will have enormous impacts on subordinate issues, such as the selection of appropriate operational doctrine in Europe.

Adjustments at the strategic level would certainly be possible by abandoning modernization of the entire triad of strategic offensive systems, and emphasizing, for example, the Trident and the cruise missile. Such a reversal is, however, implausible, given the funds that have already been committed for other systems. The Strategic Defense Initiative could be abandoned, or negotiated away, but that also seems highly unlikely given the key role that it has been given by President Reagan. As a result, strategic systems should continue to take a growing share of total defense outlays.

The real alternatives appear to be in the priorities assigned to different regions, particularly as those priorities relate to strategic mobility. This debate has been presented in terms of a "continental" or "coalition" strategy that would emphasize the key role of the forward deployment of forces in NATO, and a "maritime" strategy that would give more relative importance to other contingencies.[39] These are not stark alternatives, but issues of relative balance, and the different perspectives, and resource implications, have advocates in each of the services. The central questions relate to the desired size and structure of the Navy, the deployment and reinforcement responsibilities that will be given to ground units in the United States, and the relative importance of strategic lift and strategic mobility. The naval issue has essentially been settled by the obligation of funds for the 600-ship force, although some issues of manning this force remain. One of the most important remaining strategic judgments, then, relates to the priorities to be assigned to different types of Army forces.

Advocates of "deep attack" or "follow-on forces attack" argue for the need to begin production of new high-technology systems designed to locate and destroy second echelon forces on the Central Front. The key decision here is how long to press on with research and development, and when to shift to actual procurement. Advocates of greater strategic mobility, on the other hand, suggest that light forces will have more utility in a variety of possible contingencies, and that scarce resources should be targeted first on systems that increase the firepower and sustainability of those forces. The outcome of this decision on resource allocation will have a direct impact on the evolution of operational doctrine in NATO.

Resource Implications of Potential Revisions in NATO Operational Doctrine

There are two fundamental issues in the current debate over conventional operational doctrine for the Central Front. The first concerns the relative priority that is to be given to the attack of second echelon forces, given the simultaneous requirement to repel a first echelon attack that could conceivably be launched with very little warning. The outcome of this debate will influence procurement decisions and the missions assigned to air forces early in the battle. The second concerns the way in which forward defense should be implemented to defeat the first echelon attack. The key issues here are the acceptable depth of the battlefield, the requirement to form reserves for counterattacks, the disposition of allied forces, and the relative importance and structure of barrier planning. These issues tend to be somewhat less resource, but more politically, sensitive.

As noted earlier, these operational doctrine debates will be more heavily influenced by prior decisions on strategic priorities than by tactical considerations. Within those constraints, the issues of priorities given to different echelons and approaches to the first echelon battle must be treated together. Judgments on the ability to manage the immediate first echelon battle will inevitably influence the decision on whether or not resources can be freed for the early attack of second echelon forces.

Follow-On Forces Attack—The Deep Battle. Emerging and emerged technologies suggest that it may well be possible to identify targets far behind enemy front lines and destroy them with precision-guided conventional weapons. That capability would permit NATO forces to limit the Warsaw Pact's ability to exploit gaps created by first echelon units, and to buy time for mobilization and reinforcement. The development of such a capability would therefore be expected to improve the deterrence of any such Warsaw Pact attack.

General Bernard Roger's initial arguments in favor of follow-on forces attack (FOFA) suggested that substantial improvements in interdiction, war reserves, and electronic warfare could be accomplished with annual increases in Alliance real defense spending on the order of four percent per year over the period from 1983 to 1988.[40] That pace of expenditure would roughly correspond to the challenge level incorporated in the NATO force goals process. These estimates did not include research and development and procurement costs for the new generation of technologies that would make effective implementation of FOFA possible. Attack of Pact airfields might, for example, exploit new missiles (the Medium-Range-Air-to Surface-Missile and the CAM-40 missile are candidates) to deliver cratering munitions. The attack of tactical formations could be based on information from the joint surveillance and attack radar system (JSTARS) that was quickly processed by computers in tactical information centers and passed on to appropriate weapons systems. For example, submunition-bearing missiles from the joint tactical missile system (JTACMS) program might be launched to deliver acoustically-activated mines, infrared-seeking missiles, or radar-guided munitions to attack enemy systems.[41] There is little question that such technologies will ultimately be developed to the point where they can be reliably incorporated in operational systems, but there is a great deal of question about the current capabilities of such systems and productions costs.[42]

The resource question focuses on whether NATO should proceed with the procurement of systems that are currently available, or whether funds should be devoted to further research and development before systems are actually procured. This issue, in turn, hinges on estimates of NATO's current capability to contain first echelon forces and on forecasts of funds that will be available to procure conventional systems. The development of an acceptable Conceptual Military Framework is the key to resolving this fundamental issue of resource priorities.

Air-Land Battle. In the 1970s U.S. doctrine for fighting a conventional war on the Central Front was often criticized in West Germany as anticipating too hasty a withdrawal through a series of defensive positions, which were organized in depth, in what was labeled a war of attrition. Trading space for time to permit the arrival of reinforcements was seen, by many West Germans, as an unacceptable way of implementing forward defense.[43]

The development of the revised Air-Land Battle doctrine raised an opposite set of fears. The new doctrine called for exploitation of uncertainty on a highly mobile battlefield through more emphasis on counter-attacks, and through earlier priority in the use of air resources to support ground maneuvers. Early descriptions of the doctrine suggested that deep counter-attacks were envisioned. That prospect raised political fears of a new offensive strategy which might trigger counterproductive responses by the Warsaw Pact on the one hand, and which seemed unsupportable given available NATO resources on the other. Such fears have been quieted by greater understanding of the limited objectives envisioned by the Air-Land Battle doctrine, and indeed the emphasis on greater battlefield mobility and exploitation of counter-attacks is very consistent with emerging German doctrine.

There is considerable controversy, however, over how limited forces will be freed from responsibilities to maintain a stable front in order to mass forces for anticipated counter-attacks. German analysts stress the use of mines that would be emplaced through new technologies as the battle developed, a view that is consistent with political constraints on prior preparation of the battlefield. U.S analysts are more apt to discount those political constraints and to argue for the preparation of barriers and obstacles in advance of hostilities, so that limited forces can be freed from the outset to move quickly to possible avenues of attack.

The resource issues here concern the relative importance of different types of units—helicopters, light infantry, heavy infantry, armor—in more mobile defense, and the mix of the procurement of those systems, which are available now, with more sophisticated systems for deep attack, which will be available in the future. There is also a question of the appropriate role of reserve forces early in a potential conflict. Rather than using reserves for area defense of installations in the rear, or for replacements of active forces, more thought has been given to the early use of reserves to defend organized positions forward on the battlefield, thus freeing better trained and equipped active forces for more mobile responsibilities. Such alternatives may become more convincing as the manpower structure of West German forces shifts toward greater emphasis on reserves. The trade-off between political and resource constraints will also become increasingly important as the resource limitation becomes more binding.

Burden-Bearing and Burden-Sharing:
Risks and Opportunities

Recent trends in the conventional balance between NATO and the Warsaw Pact have not been favorable, despite rapid growth in defense outlays in the United States. There is an apparent consensus for expanding defense capabilities, based on recent NATO Ministerial pronouncements, but this depends on expanded resources for conventional forces, and such an expansion is highly unlikely. From the German perspective there is little near term flexibility in force structure, and indeed it will be difficult to maintain even the current level of active forces. Moreover, fiscal constraints will continue to limit defense outlays to roughly current levels in real terms. From the U.S perspective, there will be substantial budgetary pressure to limit conventional force outlays focused on Europe, given resource constraints, other priorities, and the structure of procurement and force structure decisions made in the early 1980s. These constraints will heighten the search for military reforms that suggest to some the promise of more defense for less expenditure. They will also increase the pressure for adjustments in the relative contributions of different members to the Alliance. Such adjustments in the distribution of burdens, however, will be very difficult to achieve, because national military structures are the result of complex differences in national environments.

Similarities and Differences
in U.S. and West German Approaches

Sources of National Perspectives. As noted in Chapter 1, differences in the international and domestic environments of the United States and the Federal Republic of Germany have significant impacts on their security policies. At the international level, geography made the United States an "Island Continent" with considerable emphasis on air and naval power, while the Federal Republic's position on the Great European Plain has made it primarily a land power. As a major economic and political power, the United States has developed global interests in contrast to the Federal Republic's primarily regional interests. The United States, with its global interests and global capabilities, has tended to view the economic, political, and military "correlation of forces" with the Soviet Union in global terms, while the Federal Republic has viewed the threat in more narrowly military and regional terms.

At the domestic level, the Federal Republic is far more dependent than the U.S. on external sources of raw materials and fuel. Both countries have relatively open economies, but international trade plays a significantly larger role in the Federal Republic's economy. Differences in political structure are also important. In the United States the President has more ability to shape security policy, while the German Chancellor is more constrained by a parliamentary system that resists short-term shifts in policy. Moreover U.S. public and elite opinion has generally been more supportive of an active foreign policy and strong defense forces than in West Germany.

Competing Views of Burden-Bearing and Burden-Sharing. The last half of the 1980s finds both countries facing severe fiscal constraints, which will hold increases in real defense outlays below levels that most defense analysts feel are required to sustain an adequate conventional deterrent in NATO. Disputes over economic relationships will inevitably spill over into criticisms of relative defense contributions at a time when the United States is forced to review its strategic priorities. The structure of U.S. procurement commitments made during the buildup of the early 1980s, moreover, suggests that there will be intense pressure to reduce allocations to ground forces on the critical Central Front, at a time when the Federal Republic will be hard-pressed to sustain its current active force.

In this environment, U.S. critics of the Federal Republic's defense contributions will emphasize real increases in defense outlays, share of total NATO defense spending, achievement of NATO force goals, support of NATO's Conventional Defense Initiative, and coordination of operational doctrine consistent with a new Conceptual Military Framework. West German resource constraints will be most obvious in the standard statistical comparisons, and they will inevitably be reflected in reluctance to embrace resource commitments for follow-on forces attack programs in the face of other shortages. West German responses to U.S. criticisms will emphasize levels of military contributions, rather than trends, the importance of social and economic balance as components of security policy, and contributions to the Alliance that are more difficult to measure, such as support of INF modernization and economic assistance to NATO's southern tier.

These differences in perspective are understandable and inevitable, but they still pose risks for the Alliance. The ways in which adjustments in force structure and levels are explained and perceived will be just as important as any absolute changes in defense capability. If, for example, the U.S. were forced to implement marginal reductions in its troop strength on the Central Front as part of a general adjustment to fiscal constraints, the changes would probably be seen in Europe as acceptable. If, on the other hand, the same reductions were explained as part of a strategic shift that required the reallocation of resources to contingencies in other regions, the impact would be quite different. Similarly, adjustments in the Federal Republic that suggested a reduced commitment to conventional deterrence would have important impacts in the United States.

Reconciling Differences in Perspectives

The first step in reconciling the differences in national perspectives is to understand them. Both countries are committed to the same principles of economic and political freedom, and both have committed their mutual security to the other's hands. Neither can achieve its security objectives without the other. Within that overarching reality, both countries must work to resolve real differences of opinion in ways that strengthen their common security yet preserve and protect national integrity.

Regional Priorities and Division of Labor. A substantial division of labor already exists within the Alliance. Although U.S. global interests do not always match West German interests, it is understood that NATO security does require military capabilities outside the formal NATO boundaries, and that the United States is in the best position in terms of interests, resources, and geography to provide those capabilities. Differences of opinion do arise, however, when the organization of U.S forces suggests that reinforcements traditionally targeted on Europe might become committed to other contingencies. Deployment priorities are crucial, because without anticipated U.S. reinforcements the whole structure of conventional deterrence, and the justification for large German forces, is eroded. Thus it is essential that the United States preserve the current division of labor by sustaining its reinforcement commitments, and that the Federal Republic sustain its commitments on the Central Front. Neither of these commitments can be maintained in the long run without the other.

Disagreements over operational doctrine for the Central Front will be driven more by economic and political constraints than by arguments over military strategy. Proponents of deep attack, on both sides of the Atlantic, must show how additional resources can be freed without jeopardizing the ability to contain first echelon forces. The resulting debate has already produced significant convergence between U.S. Air-Land Battle concepts and West German suggestions for greater emphasis on mobility and flexible mining. There is an apparent consensus for continued research and development of the systems that will ultimately make deep attack possible, but other resource constraints suggest that it may be prudent to emphasize continued development over immediate procurement commitments. The emerging shifts in the structure of West German forces, and the growing emphasis on battlefield mobility, suggest that the most fruitful area for the development of operational doctrine may well lie in imaginative approaches to the use of reserve forces.

The Conventional Defense Initiative (CDI) correctly focuses on the need to allocate scarce resources to meet the most pressing NATO priorities, but its emphasis on the requirement for more efficient integration of national forces is perhaps even more important. Proposals to highlight the highest priority force goals for immediate attention do reinforce and improve the normal NATO planning cycle, but they will inevitably focus on procurement. Because procurement is driven primarily by long-term national plans, and because funds for procurement will be limited by fiscal constraints, it is difficult to envision any dramatic improvements through the fine-tuning of the force goals process. Instead, the time may well be ripe for a concentrated assault on continuing problems in the integration of command-control-communica-tions-intelligence systems and logistical systems, where the constraints have been less the availability of resources than political differences that favor national approaches. Improvements in these areas would clearly help to offset the impact of perceived shortcomings in other measures of burden-sharing.

A major source of frustration in NATO is that national planning cycles are not synchronized with each other or with the NATO cycle. Hence the NATO force goals process produces substantial debate and effort, but only marginal impacts on the structure of defense outlays. The Long Term Defense Program attempted to expand the horizons of NATO planning, but as an out-of-cycle, largely U.S. initiative it had little impact on the actual planning process. There is a clear need for a long-term planning strategy to identify the most critical emerging technologies, to develop those technologies in an integrated armaments market, to coordinate long-term procurement priorities, and to tailor national procurement plans to those priorities. The enormous obstacles to the development of what Ambassador David M. Abshire, former U.S. Permanent Representative to the North Atlantic Council, has called a "resources strategy" are well known and substantial.[44] Nonetheless there has been sufficient movement—former Secretary of Defense Caspar Weinberger's 1985 Memorandum calling for greater Alliance-wide defense industry integration, the 1985 "Nunn Amendment" fencing funds for collaborative projects, the 1985 study by the NATO conference of National Armaments Directors (CNAD) on "The Enhancement of Armaments Cooperation Between the Allies," and the Independent European Program Group's cooperative technology projects—to warrant some optimism.[45] Even modest improvements in this area could go a long way toward offsetting the burden-sharing pressure that will be raised by resource shortages.

Summary

National contributions to the Alliance are most appropriately measured by the modifications of national economic, political, social and military policies that are designed to achieve common Alliance objectives, but since there is no clear baseline for such analysis the best achievable measure may be an assessment of each member's total contribution to agreed Alliance outputs. Even here, however, evaluation requires a subtle assessment of the impacts of a broad spectrum of policies, and analysts often fall back on narrow measures of national military inputs either to simplify the analytical task or to support a particular point of view.

The tendency to measure burden-sharing in narrow military terms will heighten the controversy over a fair distribution of effort within the Alliance through the end of the 1980s, because those measures of contribution are expected to grow slowly as a result of budget restrictions on both sides of the Atlantic. Arguments over Alliance contributions could therefore peak at a time that many critics of U.S defense policy argue for greater emphasis on the Pacific Basin and a conservation of force with less emphasis on ground forces in Europe.

These pressures make it more important than ever to use available defense resources wisely, both to build public support for future defense outlays and to compensate in part for the near-term slowdown in defense spending. The steps required to do this are clear. First, the Alliance must make decisive judgments on its operational doctrine. Here the most pressing issue is the balance between containing attacking first echelon forces, and the weight that will be given to engaging follow-on forces, because that decision will have the greatest impact on future procurement. Second, the operational doctrine must be implemented by adjusting national force goals to reflect Alliance priorities. This requires a careful assessment of competing emerged and emerging technologies. Third, in order to achieve the second objective, the Alliance needs a resource strategy that can influence long term national procurement policies, based on a clear assessment of future priorities and economic incentives to support those priorities.

The mechanisms for implementing these steps are crystallizing within the NATO planning structure in the form of a Conceptual Military Framework, the Conventional Defense Initiative, and the Resource Strategy that has been urged by Abshire and others. The risk is that the Alliance will choose to delay the difficult choices on operational doctrine, to follow the traditional pattern of identifying all programs as top priorities, and to argue over next year's budgets while national policies are locked in concrete by long-term procurement decisions outside the Alliance planning process. The steps required to solve the Alliance's problems of doctrine, planning, and procurement will not be met through incremental increases in narrowly defined defense inputs. They will demand political courage, social sacrifice, and economic vision. Burden-sharing and burden-bearing take many forms.

Notes

1. For a more complete discussion of this set of interrelationships see Daniel J. Kaufman, Jeffrey S. McKitrick, and Thomas J. Leney, eds., *U.S. National Security: A Framework for Analysis*, (Lexington, Mass.: Lexington Books, 1985), 3-26.

2. For a detailed analysis of the changing role of conventional deterrence see James R. Golden, Asa A. Clark, and Bruce E. Arlinghaus, eds., *Conventional*

Deterrence: Alternatives for European Defense (Lexington, Mass.: Lexington Books, 1985).

3. Lester Thurow, "A Time to Dismantle the World Economy," *The Economist*, 9 November 1985, 21-26.

4. For an overview of related adjustments in U.S. policies see "The New Trade Strategy," *Business Week*, 7 October 1985, 90-96.

5. Caspar W. Weinberger, *Report on Allied Contributions to the Common Defense: A Report to the United States Congress* (Washington, D.C.: Department of Defense, March 1985), 31.

6. These points are summarized from Catherine McArdle Kelleher, "The Defense Policy of the Federal Republic of Germany," in *The Defense Policies of Nations: A Comparative Study*, Douglas J. Murray and Paul R. Viotti, eds. (Baltimore, MD: Johns Hopkins Press, 1982), 268-296.

7. OECD, *Economic Surveys, 1983-1984: Germany*, 28.

8. "Pentagon Spending is the Economy's Biggest Gun," *Business Week*, 21 October 1985, 60.

9. German Information Center, *Germany's Contribution to Western Defense* (New York: German Information Center, 1984) 5, 6, 12-13.

10. Weinberger, *Report on Allied Contributions*, 110.

11. *Ibid*, 84, 90.

12. *Ibid*, 21, 96, 102.

13. *Ibid*, 82.

14. Caspar W. Weinberger, *Annual Report to the Congress, Fiscal Year 1986* (Washington, D.C.: GPO, 4 February 1985), 226.

15. James Moray Stewart, "Conventional Defense Improvements: Where is the Alliance Going?", *NATO's Sixteen Nations*, 30 (March 1985), 1-7.

16. Weinberger, *Annual Report to the Congress, Fiscal Year 1986*, 226-227, and German Information Center, *Germany's Contribution*, 11-12.

17. The Federal Minister of Defence, *White Paper 1985: The Situation and Development of the Federal Armed Forces* (Bonn: Federal Ministry of Defense, 19 June 1985), 53.

18. Bernard W. Rogers, "The Atlantic Alliance: Prescriptions for a Difficult Decade," *Foreign Affairs*, 60, (Summer 1982), 1151-1152. See also Flora Whit, "Nuclear War Escalation Seen Likely," *Washington Post*, 14 March 1983, 2, and Anthony H. Cordesman, "An Exclusive Interview with General Bernard W. Rogers," *Armed Forces Journal International*, 120, 2 (September 1983), 74.

19. Bernard W. Rogers, "The Attack of Warsaw Pact Follow-On Forces," *Military Technology* (May 1983), 39.

20. European Security Study Group, *Strengthening Conventional Deterrence in Europe: Proposals for the 1980s* (New York: St. Martin's Press, 1983), 34-35.

21. *White Paper, 1985*, 79.

22. *Ibid*, 340-342.

23. *Ibid*, 343.

24. "Eurofighter," *The Economist*, 7 September 1985, 56.

25. For a brilliant exposition of defense options by a leading West German analyst, see Peter Stratmann, *NATO Doctrine and National Operational Priorities: The Central Front and the Flanks*, SWP-LN 2447 (Ebenhausen, Federal Republic of Germany: Stiftung Wissenschaft und Politik, September 1985). For a brief summary of the role of barriers and mobility in current West German operational doctrine, see Lieutenant General Hans-Henning Von Sandrart, "Forward Defense -

Mobility and the Use of Barriers," *NATO's Sixteen Nations*, 30, Special Issue 1/85, 37-43.

26. Von Sandrart, "Forward Defense," 40.

27. Stratmann, "NATO Doctrine and National Operational Priorities," 27.

28. For a discussion of the potential uses of light infantry divisions in mid- to high-intensity conflict, as well as low-intensity conflict, see General John A. Wickham, Jr., "Light Infantry Divisions in Defense of Europe," *NATO's Sixteen Nations*, 30, Special Issue 1/85, 100-107.

29. Peter Stratmann, "NATO Doctrine and National Operational Priorities," 18-19.

30. William W. Kaufmann, *The 1986 Defense Budget* (Washington, D.C.: The Brookings Institution, 1985), 14.

31. Weinberger, *Annual Report to Congress, Fiscal Year 1986*, 155.

32. *Ibid*, 156.

33. *Ibid*, 181.

34. *Ibid*, 139.

35. *Ibid*, 109.

36. Department of Labor, *Abstract of the United States Census* (Washington, D.C.: Bureau of Labor Statistics, April 1980), 4.

37. *Ibid.*

38. Weinberger, *Annual Report to Congress, Fiscal Year 1986*, 110.

39. See, for example, Robert W. Komer, "Maritime Strategy versus Coalition Defense," *Foreign Affairs*, 60 (Summer 1982): 1124-1144.

40. Rogers, "The Atlantic Alliance: Prescriptions for a Difficult Decade," 1155.

41. Michael R. Gordon, "Technology and NATO Defense: Weighing the Options," in *Conventional Deterrence: Alternatives for European Defense*, 150-153.

42. *Ibid*, 154-157.

43. Stratmann, "NATO Doctrine and Operational Priorities," 25-26.

44. David Abshire, "A Resources Strategy for NATO," *NATO's Sixteen Nations*, 30, (October 1985), 62-70.

45. For a recapitulation of these, and other actions, see Wolfgang Tebbe, "The Transatlantic Dialogue and the European Defense Industry," *NATO's Sixteen Nations*, 30 (October 1985), 52-61.

6

Alliance Roles and Responsibilities

Dieter Dettke

Introduction: The Need for Adjustment

Ever since the Atlantic Alliance was founded in 1949, its internal structure as well as its policies towards the outside world have been a matter of dispute either in Europe or in the United States, or in both. Although adjustments have been made—often very successful ones like the institution of the Nuclear Planning Group, the Harmel Report or the creation of the Special Consultative Group for INF negotiations—a stable equilibrium within the Alliance and a consensus on policies to pursue outside it do not exist. Henry Kissinger has even warned that, today, "there is less intellectual or philosophical agreement than in any previous period."[1]

There is a clear need today, to seek a new political consensus within the Alliance and to develop convincing and acceptable political and military strategies vis-à-vis other countries, especially for East-West and North-South relations. Two developments with a potential danger for NATO's internal cohesion seem to converge: a stronger U.S. that will act unilaterally, if necessary, and greater European self-assertiveness. In theory, these two trends do not necessarily have to upset the cohesion of NATO. For instance, a deliberate process of internal reform leading to a different distribution of roles and responsibilities within NATO could well create a new consensus.

But such a process would require profound adjustments in the Alliance. Internally, NATO would need to be restructured so that a greater European responsibility for the defense of Europe would be the result. One way, as Henry Kissinger has suggested in the article mentioned above, would be to create a European SACEUR. Another possibility would be the creation of additional European defense mechanisms with U.S. support, either on the basis of the European Community, the Western European Union or through bilateral efforts.

However, enormous efforts are also necessary in order to create a new consensus about NATO's military strategy. The events leading first to the beginning of a deployment process for 108 Pershing II missiles and 464

Ground Launched Cruise Missiles (GLCMs) in Europe after the failure of the Geneva INF-negotiations in 1983, and then to an INF agreement on the basis of a global zero-solution for INF systems between 500 and 5500 km in range in 1987, constitute quite a strong coherence-test for NATO. There is no doubt that the INF agreement to eliminate nuclear systems of a range between 500 and 5500 km is welcome news in Europe and has overwhelming support in European public opinion. Yet, even that agreement has its critics. This time, it is the pro-nuclear European right wing which perceives the danger in an arms control agreement that could, in their view, "decouple" the strategic deterrent and weaken the nuclear guarantee. The opposition in Europe against the zero-solution is, however, minimal compared to the opposition against deployment, which is led by the left wing peace movement that was so active in the early 1980s. Although it is probably premature to announce the beginning of the post-nuclear era, as Edward Luttwak has done,[2] a process of delegitimization of nuclear weapons with fundamental consequences for the defense of Europe is clearly under way.

These differences have many causes and take many forms. Although the emphasis on "conventional deterrence" has (as noted in Chapters 2 and 4) gained increasing acceptance, there are still divergent views as to how to operationalize this concept, as well as over when and how to implement the "nuclear guarantee"—divergences which the U.S. adoption of the Strategic Defense Initiative has seemingly exacerbated rather than diminished. And the controversy over "burden sharing" has, as noted in Chapter 5, grown as the resources allocatable to defense have shrunk and the willingness to spend monies for arms, rather than for the revitalization of industry or the retraining of laborers, has diminished.

Another factor adversely affecting U.S.-West European relationships was the lack of progress on arms control between 1979 and 1987, for which many Europeans blamed the United States. Although this judgment may be overly simplistic, there can be little doubt that American leaders since 1980 have taken a much harder-nosed approach to negotiations than have many of their European counterparts. And one result, as shown in Chapter 7, was that official unanimity frequently cloaked significant disagreements over both objectives and tactics.

All this would not matter so much if one could anticipate a new period of superpower understanding and cooperation, which would create an optimal situation for the Europeans in terms of security guarantees. The INF agreement of December 8, 1987 has the potential of opening up such an opportunity; however, it is not yet clear where we are in the familiar cycle of superpower relations. Earlier, the *hostile bipolarity* during the Cold War period from 1947 to 1962 was followed by greater *multipolarity* in a period of loosening alliance systems from 1962 to 1969, and *cooperative bipolarity* during the period of Soviet-American bilateralism and détente in Europe from 1969 to 1979. Since 1979 the world seems to have entered a new period of *hostile bipolarity* that for many is very close to a new cold war,[3] with only a glimmering of hope for cooperative bipolarity. And typically, we have also seen new elements of multipolarity, such as the economic dominance of Japan in the 1980s, new efforts at integration in Europe—as the intensification of Franco-German military ties in the mid 1980s shows—and the consolidation of China as a coming "superpower" since the late 1970s.

Europeans and Americans have very different ideas as to how to cope with this old/new situation. Whereas the Europeans, even after the Soviet invasion of Afghanistan, still believed that détente on the basis of the Harmel Report formula of 1967 was a meaningful and necessary approach towards the Soviet Union, the United States since the middle of the 1970s has perceived a global strategic challenge that needs a different response to the USSR than the Harmel Report offered. Contrary to what many Americans expected on the basis of the Soviet-American communiqué of May 1972, détente did not work globally. For the United States, the success of détente in Europe visible in the Berlin agreement, the Moscow and Warsaw treaties and in the Final Act of the Conference on Security and Cooperation in Europe (CSCE) was soon overshadowed by Soviet and Cuban actions in Africa, increasing Communist influence in the Arab world and a continuing arms modernization and buildup on the Soviet side. The fatal blow was the Soviet invasion of Afghanistan which, from an American perspective, not only put an end to the détente process but also became a watershed in Alliance relations. (For further details, see Chapter 7).

In the United States, the "failure" of détente generated disappointment, frustration and a widespread feeling of lack of support by the European allies. It also spurred a tendency toward "global unilateralism" which had deep roots in the American political psyche and which was further intensified by the growing Soviet challenge. Together with other influences ranging from alterations in economic relations (with Asia replacing Western Europe as the primary trading partner of the United States) to the development of a new "maritime strategy" emphasizing operations in the Indian Ocean and the Pacific Basin this led to a "turning away" from Europe—at least as the Europeans saw it.

In this context, European self-assertion[4] is seen again by many as a way out of a new security dilemma. Just as the short period of multipolarity in the middle of the 1960s coincided with the first sign of greater European self-assertion—the well known examples at that time being France and Romania—today, new signs of willingness to defy the superpowers are developing in Europe, this time mainly in the two German states. Both German states talk about a *"Verantwortungsgemeinschaft"* (common responsibility).[5] In West Germany, the Federal President Richard von Weizsaecker used the word *"Verantwortungsgemeinschaft"* in a geopolitical sense and declared: "We have a geopolitical consensus in the interest here in Central Europe not to contribute to an increase of tensions but rather to reduce them."[6] On the other side, Erich Honecker, head of state and party leader of the German Democratic Republic, only two days later made a statement that employed the word *Sicherheitspartnerschaft* (security part-nership) in order to underline the proposition that the two German states, in spite of the missile deployment, should cooperate for the benefit of all of Europe.[7]

The word *"Verantwortungsgemeinschaft"* (sometimes also used in a wider European context to include Western Europe and the GDR, Poland, Hungary and Romania on the Eastern side) clearly indicates that the behavior of the superpowers is seen as at least partly irresponsible, from a German and even from a European perspective, on both sides of the dividing line between the blocs. Not only did the initial deployment of Pershing II's and GLCMs in the Federal Republic of Germany meet opposition, Honecker himself several times stated very clearly that he was not enthusiastic about the additional nuclear systems (SS-21, SS-23 and also for the first time SS-22) that were stationed in the GDR as a so-called countermeasure of the Soviet Union to Western deployments. The same is true for Czechoslovakia, and even Bulgaria indicated unhappiness about additional deployments of nuclear-armed missiles in countries other than the Soviet Union.

How far that defiance of the bloc system can go and will go is an open question; certainly it will not lead to the creation of a new "third force" in Europe. If one looks to Western Europe, there is far from total support for a superpower Europe; indeed many West Europeans are uncomfortable with such aspirations. And while some view the American presence as unnatural, others are fearful that a U.S. withdrawal would lead to total disintegration rather than to political unity. Thus the question is not whether a "new Europe" should be created but rather whether the old (Western) Europe can gain sufficient cohesiveness to bring about a major adjustment of Alliance roles and responsibilities. This chapter will first examine some of the proposals for enhancing the position of Western Europe within the Atlantic Alliance and then some of the substantive issues which will affect that possibility, notably with respect to the "out-of-area" question.

The "Two-Pillar" Concept

Historical Background

One should never forget that the American-European security community was forged during and as a result of the Cold War.[8] The European state system as a power center virtually broke down as a result of the Second World War and all European states, not only defeated Germany, were left in a deep political, economic and moral crisis because of Hitler's violent aggressiveness that ended in an almost total destruction of political and economic systems as well as social, political and human values. Not only did the European states lose a great part of their colonial empires, they had to turn to the U.S. in order to survive because only the United States was in a position to remain intact after the Second World War. Even the Soviet Union as a victor with a loss of more than 20 million people was seriously crippled as a society.

Under these circumstances, the United States emerged as the dominant power, not only among Western democracies but world-wide. The Soviet Union was certainly the strongest power in Europe militarily but clearly not in a position to compete with the U.S. on a global level. At the end of the Second World War the United States was in possession of the atomic bomb, and economically two thirds of the total industrial capacity was American. In 1938, U.S. exports amounted to about 14% of the world's trade; in 1947, they totaled 33%.[9] Bipolarity in the sense that there were two equally strong powers dominating the rest of the world did not exist in the real world. It was the political, military and ideological perception of the early post-war period that led to the notion of a bipolar international system. That system began to emerge in 1947 when the war-time alliance with the Soviet Union, the "strange alliance," as it has been so aptly called,[10] definitely broke down over the question of Poland, Germany, Berlin and the future of Europe including economic recovery.

When the Atlantic Alliance was founded in 1949, there was not much of a two-pillar system. Rather, the European nations flocked together around the United States for protection. The internal structure of the Alliance according to a symbol that has often been used can best be described by the analogy of spokes and the wheel. Everything centered around the United States. However, it was not a U.S. initiative to create the Atlantic Alliance but an European one, particularly from Great Britain. At that time, a firm commitment from the United States in the form of a substantial troop presence abroad was almost unthinkable and, if at all, not as a permanent commitment. The U.S. reluctance to make such a commitment, on the other hand, acted as an element of change, even pressure, to promote European defense efforts.

One of the most important efforts in that direction was the abortive European Defense Community of 1951. Theoretically, the European Defense Community proposal can be seen as a two-pillar effort. The political language of that time clearly supports that point and the fathers of European integration, especially Jean Monnet, who was instrumental in the creation of the Coal and Steel community in 1951, even talked about Europe as being capable of assuming responsibility for her own economic development and collective security in order to gradually become a power of equilibrium.[11] Others went even further and had a Third Force Europe in mind. However, that rather ambitious language cannot obscure the fact that the European Defense Community idea had only one important objective and that was to legitimize the rearmament of the Federal Republic of Germany in French eyes. In the early 1950s, with a fresh memory of what Hitler's armies had done in Europe, that was no easy undertaking in France and elsewhere in Europe. German troops had occupied almost every European country during the war. But how to control the Germans without also integrating them into the West militarily?

France at that time oscillated between a greater Atlantic solution of the problem of Western defense and a European approach. The option of a European Defense Community was attractive to France because it prevented the Federal Republic at least for the time being from achieving an equal status with France in the Atlantic Alliance. France wanted to control the German army according to her specific security needs and British participation in that European effort was essential. Together with Great Britain, France would have felt comfortable enough to deal with the German problem.

So when it became obvious that Great Britain would *not* participate in the European Defense Community, the project lost almost all its attractiveness. A West European military integration with the Federal Republic but without Great Britain was not acceptable to France. The fact that the Atlantic Alliance, too, in 1950 decided to create a military integration based on a substantial American troop presence beginning in 1951 certainly made it easier for France to finally live with the NATO solution of the German rearmament problem. The treaties of Paris in 1954 also made sure that the revised Brussels Treaty (which then formed the basis for the Western European Union including Great Britain) contained at least some elements of control of Germany and her military capability. Most important was the German renunciation of nuclear, chemical and bacteriological weapons plus a ceiling for the peace time strength of the new German *Bundeswehr* (495,000) and wartime forces of 1.2 million.

Failure of Structural Change

When the European Defense Community failed in 1954 and the decision was taken to make the Federal Republic of Germany a member of NATO, the Atlantic system prevailed over European hopes for a restoration of their role as an autonomous force in world politics. American protection was not only perceived to be more effective and reliable than European efforts to meet the Soviet threat, in every respect that situation was more comfortable and advantageous for Europe because it enabled the European nations to concentrate fully on their economic recovery and social development. But the inevitable consequence of European failure to extend the process of integration into the security area also was that the power structure within the Alliance, which is American dominated, was consolidated and not changed as the founding fathers of European integration had intended.

In contrast to the Eastern Bloc, West European integration from the beginning was conceived as a process to change the structure of the Atlantic System and to establish a new decision-making center in Europe. The inbuilt evolutionary objective of the Atlantic Alliance always was to help Europe to become an autonomous force again.[12] In the military field, however, the commitment of the United States based on a strong physical presence in Europe and a firm nuclear guarantee clearly blocked integration efforts.

That the two-pillar concept never really worked has structural reasons in Europe and in the international system. It is not only a lack of European efforts. Even after the failure of the European Defense Community, the discussion about the need to change the internal structure of the Alliance and to increase common European defense efforts never stopped. For example, in 1958, immediately after his return to power, de Gaulle suggested a new NATO directorate and thereby opened the first great Trans-Atlantic debate of the early 1960s. That debate took place in the aftermath of the experience of France and Great Britain in the Suez Crisis where for the first time limits on the U.S. political commitment to Europe (or, more precisely, to the support of British and French interests in the Middle East) became visible and the U.S. for the first time effectively cooperated with the Soviet Union in order to put down a fire that had the potential to invite Soviet intervention and to pull the U.S. unintentionally into a conflict with the Soviet Union. Whereas at that time Western protests against the Soviet intervention in Hungary remained purely verbal and, therefore, ineffective, the common U.S.-Soviet action against a "colonial hiccup" that could only diminish the position of the U.S. in the awakening Third World if it would have supported British and French policies, proved to be extremely powerful and strong. The Suez Crisis clearly underlined the need for better consultation within the Alliance. In 1956, the Report of the Committee of the Three, adopted by the North Atlantic Council on 13 December 1956, made some interesting proposals, for instance:

- A member government should not, without adequate advance consultation, adopt firm policies or make major political pronouncements on matters which significantly affect the Alliance or any of its members, unless circumstances make such prior consultation obviously and demonstrably impossible;
- In developing their national policies, members should take into consideration the interest and views of other governments, particularly those directly concerned, as expressed in NATO consultation, even where no community of views or consensus has been reached in the Council;
- Where a consensus has been reached, it should be reflected in the formation of national policies. When for national reasons the consensus is not followed, the government concerned should offer an explanation to the Council. It is even more important that where an agreed and formal recommendation has emerged from the Council's discussions, governments should give it full weight in any national actions or policies related to the subject of that recommendation.[13]

In addition to the Suez Crisis, the background of the first Trans-Atlantic debate was also marked by the beginning strategic reorientation in the United States which led from a strategy of massive retaliation to a strategy of flexible response. The Sputnik shock in 1957 which caused an almost hysterical reaction in the West certainly revealed a very important new factor in Alliance relations: the vulnerability of the United States to Soviet nuclear weapons. The United States quite understandably wanted to avoid a situation without room for maneuver, for reliance on massive retaliation in a position of strategic vulnerability leaves almost no military option between general war and capitulation. Flexible response and the concept of limited war, however, created the impression of a less firm commitment of the United States to Europe. The French General Pierre Gallois even made the point that Europe on the basis of a strategy of flexible response would lose the advantage of being an integral part of the American security area.[14]

Kennedy's MLF proposal and his concept of a new Atlantic partnership, the grand design, based on two pillars, tried to respond to European strategic concerns as well as to nuclear ambitions, real ones in France and anticipated ones in Germany.[15] Already immediately after the Suez crisis, France had decided to become an independent nuclear power. De Gaulle's Europe "from the Atlantic to the Urals" was a kind of antithesis to the grand design and at least in three respects different from American objectives. It was anti-Atlantic, anti-British and anti-integrationist as far as the organization of the Europe of the Six was concerned. Both concepts failed. The grand design and MLF did not succeed because—as Henry Kissinger correctly observed—"The MLF became the focus for many diverse hopes, and its supporters had many contradictory motives. It was supposed to revitalize NATO, yet reduce the role of France in Europe. It was to prevent nuclear proliferation and yet satisfy alleged German desires for a share of nuclear control. It simultaneously sought to meet requirements of the Pentagon for central control over nuclear weapons and the hopes of many Europeans for the emergence of a European nuclear force."[16] It was, as he concludes, the wrong answer to the wrong problem.

De Gaulle's concept failed because it would not only have deprived Europe of the necessary American protection for the intended cooperation with the Soviet Union but would also have created a Western Europe that without Great Britain automatically would be dominated by France as the only nuclear power. Taking such a risky step was unacceptable for the non-nuclear neighbors of France which, in addition, saw its own nuclear power as a purely national instrument. In the last analysis the United States, too, did not want to share the nuclear decision. Even under MLF the control of the nuclear weapons was in the hands of the American president. However, when the MLF project failed, NATO created the Nuclear Planning Group to share at least information about nuclear planning and targeting.

As a result, both European integration and the Atlantic Alliance stumbled into a crisis. In 1966, France decided to leave the military integration of NATO and in Europe a long crisis began over the question of British participation in the EEC.

However, NATO got back on its feet rather quickly. The strategy of flexible response finally was adopted in 1967 and, together with the Harmel

Report, approved in the same year, gave NATO a political strategy of détente and defense that proved to be extremely helpful in adjusting Alliance policies to the new international environment. The Alliance learned to live with the new Nuclear Planning Group and finally the controversial nuclear issue of the early sixties calmed down. The two superpowers also began to take effective steps to control nuclear proliferation. The first step was the Partial Test Ban Treaty of 1963. The Nuclear Non-Proliferation Treaty followed in 1968.

The crisis of European integration lasted for a longer period of time. The turning point was the beginning of the process of enlargement in 1969 which led to the entry of Great Britain, Denmark and Ireland into the European Community in 1973. But even after enlargement, the Community, according to its self-assessment, remained a genuine civilian power.[17] The global extension the U.S. has always hoped for did not take place, and, in spite of enlargement, first from 6 to 9 members, and then from 10 to 12 members (so that the EC now includes Greece, Spain and Portugal) a second pillar within the Atlantic Alliance is still more hope than reality.

The European Community as a Second Pillar

In spite of its impressive weight, the European Community has to overcome tremendous structural difficulties in order to be capable of service as a second pillar within the Atlantic Alliance. It is true that compared with the superpowers, even in military terms, the combined potential of the enlarged Community is quite strong. With a population of about 300 million (10 percent of the world population), a gross national product of over 2.5 trillion U.S. dollars, almost 40 percent of world trade, and well over 2.5 million men and women in the armed forces, the enlarged European Community matches the two superpowers in almost every respect except nuclear weapons and defense expenditures.[18] The armed forces of the European Community are well trained and have modern equipment. Two of the five nuclear powers belong to the Community. It is a legitimate question why a group of nations with such potential, enormous social and economic progress, and a high standard of living is militarily so dependent on the U.S. and vulnerable to the Soviet Union.[19]

One reason, as Ian Smart wrote some time ago, is the basic strategic truth that Europe has to face, namely the weakness of the British and the French nuclear forces.[20] Under such strategic conditions, Europe seems unlikely to be able to develop a credible deterrent of its own. However, after the modernization of the French and British nuclear forces that is now under way, and will be effective in the early 1990s, the picture as far as nuclear capabilities are concerned might look a little different. The former head of ACDA, George Seignious, even expects France and Great Britain to become Europe's nuclear superpowers.[21]

A second, and perhaps even more fundamental, reason is that the European Community is today by character a profoundly civilian entity with a high standard of living, the status of an important trading partner, relatively stable democratic structures, and enormous social progress. It is difficult to see how a civilian community such as this can make sustainable efforts to project power to the outside world. Part of Europe's attractiveness as a partner in other regions is in fact its lack of power projection.

Third, the degree of integration is still not sufficient for a political and military union. There seems to be a solid public majority for European integration in the member states of the European Community, but it is a permissive consensus, to say the least. In fact, one should rather acknowledge that fragmentation prevails. A European authority legitimized by majorities in every country is almost unthinkable if you look at the summit meetings and the fragile compromises they produce. It is possible that the process of integration could break down if there were a serious attempt to build a defense community, partly because the nuclear question is so controversial and divisive. The smaller and non-nuclear countries of the European Community could well live with U.S. dominance. It is doubtful whether they would be willing to live with French and British dominance that would hardly fulfill their security needs, especially since there is no credible conventional deterrent as an alternative.

Fourth, Europe's military, political, and economic vulnerabilities obviously contribute to discourage any attempt at military integration. As a result, there is a strong need to influence events diplomatically, not militarily. This is visible in the European Political Cooperation (EPC), but from there it is a long way to a defense community. Political cooperation within the European Community has worked quite successfully since the early 1970s and has produced common foreign policy positions in a number of areas, some even involving security matters.

For instance, the European Community from the beginning played a very active role in the CSCE-process and continues to do so. Other areas of effective European political consultation have included the Middle East, the dialogue with the Arab states, developments in Portugal and Spain, a common attitude towards South Africa, trade with Eastern Europe (an agreement between the European Community and COMECON remains open), and energy. Also, the European Community is trying to speak with one voice in international organizations such as the United Nations. The internal structure of the EC and also the way in which it looks at the outside world will necessarily change quite fundamentally now that Spain and Portugal are full members. Enlargement towards southern Europe is a fundamental process, and although it is difficult to determine what the final outcome will be, a number of internal and external consequences are clearly visible.

Integration of Southern European agricultural states into a community of predominantly middle and northern European nations is bound to cause not only institutional headaches but problems for European integration as such. The social, economic, and political structures of the new countries are closer to those in Third World countries. Pierre Hassner even talked about a "Third-Worldization of Europe" in connection with enlargement.[22]

That may be an overstatement of the case but it points to the important fact that the internal balance of the enlarged EC will be a new one, probably less stable than the existing balance. There will be increased heterogeneity and more disparity between societies, while differences of culture, religion, and tradition will add to the disparity and thus create more difficulties for a decision-making process that is already slow and delicate, not to mention the financial troubles that will result as a consequence of the present system for handling agricultural products. The European agricultural market by nature has a tendency to overproduction, and that tendency will be reinforced. In addition, the ten EC nations already have a strained labor market, with almost 13 million people unemployed. With the inclusion of Spain and Portugal into the EC, this problem will intensify. In sum, enlargement for the European Community is an additional internal burden.

Externally, however, and politically the weight of the EC will grow, although enlargement holds an enormous potential for conflict. The EC is already directly involved in the Cyprus conflict and the disputes over maritime jurisdictions between Greece and Turkey. In addition to that, the EC cannot avoid sharing responsibility for Turkey, a country of great strategic importance for the West. However, economic and domestic developments in that country, especially after the military coup of October 1980, prevented the EC from offering what ultimately might be the last chance to stabilize relations with the West, namely a closer relationship with the EC. Under normal circumstances, something less than membership but certainly more than association with the EC would be the ideal solution. Even though Turkey is moving back toward a democratic government, such a step is practically out of reach as long as Greece and Turkey are at loggerheads and as a consequence Turkey might well drift away from the West.

But enlargement does not only mean greater potential for conflict and instability in Southern Europe and the Mediterranean. It also means greater involvement in adjacent regions that directly affect European security, namely the Middle East and the Persian Gulf. Greece and Spain in particular have always had, and will continue to have, a close relationship to Arab countries. Traditional relations with the Arab world and new economic necessities come together here, and this will add momentum to efforts of the EC to play a greater role in a region that is extremely explosive. As a result of the process of enlargement, the Atlantic orientation of the European Community will decline.

It is true that Greece and Portugal are members of the North Atlantic Treaty Organization. Greece even returned to the military integration of NATO after half a decade of aloofness, and Spain recently joined NATO. (Spain's membership of NATO was even confirmed in a delicate referendum.) But at the same time, one should not overlook the fact that the security needs and concerns of the new members are primarily related to Mediterranean problems and the Third World. Nonalignment plays an important role in the foreign policy perspective of these countries. Spain obviously seeks a special status within the Alliance similar to the French model or like those of Denmark and Norway. Neutralism has a long tradition in Spain, and full membership in the Alliance could be a burden rather than an asset.

Institutional Initiatives
Towards a Two-Pillar Concept

It is doubtful whether on such a structural basis the European Community will ever find a way to autonomy in defense and security. Although peace and security, including common defense, have been from the beginning a decisive incentive for European integration, it should be acknowledged that there is no shortcut to military and political union. There are limits to military union and cooperation in defense matters in spite of several existing institutions which deal with the issue.

The oldest of these institutions is the West European Union, which after the failure of the European Defense Community was created as an alternative. The modified Brussels Treaty, from which the Western European Union originated, foresees far-reaching consultations of the participating states even in the non-military field and, in contrast to the North Atlantic Alliance, has an automatic assistance clause. However, that institution never became the heart of European defense cooperation. The reasons for that are obvious. There is no military organization in the Western European Union; that was left to NATO when the treaty was concluded. With such a construction the effectiveness of the WEU is extremely limited. Also, membership is limited to seven European countries (Great Britain, France, Germany, Italy, Netherlands, Belgium, Luxemburg). Important decisions on defense policy and arms cooperation are taken in NATO, not in the WEU. It is difficult to assume that other European states would consider becoming members of the Western European Union. Therefore, membership in the European Community and in the Western European Union will probably never be identical. Denmark, Greece and Ireland did not become members of the WEU when they entered the EC and it is difficult to see Spain and Portugal asking for membership in the WEU, even though they have now joined the EC. As a consequence, the Northern and Southern European flanks would not be included.

However, that does not mean that the WEU should be written off as a possible European defense organization. Good work is done in the permanent armament committee and the arms control office is a meaningful institution. The treaty is also the basis for the British troop stationing on the Continent and the British forces in Germany are even committed for fifty years until the year 2004. Recently, France and the Federal Republic of Germany have started to look again into possibilities of reviving the WEU and, amazingly enough, at its thirtieth birthday the WEU might suddenly become the focus of a new effort to coordinate defense policies in Europe.

Such an effort to strengthen the European pillar within NATO can hardly be dangerous for the NATO Alliance. Military and strategic planning would still be NATO's task. The WEU is certainly no *ersatz*-NATO, but it might become a useful forum for a greater European commitment in security matters.

Another successful effort at European defense cooperation has been the Euro-Group. The Euro-Group was the result of a British initiative in 1968 when defense minister Dennis Healey suggested an informal meeting of the European defense ministers immediately before the NATO meetings. Since then, that form of cooperation has become an "institution."

Important initiatives such as the European Defense Improvement Program (EDIP), the Euro-Package, which led to modernization efforts, and many arms cooperation projects came from the Euro-Group.[23] The advantage of the Euro-Group certainly is that the European NATO partners clearly work and proceed in an Alliance framework. Therefore, no real problems exist vis-à-vis the United States. A clear disadvantage, however, is that France does not participate. Any participation of France in the Euro-Group would be considered in France as a return to the military integration of NATO, and that, for domestic reasons, is not feasible in the foreseeable future. Also if the Euro-Group would be the only possible defense institution acceptable for all, then defense and security would be excluded permanently from the European Community.

How to bridge the gap between France's opposition to military integration in NATO and a kind of European defense cooperation that would still work in an Alliance framework, remains a question to be solved. Former French ambassador to NATO de Rose recently made a very simple and yet even ingenious proposal when he suggested that the competence of the Defense Planning Committee of NATO should be transferred to the Atlantic Council, of which France has never ceased to be a member.[24]

France does already participate in another institution, the Independent European Program Group (IEPG) which was created in 1976 in order to improve European cooperation in arms production. All thirteen European NATO members participate in the IEPG but the Group does not operate in the framework of the Euro-Group in order to enable France to be fully engaged. For European arms cooperation the IEPG is the optimal framework because its composition reaches the greatest market possible in Europe. At the same time a clear contribution to the Atlantic Alliance is made, even although the cooperation takes place outside the Alliance institutions.[25]

None of these institutions, not even the European Community, today is in a position to become a second pillar in the Alliance. One fundamental reason for the lack of common ground is that the European consensus in security matters is still a fragile one, *especially* in nuclear matters. The non-nuclear European states can live with an American nuclear dominance but they would have difficulties in uniting under a French and/or British nuclear deterrent which cannot become an alternative for the nuclear guarantee of the United States. Also, the fact that Europe, like Japan, is so vulnerable militarily and so dependent on foreign trade and raw materials discourages almost any attempt to unite militarily. Furthermore, to the degree that there's a permanent American presence on the European continent, incentives to organize an independent European defense can hardly emerge. A reappraisal of the American commitment to Europe, however, cannot be excluded for all time. Whether in that case the developments would necessarily lead to greater European defense efforts is an open question. An automatic evolution in that direction is not the only possibility. It is also possible that under these circumstances the process of European integration could come to an end. Also a lessening of international tensions could produce a feeling there that new defense efforts are not really necessary.

On the other hand, what became visible in Europe as a result of renewed international tensions and unrest in the Atlantic Alliance since the beginning of the 1980s is another *'rélance européenne'* in security matters. Already in 1981 the study of the four institutes for foreign policy (the Council on Foreign Relations in New York, the German Society for Foreign Affairs in Bonn, the French Institute for International Relations in Paris and the Institute of International Affairs in London) came to the conclusion that the good old days of the Atlantic system were over and that a new Alliance structure had to be created.[26] When, as a result of the Soviet invasion of Afghanistan, the hostage crisis in Tehran, and developments in Poland and in Central America, the international constellation began to change back to the pattern of hostile bipolarity, concern in Europe increased that stability and cooperation there was endangered by developments outside of the European region. European security interests were seen differently and they were articulated in opposition to American concerns over Soviet policies. This was very openly expressed in a communiqué of Chancellor Helmut Schmidt and French President Valery Giscard d'Estaing on February 6, 1981, when they declared that they were determined to act together against the factors that led to destabilization and against the dangers for peace which could result from those factors in the future.[27]

No doubt, the beginning of the *rélance européenne* in security was the crisis experience of the years 1980 and 1981, when both globally and within the Alliance there was an increasing American inclination to confront the Soviet Union more forcefully politically and with a substantial arms buildup. When the United States in 1982 tried to stop the European gas-pipeline deal because of developments in Poland, the American embargo policy met determined European resistance, and finally in 1983 that policy collapsed under successful European pressure.

Instead, France and Germany decided to intensify their exchange of views on security matters and to cooperate more closely on these matters. Even after the changes of government in France in 1981 and in Germany in October 1982 that subject remained on the agenda of French-German consultations. French Prime Minister Pierre Mauroy declared in October

1981 that it was necessary to think about the prospect of a European political system which would have its own autonomous defense.[28] Mauroy also combined this statement with an indication that an attack on France does not begin with the enemy entering French territory but before that happens. The new German government continued, too, with the Schmidt-Giscard d'Estaing initiative.

In October 1982, the French-German consultations for the first time started with a joint meeting of the foreign and defense ministers. Study groups for security cooperation were created that had been part of an agreement concluded in 1983 but never realized. Progress was made very quickly in armament cooperation, the first new project being a common anti-tank helicopter. But the most visible effort of military cooperation between the two countries is the 3000-man *Franco-German brigade*, officially created at the 25th anniversary of the 1963 Franco-German treaty in January 1988. (The idea for a Franco-German force was advanced in June 1984 by former Chancellor Helmut Schmidt and separately by former French Defense Minister Charles Hernue.)

The problem with this highly symbolic military force, however, is that its command structure and its role vis-à-vis NATO need to be clarified. The brigade will be under French command initially, but the objective is the creation of a transnational military instrument with a European mission. Finally, the two countries decided to create a *Franco-German Defense Council* to coordinate defense policies. This new institution, too, was conceived in a European perspective so that other European countries could join should they wish.

Progress on the European level was less rapid. Foreign Minister Hans-Dietrich Genscher started an initiative to create a new European Union that would include security matters. The initiative soon became known as the Genscher-Colombo initiative because the Italian government was willing to go along with it. But during the course of deliberations among the member states of the European Community it soon became evident that there was not sufficient support for including security issues into political cooperation. One specific idea in connection with the Genscher-Colombo initiative was a regular meeting of European defense ministers. That proposal was particularly supported by a study of European institutes on foreign relations on current problems of European integration.[29] In that same study the idea of a two-pillar Atlantic system was taken up again and suggested as a solution to present European and Atlantic problems. However, when the EC met in Stuttgart in 1983 to decide among other things about the Genscher-Colombo initiative, all that was said about security in a solemn declaration on the European Union was "coordination of the position of member states in view of the political and economic aspects of security."[30] Given the fact that at the same time concern in Europe about security was so great because of renewed superpower confrontation, the result of the Stuttgart summit meeting was more than disappointing.

However, recent developments indicate that the movement toward closer European cooperation cannot be stopped. The Milan summit meeting in June 1985 clearly kept the interest of the EC in security matters alive but the formal inclusion of security issues into the EC decision-making process still created problems. When the member states, as a result of their discussions about the need for closer political cooperation, including security matters, finally agreed on the Single European Act in February 1986 the mechanism for political cooperation was strengthened, especially through the institution of a special bureau within the Council of Ministers, but security was left out again.

West Germany and the "Two-Pillar" Concept: Between Political Hopes and Security Fears

The two-pillar concept always had strong support in Germany. The idea seems to be attractive for several reasons:

First, in theory it would allow West Germany a more independent role in Europe, where her Atlantic foreign policy orientation limited her room for manoeuvre in East and West as well as in the Third World. It could even serve as a bridge between France and the U.S.

Second, on a practical level the concept allows the Federal Republic to push more convincingly for progress in European integration. Progress here is a necessary pre-condition for success of the two-pillar concept.

Third, it could help to develop bipartisan domestic support in one important foreign policy area.

And yet, the German support for the two-pillar concept—as by the way in the U.S.—has at best been ambivalent. An interesting illustration of that was the famous debate between Gaullists and Atlanticists in Germany in the early sixties when the Franco-German treaty of January 1963 had to be ratified in Parliament. At that time Adenauer and the more conservative wing of the German Christian Democrats and the CSU in Bavaria supported the European foreign policy option, whereas then Foreign Minister Gerhard Schröder and the SPD opted for continuity of the German commitment to the Atlantic Alliance. Atlanticists feared that the Franco-German treaty, if not amended by a preamble reaffirming the German commitment to NATO, would send the wrong signal to the U.S. and would ultimately undermine the security basis of West Germany. The debate ended with a clear victory for the Atlanticists.

In the meantime, hope for and confidence in a two-pillar concept has grown considerably. If a new initiative with a truly European perspective would offer itself, the constellation of the domestic political forces in Germany would be quite different. Probably because of that, the willingness in Europe to push for political change of that kind has diminished, particularly in France.

However, if the initiative for a two-pillar system would come from the U.S. and not from a European country a different kind of policy might appear: the European neighbors of West Germany would probably reinforce the Atlantic orientation in Europe whereas Germany—under these circum-stances—would be more than tempted to play the Gaullist part, regardless of who is in power. The new pressure of the Greens for a neutral foreign policy course is clearly a push factor in that respect. A neutral foreign policy course for Germany, however, is clearly the worst situation for the Germans to be in. It would not only isolate them in the West; even the Soviet Union would look at the Federal Republic of Germany as a less attractive partner than a Federal Republic with membership in NATO. Even those in West Germany who desperately aim at more sovereignty and independence through a neutral course, because they consider the present security structure in Europe unnatural, have to recognize that instead of becoming more sovereign Germany might well fall back into the position of an occupied country.

The only possible conclusion is that there are limits to the room for maneuver for Germany in every direction, East, West and neutral. The difficult task is still to reconcile European aspirations to create their "own" security environment through West European integration, East-West coop-eration and Atlantic cooperation with American preoccupations with the Soviet Union on a global level. From a West German point of view the two-pillar concept needs to be able to control the dialectics of this process in order to be successful.

The American Position

Since World War II the United States has repeatedly declared itself in favor of the process of European integration and the objective of European unity. This support derived in part from the expectation that a strong and democratic Europe could both assume greater responsibility for the defense of that region and could carry part of the American burden elsewhere on the globe. This support was, however, predicated on the assumption that this European pillar would help to buttress the Atlantic Alliance, and that the Europeans would continue to share American beliefs about the role this Alliance should play, both in issuing the security of Western Europe and in upholding American policy vis-à-vis the USSR. In fact, President John F. Kennedy's "Grand Design," reflected these two presuppositions.

Many Americans questioned the viability of these assumptions, noting that a unified Europe would not only be a formidable economic competitor but also a political rival elsewhere and that it could take a neutral position in the U.S.-Soviet competition or even go along with the USSR. They also noted that even a unified Europe which did remain committed to the Alliance would have more influence than the European members now do, and that this could have many adverse implications, and limit America's political and military options rather than support them. Thus, while there have been continuous calls for larger West European contributions to the common defense, and even proposals to restructure NATO so that the burdens and responsibilities within NATO would be altered, there was very little readiness to accept the consequences in terms of power-sharing and for the global role of the U.S. When it appeared that a more unified Europe might pursue a more independent policy line the United States has either remained silent or opposed. Even the modest attempt to revive the Western European Union for security consultations among European states has been criticized rather than welcomed by the U.S.

Similarities and Differences
in U.S. and West German Positions

U.S. and German positions on the Two Pillar Concept at first glance seem to be similar if not identical. Both countries in official statements always pay tribute to the common goal of strengthening Europe to the degree that it can assume full responsibility as the other equal pillar within the Atlantic Alliance. But at closer examination the apparent similarity clearly shows substantial reservations, too, although for different reasons in each individual country.

As far as security is concerned Germany can only rely on the U.S. for nuclear protection and would always prefer a substantial U.S. troop presence on European soil in order to make the nuclear guarantee more credible. European integration at the expense of American military commitment or even with the risk of producing a reduced U.S. military commitment in the long run is something the Germans would always try to avoid. For the U.S., quite to the contrary, the European pillar in NATO has always been seen as a way to reduce the U.S. military burden including the nuclear commitment. It is less the aspect of political independence—something very desirable for Europe—which is important to the U.S. than the possibility that Europe would take a more independent political course in global matters or even turn against U.S. initiatives: that the U.S. would certainly not like. Policy differences between the two pillars, however, are not only probable, they are unavoidable. That perspective limits eagerness to push forward with European independence on both sides.

Conclusion

In spite of new pressure from the U.S. and old ambitions in Europe to change Alliance structures and enable Europe to become a second pillar with equal weight and responsibilities, political efforts to realize this common objective have not been very successful. Although there also exists a certain degree of ambiguity on the American side when it comes to practical steps in that direction, the main responsibility for the failure of Alliance reform is the incapability of Western Europe to bring her impressive political and economic potential to bear also in the field of security.

Military integration in Western Europe has not been a success story. Internal as well as external factors contributed to discourage attempts to change Alliance roles. Although the distribution of power within the Alliance changed considerably over the years both on the European and on the American side, Alliance institutions basically remained untouched. Adjustments were made through additional consultation channels, like the

Nuclear Planning Group, but Europe never succeeded in determining and defining her own role within the Alliance as a true second pillar. Efforts like those of the Euro-group, the Independent Program Group, and the latest initiative to revitalize the Western European Union are far too modest in perspective to satisfy the hopes and expectations on both sides of the Atlantic.

The European Community, on the other hand, is still too weak internally to produce a consensus in security matters or become the basis of a second pillar. A possible concept to overcome the internal weakness of the European Community would be the Schmidt-initiative to put together additional French and German divisions on the basis of common operative planning as a first step to greater European military autonomy. However, the prospects of this initiative catching fire are not good. Therefore, Henry Kissinger's call for adjustment of Alliance roles might well end in another disappointment over missed opportunities and lead to more frustration than change, at least in the short term perspective. The longer-term developments clearly indicate another direction, but that is a matter of piecemeal and slow progress.

Europe, the U.S., and the Out-of-Area Challenge

There is widespread agreement today that as the 1980s begin we live in a new strategic environment. The most important new element seems to be the possibility of confrontations arising in the Third World overlapping with the East-West relationship and/or with economic security, or more accurately, with economic vulnerabilities, partly as a result of economic systems that created dependence on oil and raw materials. This new type of overlapping conflicts can be seen in the Gulf region, in the Middle East, in Africa, in Asia, and even in Central and Latin America.

Can and should Europe, on the basis of an enlarged community, play a greater role in coping with this new situation? Part of the difficulty of the trans-Atlantic dialogue has to do with an uneasiness about the consequences of greater European responsibilities. When these were only aspirations of "professional Europeans," and mere pronouncements rather than imminent reality, there was no great problem. However, increased U.S. interest and even pressure, particularly since Afghanistan, for expanded European responsibility have prompted controversy. Many people fear that Europe, having just rid herself of her colonial past, might risk falling back into colonial attitudes again as she assumes military tasks outside the NATO area.

The current debate about the out-of-NATO-area-challenge sometimes looks like a frustrating reversal of positions in Europe and in the United States.[31] Today, it is the United States that complains about European reluctance to contribute to an Alliance effort and involvement outside the NATO boundaries, but when NATO was founded, the U.S. strongly resisted European attempts to expand the treaty area.[32] The former European colonial powers, particularly Great Britain, France, the Netherlands and Belgium, certainly would have preferred to engage the Atlantic Alliance in protecting and securing their colonial possessions. But the North Atlantic Treaty, because of the anti-colonial attitude of the United States, clearly did not include colonial possessions, as Theodore Achilles, who participated in the deliberations that led to the creation of NATO, has observed.[33]

European experience in the first Indochina War and the Suez Crisis are illustrations of the long shadow of history. In 1952, the French cabinet was arguing that her allies should support French military actions in Indochina, but when it came to a decisive battle in Dien Bien Phu in 1954, the United States declined to provide military assistance.[34] The Suez Crisis was probably even more frustrating because of the U.S.-Soviet cooperation against the NATO Allies and, even if one is not in sympathy with the French and British colonial-style adventure, the violation of prestige and the painful demonstration of a limited sovereignty of middle powers through the two superpowers certainly caused wounds that had dire consequences. One, as already indicated, was the French decision to become an independent nuclear power.

When in the 1960s the United States became more and more involved in Indochina up to a point where Europeans felt pressure from their own publics to take a position against the war, the threat, mainly from Congress, to withdraw troops from Europe contained European opposition. What eased the pressure on NATO was first that Vietnam was part of SEATO and not NATO and further that the U.S. never declared war, a fact which put the U.S. in a weaker position to ask for support. Yet in spite of these factors a good deal of disappointment and bad feelings about the lack of European support clearly remained in the U.S., especially when domestic American opposition and European opposition together really made an impact on American decisions.

There are still other historic examples of Alliance misunderstandings and misperceptions over out-of-area conflicts. North Africa, for instance, is a case where the NATO treaty even gave France a legal basis for assistance, since Article VI on territories covered by the treaty included the Algerian Departments of France. Here, as Lincoln Bloomfield writes, "Paris came to regard alliance support for its savage war against Algerian independence as a test of NATO, Washington took the lead in rejecting any definition of the NATO commitment that included Algeria, despite Article 3 [Article VI is meant, D.D.] of the treaty itself."[35] True, all these strains on the Alliance about out-of-area problems were related to the process of decolonization and Britain with her huge colonial empire, France, Belgium (problems with the U.S. over policies in the Congo) and the Netherlands (problems with the U.S. over the Dutch East Indies and West Irian) all had difficulties with Alliance partners who did not support their positions there.

Of course, American opposition against European colonial policies is no justification today for rejecting joint policies or even military action outside the NATO-area. But it is probably very difficult, if not impossible even, to establish a political consensus within NATO which would be strong enough to allow joint military action. When the United States attacked Libya in April 1986 in order to stop Libyan support for terrorist acts— which was the official justification for the military raid against Libya— European governments with the exception of Great Britain were clearly against the use of the military in order to combat terrorism. The predominant expectations in Europe—both in government circles and in the general public—was that military action would lead to more terrorism and could even lead to a war that Europe did not want.

The only lesson that history can teach is that one should not too quickly become impatient or even frustrated over a lack of unity and consensus within the Alliance concerning out-of-area problems. It would be wrong to state today, as Lincoln Bloomfield does—not without chutzpah—"If NATO had in fact always been doubtful as a coherent extra-European coalition, Afghanistan threw into vivid relief the conflicting interpretations of Soviet military activity, the differing stakes in the détente process, and the growing psychological chasm between those living near the Red Army and those an ocean away."[36]

Outside the NATO area the Alliance will probably have to live with a situation where there is neither total agreement nor total disagreement about policies to pursue. How much unity the Alliance can produce concerning issues outside the NATO area certainly is an important question but not the only one. In terms of conflict resolution the Alliance must also live with different approaches in Europe and the United States, and in some cases these differences of approach might even be helpful.

The Persian Gulf

American policy in the Persian Gulf, today, is directed by the Carter Doctrine which stipulates that "an attempt by an outside force to gain control of the Persian Gulf region will be regarded as an assault on the vital interests of the United States of America. It will be repelled by the use of any means necessary, including military force."[37]

The Carter Doctrine was the immediate consequence of the Soviet invasion of Afghanistan and it tried to give a clear signal to the Soviet Union that there were limits to expansionist moves. The invasion of Afghanistan was seen in the U.S. as such a move particularly after the Shah's regime had collapsed in Iran, and that country, once a strategic pillar of the United States in that region, became utterly unstable and unpredictable. President Reagan, therefore, added a corollary to the Carter Doctrine saying that we will not permit "Saudi Arabia to be an Iran."[38]

Obviously, the United States interpreted events in that region from a global perspective. Perceptions in the U.S. centered around the notion of a crisis of the West after Vietnam and the Arab oil embargo of 1973 caused mainly by the following factors:

- The collapse of Europe's colonial empires and the emergence of largely unstable states incapable of providing the necessary assurance of access to vital raw materials;
- The recession of the Western military power outside the NATO area, as demonstrated by the withdrawal of the British forces East of Suez;
- The establishment of Soviet military power in areas vacated by the West.[39]

And former Secretary of Defense James R. Schlesinger saw in them a totally new form of threat, namely the "domination of Western Europe by the Soviet Union . . . through the Persian Gulf."[40]

The new and more difficult strategic environment the West had to deal with was visible well before the Soviet invasion of Afghanistan. At the latest after 1973 the new vulnerabilities of the Western industrial nations became evident. At that time, however, it was clearly an indirect, non-military threat. With the Soviet invasion of Afghanistan and the fall of the Shah it became a multifaceted East-West, North-South and geostrategic problem at the same time and the response of the Alliance to that type of crisis was indeed poor, to say the least. It was a tragedy, characterized first of all by lack of a sense of political direction but also by misunderstandings, misperceptions, frustration and open mistrust and egoistic self-assertion. A mild summary is what Simon Lunn wrote:

> For most Americans, the events of late 1979—the seizure of the hostages in Tehran and the invasion of Afghanistan—symbolized the decline of the United States and the failure of past politics based on accommodation and negotiation. From this period on, the United States began to move on a new track towards a national revival, a trend intensified under President Reagan. Unfortunately, this mood did not carry across the Atlantic, since the NATO allies did not suffer the same sense of outrage and frustration, and were reluctant to follow policy prescriptions that derived from analysis and a public mood which they did not share. If this period did not mark a parting of the ways, it certainly laid the foundations for the tension and recrimination that currently affect the alliance.[41]

Clearly, Europe, confronted with the Afghan crisis, first of all wanted to avoid spill-over effects and to insulate stability in Europe as much as possible against factors capable of interrupting processes that are clearly in the interest of the Alliance in Europe. What many Americans interpreted as an egotistic, even cowardly and timid reaction after all makes sense insofar as nobody rationally can have an interest in opening a new front of confrontation at a time when the Alliance is already in difficulties elsewhere. A characteristic statement, often cited, was that one should not endanger Berlin because of Kabul. Later, the debate over *horizontal escalation* made clear what the issue really is: crisis interdependence does not only and necessarily work in favor of the West. It is also possible that the

Soviet Union could become interested in conflict escalation if NATO forces were deployed in the Middle East at the expense of the defense of Europe.

The need to develop military precautions for crises outside the NATO area has been generally accepted in NATO. Nobody in NATO wanted the United States to be weak in the face of global challenges. In fact, one of the problems of U.S. preparedness has been the conventional weakness of the United States after Vietnam. The desirability for the U.S. to act worldwide was certainly recognized in Europe. But it took the U.S. quite a long time to develop the necessary instruments. The Rapid Deployment Force which then became the chief instrument was clearly designed before the Soviet intervention in Afghanistan. What concerned Europe was not so much the building of that kind of military instrument but rather the general political implications of its creation and, of course, the impact on the defense of Europe. The United States clearly wanted greater military flexibility without creating many new divisions. Consequently, the bulk of the seven divisions that ultimately will comprise the Rapid Deployment Force under a new U.S. Central Command have to be taken out of the existing potential.[42]

Since some of the units assigned to the Central Command are also earmarked for NATO, their use in one area means that they would be unavailable for employment in the other. If, in case of a crisis, the Central Command would not only ask for support elements such as sea and air transport but would also need forces assigned to NATO, the conventional defense in Europe would certainly be weakened. What everybody in Europe tries to avoid, namely a lowering of the nuclear threshold, might be the unavoidable consequence of American military planning. To guard against this the United States has asked its allies to take compensatory measures should U.S. forces be engaged out-of-area. However, Wartime Host Nation Support, designed for conventional improvements in Europe and other support measures that could be taken under these circumstances, appear in a different light in a Rapid Deployment scenario. That support might now be considered as a contribution to RDF strategic needs.

The Federal Republic of Germany, in this respect, is in a difficult position for several reasons. First, there are legal restrictions concerning any deployment outside the NATO area. According to the Federal Constitution, the use of the *Bundeswehr* for military operations not directly related to the defense of the homeland is unconstitutional.[43]

Second, the *Bundeswehr* from the late 1980s on will have a rather dramatic manpower problem. It has to deal with a shortfall of up to 100,000 servicemen, which will not be easy to fill. This will probably lead to a reduction of the peace-time strength of the *Bundeswehr* in the years to come. Robert Komer, therefore, correctly observes that:

> Our allies are severely inhibited politically from assuming out-of-area strategic obligations by their own domestic preoccupations, their consciousness of their own limited capabilities, their fear of he USSR, their concern over irritating Persian Gulf states on whom they depend for oil, etc. These reasons vary

from country to country, but only France and perhaps Britain contemplate even limited military commitments to PG/IO deterrence and defense. Insofar as security is concerned, Europe's overall outlook has become increasingly regional and less global.[44]

This last point is probably the most important source of friction. That Europe, today, after a long period of influence world-wide restricts itself to a regional role and, therefore, also sees the Atlantic Alliance as a regional defense organization with the main task of protecting Europe, is for many Americans hard to understand and to believe. Particularly, the free-rider accusation in the U.S. is fueled by the regional/global dichotomy and the even higher dependence of Europe on oil supplies in the Middle East and the Persian Gulf evokes a similar type of accusation. Lincoln Bloomfield provides another example of a destructive dialogue when he says:

> If logic were the guide, Europeans should be acting to protect those interests, while Americans should be taking steps to avoid being lured once again into pulling European chestnuts out of the neocolonial fire.[45]

If the problem is dependence on oil from the Middle East and the Persian Gulf, a dependence that the Western industrial states have created themselves through their own industrial structure, then the logical answer to the problem is not necessarily a military one. The logical answer to the problem would be to reduce dependence through energy conservation, alternative energy sources and diversification. These economic steps, however, as we all know, have met with difficulties, because there is no quick solution through conservation and diversification. Also, alternative energies, like nuclear energy, produce severe domestic strains in almost every industrial society. Therefore, complacency on the basis of the formula that the Arabs can't drink oil is not enough.

Economic cooperation between Western industrial countries and the oil-producing states has to be fostered, cultivated and developed and the West is in a much more advantageous position in that respect than is the Soviet Union. A meaningful Western strategy in the Persian Gulf region has to be a combination of economic measures in the industrial states (conservation, alternative energies and diversification) and incentives for cooperation (trade and monetary policy).

The U.S. must be militarily prepared to be available at the request of local states. The military role of the United States as the only Western world power cannot be replaced by the Europeans, although France, Britain and to some degree also the Netherlands are involved in out-of-area contingencies. The more effective European contribution would be to prevent a denudation of the European front in the case of a use of Rapid Deployment Forces in order to discourage Soviet conflict escalation should she be interested in taking advantage of any drawdowns in U.S. troops in Europe or feel she is forced to do so. It would be a mistake, however, to seek again a permanent Western military presence in the region after the

British withdrawal from East of Suez. The British withdrew precisely because their presence ultimately was "encouraging tensions rather than bringing added stability to the area."[46] That lesson should be kept in mind.

The Persian Gulf area is too complicated a region to look at it as a power vacuum that necessarily has to be filled by either one of the two superpowers, and if it is not the U.S. then it is automatically the Soviet Union. That kind of crude basis for policy, perhaps enriched with another, the domino theory of the Khomeini-revolution, is too simple to be effective in the region itself. What satisfies strategic thinkers in Europe or the U.S. may not necessarily convince the local states in the Gulf region. Capabilities for military intervention of the West seen from the Gulf region are not only stabilizing factors; these capabilities clearly have a tendency to provoke the build-up of corresponding capabilities by the other superpower and turn the Gulf region into another area of superpower rivalry. And should U.S. troops be used in the case of internal upheavals, their presence might well be another source of radicalism.

Those who argue in favour of a strategic consensus with Israel and the moderate Arab states often overlook the fact that the communist threat is seen as a very distant danger and that too much and too close cooperation with the U.S. could make it a more imminent one. So, in addition to military capabilities one certainly needs political vision to develop a kind of stability that does not produce domestic sclerosis. It might well turn out that the real security risk there is not communism or the Iranian revolution but rather the lack of democratic institutions.

The Middle East

Alliance actions are, and probably will be, measured by the degree of unity and identity of approaches. It is seldom that some degree of difference is seen as being productive. (One only has to recall Henry Kissinger's complaints about the lack of Allied support for U.S. initiatives in the Middle East in 1973 when he, with his sense of history, interpreted European resistance to the use by the United States of European airfields and space during the October war as a "change of roles" compared to 1956.[47]) However, in the Middle East a different policy of the European Community toward that region might even carry some advantages.[48]

Alliance history in the Middle East is definitely not a success story. What made things worse after 1973, however, was that the oil embargo on the one hand demonstrated economic dependence on the region, and on the other hand, that there was no protection or insulation from the conflicts of the region even if the Europeans wanted it. Since then, Europe has tried to find some sort of accommodation with the Arab world, bilaterally or unilaterally (Euro-Arab dialogue) in order to prevent repetition of the 1973/74 events.[49] No doubt, a policy of that kind would have consequences for Israel, too. That became evident in the course of the Camp David process, where serious Alliance differences appeared. Part of the problem within the Alliance was certainly that the U.S. administration under Carter until

1977 acted on the basis of an inclusion of the Soviet Union in the peace process. That was the message of the Soviet-American declaration on the Middle East of October 1, 1977, which was supported in Europe.[50]

But soon after that declaration, and in light of Anwar Sadat's move in November 1977, the U.S. changed from a comprehensive approach to the Camp David process which excluded the Soviet Union. Of course, the Camp David process did not include the Europeans. That would have been difficult because of a lack of consensus here, too. The Europeans hoped to regain a role in the peace process when the Camp David process got stuck over the autonomy question. It was then that the EC, or, more precisely, Great Britain and France as members, tried to amend U.N. resolution 242, which, as it stood, still treated the Palestinian question as a refugee problem. The EC tried to include the right of self-determination in that resolution in order to break the impasse on the autonomy neogotiations.[51] President Carter clearly wanted the Europeans to stay out of the Camp David process and even announced his intention to veto any move to change resolution 242.[52]

With the Venice Declaration of June 1980, the EC then tried to launch its own initiative to renew the peace process stating, however, that the new initiative should complement rather than replace the Camp David process. The main new element in the European effort was to include the PLO in the peace process. In view of Israel's massive opposition and even hostility towards the Venice Declaration, but also because the PLO was not ready to accept Israel's right of existence in advance, the European initiative did not work. In addition, support in Europe, which had never been unanimous, was diminished with the change of government in France in 1981 when French President Mitterand decided to support the implementation of the Camp David process and refused to engage in a European role separate from that of the U.S. With the creation—by the U.S. and Europe—of a Multinational Force and Observers (MFO) in the Sinai, the U.S. and European positions became less different again temporarily. The participation of four European states in the MFO for the Sinai is a clear evidence that the nations of Western Europe had given up attempts to push forward with their concept of broadening the peace process. However, Europe continued to put more emphasis on a United Nations role than did the U.S. Different negotiating concepts between Europe and the U.S. do continue to play a role in the Middle East and these differences may come up again.

Israel clearly emerged as a strategic ally of the United States in the Middle East, and so did Syria as a bridgehead of the Soviet Union. Today, in Europe, support is growing for a position that not only the Syrians but also the Soviet Union and the Palestinians should be included in the Middle East dialogue and peace settlement.

The tense relationship between Israel and Syria clearly bears the risk of military confrontation at almost any time, especially in view of their rivalry in Lebanon.[53] Lebanon still suffers from an imported civil war, with Syria and Israel as the dominant outside powers. But even the Israeli invasion of Lebanon in 1982 could not end the tragic situation of that country. On the contrary: not only did Israel fail to reach the goal of pushing out the Palestinians and the Syrian troops and of establishing a pro-Israeli government in Lebanon, the invasion was stopped by the U.S. before a decisive blow against Syria could be struck. Today Israel, despite a partial disengagement, seems to be drawn into a situation similar to that of the U.S. in Vietnam.

Even the Reagan Initiative of September 1982 did not help to revitalize the Camp David process. The initiative clearly ignored Syria and did not offer enough for Jordan in order to bring that country—like Egypt before it—into the peace process. The last hope for success of the Reagan initiative disappeared with the failure of the American and European peace-keeping forces troops to produce stability in Lebanon. Under heavy domestic pressure after the loss of 270 marines, the U.S. forces had to leave Lebanon in February 1984 and the European forces under the circumstances had no other choice but to leave too. What was left of a common U.S.-European peace effort in that region was consternation and disappointment in the Arab world.

Especially in light of the U.S. strike against Libya to fight state supported terrorism, the gap between the Western Alliance and the Arab world seems to be widening and new efforts have to be made to bridge the gap. So far, however, neither widespread condemnation in the West of the methods used by Israel to supress the demonstrations by Palestinians in the West Bank and Gaza nor the American efforts, spearheaded by Secretary of State Shultz, to arrange for negotiations which could restore a measure of tranquility to the area, have either narrowed that gap nor furthered the aspirations of all the Western governments for peace, security and justice in the Middle East. Perhaps the U.S. decision to talk to the PLO will do so but that has yet to be seen.

Africa

The single most important problem in Africa for the Alliance remains the relationship to, and with, the Republic of South Africa. If the Soviet Union has a chance to get a foothold in Africa, it will certainly be because the West appears to deprive black Africa of any hope of support in the efforts to change both the racist policies of the Republic of South Africa and its attempts to prevent a democratic solution for Namibia. Even those who argue for historical understanding of the oppressing and tragic domestic situation in the Republic of South Africa, and for acknowledgement of the geostrategic importance of that country, must caution against a course of the West that lends increasing support for South African positions. The recent understanding between the Republic of South Africa and the front line states should not obscure the fact that what needs to be strengthened is not South Africa's legitimacy but rather black Africa's economic, social, and political conditions. Here is where the credibility of the West in the Third World is going to be tested.

The sanctions imposed on South Africa by the U.S. Congress in the summer of 1985 were clearly an indication of decreasing patience on the U.S. side with the lack of success of "constructive engagement" vis-à-vis South Africa. Pressure for reform in South Africa towards majority rule is important, but so is cooperation with the frontline states.

Moreover, it is not enough to see Africa as an arena in which the West confronts Soviet and Cuban military presence; though these may add to the problems of the area they are not their prime cause. The number of people living in poverty in Africa is growing dramatically and, for a majority, even basic human needs cannot be met.

Europe does have a kind of model institution to organize improved cooperation with Africa and other developing countries. It is the so-called Lome Agreement which gives more than sixty states of Africa, Asia, the Caribbean and the Pacific better access to European markets. However, agricultural access remains a problem with the present agricultural system of the European Community. Also, problems like energy, monetary relations, and transfer of technology have to be solved in order to establish a system of relations that could increase the chances of enabling the Third World countries to progress.

There are also traditional relations of European states dating back to the colonial period; not only France and Great Britain but also Spain and Portugal still have close ties with the African continent. It is interesting to see that today Angola and Mozambique, former Portuguese colonies, are renewing their contacts with Portugal. The Soviet and Cuban influence there seems to have diminished after successful revolutions and both countries obviously see a better future in closer economic ties with the European Community.

France, for example, has not only kept a strong influence in Africa through cultural heritage, language, and administration systems but it has also built strong economic ties. The French military presence in Africa even led to several small-sized military interventions, for instance in Chad. Such interventions have occurred as a result of national considerations without any formal consultation within the European Community.

American policies toward Africa seem to be more determined by the global competition with the Soviet Union.[54] Strategic concerns of the U.S. are obvious in the Horn of Africa where Europe and the U.S. have to secure their oil supply. Both Europe and the U.S. also have an interest in helping to contain Libyan expansionism in Africa, where France with American backing helped to stop a political group supported by Colonel Ghaddafi from conquering Chad. Both France and the U.S. have economic interests in Chad but there are also political differences between France and the U.S.. Paris does not want to be replaced by Washington in Africa and would be willing to compromise with Ghaddafi. The U.S. would oppose any compromise with Ghaddafi. Another possible crisis area because of

Libyan intervention is the Sudan, a country which is bordered by two anti-American powers in Africa: Libya and Ethiopia. Here, the U.S. clearly stated through President Reagan that aggression against the Sudan would not be tolerated. Strategic and ideological considerations play a much greater role in American policies than in European policies where the developing needs of Africa are more respected. Given the fact that most African states, except perhaps in the case of civil war, do not like superpower involvement, differential Alliance policy which would give Europe a special non-military role in that region might well work and even be advisable.

Central and Latin America

For the United States, the strong interest of Europeans in Central and Latin America certainly came as a surprise. Ever since the Monroe Doctrine, the United States had asserted its dominant, hegemonial power in the Western hemisphere. "American preeminence in the hemisphere was not challenged until Fidel Castro's revolution in Cuba and his alignment with the Soviet Union."[55] For the U.S., Central and Latin America are still seen as zones of influence in a geopolitical sense. Seen from a European perspective, the renewed interest in a region where Europe, because of the strong American opposition to European colonialism, lost almost every influence except a cultural one is perhaps less surprising precisely because the Europeans stopped looking at that region as a zone of influence. That privilege, today, is left to the two superpowers alone. Why does and why should Europe at all be interested in the region again, instead of leaving things as they are? And if there is a need to act, why not let the U.S. deal with it? Some Europeans would even agree to that. The explanation has to be seen in several developments.

First, there is a general increased awareness in Europe about developments in the Third World since the first oil embargo, which was a dramatic demonstration of European economic vulnerability, led to greater sensitivity to events in the Third World in general.

Second, as Wolf Grabendorf points out, there were a number of factors which in his view made a European involvement unavoidable:

- The domestic political environment;
- Popularity of the revolution in Nicaragua, at least at the beginning;
- Human rights and humanitarian commitment;
- The attractiveness of Europe as a market and a source of investments and aid;
- General support of the public in Europe and assurance for opposition forces fighting military regimes often supported by the U.S.[56]

For its part, the United States has long regarded the Caribbean as a region of great strategic significance, especially since the opening of the Panama Canal, and has long played the role of "international policeman," a role which has led to military intervention, to extended periods of occupation and to the creation of what some historians have called a "Caribbean empire."[57] Hence, even before Castro came to power, the United States had been concerned over the intrusion of Marxism-Leninism (which it regards as an extra-continental political system) into the Western Hemisphere and had taken steps to oppose it. Since 1962, Washington had intensified its efforts to contain Cuban influence and to head off the establishment of new states oriented toward the Soviet Union, and when these efforts failed, it took counter-actions, such as supporting the overthrow of Allende in Chile, intervening in Grenada and organizing the "Contras" against Nicaragua. These moves reflected not only a desire to check Soviet "expansionism" but also a belief that the further extension of Soviet influence could, at a minimum, result in a military threat to American lines of communication with Europe and might even eventuate in a direct threat to the United States through its "back door."[58]

Although American policies include the provision of economic assistance to countries of Central America, efforts to assure the widest possible distribution of the benefits of growth and support for democratic processes and institutions, they also include arms transfers, the dispatch of military trainers and advisers, the construction of air bases and other facilities for use in an emergency, and, as noted earlier, support for partisans operating against the Sandinistas. That these measures require cooperation with right-wing governments is deemed deplorable, but necessary: reforms are both uncertain and slow to take effect, especially in strife-torn countries. Ultimately, therefore, the United States judges that it cannot exclude the use of force to preclude the further extension of Soviet-Cuban influence, if not to change the Sandinista government in Nicaragua.

The difference of perspective in looking at Central and Latin America between Europe and the U.S.—in the U.S. from a strategic and geopolitical perspective, in Europe from a Third World perspective—leads to different policy orientations within the Alliance. The United States is concerned about the thrust of social and political change because of its possible consequences for the global competition with the Soviet Union. Cuba in the late 1950s and Nicaragua now are alarming events for the United States. In Europe, on the other hand, social change is seen as being inevitable because "attempts by the U.S. to preserve the status quo or to stabilize pre-revolutionary situations will most likely lead to more radicalization and violence and increase the tendency in the region to turn to the socialist bloc for help."[59] The *Strategic Survey*, published by the IISS in London, therefore warns that the policies of the United States appear likely to alienate the left further, but without defeating it, and to increase U.S. dependence on the right, but without assuring that the changes that are necessary for any genuine prospects of improvement will occur.[60]

Traditional relations of individual European states add to European special attention to Central and Latin America. France, Great Britain, and the Netherlands still have some colonial territories. Both Britain and the Netherlands have more or less withdrawn from the region but France still keeps its islands in the Caribbean and Guyana on the mainland.[61]

Spain in Europe is expected to build a bridge to Latin American as a full member of the European Community. There are already many indications, for example, of the particular interest of the Spanish Prime Minister Felipe Gonzales in Central America which support the thesis that the EC will be even more active in Central and Latin America now that Spain has joined the community.

For some time, the United States even tried to bring in the EC deliberately, for example, to help to support development projects. Now, with so much criticism of the policy of the Reagan Administration in the region, there seems to be greater reluctance in the U.S. to involve the Europeans. Given the tensions in the Caribbean particularly, and the obvious attempt at self-assertion against great power influence, a special and different role of Europe to contribute to change might be beneficial for the West in the long run. The European Community, for instance, is gradually stepping up its commitment in Central America, including Nicaragua. The EC now meets on a more or less regular basis with all Central American governments, alternately in Europe and in Central America. In addition to that, the Arias-Peace Plan for Central America, or the Esquipulas II Agreements, as they are officially known, opens up a new perspective that might even lead to greater convergence of U.S. and European policies. However, to date, it remains to be seen whether the Arias-Plan, for which its author received the Nobel Peace Prize in 1987, will be successful.

Institutional Aspects

There are obvious shortcomings in the existing institutions of the West to deal with out-of-area problems. NATO, OECD, EC and European Political Cooperation (EPC) and also the annual Economic Summit of the seven Western industrial nations (U.S., France, Great Britain, Germany, Japan, Italy, Canada, and the President of the EC-Commission) are all relevant, at least partly, but there is no comprehensive and competent institution with sufficient authority to bring about the necessary decisions. Out-of-area problems are typically overlapping issues, political, economic and military at the same time. The main problem, of course, is that the nature of out-of-area problems simply transcends any one of the above mentioned institutions and that in order to be effective, a degree of flexibility is necessary that can only be achieved on the basis of *ad hoc* political consultation between national governments. Under these circumstances, the key-country concept developed by the four institutes is probably the only realistic approach possible.[62]

The primary concern of the Western Alliance outside the NATO area is not to develop additional capabilities for military intervention. The area outside the boundaries of NATO is not void of self-determination and free for intervention. For this reason, the Rapid Deployment Force as an instrument for intervention has to be handled very carefully. If far enough away, the existence of Rapid Deployment Forces might well be accepted by local states but in general the physical military presence of both super-powers is rejected.

What has to be achieved in the first place is crisis management and conflict resolution. All the recent examples, like the Multinational Force and Observers in the Sinai (MFO), the Multinational Force in Lebanon (MNF) and the Western naval presence in the Persian Gulf show that key-countries with specific geographic, strategic and/or traditional political interests in regions outside the NATO area really matter, whereas existing institutions like NATO, the EC, and EPC tend to prevent decisive action. They can take positions and support or discourage actions diplomatically but they would have difficulty in providing crisis management. There are sufficient technical means of communication today to assure that key-countries of the West, including Japan, can consult on an *ad hoc* basis.

For some observers the Economic Summit Meeting on the basis of experience since 1975, when the first Meeting took place in Rambouillet (France), seems to be the ideal solution. Indeed, with a permanent secre-tariat and staff, the Economic Summit could become a sort of Trilateral World government which many trilateralists probably have hoped for. Since the last meetings in Williamsburg, Tokyo and Venice, the Economic Summit has definitely become more political than it used to be when it started. The economic issues in Williamsburg clearly had a second rank compared with defense, arms control, and the deployment of Pershing II and Cruise missiles in Europe. That step seemed to indicate an implicit extension of the Western security alliance to include Japan.[63] However, since there is no permanent secretariat of the summit meeting, and the summitry seems to be at a crucial juncture because of a lack of economic success at the meetings, one should not place too much hope in the summit as *the* institutional solution for out-of-area questions. There is also the fact that the summit meetings were successful at the beginning precisely because of the lack of bureaucracy and organization. The more these meetings became part of routine diplomacy, the less successful they were.

Another potential institution might be the Guadeloupe type of meeting between the U.S., France, Great Britain and Germany. This idea comes very close to a kind of NATO directorate. For European and Atlantic East-West issues this type of meeting certainly makes sense and should be kept in mind in the case of East-West crises. However, it is difficult to see that a Guadeloupe type of meeting could be efficient enough to deal with out-of-area problems in general. It is obvious that different regions outside NATO demand different participants in order to provide successful crisis management. As has been suggested by the four institutes, the permanent key-members should be the U.S., France, Great Britain, Germany, and Japan but the regional circumstances should really determine the make-up of the group that tries to deal with the issue. It would certainly be very attractive if the key groups and possible regional groups could provide what might best be called "preventive diplomacy." That, however, is a question of substance and not institutions. Institutions cannot replace the right kind of policy and they, too, cannot create consensus if it is not already there.

West Germany and the Out-of-Area Challenge:
A Low-Key Approach

For obvious reasons, West Germany cannot play an active military role out of the NATO area and yet she is the object of many hopes in that respect. This discrepancy is at the heart of the out-of-area challenge as seen from Germany. According to the Basic Law of the Federal Republic of Germany the use of the *Bundeswehr* for military operations outside the NATO area is unconstitutional.[64] That is also the official position of the Federal Government.[65] In addition to that, manpower shortages in the late 1980s and early 1990s will create tremendous problems in keeping up the peace-time strength of the *Bundeswehr*, which will probably shrink in the years to come. Also, to prepare for contingencies outside the NATO area would make necessary a reorientation of present policies for armaments and equipment. That, for financial reasons, is not in the cards in the near future. And there is one great danger of such a policy even if it were financially possible, namely that the Alliance will be weakened as a result of trying to equip the *Bundeswehr* for out-of-area missions. The most beneficial contribution of the *Bundeswehr* to NATO is the defense of the Central Front. There the West Germans are sufficiently equipped and, what is more important, they are motivated. The specialization of the *Bundeswehr* for defending the Central Front should not be changed. Otherwise, the whole concept of integration of forces in West Germany could be weakened because the nations whose troops are stationed on German soil would have difficulties in justifying their presence in Germany while Germany's own home forces are preparing to fight elsewhere.

The more important question, today, is what NATO can do in order to compensate for U.S. military activities outside the NATO area which take out forces assigned to NATO. Since the seven divisions that ultimately comprise the Rapid Deployment Force under a new U.S. Central Command will be taken out of the existing potential, most of that force will probably have to be taken out of forces allocated to NATO. The German concern in that respect is that Europe does *not* become the second most important area of NATO's defense efforts. Two more specific concerns are these: first that Host Nation Support is clearly an effort to strengthen the defense of Europe and that the corresponding agreements are not considered as a mere service for RDF strategic needs. Even more important is a second concern related to the role of nuclear weapons. A lowering of the nuclear threshold in Europe as a consequence of American military planning for South West Asia must be avoided.

For West Germany, the Atlantic Alliance is a regional defense organization whose main task is to defend the Central Front. Seen from Germany, the military role of the United States as the only Western world power cannot be replaced by Europeans, although European nations like France and Great Britain are involved in out-of-area contingencies. The more effective European contribution to the Western defense beyond the NATO-area would be to prevent a denudation of the European front in the case of a use of Rapid Deployment Forces. It would be a mistake to seek a permanent Western military presence. The lesson of the British presence East of Suez should be kept in mind.

Similarities and Differences

Obviously, as a global power, the U.S. is much more concerned about out-of-area challenges than are the European members of the Alliance. In fact, the U.S. has difficulties accepting the notion of a NATO-first-strategy because such a regional approach would be an impediment to the global role of the U.S.. From the U.S. perspective, a conflict originating outside the NATO area is in principle not different from NATO-area conflicts; for Europe it makes a great difference, in fact it makes all the difference. Concerning the out-of-area challenge, differences between Europe and the U.S. seem to outweigh by far the similarities. This is no surprise because geography, power and historical experience seem to pull powerfully in different directions. In the case of the Persian Gulf, the reasons for differences in the German and American approaches have been laid out in some detail. In addition to the German legal restrictions, it is most importantly the manpower shortage of the *Bundeswehr* and the fear that the defense of the Central Front, where Germany's most vital interests are located, could suffer from Persian Gulf military activities. But there are also different perspectives on what military activities can achieve. This has a lot to do with the difference in the power status of the two countries. There is not much hope that Germany could positively influence events militarily and hence there is a reluctance to join the military efforts of the U.S.

In the case of Central America similar factors are at work. First, geography and geopolitics lead the U.S. to see political changes in that region as a matter of national security and more often than not in the context of the East-West conflict. Germany and Europe, on the other hand, from a geographical distance see the Central American issue as a North-South conflict in which they have no vital stake. The use of military force is seen as a necessary option from the U.S. perspective. For Germany and Europe such an option seems to be self-defeating. On that basis greater European involvement in the Central American region could well lead to a strain in Alliance relations rather than to burden-sharing.

In the Middle East and Africa too, the differences in power status and conflicting views concerning the use of force are responsible for the lack of agreement among allies. In addition to that, the U.S. constantly plays down the role of economic measures and/or the positive role international organizations can play in conflict resolution, thus it fails to make full use of the contributions its European allies are best fitted to make.

Conclusion

The out-of-area challenge is an integral part of the difficult task of adjustment of Alliance roles, and it is not at all a new one. The only new thing is that today positions about the proper role of the Alliance beyond the treaty area seem to have changed 180 degrees, so that a frustrating reversal of positions in Europe and in the United States can be observed. Whereas the U.S. strongly resisted European attempts to expand the treaty area when NATO was founded, today it is the European reluctance to contribute to Alliance efforts outside the NATO boundaries which leads to complaints by the United States.

The main obstacle to having a coherent Alliance policy towards the outside world, or, more precisely, beyond the treaty-area, is the question of which political, military and economic strategy NATO should adopt and how such a strategy should be implemented. In that connection, particularly, the following observations are important:

1. Any meaningful Western strategy vis-à-vis Third World countries has to be an attempt at economic and political cooperation in the first place.
2. Although it is still important, the capability of military intervention at the request of local states (not as an imperial act) is not *per se* a stabilizing factor. It can also encourage tensions, particularly if the West should seek a permanent military presence. The lesson of the military presence of Great Britain East of Suez should not be forgotten.
3. The military role of the United States as the only Western world power cannot be replaced by the Europeans, although France, Britain and to some degree also the Netherlands are involved in out-of-area contingencies.
4. The more important and effective European contribution in the Alliance is to prevent the denudation of the European Front in case of a use of Rapid Deployment Forces. In such a case, conflict escalation is definitely not favorable for the West. Rather in the case of crisis interdependence in the Gulf area and elsewhere, conflict escalation in Europe could be a possible Soviet move that has to be discouraged.
5. European and American interests beyond the treaty-area are neither totally identical nor completely opposed. Under these circumstances, political unity within the Alliance should not be the first priority or prerequisite for action. In terms of conflict resolution, the Alliance might live better with different approaches by Europe and by the U.S. because different approaches here and there can be helpful in some cases, i.e., in the Middle East and Africa and in Central and Latin America.
6. Since out-of-area problems are typically overlapping issues and political, military and economic in character at the same time, the best

institutional approach for crisis management and conflict resolution is the key-country approach. This avoids both the problem of finding an appropriate body to deal with the issue and the fact that none of the bodies now extant have anything like the full range of power and authority required to cope with virtually any out-of-area question.

In general, one can conclude that in spite of an increased potential for conflict within the Alliance and the divergent interests of Europe and the United States, chances for successful adjustment exist because, today, for the first time in Alliance history there is a parallel, although not necessarily identical interest, on both sides of the Atlantic, in changing and redefining Alliance roles.

Notes

1. Henry Kissinger, "A Plan to Reshape NATO," *Time*, (5 March 1984), 47.
2. See Edward Luttwak in the *Washington Post*, 29 November 1987, L 1.
3. I am taking up an idea that Carl Friedrich v. Weizsäcker developed in 1966. See his article *"Über weltpolitische Prognosen," Europa-Archiv*, 1, 1966.
4. Title of a paper by Horst Ehmke, Bonn, January 1984.
5. See Richard v. Weizsäcker, Speech on the occasion of taking office as President of the Federal Republic of Germany, *Bulletin des Presse- u. Informationsamtes der Bundesregierung*, 80, 3 July 1984.
6. Interview with the Radio Station *Deutschlandfunk*, 20 August 1984.
7. Interview with *Neues Deutschland, Berliner Zeitung* and press agency ADN, 18 August 1984.
8. Karl W. Deutsch *et al.,Political Community and the North Atlantic Area*, (Princeton: Princeton University Press, 1957), 3-21.
9. Economic data in *Europa-Archiv*, 12, 1948, 1736.
10. John R. Dean, *The Strange Alliance. The Story of the Efforts at Wartime Cooperation with Russia*, (New York: The Viking Press 1947).
11. Memorandum of Jean Monnet of 3 May, 1950. Text in Gilbert Ziebura, *Die deutsch-franzosischen Beziehungen seit 1945—Mythen and Realitaten* (Pfullingen: Neske, 1970), 195-200.
12. See Karl Kaiser, "The U.S. and the E.E.C. in the Atlantic System: The Problem of Theory." *Journal of Common Market Studies*, V, 4 (June 1967), 413.
13. North Atlantic Council, *Report of the Committee of Three on Non-Military Cooperation in NATO*, 1956.
14. See his article, "U.S. Strategy and the Defense of Europe," *Orbis*, 7, 2 (Summer 1963), 231.
15. The two-pillar concept was Kennedy's message in his speeches on Independence Day, July 4, 1962, in Philadelphia and in Frankfurt, June 25, 1963. See also Ronald Steel, *Pax Americana*, (New York: The Viking Press, 1967), who tries to explain the U.S. foreign policy approach in the 1960's and the two-pillar concept.
16. Henry A. Kissinger, *The Troubled Partnership* (New York: McGraw-Hill Book Company, 1965), 139.
17. See Francois Duchêne, *"Die Rolle Europas im Weltsystem: Von der regionalen zur planetarischen Interdependent,"* in *Zivilmacht Europa—Supermacht oder Partner?* (Frankfurt: 1973), 33.
18. *Ibid.*

19. I have dealt with that problem in a contribution to *The Contemporary Mediterranean World*, ed. by Carl F. Pinkele and Adamantia Pollis (New York: 1983) and elsewhere. The following arguments draw heavily on my article "Security in the Context of an Enlarged European Community," 50-58.

20. Ian Smart, "Future Conditional: The Prospect for Anglo-French Cooperation," *Adelphi Papers* No. 78 (London: Institute for Strategic Studies, 1971), 3.

21. See George M. Seignious II and Jonathan Paul Yates, "Europe's Nuclear Superpowers," *Foreign Policy*, 55, (Summer 1984), 40-53.

22. Pierre Hassner, "Détente and the Policies of Instability in Southern Europe," in *Beyond Nuclear Deterrence*, ed. by Johan Holst and Uwe Nerlich (New York: Crane, Russack, 1977), 46.

23. See *Westeuropaische Verteidigungskooperation*, ed. by Karl Carstens and Dieter Mahncke (München, Wien: Oldenbourg, 1972), 217 ff.

24. See his article in *Strategic Review*, XI, 4 (Fall 1983).

25. See *Adelphi Papers* No. 129, "The Alliance and Europe, Part VI: The European Programme Group" by D.C.R. Heyhoe. (London: The International Institute for Strategic Studies, 1979).

26. Karl Kaiser, Winston Lord, Thiery de Montbrial, David Watt, *Security: What Has Changed: What Should Be Done?* (London: Royal Institute of International Affairs, 1981), 13.

27. Communiqué of the Franco-German consultations in Paris on February 5 and 6, 1981. Full text in *Bulletin des Presse und Informationsamtes der Bundesregierung,* 1 February 1981, 101.

28. See Michel Tatu, *"Europaische Verteidigung—eine gemeinsame Aufgabe?,"* *Dokumente*, 22 January 1983, Special edition, 47.

29. *Die EG vor der Entscheidung: Fortschritt oder Verfall?,* (Bonn: 1983), 48.

30. See text of the declaration in *Europa-Archiv* 15, 1983, D 420-427.

31. Gregory F. Treverton, "Defense Beyond Europe," *Survival*, 25,5 (Sept./Oct. 1983), 216.

32. See the interesting article of Stanley R. Sloan, "The Alliance and the Third World," in *Die Europaisch-Amerikanischen Beziehungen bei Sicherheitsfragen in der Dritten Welt*, Stiftung Wissenschaft und Politik, SWP—K 2378, December 1983, 8.

33. Cited by Sloan, *ibid.*

34. See Treverton, "Defense Beyond Europe," 217.

35. Lincoln Bloomfield, "Crisis Management Outside the NATO Area: Allies or Competitors?" in *Allies in a Turbulent World*, ed. by Frans A. M. Alting von Geusau (Lexington: Lexington Books, 1982), 51.

36. *Ibid.*, 53.

37. 1980 State of the Union Message, 23 January 1980.

38. See Robert Litwak, "Persian Gulf Security and European-American Relations," in *Die Europaisch-Amerikanischen Beziehungen bei Sicherheitsfragen in der Dritten Welt*, 36.

39. See Jeffrey Record, "The Impact on NATO of Security Requirements Outside the Treaty Area," in *Strengthening Deterrence. NATO and the Credibility of Western Defense in the 1980s* (Cambridge: Cambridge University Press, 1981), 165.

40. Cited in Record, *ibid.*, 163.

41. Simon Lunn, *Burden-sharing in NATO*, Chatham House Papers No. 18, (London: 1983), 19.

42. See Robert Komer, "Prospects for Allied Cooperation Outside the NATO-Area," in *NATO: Agenda for the Next Four Years* (Santa Monica, CA: RAND Corporation, January 1982.)

43. See Herbert J. P. Woopen, "Legal Restrictions on the Deployment of European Forces Outside the NATO-Area," unpublished paper, Washington, D.C., 1983, 14.

44. Komer, "Prospects for Allied Cooperation . . . ," 14.

45. Bloomfield, "Crisis Management Outside the NATO Area . . . ," 52-53.

46. Philip Darby, cited by Litwak in "Persian Gulf Security and European-American Relations," 41.

47. See his memoirs 1973-1974, German text, 830.

48. Treverton, "Defense Beyond Europe," 220.

49. See Reinhardt Rummel, "The Arab-Israeli Conflict," in *Die Europaisch-Amerikanischen Beziehungen bei Sicherheitsfragen in der Dritten Welt*, 56.

50. See text in *Europa-Archiv* 4, 1978, 97-98.

51. See Rummel, "The Arab-Israeli Conflict," 61.

52. *Ibid.*

53. See the excellent analysis by Helmut Hubel, *Turkei und Mittelost-Krisen*, Paper, Research Institute of the German Society for Foreign Affairs (Bonn: August 1984).

54. See Sloan, "The Alliance and the Third World," 16.

55. *Ibid.*

56. See for this and the following Wolf Grabendorff, "The Role of Western Europe in the Caribbean Basin," in *Die Europaisch-Amerikanischen Beziehungen bei Sicherheitsfragen in der Dritten Welt*, 88.

57. *Ibid.*

58. Gordon Connel - Smith, "President Reagan and the Caribbean Crisis," *Washington Quarterly* 7, 4 (Fall 1984), 14.

59. Grabendorff, "The Role of Western Europe in the Caribbean Basin," 90.

60. *Strategic Survey 1983-1984*, London 1984, 116.

61. Grabendorff, "The Role of Western Europe in the Caribbean Basin," 102.

62. Kaiser *et al.*, *Western Security: What Has Changed? What Should Be Done?*.

63. See Robert D. Putnam, "Summit Sense," in *Foreign Policy*, 55 (Summer 1984), 87.

64. Woopen, "Legal Restrictions on the Deployment of European Forces . . . ," 14.

65. *Ibid.*

7

Détente and Security

Gale A. Mattox

Since World War II the United States and the Federal Republic of Germany have defined as acceptable and desirable a security regime which at the same time offers physical security to Western Europe and permits the continuation of democratic processes. This concept is embodied in Articles 1 and 5 of the NATO Treaty[1] of 1949. Obviously this security regime requires political as well as military stability and both countries have defined their requirements in political and military terms.

The earlier chapters of this book dealt with the similarities and differences in American and West German perceptions of the military contribution to physical security. Whatever the differences between the two countries, the U.S. and the FRG have been in fundamental agreement since the mid 1950s, when Germany assumed responsibility for its own defense, over the need for a staunch bulwark against the East Block or, indeed, any other threats to their security. However, agreement on the need for physical security and on the way to achieve it has been much easier to attain than agreement on the much more vague concept of political security. In this chapter we will attempt to consider these differences over the political requirements of security in the East-West context (i.e., over détente) and over the interlinkage of the political and military aspects of the security regime in Europe as pursued through arms control. It is in this interlinkage of political and military aspects that the similarities and divergences between U.S. and FRG perceptions of defense and détente become most striking and most revealing.

The motivations behind support of a policy direction, the approach to policy objectives and even basic perceptions or interpretations of policy have varied from country to country and at different periods in time. The priority given either political or military approaches to the construction of a security regime (i.e., to the balance between defense and détente) has accounted in large part for the contradictions often evidenced in different FRG and U.S. stances toward the East Block. Thus, it may be useful to begin with a brief review of prior policies.

Détente and Security: Two Approaches

The Early Days of the NATO Alliance

While the U.S. and FRG jointly pursued the same objective, that of establishing a security regime, there were clear differences in approach during the postwar period, reflecting their divergent motivations based on their respective evaluations of national interests. For the West Germans, a security regime in the 1950s was also to serve the further goal of reunification of Germany within a democratic framework. Proper political conditions would lead then to the necessary conditions for physical security. For the United States, a security regime was regarded as a necessary protection of American interests in a physical and then political economic sense. Although the United States formally adopted the concept of German reunification, it clearly was not a priority and, some critics have asserted, not even a particularly desirable goal, given the experience of the 1930s and 1940s. Above all, the United States regarded a militarily secure Europe to be the prerequisite to any political solutions.

To complicate matters still further, the Adenauer government was also clearly concerned early in the 1950s with assuring German political sovereignty and legitimacy and later with their maintenance. Furthermore, the security regime envisioned by Chancellor Adenauer was to be one in which Germany would play a significant political role within the Western Alliance. Indeed, the desire for legitimacy within the Atlantic Alliance often appeared even more important than reunification, particularly a reunification which might threaten the carefully constructed democratic basis in the Federal Republic and its resumption of sovereignty.

The differences in U.S./FRG conceptions of a European security regime were especially evident during the talks between the Western Allies and Germany in the course of the attempt to create a European Defense Community. Not only was the issue of German sovereignty a focal point, the question of borders in the event of reunification was also fiercely debated.[2] From the point of view of the United States, but even more from the French perspective, mention of the 1937 borders, even within the context of future reunification, would only aggravate East-West relations, not to mention the fears and concerns of the non-German population of Western Europe. While German entry into NATO in 1955 resolved finally the question of FRG sovereignty and tied West German security to the Atlantic Alliance, the process of acceptance as a partner in the Alliance was slow and FRG/U.S. perceptions of the broader issue of reunification remained split.

Constructing a Dialogue with the East

The situation began to alter in the 1960s and 1970s as three changes occurred: 1) U.S. nuclear superiority came under challenge, 2) the Federal Republic assumed a greater economic and political role both within Europe and internationally and 3) the U.S. interest in closer relations with the East was followed by German initiatives toward Moscow and its allies, particularly on inter-German issues.

In the first case, the nuclear superiority of the United States until the late 1960s and early 1970s meant that détente (i.e., a relaxation of tensions leading both to greater security and to closer political and economic cooperation) was not essential to the physical security of the FRG-though it might be significant for reunification, or at least for some improvement in relations between West and East Germany and in the lot of the inhabitants of the latter state. As noted in Chapters 2 and 4, the impending loss of American nuclear superiority led to a change in concepts for the defense of Western Europe, from "massive retaliation" to "flexible response." It also led to (or at least influenced) two other changes in policy: one a renewed interest in arms control (which will be discussed later) and the other a greater emphasis on détente. The equal focus on "defense and détente" embodied in the Harmel Report[3] of 1967 (See Chapter 6) brought the European allies and the United States to possibly the closest consensus since NATO's founding. On the one hand, NATO was to permit more room for military maneuver in responding to a Warsaw Pact threat while, on the other hand, it would seek greater political flexibility through closer relations with the East, and, if possible, through arms control.

The gradual loss of U.S. nuclear superiority came concurrently with a second instance of change: the increasingly greater role of the Federal Republic in economic and political affairs. The economic miracle of the 1960s had prompted a resurgence of FRG confidence. Its stature increased within the European Community as well as outside Europe as its trade grew. With the change of government in 1969, a new SPD/FDP coalition emerged with a vision of improved East-West relations in which the FRG would actively participate. A strengthened economy forged for West Germany a leading political role within Europe and the Common Market which gradually also drew international recognition. At the same time, the Federal Republic expanded its role within NATO. With the withdrawal of the French from the integrated military structure of the Alliance and the preoccupation of the United States in Vietnam, its ascendance as a more influential partner was natural.

In a third example of change during the late 1960s, the Federal Republic followed the U.S. lead and began a more active policy of relations with the East, including improved German-German relations. The canopy under which the improvement in East-West relations occurred was the process of superpower strategic arms limitation talks (SALT). After President Johnson's "bridge-building" speech of 1966, it had become obvious that closer U.S.-USSR relations in a number of areas, including arms control, were likely. If the U.S. was going to open a dialogue with the East, then Western Europe could also benefit—and the West Germans could use the improved climate of U.S.-USSR relations in strategic arms negotiations to achieve movement on the German question.[4]

As it had become obvious since the building of the Berlin Wall in 1961 that the Soviet Union would not soon relinquish control of the East Block, the Federal Republic of Germany decided to pursue German-German relations based on *de facto*, if not *de jure*, recognition of the Eastern borders. The 1972 treaties according that recognition between Bonn-Moscow and Bonn-Warsaw came only after a Quadripartite Agreement on the Status of Berlin in 1971. What became known as the *Ostpolitik* of the Brandt government was undertaken within the broader framework of improved U.S.-USSR relations and from the time of the definitive West German adoption of détente to the U.S. move away from that policy in the latter half of the 1970s, there existed a consensus—although one not shared at the time by the opposition CDU/CSU fraction[5]—in FRG-U.S. official concepts and relations with the East. But the consensus did not mean that the U.S. and German motivations in pursuing détente were identical, and indeed this fact was later the root of difficulty in U.S.-Allied relations over approaches to East-West issues.

For the Germans, détente, translated as *Entspannung* (literally a "relaxation of tensions") has clearly been regarded as a long-term process[6] leading to enhanced security and to better East-West relations. For the Americans, détente has held various meanings and has become an even more ambiguous word since President Ford took it temporarily out of the official U.S. vocabulary. Whereas it has been used in the sense of a "relaxation of tension" without real change, it has been employed more often in the sense of a certain degree of accommodation between the two blocks; thus, then Secretary of State Kissinger declared that it was "the search for a more constructive relationship with the Soviet Union reflecting realities . . . a continuing process, not a final condition that has been or can be realized at any one specific point in time."[7] Finally, grappling with the concept, the North Atlantic Assembly Subcommittee on Détente defined it as a political and strategic process with bilateral and multilateral dimensions involving both competition and cooperation in the interest of reducing the risks of nuclear war and with limits which are indefinite and unclear.[8] In contrast, the Soviet Union has preferred the term "peaceful coexistence . . . a form of struggle between states with different social systems without resort to war, but specifically emphasizing the continuing ideological conflict . . . a long-term political strategy."[9] In adapting these approaches of détente to often different perceptions of long-term security interests, U.S. and Allied divergences often have emerged.

The Adoption of Ostpolitik

The result of the difference in German and U.S. perceptions of the potential benefit of normalization through *Ostpolitik* had also an effect on their concepts of a security regime in Europe. For the United States, the primary objective of the Atlantic Alliance remained the physical defense of Europe. Normalization of relations with the East was seen as merely a tool that could be and was discarded when it no longer appeared to serve that purpose. For the Federal Republic, however, the adoption by the Atlantic Alliance of the two objectives of defense and détente suggested the possibility of change, rather than maintenance of the status quo. More specifically, for the West German government, *Ostpolitik* embodied the concept of reunification in more realistic terms. It confronted Germans with the fact that reunification could not and should not be expected in the near future. Rather, the general normalization of relations or détente between the Blocks could be used to promote and facilitate better conditions in the East. This possibility held a personal meaning for the large percentage of the German population with relatives in the East, as well as the two million West Berliners.

These divergent views on the purpose of détente also affected U.S. and FRG perspectives on arms control. For the United States negotiations on arms control were seen as a means to the larger end of enhancing physical security, preferably on a global basis; in the words of then Secretary of State Henry A. Kissinger:

> In moving forward across a wide spectrum of negotiations, progress in one area adds momentum to progress in other areas . . . we have looked for progress in a series of agreements settling specific political issues, and we have sought to relate these to a new standard of international conduct appropriate to the dangers of the nuclear age. In acquiring a stake in this network of relationship with the West, the Soviet Union may become more conscious of what it would lose by a return to confrontation.[10]

For the West Germans, arms control was one among a number of instrumentalities for promoting détente, or at least avoiding a worsening of relations which could jeopardize the hard-earned gains in relations with East Germany. It enabled smaller gains toward the improvement of the daily lives of those in the East as broader East-West issues received attention by the superpowers. Thus, a failure in arms control negotiations would have very different meanings for the two countries, as will be seen later.

For some years, however, progress was made on both fronts and this divergence had little perceptible effect. The new *Ostpolitik* of the 1970s was manifested first and foremost by a range of arms control talks even beyond the SALT negotiations. The initiation of the Conference on Security and Cooperation in Europe (CSCE) in 1972 was followed by the talks on Mutual and Balanced Force Reduction (MBFR) in 1973, the Vladivostok Agreement of 1974, the SALT II negotiations, concluded in 1979, two CSCE review conferences, the Strategic Arms Reduction Talks (START) and those on Intermediate-Range Nuclear Forces (INF) (the latter two begun in 1982, broken off in 1983 and reinitiated in 1985 to include strategic defensive systems) the Conference on Disarmament in Europe (CDE), begun in 1984, and, most recently, the Conventional Forces Talks (CST). For the United States, whose policies during the initial stages of these negotiations were guided by Secretary of State Henry Kissinger, the arms control process was very critical to the concept of détente. Within the framework of those negotiations, relations between the Blocks had improved by the mid-1970s, albeit less in avoiding confrontation than had been perhaps hoped. As President Georges Pompidou commented at the time of the October 1973 U.S. nuclear alert during the war in the Middle East only months after the Nixon-Brezhnev Agreement on the Prevention of Nuclear War "the *tête-à-tête* of the two big powers, the United States and the Soviet Union, can as well help détente as lead to a confrontation."[11]

There were, in any case, improvements in a number of limited areas. Above all, trade and credit between individual Western states and the East Block increased. Meetings of heads of states from the two Blocks became more frequent and conditions under which many East Europeans lived improved economically, thanks in part to Western credits, and politically through negotiations such as CSCE. But at the same time, the Soviet Union retained its interest in influencing the developing world and in matching the U.S. nuclear arsenal. It continued its activities in Asia and Africa, and was especially engaged in Angola, Ethiopia and Vietnam. Furthermore, not only did the Soviet Union begin to "MIRV" its strategic arsenal in 1974/75, two years before expected, it obviously tried at the same time to improve its advantage in intermediate-range nuclear weapons in Europe with the introduction of the SS-20 in 1976. All these events impacted adversely on détente.

The Death—and Rebirth—of Détente

Disillusionment with the "era of détente" grew in the late 1970s within both the United States and the Federal Republic. When it became evident that the promises Schmidt believed Brezhnev made during his first visit to Bonn in May 1978 to maintain the existing balance of forces, i.e., to halt new deployments of SS-20s, were not being kept, German skepticism grew. The disillusionment of the FRG, even after the Soviet march into Afghanistan, however, was never as intense as that experienced by the United States. (Perhaps détente had not raised in the German population the expectations raised in the American population, or, as suggested earlier, other German interests would be jeopardized by a return to the cold war.)

The coincidence of Afghanistan and the Iran hostage crisis, moreover, compounded the U.S. aggravation with its declining military power relative to that of the Soviet Union. There is no question that the occurrence of these events in an election year, with the incumbent President Carter under fire from the right by Ronald Reagan, brought pressure to reassert U.S. strength vis-à-vis the Soviet Union at the price of détente. Even before the 1980 election, however, the U.S. had begun a buildup of nuclear arms and experienced a cooling of relations with the East.[12] In contrast, while Afghanistan and the hostage crisis sobered the West Germans, both demonstrated even more strongly to them the need to maintain ties to the East. A comparison of U.S. and German comments on the Fifth Anniversary of the Helsinki Accords in 1980 is instructive; whereas Carter underlined Soviet misuse of the accords, Genscher made only fleeting reference to Afghanistan and concentrated on the significance of the Helsinki process.[13]

In the early 1980s, the Kohl government appeared initially to move in the direction of the United States and, in fact, adopted a more sober assessment of the Soviet Union. It continued, however, to advocate a policy of dialogue with the East, particularly with the German Democratic Republic (GDR), to a far greater extent than did the United States, and encouraged arms control negotiations. Unfortunately, the result of these shifting and sometimes contrasting approaches was often misunderstood signals, or, on some issues, strained relations.

The 1984 biannual NATO Foreign Ministers meeting could not have underlined more clearly the prevailing divergence in U.S. and FRG perceptions of approaches to relations with the East. The attempt to fashion a consensus before the meeting uncovered strong differences of opinion over the meaning of détente for the future. Those differences prompted a letter from U.S. Secretary of State Shultz to Foreign Minister Genscher purportedly acknowledging the contributions of détente in the past, but rejecting Genscher's contention that the past could be used as a model for the future.

Meetings on reopening arms control talks held between Secretary Shultz and Foreign Minister Gromyko in January 1985 marked a new era in East/West relations. The subsequent superpower summits in Geneva (1985), Iceland (1986), Washington (1987), and Moscow (1988) resulted not only in a treaty dealing with intermediate-range nuclear forces, but also in progress, albeit sometimes slight, in other areas as well, including human rights, Afghanistan (with more success) and scientific/cultural exchanges.

For the West Europeans, the thaw in U.S.-Soviet relations opened the door also to improved dialogue with the East. Although the West Germans had maintained working relationships at a low level with the East during the first Reagan Administration, they now felt confident in pursuing those contacts more actively. Just as the United States used the framework of arms control to expand its relationship into other areas, the West Germans felt less constrained in pursuing improved German-German contacts, attempting to address the conventional imbalance in Europe through a new forum, and expanding trade and other ties to the East Block generally. Though both were more cautious than in the 1970s, the United States and West Germany approached contacts to the East pragmatically and with specific objectives which were political and economic as well as military.

U.S.-FRG Approaches to Relations with the East

As indicated by this brief review, at some points the U.S. and the FRG have differed in defining an appropriate security policy while at other points they have coincided.

They diverged in the 1950s and early 1960s, when the United States saw security policy in largely military terms, from the perspective of a superior nuclear superpower with the objective of containing the Soviet

Union through the construction of a system of alliances around the world, whereas the Federal Republic, as a divided state, sought gains on the issues of political sovereignty and legitimacy through political means;

They coincided in the late 1960s and early 1970s, when the security policies of the United States and the Federal Republic emphasized closer contacts with the East, particularly in the area of arms control;

They again diverged at the end of the 1970s, when there was an abrupt change in U.S. perceptions of the East Block and U.S. policy shifted to place priority on an increase in military capabilities through which political benefits would eventually accrue, while the Federal Republic essentially maintained its policy of pursuing security with political means, backed by military might.

They have converged in the second half of the 1980s in a more pragmatic approach to the Soviet Union which has been based initially on the U.S.-Soviet arms control negotiations but which has since resulted in a broader dialogue for the Americans and the West Germans with the Soviets, on trade, human rights, the European conventional balance and other issues.

Arms Control, Détente, and Security

As noted earlier, the United States and the Federal Republic of Germany have very different views as to how arms control can enhance security and hence as to the purposes of arms control negotiations. While both countries are interested in measures which can improve physical security, the U.S. has been less interested than the FRG in the contribution of arms control to détente—or, indeed, in the implications for détente of failure to reach agreement on measures for the limitation and reduction of armaments. Moreover, the United States is inclined to judge the outcomes of arms control negotiations on a global scale, the Federal Republic on a regional one. Thus to all the differences of opinion that might derive from asymmetries in armed forces, size, location, etc., must be added those that derive from divergent judgments as to how best to enhance security, with the West Germans emphasizing political security through détente as well as physical security, through some mixture of arms control and force postures, and the United States much more concerned with the military balance than with political relations.

The following sub-sections examine four of the ongoing sets of arms control talks which contrast the U.S. and German approaches to East-West relations and particularly East-West negotiations. Two are multi-lateral: the negotiations on Mutual and Balanced Force Reductions (MBFR) and the CSCE and CDE processes, which deal with human rights as well as with military issues, and two are bilateral: the INF process dealing with nuclear weapons in Europe, and the negotiations over strategic defenses. All are significant but the last has initiated a serious U.S.-German debate over the future of deterrence and the essence of the prevailing security regime in Europe.

The Conference on Security
and Cooperation in Europe (CSCE)

The "Helsinki Process" which started in 1972 spanned a period of consensus in U.S. and FRG approaches to East-West relations from the late 1960s to mid-1970s and a period of divergence in approach beginning in the late 1970s. The first years of the conference were marked by considerable agreement on the issues raised during the CSCE negotiations; in fact, the Final Act[14] of the CSCE, signed in 1975 in Helsinki, is often heralded as the high point of East-West and West-West cooperation. For its agreement in the area of military, technical-scientific and human rights, the Act has also been cited as a model for longer-term Block-to-Block relations. This congruence of views continued, albeit to a lesser extent, during the first follow-up conference, held in Belgrade in 1978. The second follow-up conference, however, in 1980 in Madrid, witnessed a greater divergence in approaches, which carried over to the Stockholm Conference on Disarmament in Europe as well as to the Helsinki Ten-Year Anniversary and is characteristic of the general differences in U.S. and West German perceptions.

CSCE, 1975

The CSCE conference was an Eastern initiative aimed at gaining recognition for the borders which evolved after World War II, in particular the borders of the German Democratic Republic (GDR) and the western borders of Poland,[15] at achieving formal recognition of the GDR, and at striking an agreement with the West for a renunciation of force and non-intervention. In addition, the East saw an opportunity to weaken NATO by establishing a permanent organization for European security designed to transcend East and West Blocks. The Eastern objectives were to be reinforced through a strengthening of scientific, cultural, political, and economic ties.

The objectives sought by the West in the negotiations changed and evolved from the initiation of the conference in 1972 to its conclusion in 1975 and in the follow-up conferences in Belgrade and Madrid. In the late 1960s and early 1970s, the initial impetus for Western participation in a conference dealing with security and cooperation in Europe was to assure simultaneous discussion of mutual and balanced force reductions (MBFR). The West Germans were interested in avoiding any unilateral U.S. pullout, as advocated by the Mansfield Amendment. The United States wanted MBFR to assure that any troop reductions would be bilateral and to subvert congressional pressure for unilateral cuts. Under the prodding of the West Europeans, Washington struck a compromise with Moscow of MBFR for CSCE.

The CSCE conference convened with "active, if reluctant, American participation."[16] As the conference progressed, however, the perception of CSCE as a concession to the East for MBFR changed and the West became aware of the possibly wider implications of the talks, particularly with regard to human rights, an issue which drew intense Congressional interest in 1974 in the debates on the Jackson-Vanik Amendment. (In fact, even before the official meeting began, the last issue resolved in the preliminary talks was the Soviet concession to drop its demand for "due respect for the sovereignty, laws, and customs of each country," which might, as one diplomat phrased it, "have prohibited the full conference from even talking about more human contact."[17])

For the West, the recognition of the permanence of the borders of the East Block could only be acceptable if coupled with measures which would accord the populations of Eastern Europe greater freedom of movement and increased communication of ideas and information. The acceptance of the German and Polish borders was a particularly difficult issue for the Federal Republic of Germany[18] since the concept of reunification (and, to a lesser extent, of re-establishment of the 1937 borders) had been a constant element of its domestic and foreign policy since World War II, as already noted in Chapter 3. Would not such an acknowledgement directly contradict the Basic Law and even create the impression of abandonment of those Germans within the Eastern Block? In the early Warsaw Pact initiatives for a European security conference, the objective of the East with regard to the question of reunification had been clear and unacceptable:

> A German peace settlement is in accord with the interests of peace in Europe. . . . A constructive approach to this question, just as to other aspects of security in Europe, is only possible if it proceeds from reality, above all, from recognition of the fact of the existence of two German States. At the same time, such a settlement requires recognition of the existing frontiers and the refusal of both German states to possess nuclear weapons.[19]

This issue had confronted Chancellor Brandt on his assumption of office in 1969 and, in large part, the German government had come to terms with the dilemma in 1970/71 with the signing of the Warsaw and Moscow treaties and their ratification in 1972. Through those treaties, and again in the Helsinki Agreement, West Germany recognized *de facto* the Eastern borders and renounced the use of force to change those borders in the future. Upheld later by the Constitutional Court, the treaties and the later CSCE agreement did not rule out future peaceful change of the territorial boundaries. The concept of "two German states, one German nation" was adopted by the SPD/FDP government and was eventually recognized by the CDU/CSU opposition.[20]

For the United States as well as the Federal Republic, the 1975 agreements in the area of human rights served to assure the East Block populations that abandonment was not the intention of the West. The conference participants in both delegations came to perceive human rights as a vital step to political stability and a move overall for security.

In other areas, the conference members agreed in scientific-technical matters on, among other things, improved cooperation and coordination of scientific and commercial exchanges and protection of the environment, as well as provisions for trade and industrial cooperation. In military affairs there was agreement to give advance notice of troop movements involving in excess of 25,000 men as a way of reducing the possibility of surprise attack and to encourage voluntary exchange of military observers, as well as on other more general provisions. The main result of the Helsinki Conference was to place East-West relations in a new context based on the resolution of conflict by pragmatic consultation rather than by military threats—and thus to extend areas of cooperation.

The Belgrade Conference, 1978

A subsequent follow-up conference in Belgrade in 1978 reviewed adherence to the agreements and pursued without notable success improved human rights provisions. Its Concluding Document and Statement reflected the mounting caution of the West, and especially the United States, with regard to the Helsinki process in the comment that "the representatives of the participating states stress the importance they attach to détente, which has continued since the adoption of the Final Act *in spite of difficulties and obstacles encountered* (author's italics)."[21] But while the FRG and U.S. did not agree on every issue, there did exist a basic consensus with regard to the necessity and desirability of designing a political framework which could bind the East to international rules of conduct and thereby promote greater political stability.

Madrid, 1980

The second follow-up conference in Madrid in 1980 was far less consensual and exposed divergences in U.S. and FRG approaches to East-West relations, divergences which were aggravated by the Soviet invasion of Afghanistan. The difference in approach was evident in the opening statements at the Madrid conference. Although the U.S. and the Federal Republic both concentrated on regulating East-West relations through the provisions of Basket 1 (dealing with security in Europe), the American emphasis (70%) on military issues was almost twice that of the Federal Republic (47%) while FRG interest in Basket 3, relating to human rights issues, (19%) was over three times that of the United States (6.3%).[22] The review of the agreement became, moreover, even more difficult after the imposition of martial law in Poland in December 1981.

Where there had already been skepticism within the U.S. over the détente process, there was now rejection. Having previously voiced complaints in the opening months of the Madrid conference over violations of the human rights clauses governing treatment of dissidents and of the military clauses requiring exchange of observers during maneuvers, the United States considered walking out of the conference over the issue of martial law in Poland. In contrast, the Federal Republic of Germany viewed continued East-West contacts as even more vital. While joining the United States in its boycott of the Olympics after Afghanistan and in other selected sanctions after Poland, it pointed out that it was only through the increased contacts with the East in the foregoing decade that the West had any trade to cut in protest. A retreat entirely from the negotiating table would be foolhardy.

It is on this point that the differences in U.S. and FRG approaches to the talks in Madrid were perhaps most evident. For the United States, the Soviet actions in Poland warranted the most severe diplomatic counter-measures. Why not leave the conference? For the Federal Republic and most European allies, however, the conference itself offered both a platform for the airing and discussion of the Soviet actions and the only means of undertaking positive measures to signal support for the Polish cause. In the end, the European allies and the United States compromised by re-convening the conference and using it as a platform to demonstrate the displeasure and condemnation of the events in Poland by the West. There-after, this stance aided the passage of stricter measures governing human freedoms in the East.

The Conference on Disarmament in Europe (CDE)

A major issue in Madrid was whether to convene a conference to set conditions to extend military détente in Europe. A French proposal gained the broadest support and became the basis for the Conference on Disar-mament in Europe (CDE), convened in 1984 in Stockholm. The CSCE, with the exception of the military provisions, had attempted to achieve a cooperative political basis for Europe, while CDE was to regulate more specifically the military basis and, at a minimum, establish Confidence-Building Measures (CBM) to stabilize the security regime in Europe.

The proposals for a Conference on Disarmament in Europe had been received with mixed emotions in the United States and with far from immediate acceptance. There were several reasons for the skepticism. First was the fear that such a conference could be manipulated by the Soviet Union to improve its position in Europe by using CDE against NATO and/or by sowing discord between the United States and its allies. Second was the dim prospect of 35 nations striking an agreement satisfactory to all. Might not the United States become boxed into positions not necessarily in its best interests?

The most convincing argument for the United States to attend CDE was that the conference had overwhelming support within Europe and could provide an opportunity to demonstrate alliance cohesion. The West German Schmidt/Genscher government had indicated strong support as early as the first French proposal for a CDE in 1980 and Chancellor Schmidt supported the concept at the UN in June 1982.[23] As the internal INF debate grew, CDE gained added importance as a forum for arms control. After the change of government in October 1982, it received mention in Kohl's first official remarks.[24] The Kohl/Genscher government has approached CDE as a potentially stabilizing factor in Europe and a component of its overall arms control policy. The CDE offered the oppor-tunity to continue the arms control process and, importantly, later to continue the superpower dialogue broken off in November 1983 when the Soviets walked out of INF and adjourned START without setting a date to reconvene. While CDE in the post-Afghanistan and post-Poland era, and under the more conservative rule of a Christian Democratic government, was approached far more cautiously than had been true in 1972 for CSCE, it found considerable resonance.[25]

A two-phase approach to CDE was adopted with the support of both the United States and the Federal Republic. The first phase was to concentrate on designing a series of confidence-building measures to be militarily significant and verifiable. The second phase was then to focus on specific disarmament issues. In the initial discussions, the Soviets and the Americans appear to have struck a compromise by agreeing to a renunciation of force clause if significant CBMs were negotiated. (This clause has been particularly important to the West Germans, as it is perceived as a step toward eventually dismantling offensive capabilities on both sides.)[26] A short-term outcome would then include agreement on a range of confidence-building measures, many of which had been introduced unsuccessfully to date elsewhere, in an attempt to reduce the possibility of surprise attack or war by miscalculation. Specifically the West called for early notification of movements by land forces, exchanges of observers and on-site inspections. The East, in contrast, concentrated on more political measures—for instance, a declaration on no-first-use of nuclear weapons; when it did get down to specifics it sought advance notification of air and naval activities, a measure that the West deemed difficult to verify.

Despite its seemingly inauspicious beginnings, the CDE succeeded in concluding in September 1986 the so-called Stockholm Agreement, which contained provisions for the advance notification, observation and on-site inspection of exercises and concentrations in the field and for regulation of the uses to which such activities can be put. And the session of the CED/CSCE under way as of October 1988 is expected not only to outline further confidence-building measures and to schedule negotiations on their adoption but also to endorse the commencement of the Conventional Forces Talks among the 23 NATO and Warsaw Pact countries, "within the CSCE framework."[27]

From the perspective of the United States, success in CDE coincided with movement in other negotiating *fora*, such as INF and START, movement which was attributed to Western strength and determination. From the European perspective, especially the West German, these were positive steps toward a more stable European security regime, perhaps leading in time to a final European settlement ("Friedensordnung").[28] At the moment, however, the main accomplishments of the CDE have been to promote allied coordination of policy on thorny issues and to provide a forum for East-West contact; as even its supporters agree, more extensive CBMs are needed to give unambiguous warning of threats to security.

Conclusions

In sum, although the Federal Republic and United States initially approached the CSCE process with broadly similar objectives, their consensus on ends did not always lead to agreement on means; instead, they often "agreed to differ," particularly with regard to the most appropriate approach in East/West relations. The West Europeans, albeit more cautious than in the early 1970s, saw in the CSCE/CDE negotiations an opportunity to reduce tensions in Europe and to increase in a limited manner their ability to influence internal conditions in the East Block. In particular, West Germans point to the events in Poland created by Solidarity as a spin-off of Western contacts with Eastern Europe. Furthermore, the West Europeans have continued to view the 35 nation CSCE negotiations, and subsequent CDE talks, as a chance for them to participate in defining East-West relations and, even if peripherally, in influencing European security policy. For the Federal Republic, and especially for the smaller West European nations who only infrequently are consulted on security matters, their presence at the negotiating table with the U.S. and the USSR was significant, particularly for their domestic publics.[29]

For the United States, the negotiations offered an opportunity; first, to demonstrate U.S. willingness to negotiate with the East when other talks were stalemated; second, to promote allied cohesion; and, third, to create a more stable military situation in Europe through confidence-building measures.

Certainly there is an overlap in U.S. and German objectives and the policy pursued by the Kohl government has more closely paralleled that of the United States than might have been the case with an SPD government. (The CDU, for instance, has been more insistent on verifiable measures for any "renunciation of force" statements in a final accord.[30]) But one need only compare the FRG and U.S. approaches to Eastern Europe (especially the GDR) and the Soviet Union in the early 1980s to discern a difference in approach and, in part, even in long-term objectives.

The Talks on Mutual and Balanced Force Reductions (MBFR)

The talks on MBFR (or, to give them their correct title, the Conference on Mutual Reductions in Forces and Armaments and Associated Measures in Central Europe) have been focused on conventional ground and air forces in that region. Specifically, they have sought to impose ceilings of 900,000 on the NATO and WTO troops stationed in the Federal Republic of Germany, Belgium, the Netherlands, Luxembourg, the German Democratic Republic, Poland, and Czechoslavakia, and involve representatives from these countries, delegates from the USSR, the U.S.A and Canada and observers from other European countries; thus they are essentially inter-block negotiations.

The genesis of the MBFR talks can be traced back to the mid-1960s, when NATO confronted a number of problems. First, Western European countries were searching for ways to reduce costly defense expenditures, whose effects were compounded by high rates of inflation. Second, the United States was becoming increasingly embroiled in the Vietnam conflict and many Americans (led by Senator Mike Mansfield) began questioning the rationale for maintaining a large U.S. troop presence in Europe. Third, there was a growing belief that political accommodation with the East was essential to the maintenance of stability in Europe, embodied in the Harmel Report on the future tasks of the Alliance. And since both accommodation and stability could, it was believed, be effected through a reduction in conventional forces, it is understandable that in June 1968 a NATO Ministerial Conference at Reykjavik, declared that "it was desirable that a process leading to mutual force reductions should be initiated."[31]

Although the Soviets were not initially interested in this invitation, they were interested in a Conference on Security and Cooperation in Europe (for which, see above), and in May 1972, at the Moscow Summit, Mr. Brezhnev and President Nixon struck a bargain: CSCE for MBFR. After months of preparatory talks, formal negotiations opened in Vienna on October 30, 1973 and continued until the Fall of 1988.

Although it would be fruitless to restate all the arguments made by each side, it might be helpful to outline some of the principles which underlay these arguments. The West, confronted by what it perceived as larger and more heavily-armed Warsaw Pact forces, sought parity, which, in its judgment, could only be achieved by disproportionate cuts in Soviet and allied troops, preferably in the form of organized units, with all their equipment. Since, moreover, NATO negotiators were concerned about geographic asymmetries (Soviet reinforcements need travel only 500 miles, while American ones have to cross the Atlantic Ocean), they sought, at least initially, to offset this Soviet "advantage" by removing only men from American forces and retaining their weapons in Europe. They sought also to impose strict limits on Soviet troop strength, while avoiding constraints on the armed forces of individual NATO nations, a position held strongly by the Federal Republic. And they were (and are) insistent on verifying the levels of forces in the area at all times, to which end they have proposed establishing control points through which troops must pass, coming or going, authorizing air or ground inspection trips and introducing other "associated measures" to insure compliance.

For their part, the Soviets and their partners in the Warsaw Treaty Organization opposed what they called "intrusive" means of verification. They were insistent that there be some limitations on the size of the *Bundeswehr*. In fact, it is generally accepted that a major Soviet objective at the outset was limiting German forces while at the same time driving a wedge between the U.S. and Europeans. The Soviets disputed Western claims of disparities in the forces of the two blocks and maintained that if geography favored either side, it favored the West, because of the relative advantages offered by ocean transportation and the proximity of powerful French forces.

Given these fundamental differences in perceptions, interests and positions, it is surprising that the MBFR talks have made the limited progress they have. Over the years, a series of proposals and counterproposals[32] have resulted in significant modifications in initial positions and some measure of agreement, to include: 1) acceptance of common manpower ceilings, tentatively set at 700,000 for ground forces and 900,000 overall; 2) a general accord that any arrangement should include methods for verifying compliance (Confidence Building Measures or Associated Measures) which also help to reduce fears of surprise attack; 3) an understanding that there should be initial U.S.-Soviet reductions, followed by reductions in indigenous forces; 4) an undertaking not to re-deploy in a "threatening manner" (to the flanks) forces withdrawn from the reduction zone; 5) agreement in principle to establish a consultative commission to guide and review implementation.[33]

Issues on which the two sides have disagreed are: 1) data, with the West charging that the East has about 150,000 more soldiers in the area than it admits to having; 2) limitations on residual forces, with the East seeking a sub-ceiling on national forces within NATO, a measure aimed especially at the Federal Republic. (NATO is against this proposal because it will prevent one nation from making up any reductions in troop strength by another once an agreement has been signed);[34] 3) associated measures for verification and compliance, where there is general agreement for the need for verification but disagreement over the details of how and in what manner verification should be effected; 4) armaments reductions, with the West[35] opposing cutbacks in weaponry (so as to avoid depleting its own stocks of material without being able to touch that stored in the Soviet Union) and the Soviets insisting that both sides draw down armaments.

Recently, both East and West sought to capitalize on the areas of agreement by taking small, first steps toward reduction and verification. Thus the WTO in February 1985 proposed initial cuts of 20,000 Soviet and 11,000 American servicemen, 10% as individuals and 90% in units, accompanied by a freeze on remaining forces. Verification would be accomplished by notification of reductions, which would be monitored at "three or four observation points on each side," with further procedures for counting forces to be negotiated along with subsequent cuts.[36]

In December 1985, the Western powers replied with a counter-proposal, calling for somewhat smaller initial reductions (5,000 Americans and 11,000 Soviets) followed by exchanges of information on troop strength, and somewhat more extensive "associated measures," including "challenge inspections," to be installed *seriatim* over the succeeding three years. Only after these verification measures had been applied and proven effective would further negotiations on reductions ensue.[37]

This proposal was hailed by some (including Margaret Thatcher and Helmut Kohl, both of whom pushed for its acceptance by the United

States) as offering new possibilities for agreement and castigated by others (including officials in the U.S. Department of Defense) as a retreat from principle with dangerous implications—the most dangerous being a three year freeze on forces while further negotiations took place. However, the Soviets showed little enthusiasm for the proposal, even though it would, in conjunction with an earlier NATO offer to count only men in combat and combat-support units rather than total manpower, have provided a graceful way out of the long dispute over data in terms favorable to the WTO.

The relevant question is not, however, whether the proposal is acceptable but whether it is meaningful. The cuts are so small as to be insignificant, there would be no further reductions for at least four years, the verification measures would add little to the ability to detect preparations for surprise attack (especially since the West did not push an earlier requirement for notification in advance of "out-of-garrison" troop movements by division-sized units) and the freeze, even if faithfully observed, would do nothing to alleviate the disparities in ready forces which so trouble some in the West; indeed, given manpower and budgetary constraints, the European Allies are likely to fall below present manning levels. Thus MBFR, whatever its importance politically, offers little prospect of affecting the military balance on the Central Front.

This latest proposal nailed down the coffin on the optimum U.S. objective in the MBFR talks: to obtain disproportionate reductions in WTO forces. It may not even uphold the minimum objective of "damage-limitation," i.e., of holding talks as a means of staving off pressures for unilateral draw-downs in U.S. and other NATO forces; a four-year suspension of the bargaining process is unlikely to persuade critics that they should defer changes in the U.S. force posture because these might adversely affect the conduct of future negotiations! Moreover, it has been apparent for some time that the United States is seeking to strengthen Allied forces on the Central Front, an aim which would be jeopardized by any far-reaching agreement on MBFR. Hence, in recent years, U.S. proposals have been designed more to satisfy the Allies and to influence public opinion than to achieve any significant military results.

To some extent, this has also been true of the approach taken by the Federal Republic. Although at one time it might have hoped for disproportionate reductions in Warsaw Pact forces or for WTO acceptance of measures that could provide warning of surprise attack, this hope was short-lived; indeed, the West German government had to spend a great deal of effort in fending off proposals which would have imposed limits on *its* forces, proposals which were politically unacceptable in the Germany of the 1970s. Although the climate has changed somewhat, with the SPD now suggesting a restructuring of the *Bundeswehr* which would make it defensively-oriented the official position is that a decision on reductions will be made only in the context of an agreement. However, the Federal Republic, even more than the United States, is cognizant of the pressure of public opinion, and hence willing to be flexible on issues such as data discrepancies and verification procedures, if this flexibility will keep the negotiations going. It is also conscious of the impression that adamancy will make on the East (which regularly castigates German "militarism" and "revanchism") and of the potential contribution of "military détente" to better relations with its socialist neighbors—an awareness which prompted Helmut Schmidt, in the 1970s, to press for an agreement, even at the price of accepting limitations on the *Bundeswehr*. By and large, however, West German approaches to MBFR have been much closer to those of the United States than has been true in other areas of arms control.

More importantly, this closeness seems likely to continue once MBFR is phased out and the yet-to-be started Conventional Forces Talks get under way. For the United States, the CFT promise to provide a forum in which negotiations can redress the persistent imbalance in conventional forces in Europe, thereby achieving greater military stability. This also is a primary objective of the West Germans, in fact, NATOs "opening gambit," which proposes disproportionate reductions in tanks and artillery held by the two sides, was advanced by the Federal Republic. (In this connection, Dr. Ernst F. Jung, Head of the FRG Delegation at the MBFR negotiations from 1978 to 1981, has advanced the view that the CFT should place greater importance on the geostrategic factor and on fighting power than has been true in MBFR.)[38] However, from Jung's perspective—as well as that of the West German government—stability should be pursued within a political framework as well as a military one; whether this issue will prove divisive only time will tell.

Negotiations on
Intermediate-Range Nuclear Forces (INF)

The divergence in perceptions of the contribution of arms control to the establishment of a security regime in Western Europe is possibly nowhere clearer than in the contrast of U.S. and West German approaches to the INF negotiations. Whereas the CSCE and CDE negotiations have been among 35 nations, and those on MBFR between the military alliances, the INF talks have been strictly between the superpowers, but dealing with weapons systems of intense interest to the Europeans, West as well as East. For the Federal Republic, the West-West consultations over INF have taken on almost as much importance as the West-East discussions. Furthermore, the INF talks have been influenced by a dimension which had played only the most minimal role in past negotiations: public opinion. The role of the public, especially the German public, has been unprecedented not only for its influence on the postions taken by the Federal Republic but also for the impact it has had on the state of U.S.-FRG relations and even on the conduct of the superpower negotiations generally. Hence, it is worth examining the course of these negotiations and, indeed, the whole question of intermediate-range nuclear forces in Europe.

Concern over the European Balance of Forces

The concern in the early 1970s over INF imbalances in Europe arose from three developments: one, the modernization of (and consequent increase in the capabilities of) Soviet theater nuclear forces; two, the demise of U.S. nuclear strategic superiority and the realization of superpower strategic parity; and, three, the frustration of the Europeans generally with the lack of U.S. leadership and their own lack of influence in Alliance affairs, and specifically with the limited European role in the Strategic Arms Limitation Talks (SALT) despite obvious U.S.-USSR discussion of European weapon systems.

The oft-cited Schmidt speech of October 1977 at the International Institute for Strategic Studies (IISS)[39] dealt precisely with the latter two points. First and foremost, Chancellor Schmidt was concerned with the progress of the SALT talks. Not only did the SALT treaty virtually codify U.S.-Soviet strategic parity but the negotiations appeared to be proceeding without sufficient consideration by the United States of the impact the change in the strategic nuclear balance might have on the European balance of forces. This was not only a German concern: a 1976 Conference report by the Chicago Council on Foreign Relations concluded that West European allies had been growing "more uncertain and restive concerning [the] policies and general reliability of the superpowers" and feared "that the results of Soviet-American accommodation will weaken ties and undermine security."[40] Not only were European issues (transfer of technology, forward-based systems (FBS), etc.) themselves often the subject of discussion, decisions on the provisions of SALT dealing with strategic nuclear systems did not appear to be taken with regard to the global balance or even the theater nuclear or conventional force balances.

The accumulated European concern in government and expert circles over the European balance of forces and the impact of Schmidt's comments were compounded by the Soviet deployment of a new intermediate-range nuclear weapon system: the so-called SS-20. This not only aroused worry that the Soviets were gaining the capability to dominate the escalation of any conflict, and thereby to neutralize the NATO nuclear deterrent, but also generated fears that this capability might give them a political advantage. As the present State Secretary Lothar Rühl, then a journalist, noted at the time: "If Washington does not counter the Soviet weapons aimed at U.S. allies, there will be a fundamental change in NATO political relations between the United States and Europe."[41]

Discussions among the allies became more intense in 1977 and steps toward improvements in NATO defenses were articulated by the NATO Ministers in their communiqué of May 1978.[42] The steps decided upon by the Ministers included theater nuclear modernization (Article 10), although the form it would take remained unclear[43] and a final decision was not reached until December 1979.

Formulating a Response

The West Germans looked first to agreement with the East to try to stabilize the balance and in May 1978 Chancellor Schmidt met with Premier Leonid Brezhnev in Bonn. The joint communiqué issued on the occasion of that visit reflected Schmidt's concern that the Russians would achieve superiority in theater nuclear forces, with unsettling consequences for the Federal Republic, warned that no nation should attempt to obtain military advantages, and insisted that defense could be assured by essential equality and parity (Article III), i.e., further deployments of the SS-20 were unnecessary. (The communiqué also reiterated the importance of the Four-Power Agreement on Berlin of 1971 and the continuance of German-German relations for the maintenance of détente [Article IX].[44]) When, however, SS-20 deployments continued, the West German leaders felt betrayed and were in consequence prepared to consider other measures.

While the United States had initially not felt the modernization of theater nuclear forces to be necessary, by January 1979 the Carter Administration had become convinced of the growing unease in Western Europe over the nature of the existing systems and the state of the balance. At a summit meeting that month in Guadeloupe with Chancellor Schmidt, President Giscard d'Estaing, and Prime Minister James Callaghan, President Carter proposed formally the modernization of theater nuclear forces and suggested that this be done by deploying Pershing II SRBMs and Ground-Launched Cruise Missiles (GLCMs), which together would provide a visible deterrent but one not threatening to the Soviets. While Chancellor Schmidt argued in Guadeloupe and afterwards for a sea-launched cruise missile, the U.S. offer of Pershing IIs and ground-launched cruise missiles gained backing from all NATO representatives to the High-Level Group. It was felt that the presence of those weapons on European soil would couple the U.S. and Europe more securely in defense. Since the West Germans were insistent that they not be the only continental European power to deploy the new weapons it was, therefore, decided to place cruise missiles also in Italy, Britain, Belgium and the Netherlands, though the Pershing IIs would be based only in Germany.

While supporting the decision of the High-Level Group, the Dutch and the Germans in February 1979 proposed the creation of a Special Group (SG) in NATO to investigate possible avenues of arms control negotiations as an alternative counter to the SS-20. The group would overlap in membership and purpose with the existing NATO High-Level Group and would work in tandem to give NATO proposals for possible arms control measures which could complement, and perhaps substitute for, a modernized defense program. The Dutch-German proposal was accepted in record time and the deliberations of the Special Group led to the "Double-Track" decision of 1979, with one track bearing proposals for arms control and the second one the agreement to deploy PIIs and GLCMs.

It is important to the later political debate to note that while the U.S. bureaucracy was divided on the necessity for INF modernization up to 1978, by the time of the 1979 Guadeloupe meeting, there was essential agreement that even if modernization was not militarily necessary, there was at least a strong political case for it on the basis of European and alliance cohesion. In contrast, there was little to virtually no major West German internal debate of the issue until the period of discussions over the most appropriate weapons in 1979.[45] Indeed, while Chancellor Schmidt aimed at consolidating support for INF modernization by NATO within the SPD, the Free Democrats recognized at the party defense conference in Munster that "new weapon systems by the Warsaw Pact increases our concern for our security."[46] And CDU chairman Helmut Kohl stated in June 1979[47] that the force imbalance in Europe required modernized theater nuclear weapons.

Implementing the Double-Track Decision, 1979-1983

In December 1979 the NATO foreign and defense ministers agreed to the deployment of 572 (108 Pershing IIs, 464 GLCMs) intermediate-range theater nuclear weapons in Germany, Britain, Italy, Belgium, and the Netherlands beginning in 1983 if arms control negotiations were not successful.[48] If the decision marked a clear FRG-U.S. coincidence of objectives and agreement on appropriate means to achieve those objectives, it did not necessarily indicate identical priorities.

The West Germans viewed the INF decision as one which would first, counter the SS-20 deployments either, in order of priority, through arms control negotiations or modernization of NATO arms; second, achieve arms control through the declared preference for inclusion of INF talks in the broader framework of a SALT III,[49] and encourage continuation of the strategic arms control process with greater consideration for European issues and input; third, reaffirm the U.S. guarantee for European defense; fourth, demonstrate the FRG role and responsibility on NATO defense issues; and fifth, show NATO resolve and cohesion *vis-à-vis* the East.

For the United States, its priorities had remained first, to reaffirm the U.S. commitment to European defense and demonstrate U.S. leadership especially in light of the recent hostage crisis, and secondly, albeit increasingly more important, to counter the Soviet military threat posed by the SS-20 with a NATO modernization and/or, if possible, alternatively to remove the Soviet threat through arms control. It was recognized that this could only be successfully achieved with a coordinated and cohesive Alliance resolve. The NATO decision was celebrated and lauded both by the governments of Western Europe and the United States. Despite the differences in ordering of priorities, consensus on defense *objectives* seemed as close as it had ever been.

The euphoria was short-lived. By the end of December 1979 the U.S.-FRG consensus on the double-track decision began to experience problems. Even if the Carter Administration had viewed the initiation of INF negotiations to be a top priority, arms control with the Soviet Union was clearly out of the question after Afghanistan. Even SALT II, which had held a high priority, was withdrawn from Senate consideration, and it was left to the new Reagan Aministration to begin talks in earnest.

West German policy not only took different directions but was influenced by something largely lacking in the United States: wide-spread public opposition to INF. Beginning in late 1980 the issue stimulated a mobilization of public opinion notably more influential than any one previous German post-war experience and without parallel in U.S. public activism on a single defense decision. In October 1981, approximately 300,000-500,000 demonstrators gathered in Bonn to protest the planned NATO deployments and to urge superpower negotiations. (Similar demonstrations were also held in London, Brussels, Amsterdam and Rome.) Widespread smaller protest actions occurred simultaneously and thereafter throughout West Germany which mobilized not only a core of anti-nuclear activists, but also concerned citizens from the mainstream of German politics. While their numbers did not always, or even most of the time, translate into votes, the protestors unquestionably had a significant impact on the German political scene.

Above all, they provided the impetus for the emergence of the Greens as a national party. Although not successful in halting the deployment of Pershing and cruise missiles in the Federal Republic, the Greens influenced the debate and the security policies of both the Schmidt and the Kohl governments and at least indirectly played a role in the change of regime in the Fall of 1982. Furthermore, none of the four traditional parties in the past few years has been able to ignore the issue on which the Greens have attracted voters: that of opposition to nuclear weapons. Although rejecting the Greens' calls for withdrawal from NATO and for an end to German participation in the Atlantic Alliance, the major parties have, by necessity and design, been outspoken in their support for arms control to the extent, in the case of the SPD in November 1983, of even proposing deferral of the INF deployments in order to enable a prolongation of the negotiations.

In contrast to the European demonstrations, the U.S. public in 1980 was involved in a heated Presidential campaign which focussed on increased defense spending rather than on arms control. The election of Ronald Reagan was interpreted as a signal of support for rebuilding U.S. forces. It was only in November 1981 that the new President announced his intention to commence INF negotiations at the beginning of 1982. This came only after the initiation of major U.S. defense programs which enabled the United States to maintain that it was "negotiating from strength." And while a significant nuclear freeze movement had begun to pressure President Reagan, its activities were directed at *strategic* weapons and specifically left European INF out of the call for an "immediate, verifiable freeze."

Although the period 1979-1983 was marked by official agreement to pursue *both* tracks of the double-track decision, there was a clear difference in emphasis between the Reagan Administration and the government of the Federal Republic, even after the CDU assumption of power in 1982. In part, the further adherence of the FRG to *Ostpolitik* and its attendant posture with respect to arms control can be explained by the continued presence of FDP Foreign Minister Genscher in the Cabinet, but it can, in large part, also be attributed to an evaluation of German interests and a determination by the leaders of all parties of the importance of arms control to those interests—notably the interest in good relations with the East. In this they were backed by the public, who preferred arms control to the deployment of new missiles on German soil.

These differences were manifest in several ways, one being the German willingness to "take into account" in the negotiations British and French weapons systems, another being the acceptance by the FRG of a "zero-plus" solution, whereby all American INF would be banned from Europe but only some of the Soviet missiles would be destroyed or removed. The most significant was, however, Chancellor Kohl's dismay over the failure of the U.S. and the USSR to reach agreement on the "walk-in-the-woods" proposal of July 1982 when Paul Nitze offered—privately—radical changes in U.S. INF proposals to Soviet negotiator Youli Kvitsinsky.[50] There was an obvious German readiness at least to consider restricting deployments to GLCMs in exchange for substantial, but not total, SS-20 reductions. The rationale for support of this concept was simple; it would: one, remove the Pershing II threat to the Soviet Union in exchange for the removal of a substantial number of the missiles threatening the Federal Republic; two, retain a NATO counter to the remaining SS-20s; and three, still install a visible indication of U.S. commitment to West European defense.

Life After Deployment

The proposals made by President Reagan in Autumn 1983 were rejected by the Soviets, who again sought 'equal reductions' in weapons now deployed or to be deployed, and the two parties failed to reach an agreement on arms limitation. Then the U.S. proceeded to deploy as planned. On 23 November 1983 the first Pershing II missiles arrived in the FRG and the USSR walked out of the INF negotiations.

This situation remained essentially unchanged throughout 1984, with the Soviets insisting they would not reopen negotiations unless the West dismantled the Pershing IIs and GLCMs installed in the Federal Republic. During this period there were, however, continued expressions of Soviet interest in arms limitations, an interest which seemed to be stimulated by American development of an effective antisatellite weapon and by the adoption of a multi-billion dollar program for research on space-based defensive systems, the Strategic Defense Initiative.[51] And in 1985, following agreement in principle that SNF, INF and SDI would all be discussed concurrently, the U.S. and the USSR resumed negotiations at Geneva.

The subsequent negotiations focused on the same issues that had plagued prior meetings: the American and Soviet weapons systems to be covered by any agreement, the number to be left to each party, their location, the means of verifying both weapons destroyed and those remaining and the perennial question whether to count, to consider and/or to control British and French nuclear forces. Over time, however, these issues were all resolved,[52] with the INF treaty of 1987 obligating both countries to eliminate all existing missiles with ranges of 500 km to 5,500 km (for the U.S., the Pershing IA, the Pershing II and the GLCM, for the USSR the SS-12, SS-23, the SS-23, the SS-4, the SS-5 and the SS-20, whose deployment in 1975 had generated much of the Western concern about the theater nuclear balance), not to flight test or to produce any new systems after the treaty entered into force nor to possess any such missiles whatsoever following the dates by which designated systems must be eliminated; moreover, it provides for extensive verification procedures, including access to facilities where missiles are kept, monitoring of production facilities and short-notice inspections of suspect operations.[53]

Our concerns are not, however, with the treaty as such but rather with its impact on "defense and détente," as this is perceived by both Americans and Germans. For the latter, there were three instances where the German sense of how things should go differed from the American, two during the course of the negotiations and one thereafter.

The first came as a result of the summit meeting in Reykjavik, Iceland, in December 1985. The surprise announcement of this meeting was met with guarded satisfaction by the West Germans. Although relieved that the "September Cold War" between the superpowers appeared to have ended, they would have preferred more warning so that they could arrange again a meeting of NATO heads of state or even of a smaller group of European leaders before Reykjavik. Their hesitancy, however, was mild in comparison to their reaction (and that of other Europeans) in the aftermath of the Iceland summit. Rather than conducting broad discussions, as announced before the superpower meeting, the U.S. and Soviet negotiators in Reykjavik had met through the night on a wide range of issues, with the obvious intent to reach final agreements, particularly on INF. The concluding statements and remarks to the press after the three days of discussions were most disconcerting to the Europeans. In essence, President Reagan was understood to have agreed with General Secretary Gorbachev that the goal of the superpowers should be the elimination of all nuclear weapons. There was only slight consolation when his remarks were revised later to include only strategic nuclear weapons.

The distinctions were generally lost on the broader American public and the fact there had been U.S.-Soviet discussions and that "real" arms reductions appeared at hand was greeted with considerable enthusiasm. The president of the earlier "evil empire" speech seemed to have disappeared and there was broad support for an improvement in U.S.-Soviet relations. This is not to say that this enthusiasm was evidenced by all; to the contrary, the skepticism among Reagan's longtime conservative right supporters was considerable and vocal.

The German public reaction mirrored that of the American in its enthusiasm for what appeared to be a considerable warming of the previously very cool U.S.-Soviet relations and indications of real movement on the difficult issues holding up an INF agreement. West German official reaction, however, was restrained and cautious. The reason was quite simple—the 1983 deployments of nuclear-capable ground-launched cruise missiles and Pershing IIs had been justified as necessary elements in the maintenance of the NATO strategy of flexible response. The basis of that strategy, and therefore of European defense, was the American nuclear guarantee. Potential, realistic alternative strategies were not clear. While there was broad support for the concept of eventual elimination of all nuclear weapons in the future, the idea of a U.S.-Soviet agreement to do so in the course of brief weekend discussions was sobering, to say the least.

Unofficially, there was an interesting leak at the end of the week after the Reykjavik summit that more likely revealed the true assessment of that meeting. A high-level West German general in NATO was reported to have expressed concern for the basis of European defense—the American nuclear guarantee. Under the present constellation of forces, the comments ran, NATO was not prepared to counter the Soviets exclusively with conventional forces.[54] Not only was the military capability not present, political support for an exclusively conventional defense was questionable. Whereas nuclear deterrence had kept the peace for over forty years, conventional forces historically had not assured conflict avoidance.

While these comments never received official sanction from the Kohl government, their thrust was not lost on the Americans. European concerns were two-fold: one, European issues had been discussed in the "presummit" without the benefit of Allied consultation and input and, two, the concept of eliminating strategic nuclear weapons entirely, while attractive in the long-term, was disturbing in the short term. Nuclear systems form the basis of Western defense and will for the foreseeable future.[55] In response to the latter, official accounts of the Reykjavik meeting mentioned only a future reduction of *strategic* missiles. In answer to the first concern, U.S.-European consultations intensifed further over the next year.

The second instance of German *malaise* occurred in the Spring of 1987. As the negotiations broadened to include not only long-range INF (SS-20s, SS-4s, and SS-5s for the Soviets; Pershing IIs and GLCMs for the United States), but also shorter-range INF, the Soviets sought the dismantling of old Pershing IA (P IA) missiles, whether operated by Germans or by Americans, on the ground that these were U.S. weapons. (Actually, this was not correct: while the nuclear warhead is U.S.-owned, and controlled under the dual key system, the P IA launcher and missile are German-owned.) Making the same argument it had with the British and French forces (which the USSR had finally agreed not to count) the United States insisted on the right of the Federal Republic to decide the issue, which fell outside the scope of any Soviet-American agreement; clearly, however, it wanted the Federal Republic to give up the P IA.

The dispute over these weapons continued throughout the summer and represented the most direct Allied involvement in any phase of the negotiations. The German internal debate was substantial. There was pressure from within the government coalition to reject all attempts to place limitations on the P IA, since these would infringe on West German sovereignty as well as restrict their defense options for the future. Government and opposition proponents of including the missiles were concerned that the onus for failure of the superpowers to reach an INF agreement would fall on the West Germans. There had already been questions by the Soviets of the German right to dispose of these nuclear weapons in light of their commitments under the Nuclear Nonproliferation Treaty. This was hastily refuted by the Germans, who were obviously embarrassed by the charge.

After an extended debate, Chancellor Kohl announced Germany's intention to dismantle its Pershing IAs, contingent on a successful U.S.-Soviet INF agreement and only after the superpowers had begun to dismantle their systems. He underlined the independent decision of the West Germans on the disposition of their systems.

With this issue out of the way, negotiations intensified over 1987, with persistent signs that agreement was near. After final negotiations on the treaty language, Gorbachev travelled to Washington in early December 1987 for a triumphant signing of the final document.[56]

As might have been expected, this "victory" was attributed to different "fathers." German public opinion polling indicated a perception that progress was due to the more forthcoming attitude of the new Soviet leader, Gorbachev. While agreeing that the Soviets had indeed been forthcoming, the Reagan Administration interpreted their acquiescence rather as a response to the hard bargaining of the United States and the cohesive stance of the Alliance. Not only had the Soviets accepted on-site inspection for the first time and a strict verification regime, they also agreed to reductions requiring them to destroy two-and-a-half times the number of missiles that the United States would destroy. It was, therefore, a clear victory of the Reagan approach.

In the United States, public support for the Treaty was high and Senate debate proved far less contentious than had been anticipated. The Treaty passed the Senate by the comfortable margin of 93-5. Opponents fell into two categories. On the one hand were a small number who were disappointed that the Treaty did not go far enough. On the other hand, and representing the Senate opposition, were those such as Senator Jesse Helms who felt that the verification procedures were insufficient to preclude anticipated Soviet violations. Furthermore, opponents argued, the Treaty would leave the United States without INF in Europe while the Soviet Union continued to have a conventional superiority on the continent as well as an ability to target Europe with its ICBM force.

West German public reaction to the summit and the Treaty was enthusiastic and the official posture supportive. Clearly there was German support for ratification of the Treaty, particularly in light of 1979 and the dismay when SALT II had not been ratified. Although some shared the sentiment of former Secretary of State Henry Kissinger that the West might have been better advised to negotiate first a more equitable conventional balance,[57] the effect of not ratifying a signed treaty would be worse. Both hard-line CDU politician Volker Ruehe and left-wing SPD leader Oskar Lafontaine called publically for ratification.[58]

Behind the scenes there was, however, some notable hand-wringing. Confronted with the treaty, some officials began to question whether reductions should not have begun with conventional forces. Not only would the Treaty require a shift in European defense to greater reliance on conventional forces, the Soviets held an acknowledged superiority in this area. Furthermore, substantial and growing shortfalls in the available manpower pools in the West could be expected to increase those differences even further in the future.

A second concern lay in the verification procedures, which would require Soviet on-site inspections at West German installations and possibly even privately-owned defense firms. These were addressed in the final verification agreement. Finally, the Germans expressed concern over the quick-fix solution that the British, Americans and even French seemed ready to propose to readjust the nuclear balance in Europe—a modernization of the U.S. short-range and battlefield nuclear weapons in Europe, beginning with the Lance. This would violate the concept of non-singularity often espoused by the Germans by placing the burden of modernization only on those systems located in Germany. While the government was more circumspect with its criticism, the Opposition was clear at its party conference in September 1988. This concern across party lines reflected the conviction of many that such a modernization would prompt massive public protests similar to those in 1983 while at the same time negating the public support and enthusiasm for the INF treaty and the closer U.S.-Soviet relationship that was emerging.

The debate over force structure and the approach to future arms negotiations has already begun. It promises to be a lively one. The most immediate and fundamental issue will be the appropriate mix of conventional and nuclear systems in Europe to assure adequate deterrence while not placing too heavy a burden on any one country. Beyond the issue of the above mentioned short-range nuclear systems is the question of conventional force modernization. First, what modernization will be necessary? Second, where should the Atlantic Alliance place its priorities in the next round of negotiations?

The American position on these issues has been less contentious than the German. The United States has made it known that it considers short-range nuclear modernization desireable. The Reagan Administration has also emphasized the necessity for conventional force improvements, with a greater proportion of the burden for those improvements becoming the responsibility of the Europeans.[59] While the next rounds of arms control negotiations might alter the present calculations, there appears to be a

strong conviction that the existing conventional imbalance must be addressed first through modernization and only then through any necessary
asymmetrical reductions to minimize the Soviet advantage on the continent.

The German positions are less clear. While the Opposition SPD and
Greens have passed resolutions against short-range modernization and have
encouraged the inclusion of these weapons in future negotiations, the
Federal Government has evaded a final decision. The FDP Foreign Minister,
Hans-Dietrich Genscher, has underlined the need for conventional force
negotiations. He returned home from a trip to Moscow very optimistic
over the Soviet proposals.[60] In contrast, the CDU Defense Minister, Rupert
Scholz, noted that "Skepticism and sober attitudes are necessary in disarmament . . . we must measure the Soviets in terms of their deeds, in
terms of their actions."[61] But while the government appears to want to
avoid further modernization and has signalled its desire for nuclear as well
as conventional force reductions, it clearly feels the need for continued
nuclear deterrence in Europe. As Herr Scholz put it, "What I rule out
completely is a denuclearization. Without nuclear weapons, we cannot
guarantee our security."[62]

Conclusions

On the whole, the positions of the Kohl and Reagan governments on
INF drew closer between the deployments of November 1983 and the
approval of the Treaty in December 1987. There have been three causes
for this. From the German side, the anti-missile opposition quieted as the
Greens attempted to assure their future through identification with other
issues of more pressing interest to the voters and, from the U.S. side,
President Reagan became more forthcoming on the question of arms
control, as a result both of the 1984 elections and of considerable public
pressure.

Finally, the change in the Soviet position from refusal to conduct further
negotiations in November 1983 to acceptance of most of the Western
proposals in 1987 enabled both governments to achieve acceptable results—
although not, as noted above, without some heartburn on the part of the
Germans. The fundamental approaches of the U.S. and the FRG remain,
however, different in emphasis. Whereas the Reagan Administration continues to view weapons modernization as a prerequisite to arms control,
the Kohl government has consciously remained committed to the primacy
of arms control, even to the extent of hinting that the Lance missiles on
West German soil should (along with their Soviet counterparts) be removed
rather than upgraded.

An important reason and possibly motivating force for this difference
in emphasis lies in the issue of intra-German relations, whose impact on
FRG concepts of security has been particularly notable under the Kohl
government.[63] Although, as Christoph Bertram has noted, this interest does
not mean that the question of a divided Germany is up for revision, as
long as the Federal Republic stays within the framework of the Atlantic

Alliance, it does mean that developments in East-West relations are scrutinized with that interest in mind.[64]

Thus, the CDU/FDP coalition, while convinced of the need to offset the SS-20s deployed by the Soviet Union by counter-deployments if necessary, saw the possibility of a Soviet walk-out of the INF negotiations in as a threat to the carefully constructed structure of German-German relations, relations dependent on continued East-West dialogue. If East-West contacts were only maintained, it was reasoned, then the possibility of a misunderstanding with potentially disastrous consequences could be minimized. Might it not even be possible to avoid the *"Raketen-Zaun"* (missile fence) between the two Germanies threatened by Andropov? Could not the two German states in effect create a *"Verantwortungsgemeinschaft"* that is, a "responsible partnership" to keep open the contacts between East and West and maintain stability in Central Europe.[65] With this in mind, the West Germans in the summer of 1983 offered the GDR a credit of DM 500m, followed by a second credit offer in 1984 after the Soviets actually withdrew from the negotiations. In addition, other trade and cultural exchanges were increased. In a speech before the *Bundestag*, Chancellor Kohl emphasized the importance of those contacts[66] and subsequently underlined the continued significance of détente (*"Entspannung"*) to the Federal Republic.[67]

That the German-German initiatives were not, however, always seen in such a positive light internationally was obvious not only from the barrage of Soviet charges throughout the summer of 1984 of German *"révanchism"* but also from remarks made in unofficial comments from Paris and even official charges by Italian Foreign Minister Andreotti of "Pan-Germanism."[68] In fact, the link of INF to German relations with its allies was clearly a factor in the speech given by President Mitterrand before the *Bundestag* on January 20, 1983, in which he gave strong support to the deployment of the Pershing missiles as a necessary balance to the East in the event that the INF negotiations were not totally successful.[69] In his view, an INF modernization would assure continued U.S. presence and nuclear control in the Federal Republic.

As for the Reagan Administration, while not discouraging the German attempts to continue *Ostpolitik* it subscribed not to the concept of détente but to a policy of openness to dialogue. However, the several summits that have now occurred have opened the door wider and permitted not only German-German dialogue to expand but FRG contacts with the USSR and other East Bloc countries to increase. In 1987 East Germany permitted almost 1.5 million working age citizens to visit West Germany while 71,500 ethnic Germans emigrated from Poland, the GDR, Romania and other East European countries, with an additional 14,500 coming from the Soviet Union.[70] For the German on the street with relations in the East, the East-West dialogue has a very different significance than it does for the average American reading about an INF treaty in his local paper. Thus, the seeds of differences remain.

The Strategic Defense Initiative (SDI)

On March 23, 1983 President Reagan proposed a comprehensive program of research on strategic defensive systems which could, if successful, ultimately "eliminate the threat posed by strategic nuclear missiles," thereby "[paving] the way for arms control measures to eliminate the weapons themselves."[71] Mr. Reagan went on to postulate a situation in which security would be based not upon deterrence but upon defense, not upon killing people but upon destroying weapons. While others within the administration seemed willing to settle for lesser objectives, such as protecting missile silos against a Soviet disarming strike and/or creating uncertainty about the effects of any nuclear attack upon the United States, officers and officials alike have supported an expanded and intensified research and development program. This program has included work on particle beams, nuclear-powered X-ray lasers, electromagnetic guns and other exotic weapons, together with the surveillance satellites, battle management centers and computerized command and central facitilies necessary to tie these together in a functioning system. And though the exact nature of that system has not yet been decided upon, one official conceptualization pictured a multi-layered defense aimed at intercepting enemy missiles during boost phase, at various stages of their flight through space and when they re-enter the atmosphere (See Figure 7.1).

Although the Strategic Defense Initiative deals most specifically with strategic weapons systems and was, therefore, considered initially to be a U.S.-Soviet issue and not one directly involving the Europeans, as did INF, the American offer in Spring 1985 to include European and other allied participation expanded the scope and effect of SDI. But it is clear that even before this offer, the potential implications of SDI for European defense strategy had become a topic of debate in many of the Alliance capitals, as well as at NATO headquarters in Brussels. From the time of its announcement by President Reagan, SDI had increasingly occupied U.S.-West German discussions. If the research and development of a strategic defense system continue as anticipated, the issue can be expected to play an ever larger role in U.S.-German relations over the next decade, if not longer. It is important at several levels—from the indirect impact of a U.S. strategic defense system on the nuclear guarantee to the direct implications to European air and missile defense systems, from the potential of a trade-off on SDI for the success of START to the participation of European civilian industry in the U.S. development program. As envisaged by President Reagan, SDI poses the prospect of new security options for Europe—but as seen by others, it may adversely affect security, by stimulating a U.S.-Soviet arms race, with consequent increases in tensions, by requiring shifts of resources from other military programs, or even by "decoupling" the United States from the defense of Western Europe.

256

FIGURE 7.1 A Schematic Diagram of the SDI System

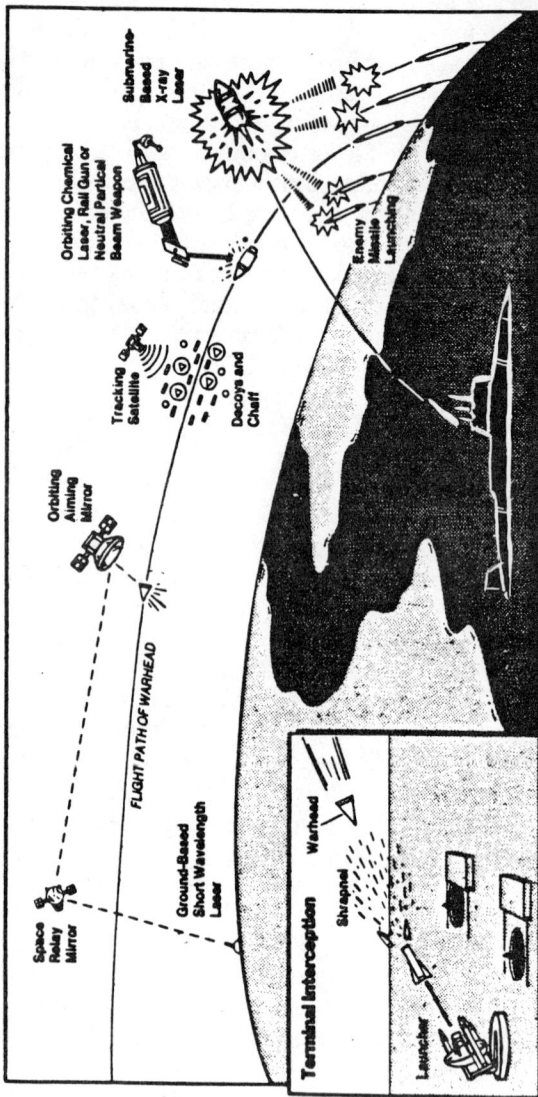

Source: The New York Times, 7 January 1985. Copyright © 1985 by The New York Times Company. Reprinted by permission.

Drawing by Brad Hamann

SDI from the U.S. Perspective

Despite SALT I, SALT II (unratified, but adhered to) and other arms control initiatives of the late 1960s and 1970s, the Soviet buildup in nuclear arms proved substantial. Moreover, by 1983 it was apparent that offsetting U.S. efforts were unlikely to change significantly the strategic balance and that the security of the United States (and of the Soviet Union) rested on the effectiveness of deterrence, as it had for the past forty years. But would deterrence continue to be successful? Would it not make sense to shift to a strategy of "security through defense?" True, this strategy had been abandoned in 1972, largely because technology had proven unequal to the task, but since that time technology had made great strides.

The Strategic Defense Initiative suggested to President Reagan by the influential Dr. Edward Teller and the Science Advisor, Dr. George Keyworth, was attractive for a number of reasons: it offered a non-nuclear defense which could, if successful, even make nuclear weapons obsolete; it could eventually replace the "immoral" strategy of deterrence; it could give impetus to the slow-moving negotiations at Geneva and it would put the United States on the "leading edge" of a new and seemingly inevitable technological development.

Although research on SDI has met with some opposition in the U.S., annual funding for the program has doubled since 1984 and would, if the administration had its way, double again; in fact, SDI holds the record for the largest R & D program ever proposed. Whether the program will actually receive the projected $26 billion over five years now seems doubtful but SDI is a politically-appealing project that promises jobs in many ailing industries and added responsibilities and new systems for the military. Its technological advancements could have significant implications for civilian industry as well, particularly in the computer field. Thus, even those opposed to SDI might find it hard to gut the research program.

Finally, if the arms control argument for SDI was intriguing in March 1983 when the negotiations were clearly stalled, it became even more interesting later in 1983 when the Soviets walked out of INF and START without setting a date to return. And when the evident Soviet concern over SDI seemingly influenced the decision to return to Geneva if SDI were included among the subjects for discussion, even its ardent opponents expressed pleasure.

Nevertheless, the degree of approval is less clear as the program moves into more advanced phases. Even within the administration there have been a number of clarifications of, and even alterations in the structure of, the SDI program[72] and there are evident divergences between Defense and State Department views and even within Defense, as, for example, between the Army and the Air Force. In the Congress there seems to be a consensus that SDI will not resolve U.S. security concerns in the near future and though basic research will undoubtedly continue the Republicans and the Democrats part ways over one, their expectations of the results of the research and two, the desirability of accepting restrictions on SDI under an arms control regime. These differences sharpened during the 1988 presidential campaign.[73] Moreover, there are significant differences over SDI between the United States and its European allies.

The West German Reaction to SDI

Aside from the inevitable uneasiness the Europeans always experience when asked to participate in a program on which the United States has not yet reached a domestic consensus, there are a few specific issues directly affecting Europe on which the U.S. has not been consistent. The most striking example of this is the question of the future of deterrence and of the U.S. nuclear guarantee, both of which could be threatened should President Reagan's dream of installing U.S. *and* Soviet defensive shields ever come true.

For the front-line West Germans especially, this posed an uncomfortable situation that quickly became evident to some U.S. officials. Among those concerned was the arms control negotiator and long-time European expert, Paul Nitze, who in 1984 gave a precise and highly visible speech in Philadelphia asserting the continued adherence of the United States to the strategy of deterrence and reaffirming its nuclear guarantee to Europe. Under no circumstances, said Nitze, was the prevailing strategy to be altered in the near future and there was no way of predicting the outcome of the SDI research in the longer-term; hence, European concerns were unwarranted.

Overall, the German reaction to SDI has been interesting and reflective of the frequent schizophrenia in German-American relations since WWII. On the one hand, the West Germans, as a non-nuclear nation in Central Europe, are dependent on the United States for their defense, to a greater extent probably than any other European nation, and are closely allied to the U.S. On the other hand, there is a serious German commitment to European integration and to German-French relations. These conflicting commitments have been in evidence throughout the SDI debate as the German inclination to follow the U.S. lead by endorsing and participating in SDI has been at loggerheads with reservations about SDI, reinforced by the British skepticism and the French rejection. With the French counterproposal to participate in Eureka, a civilian-oriented program of advanced research, the Germans have had to reconcile these conflicts without making financial commitments to SDI or Eureka that the federal budget could not fulfill. The result has been official West German endorsement of SDI, as shown by the agreement for cooperation on research signed on March 27, 1986, but a more skeptical posture in intra-German and party debate.

This debate is far from resolved. Whereas the CDU/CSU continues to experience limited intra-party disagreements on the extent of involvement in SDI (particularly financial), there is general support for the Reagan program and for German participation in research on SDI. Their coalition partner, the FDP, is less convinced and has passed several party resolutions expressing skepticism of the concept.[74] However, it was a Free Democrat,

Minister of Economics Martin Bangemann, who in March 1986 negotiated and signed the accord of cooperation on SDI with Washington, indicating perhaps that the government of Bonn sought to stress the industrial nature and "low-profile approach" of West German participation.[75] In opposition, the SPD has rejected SDI, and called for its inclusion in the Geneva talks.[76] The Greens' rejection has been most firm and their anti-NATO policy does not prompt further consideration of alternatives, should SDI become reality.

The reasons for the general German ambivalence about SDI are similar to those of the other West European nations: 1) lack of prior consultation by the U.S. before announcement of a program with potentially profound implications for the NATO alliance, 2) lack of clarity over the future of NATO deterrent strategy and the implications for the U.S. nuclear guarantee; 3) lack of clarity over the role of Europe in a "new" strategy and over the implications for German defense policy; 4) fear that SDI will complicate the Geneva arms control talks; 5) confusion over German participation in the SDI program and therefore over the economic costs to the Federal Republic.

For the West Germans, on whose soil NATO troops are concentrated, the U.S. failure to consult its allies before the 1983 SDI announcement was an embarrassment, albeit less so after it became known that the President had apparently not consulted many of his own advisors either. Future cooperation on the program will have to take forms that will ensure German input and assure consideration of German views.

In addition, many in the FRG are concerned that SDI will prompt an arms race rather than be used as a bargaining chip in Geneva. A closely involved West German general commented to John Newhouse that if SDI went forward as planned "Our leaders would have to ask the people for more money for defense. And the Americans, we think, would have to improve nuclear weapons across the entire spectrum: short-range and long-range ballistic missiles, cruise missiles—all weapons."[77] And former Chancellor Schmidt took the unusual step of writing Kohl directly, warning against an isolated participation by Germany or even a concerted European participation and underlining the importance of SDI in the arms control process.[78]

A final major issue has been the extent of FRG participation in research on SDI. There have been several difficulties. First and foremost has been the potential degree of German access to the results of the research and development of the program. Second has been the question of FRG input and influence over the program should it decide to participate and to aid in the funding. Finally has been the uncertainty of even German firms whether SDI would actually have any spinoffs for the civilian side, as proponents claim, or only "dropoffs," as IBM Vice President Lewis Branscomb asserted in agreement with former head of Siemens communications division Dieter von Sanden.[79] Finally, but not last in priority has been the issue of funding.

The Eureka Alternative

To complicate the debate, France has offered participation in the Eureka program. While seemingly proposed as an alternative to SDI, Eureka is now being touted as a complement to SDI. Its focus is the development of technology in the civilian sectors of industry rather than the military. It is this civilian nature that has made the program particularly attractive to Bonn and not a major financial burden. (As now envisaged, the costs will be borne primarily by the private sector.) The program, however, should benefit the entire country and "throw open the door to the high-tech era to ensure that European industry remains competitive in the 1990s and beyond. . . . "[80] In the most pressing area of present concern, employment, the Germans are acutely aware that the U.S. has created 15 million new jobs and Japan 5 million while the European Community has lost 1.5 million over the past decade.[81] Eureka is viewed as a possible vehicle to alter that discrepancy.

In addition, and in contrast to SDI, Eureka's civilian emphasis has attracted support across the German political spectrum, including the opposition,[82] and its French sponsorship is attractive. For the West Germans, the program offers an opportunity long sought—to intensify European cooperation and integration among the seventeen nations who attended the July 1985 organizational meeting in Paris.[83] The joint ventures advised by Eureka for the development of technology are particularly appealing, since they hold the promise of even industrial cooperation in a field that has traditionally been fiercely competitive and insular.

Conclusions

From the American perspective, SDI is viewed as a technical solution to a military problem, that of safeguarding the United States from (most of) the consequences of a nuclear exchange. If successful, SDI should in the short run enhance deterrence and in the longer run perhaps replace it, both by "eliminating the threat posed by strategic nuclear missiles" and by providing an iniative for their dismantling under arms control agreements. Given these far-reaching aspirations, it is understandable that the Reagan Administration should be reluctant to settle for lesser reductions in strategic offensive weapons at the Geneva negotiations if the price to be paid is the curtailment of SDI.

Instead, the United States has sought, by other means, both to ameliorate European uneasiness about the implications of SDI and to generate European support for it. The first has been done by stressing that SDI is only a research program, that no final decisions on deployment have been made, that the nuclear guarantee will continue for the foreseeable future and that if defenses are built Western Europe will also be shielded, either by U.S. missile interceptors based in space or by a regional system capable of coping with the various modes of attack. The second has been done largely by seeking to involve the West Europeans in the on-going research on SDI, in the hope that this would generate political support for the program.

However, the Weinberger "one-time sixty-day" offer of participation in SDI was viewed throughout Western Europe with distaste as thinly-veiled "blackmail" and as another example of poor consultation. The U.S. assurance that no coercion or deadline were intended limited damage to intra-Alliance relations but the confusion was not helpful in selling the program to European publics. Equally unfortunate was the use of the term "subcontractor" by an official when referring to West European participation. Hence, though the FRG did authorize participation in the research, it made clear that this was a commercial venture, not an instance of military cooperation.

Much more enthusiasm has been displayed for Eureka, which is viewed as a step in the direction of European integration. Its French sponsorship offers Bonn also the opportunity to increase ties to Paris. The process of French-German defense cooperation has been a high priority over the past decade and technological cooperation in Eureka could be an important contribution to that process. Moreover, it could shift the emphasis of German security policy slightly toward France.

Furthermore, many in the Federal Republic were—and are—concerned about the implications of SDI for German security. Even after Chancellor Kohl in February 1985 at the Munich *Wehrkunde* Conference resoundingly endorsed SDI, then Defense Minister Manfred Wörner reportedly expressed reservations to Secretary of Defense Weinberger during conversations the following week.[84]

For all these reasons, there is no question that the easiest solution for the SDI issue from the West German perspective is its serious inclusion in the Geneva negotiations, in the hope of a bilateral U.S.-Soviet arms limitation agreement. The issue has already brought the superpowers back to the negotiating table and the strong Soviet desire to curb SDI indicates a possibility for tradeoffs in strategic nuclear weapons. There is, in addition, great interest in Bonn in avoiding an abrogation of the ABM Treaty, an agreement considered one of the few successes of the "détente" years.[85]

Summary

In order to assure the continued stability of the security regime now extant in Europe, the United States and the Federal Republic have maintained conventional forces designed to deter Soviet aggression. The U.S. nuclear guarantee serves as an added deterrent to both conflict and conflict escalation and any potential aggressor must include this possibility in *his* calculations.

For the Federal Republic, the additional security provided by Allied forces, by the U.S. nuclear guarantee and by its membership in NATO is essential, as it could not by itself deter the USSR. Moreover, its small size, its location on the border between East and West, its relatively limited geo-economic base and its high dependence on foreign trade make it vulnerable to political and economic pressures, as well as to military operations. And while resistance to these pressures requires both a strong defense and a solid political base these are not enough; in some instances, at least, mutual political accommodation and economic interdependence may both alleviate pressures and make them less effective if tried again.

The 1980s have witnessed a broadening of the German perception of the appropriate security for Europe and its role in achieving it. Under the chairmanship of West German Foreign Minister Genscher further advances were made by the European Community toward the goal of a single market by 1992. While this goal is not yet assured, the general economic and political progress within the European Community has been impressive. Progress in both areas is clearly seen as a necessary reinforcement to the long-term security of the continent. At the same time, considerable but cautious efforts have been undertaken in the area of European cooperation on security policy. These have included the Colombo-Genscher initiative and reactivation of the Western European Union as well as more emphasis on Eurogroup and other *fora* for European coordination, including the various arms control negotiations such as the Conference on Disarmament in Europe and the forthcoming Conventional Stability Talks.

In addition, the Franco-German brigade combat group and the Defense Council have also been established to strengthen the "European identity" within the Alliance.[86] For the Federal Republic, the European pillar may be expected to have increasing importance in the future. As Jan Reifenberg advised in a December 1987 article on the INF treaty:

> Although the vital bond with America should not be severed, Western Europe should do more to establish a framework of independent European security. Europe must step up its significance so as to be able to influence developments between the two superpowers. . . . Europeans should not . . . start complaining about a new "condominium," but establish their own place in the sun instead of merely responding to what happens in Washington or Moscow.[87]

Finally, the dialogue with the East Block during the 1970s and, even more, during the latter half of the 1980s, opened the East-West border to human traffic and gave substance to the long-term FRG objective of reunification and short-term objective of normal contacts with the East. The START and INF arms control negotiations between the U.S. and the USSR, as well as the multilateral CSCE/CDE talks (and NATO-WTO MBFR talks) further increased Bonn's *"Spielraum"* (flexibility) in its relations with the East. Even during the superpower stalemate that marked the first Reagan Administration, and especially in the period of the suspended Geneva talks, the West Germans placed a high priority on continued contacts between East and West in the hope that reduced tensions would lower the threshold of possible military threat. Thus, continued negotiations on arms control are seen by Chancellor Kohl as contributing to political stability as well as to military security.

Conversely, the U.S. approach to the maintenance of the security regime defined in its alliance with the other 15 nations of NATO focused primarily on military stability and the forces needed to assure that stability. Détente was judged more likely to result from Soviet recognition of U.S. military capabilities than from political accommodation. In this context, military strength was seen as a prerequisite to arms control and to the U.S.-Soviet dialogue necessary for its success; thus the signature of the INF treaty was viewed as a direct result of the U.S. resolve to deploy the P IIs and GLCMs and to drive a hard bargain over their removal. This does not, however, mean that arms control in itself was regarded as a means of enhancing U.S. security or as a means of improving East-West relations. Instead, the Reagan Administration, which has been deeply mistrustful of, and engaged in a global competition with, the Soviet Union, preferred to rely on its industrial base and its technological and military capabilities to safeguard its interests and those of its allies.

Obviously, these differences over the importance attaching to détente and to arms control, and with respect to the approaches to ensuring security in Europe, are going to leave the U.S. and the FRG at odds over many policy issues. As indicated earlier in this chapter, this has been particularly true in the aftermath of Helsinki (most notably at the Madrid conference of 1980-82) and to some extent with SDI and INF, particularly over the issue of removing or retaining short-range and battlefield tactical nuclear weapons. Differences over constraints on conventional forces in Europe, or over the desirability of confidence-building measures, have been much less pronounced. Given the power, positions, locations and interests of the two allies, old differences are likely to persist; whether new ones will arise depends largely on political developments in the two countries.

Notes

1. The two aspects of the concept are set forth clearly in the *North Atlantic Treaty*, NATO Information Service, Brussels, 1949. Article 1 . . . to safeguard the freedom, common heritage, and civilization of their peoples, founded on the principles of democracy, individual liberty, and the rule of law, Article 5 . . . an armed attack against one or more of them in Europe or North America shall be considered an attack against them all. . . .

2. For Adenauer's account of the talks and later arms control proposals, see his memoirs. Konrad Adenauer, *Erinnerungen 1945-53*, also *1953-1955, 1955-1959, 1966* and *1967* (Stuttgart: Deutsche Verlags-Anstalt, 1965). Also Arnulf Baring, *Aussenpolitik in Adenauers Kanzlerdemokratie*, DGAP (Munich: Oldenbourg 1969), especially 124-162.

3. NATO, *Harmel Report. Report on the Future Task of the Alliance* (Brussels: NATO Information Service, 1969).

4. W. Leisler Kiep, "*Auch in Helsinki die deutsche Frage offenhalten,*" *Die Zeit*, 25 July 1975.

5. For the most thorough discussion of German policy, see Helga Haftendorn, *Abrustungs- und Entspannungspolitik zwischen Sicherheitsbefriedigung und Frie-*

denssicherung zur Aussenpolitik der BRD 1955-1973, (Dusseldorf: Berklsmann University Press 1974).

6. See FRG, *"Entspannung, ein langfristiger Prozess,"* *Sozialdemokratische Sicherheitspolitik* 8/9, November 1980, 11-20.

7. Henry A. Kissinger, "Détente with the Soviet Union: The Reality of Competition and Imperative of Cooperation," in *Détente and Defense*, Robert J. Pranger, ed. (Washington, D.C.: American Enterprise Institute, 1976), 155.

8. North Atlantic Assembly, Subcommittee on Détente, *Détente: Results and Prospects*, (Brussels: October 1979) 3-8.

9. Marshall D. Shulman, "Toward a Western Philosophy of Coexistence," *Foreign Affairs* 52 (October 1973), 36. See also *Entspannung: Der Sowjetische Standpunkt*, in *Novosti*, (Moscow: 1977). (Commentators include Ponomarjow, Proektor and Zagladin).

10. Kissinger, "Détente with the Soviet Union: The Reality of Competition and Imperative of Cooperation," 158.

11. Michel Tatu, *Détente and the Atlantic Nations* (Chicago: Chicago Council on Foreign Relations, 1977), 45.

12. Although Afghanistan proved the breaking point, relations with the Soviet Union had come into question much earlier. See essays in Fred W. Neal, *Détente or Debacle: Common Sense in U.S.-Soviet Relations*, (American Committee on East-West Accord, New York: 1979).

13. Jimmy Carter, "Speech on the Anniversary of the Signing of the Helsinki Accords, August 6, 1980," *America Digest*, Bonn, 1980, and Hans-Dietrich Genscher, "Comments on the Anniversary of the Signing of the Helsinki Accords, 31 July 1980." *Bulletin* 89, Bonn, 5 August 1980, 761-62. Compare with Leonid Brezhnev, "Helsinki Final Act was 'Major Event in History of Post-War Europe,'" *Soviet News*, 5 August 1980 (from *Pravda*, 30 July 1980).

14. For text: Conference on Security and Cooperation in Europe. *Final Act*, Cmnd. 6198 (London: Her Majesty's Stationery Office, 1 August 1975), 54.

15. The recognition of Polish and German borders is listed as a major, when not first, priority not only in Soviet press accounts, but also in East European ones. See Grzegorz Jaszunski, *Zycie Warszawy*, 15 May 1973. *Soviet News* quotes *Izvestia* correspondent Yury Goloshubov, that "the inviolability of the postwar frontiers in Europe is the basic principle for relationships between countries today." "High Time to Convene the European Conference," *Soviet News* (from *Pravda*), 22 January 1974.

16. See U.S. Congress, House of Representatives, Committee on Foreign Affairs, "Appeal to all European Countries adopted by the Political Consultative Committee of the Warsaw Pact, Budapest (17 May 1969)" *Conference on European Security*, Hearings, April 25; May 10; August 10, 17; September 7, 27, 1972 (Washington D.C.: GPO, 1972), 142-144 and v-vii.

17. Alvin Shuster, "Soviet Gives Way on Europe Parley," *The New York Times*, 28 May 1973.

18. For the cautious German approach see Theo Sommer, *"Entspannung hat ihren Preis,"* *Die Zeit*, 21 September 1973. CSCE had strong critics among the opposition, such as Richard Stucklen (CSU Party leader) *"Konferenz der Unsicherheit,"* *Bayernkurier*. 19 October 1974. For the best historical review of opposition reservations see Christian Hacke, *"Parlamentarische Opposition und Entspannungspolitik—Die Position der CDU/CSU zur KSZE"* in *Verwaltete Aussenpolitik*, Helga Haftendorn *et al.*, eds., *Wissenschaft und Politik*, (Köln: 1978), 263-278.

19. U.S. Congress 1972, "Declaration Issued at the Close of the Meeting of the Political Consultative Committee of the Warsaw Pact on the Strengthening of Peace and Security in Europe," Bucharest, (5 July 1966), 141-142.

20. U.S. Congress 1972, "Final Communiqué issued after the Ministerial Meeting of the North Atlantic Council," (Brussels: 4 December 1970), 156-158.

21. U.S. Congress, Senate, "Concluding Document of the Belgrade Meeting 1977," Report No. 95-773, *Belgrade Conference on Security and Cooperation in Europe*, 95th Congress, 2nd Sess. (Washington:, GPO, 2 May 1978), 5.

22. Daniel Frie and Dieter Ruloff, *East-West Relations*, Vol.1 (Cambridge: Oelgeschlager, Gunn & Hain, 1983), Madrid 21, Helsinki 16.

23. Heinz Brill, "*Konferenz uber Vertrauens—und Sicherheits-bildende Massnahmen und Abrustung in Europa*," *Europaische Wehrkunde* 2, 1984, 76.

24. *Ibid.*, 77.

25. Alois Mertes, "Outlook for the Conferences on Confidence Building and Disarmament in Europe," *Aussenpolitik* (English edition), 1, 1984, 13-30.

26. *Ibid.*, 27.

27. John Borawski, " 'Next Steps in Conference and Security' Building Measures," in Stan Windass and Eric Grove, eds., *Common Security in Europe 1988*. The Foundation for International Security (Adderbury, England: 1988), 1-3.

28. Mertes "Outlook for the Conference on Confidence Building and Disarmament in Europe," 28.

29. Karl Liko, "*Von Madrid nach Stockholm*," *Österreichische Militarische Zeitschrift* 1 (January/February, 1984), 1-4.

30. "Mertes in Stockholm: *Vertrauen allein starkt nicht die allgemeine Sicherheit*" *Frankfurter Allgemeine Zeitung* 5 May 1984, 2.

31. Quoted in James Macintosh, *Confidence (and Security) Building Measures in the Arms Control Process: A Canadian Perspective*, prepared for The Arms Control and Disarmament Division, Department of External Affairs (Ottawa, Ontario: Department of External Affairs, 1985), 40.

32. *Ibid.*, 41-43.

33. See *Ibid.*, 43-44 and William R. Bowman, *Limiting Conventional Forces in Europe: An Alternative to the Mutual and Balanced Force Reduction Negotiations*. (Washington: National Defense University Press, 1985), 11-13.

34. Jonathan Dean, "MBFR: From Apathy to Accord," *International Security* 7, 4 (Spring 1983), 120-121 and Macintosh, *Confidence and (Security) Building Measures*, 45-46.

35. See Bowman "Limiting Conventional Forces," 16-19.

36. *The Arms Control Reporter, 1985* (Brookline, Maryland: Institute for Defense and Disarmament Studies, 1985), 401.B.84.

37. *Ibid.*, 401B.96-97.

38. Ernst F. Jung, "Conventional Arms Control in Europe in Light of the MBFR Experience." *Aussenpolitik*, English Language Edition, 39 (February 1988), 166-167.

39. Helmut Schmidt, "Speech before the Annual Meeting of the IISS," *Survival*, xx, 1 (January-February 1978): 2-10.

40. Chicago Council on Foreign Relations, *Détente and the Atlantic Nations*, Papers from the 1976 Atlantic Conference, (Chicago: 1977).

41. Lothar Rühl, "*Im Schatten der roten Raketen*," *Die Zeit*, 4 March 1977; see also *idem*, "*Sorgen um die Graue Zone*," *Die Zeit*, 16 December 1977.

42. "NATO Long-term Defense Program, 1978," *The Military Balance 1979-1980* (London: International Institute for Strategic Studies, 1979), 112.

43. G. Philip Hughes. "Cutting the Gordian Knot: A Theater Nuclear Force for Deterrence in Europe," *Orbis*, 22, 2 (Summer 1978), 312.

44. This agreement was made under the Schmidt government and remains the case to the knowledge of the author. There was, however, sentiment voiced at the

time of the change in government by the Bavarian Minister-President Franz-Joseph Strauss (CSU) advocating renunciation of this agreement in favor of dual key controls.

45. The debate surfaced in private and public comment at a variety of forums on security policy in the winter and spring of 1979. See SPD, *Für Sicherheit und Frieden*, Security Conference, Bremen, *Bundestagsfraktion* SPD, Bonn, 19-20 May 1979; Dr. Friedrich Zimmermann (Chairman, CSU Parliamentary Party) "*Pflicht zur Verteidigung des Westens*," *Das Parlament, Bundestag*, Bonn, 17 March 1979, 1-2; FDP, *Provisorische Materialsammlung vom verteidigungspolitischen Kongress der FDP-Munster*, FDP, Bonn, 1 June 1979, Karl Kaiser, "Warning: Security of West at Stake," *International Herald Tribune*, 9 March 1979, 6.

46. FDP, *Ergebnisprotokoll Arbeitskreis II Rustungskontrolle/ Abrüstung, Provisorische Materialsammlung* (Munster, 27/28 April 1979), 117.

47. Helmut Kohl, Statement on the Signing of the SALT II Agreement, CDU *Pressemitteilung* (Bonn, 18 June 1979), 51.

48. North Atlantic Treaty Organization, "Communiqué of the Special Meeting of NATO Foreign and Defense Ministers," Brussels, 12 December 1979, (Xerox).

49. *Ibid.* The communiqué stipulates as follows: "Limitations on U.S. and Soviet long-range theater nuclear systems should be negotiated bilaterally in the SALT III framework in a step-by-step approach." See also NATO. North Atlantic Council Communiqué, Brussels, 13-14 December 1979 (Xerox). Specifically, the communiqué called for "the following wide range of initiatives particularly in the fields of confidence-building and arms control designed to improve mutual security and cooperation in Europe;—an offer to negotiate for substantial reductions in the level of long-range theater nuclear forces as well as inter-continental strategic forces within the framework of SALT III . . . ".

50. NATO Senior Consultative Group, *Report to Ministers*, 8 December 1983, 18.

51. J. I. Coffey, *Deterrence and Arms Control: American and West German Perspectives on INF*, Monograph Series in World Affairs, Vol. 21 (Denver, CO: University of Denver, 1985), 92-93.

52. A brief recital of the steps in this "mating dance" wil be found in William M. Arkin, Robert S. Norris and Thomas B. Cochran, "Implications of the INF Treaty," Nuclear Weapons Databook Working Paper 87-3. (Washington, D.C.: National Resources Defense Council, 1 December 1987), 47-51.

53. U.S. Government. *Treaty between the United States of America and the Union of Soviet Socialist Republics on the Elimination of Their Intermediate-Range and Shorter-Range Missiles.* (Washington: December 1987) (also Memorandum of Understanding regarding the Establishment of the Data Base).

54. Statement attributed to General Hans-Joachim Mack, at that time Deputy Supreme Allied Commander, Europe, by Jeane Kirkpatrick, "Grumbling About Reykjavik," *Washington Post*, 27 October 1986, A-15.

55. John J. Fialka. "Europe Debates Missile Pact's Aftermath," the *Wall Street Journal*, 7 December 1987.

56. A. Dunn. "Considerations after the INF Treaty: NATO after Global 'Double Zero,' " *Survival*, XXX, 3 (May/June 1988), 195-209.

57. Henry Kissinger. Prepared Statement. *The INF Treaty*, Part 4, Hearings before the Committee on Foreign Relations, U.S. Senate, 100th Congress, 2nd Session, February 22, 23, 24, and March 3, 1988, 178-186. See also Parts 1, 2, 3, and 5.

58. *Süddeutscher Zeitung. "Bonner Appelle an den Senat*," 9 December 1987.

59. Congress also remains convinced of this need. See especially Kenneth W. Thompson, ed. *Sam Nunn on Arms Control*, (Lanham: University Press of America, 1987).

60. Genscher's optimism received criticism in the United States as well as in Germany. See Jim Hoagland, "Rhetoric From Bonn. Why is the German Foreign Minister Saying Nice Things about the Soviets?" *Washington Post*, 18 August 1988, A23.

61. Robert J. McCartney. "Bonn's Defense Minister Cautious on Arms Talks," *Washington Post*, 17 June 1988, A19.

62. *Ibid.*

63. Robert Leicht, "*Deutsche Verantwortungsgemeinschaft*," *Suddeutsche Zeitung*, 11 September 1984, 4.

64. Christoph Bertram, "European Security and the German Problem," *International Security*, 4, 3 (Winter 1979/80), 105-116.

65. Leicht, "*Deutsche Verantwortungsgemeinschaft*."

66. Helmut Kohl, "*Wir haben mehr Kontakte möglich gemacht*," *Suddeutsche Zeitung*, 13 September 1984, 8.

67. Remarks to Robert Bosch Fellows, *Bundeskanzleramt*, 11 September 1984.

68. Enrico Jacchia, "What Was Bothering Andreotti?" *International Herald Tribune*, 22-23 September 1984, 4.

69. Francois Mitterrand, "*Rede in Bonn am 20. January 1983 anlasslich des zwanzigsten Jahrestages der Unterzeichnung des Vertrages uber die deutsch-franzosische Zusammenarbeit*," *Europa-Archiv*, 10 March 1983, D145-155.

70. Elizabeth Pond, "Kohl Hails Thaw in West German, Soviet Relations," *Christian Science Monitor*, 15 January 1988.

71. President Ronald Reagan, "Peace and National Security," Televised address to the Nation, Washington D.C., 23 March 1983, reprinted in U.S. Department of State, *Realism, Strength, Negotiation: Key Foreign Policy Statements of the Reagan Administration*, May 1984, 43.

72. The latest of these called for cutbacks in the number of space-based interceptors to be deployed in the initial defensive system, an increase in ground-launched interceptors and a reduction in costs of almost 50 per cent. Despite these changes, the system is supposed to meet the performance requirements set by the Joint Chiefs of Staff which reportedly call for "intercepting one-third of the warheads in a Soviet missile attack, including half of the warheads from the powerful SS-18 missile." (*The New York Times*, 7 October 1988, 9). Even if successful, this would, however, be a far cry from erecting an "impenetrable shield" over the United States.

73. Robert C. McFarlane, "Time Out on Defense," the *Washington Post*, 3 January 1988, R2. The former national security advisor has come to admit that "Both sides should begin by acknowledging that for the next five to ten years, there is simply no alternative to continued reliance on nuclear weapons and the basic strategy of deterrence."

74. "FDP Executive Committee: No Role in SDI without European Partners," *The Week in Germany.*

75. "Bonn's 'Star Wars' Role Draws a Soviet Protest," *The New York Times*, 5 April 1986, 5.

76. SPD, Statement of the Parliamentary Group of the SPD on President Reagan's "Strategic Defense Initiative," Friedrich Ebert Stiftung. Undated Xerox, released in April 1985.

77. John Newhouse, "The Diplomatic Round," *New Yorker*, 22 July 1985, 38.

78. Helmut Schmidt, *"Letter an Herrn Bundeskanzler Dr. Helmut Kohl,"* 23 May 1985, 2. (Xerox)

79. Newhouse, "The Diplomatic Round," 49 (The author is citing comments made at a June 6, 1985 conference in Maastricht, The Netherlands).

80. Uwe Vorkotter, "Europe looks towards New Technology Horizons," *Hannoverische Allgemeine,* 22 July 1985. Reprinted in the *German Tribune* 1189 (28 July 1985), 1.

81. *Ibid.*

82. Schmidt, *"Letter an Herrn Bundeskanzler. . . . ",* 4-5.

83. Klaus W. Growlich. "Eureka-eureka?" *Aussenpolitik,* 37, (January 1986), 24-36.

84. See News Broadcast, CDF Evening News, 11 February 1985.

85. Newhouse, "The Diplomatic Round," 52.

86. Lothar Rühl. "Franco-German Military Cooperation: An Insurance Policy for the Alliance," *Strategic Review,* XIV, 3 (Summer 1988), 48-54.

87. Jan Reifenberg. "Watershed in Arms Control: Now for the Future," *Frankfurter Allgemeine Zeitung,* 11 December 1987, translated and reprinted in *The German Tribune,* 20 December 1987, 1.

8

The United States and the FRG: Differences, Commonalities, Choices

Klaus von Schubert and Joseph I. Coffey

Dealing with the Preconditions
of History and Geography

Anyone contemplating a political map of the world wonders how it is possible for the U.S., a superpower, and the Federal Republic of Germany, a small regional power, to have much in common in terms of security policy interests and options. The differences are too great. And yet, members of one Alliance as they are, the policies of both countries reveal common elements, overlaying differences and even conducive to symbiosis. Although we are aware that a host of factors, from climate to culture, may influence the power, the objectives and the policies of a country, we have singled out for consideration a dozen which we think are of particular importance. One of these is geo-strategic position, which for the two countries is strikingly different.

The Federal Republic of Germany is no bigger than the state of Oregon, yet supports a population of over 60 million people, about 25% of the total number living in the United States. The resultant differences in area and density can lead to very different views on security and defense. So can location. The United States—and Canada—may be considered as a continent, but also as an island, giving a sense of independence which can never arise in the Federal Republic, situated as it is amid a patchwork of European states.

Furthermore, the fact that the American East and West coasts open on to the warm waters of the two biggest oceans permits it to pursue a global maritime policy. The Federal Republic of Germany has access to the North and the Baltic Seas, but can reach the Atlantic Ocean only after passing through straits and channels controlled by other powers. The U.S. showed during World War II that it could engage in military action at opposite ends of the globe, in the Western Pacific and the Eastern Atlantic. In all their history, the Germans never attained anything like this dimension of maritime power.

Through World War II the U.S. became a superpower. The Germans began World War II with the intention of becoming a world power but Hitler's megalomania led to a total loss of German positions of power. The terms of the East-West conflict have permitted the emergence of a relative German power. This power is and remains limited, being bound up in the East-West conflict and its alliances. The post-war world structure prevents the Germans from using this power on their own.

The U.S., on the other hand, can take the independent decision to use military force worldwide. On closer inspection, though, this power also proves to be restricted. Two factors have a constraining influence: firstly, the Soviet Union and its allies, as a counter-power, and, secondly, dependence on raw materials, allies and developments in other regions of conflict. To differing degrees, both the superpower U.S.A and the medium-size power West Germany are enmeshed in a web of interdependence, making absolute sovereignty a thing of the past.

A power factor which has changed the world should not be overlooked. It was not Hindenburg who gave military power a new dimension, nor was it Hitler—but the nuclear physicists of the Manhattan project. Otto Hahn was the first to split the atom in Germany in 1938. The first atomic bomb was not developed by Werner Heisenberg on the shores of the Baltic, however, but by J. R. Oppenheimer in the mountains of New Mexico. Albert Einstein and others were afraid of seeing Nazi Germany develop the weapon and thus advised the U.S. government to concert all scientific and economic efforts in order to construct the bomb itself. In time, the nuclear arsenal became the main element of America's military power and deterrence "the name of the game." Subsequently the U.S. and the USSR were dubbed "superpowers" not least because of their large nuclear arsenals. For its part, the FRG, in a statement by Chancellor Adenauer in 1954 before its entry into NATO, undertook never to possess or produce nuclear weapons. This places the West Germans permanently in another category than the Americans.

Washington's nuclear power has not given it a free hand in using it, however. At the nuclear level, power and counter-power are related; mutual deterrence also means mutual dependence on the forebearance and the prudence of the adversary. The extreme increase in military power through nuclear weapons has finally led to a lessening of the applicability of military power. The growing realization that, in the nuclear age, war is no longer an instrument of policy unites the powers in the regions where there is a threat of nuclear war, regardless of whether or not they themselves possess nuclear weapons.

The Americans have gotten to know the limits of power and the horrors of war—but not, for more than a century through war in their own country. It is no surprise, then, that military power is talked of differently in the FRG than in the U.S. The relation between people and their state or nation is not as intact in the Old World, either. The Americans have taken part in two world wars but their statehood and national identity have never been in question. The German nation was shattered after the attempted Nazi expansion, however, and split into two states. This question has not troubled the United States since 1865, though it may again arise as the U.S. becomes a multiracial state.

Because Germany was in the forefront of the East-West conflict, all attempts to reinstate German unity foundered on the intensity of the conflict. The idea of restoring unity by military force was *a priori* excluded in view of the possibility of a third world war. Here, too, the effect of the nuclear age was perceptible. The development of the German question over time and the ways in which the various crises were resolved revealed an initially tacit, and later overt, agreement between Washington and Bonn to give priority to the *status quo*, when the chips were down. The orientation to the *status quo* in the East-West conflict today links all powers involved in it.

Differences exist with respect to what may be termed geo-economic influences. Although the United States is becoming increasingly dependent on imports of common minerals like copper as well as strategic ones like chromium, it has a relative abundance of natural resources, including petroleum; in contrast, the Federal Republic is sorely deficient. The U.S. industrial base is far larger than that of the Federal Republic, as is its gross national product; in consequence, it can sustain a defense budget on the order of 300 billion dollars, a sum which the Federal Republic could never hope to match, even if it so desired. Moreover, while West German industry is as technologically advanced as any in the world, it is not oriented toward military technology, which the United States exploits for everything from the building of Stealth bombers to the development of missile defenses.

Furthermore, West Germany is, because of the density of its population and the concentration of its industry, much more vulnerable to military action than is the United States, even in an age of nuclear weapons. It is also, because of the scarcity of resources noted earlier, much more vulnerable to any interruption in the flow of imports than is the United States, much more dependent on outside sources of oil and gas and much more economically interdependent with the outside world. These factors affect the domestic environments in the two countries, in that West Germany, which exports one-third of its products, has a vested interest in maintaining a stable and secure international economic environment that will encompass the countries of the East as well as those of the West and South. Conversely, the exporters in the United States are more highly specialized, less influential (save for the farm lobby) and less committed to a world market.

More importantly, public attitudes and policy preferences exercise a different—and differential—impact upon security policy. This is not because the two publics are at odds: Americans as well as West Germans are overwhelmingly disposed toward accommodation with the Soviet Union and overwhelmingly endorse the limitation of armaments. Rather, it is because the political system in Germany, where local parties are subsets of national ones, and national ones are highly disciplined, is more responsive to changes in public attitudes than that in the United States, where local elections are seldom won or lost on issues of defense policy and where every Congressman and Senator is the determiner of his own vote. Moreover, the Chancellor of the Federal Republic is much more dependent on party and legislative support than is the President of the United States, who is arguably the most powerful man in the world. Thus, aside from the degree of responsiveness to public opinion, the personality, perspectives and ability of the political leader is of far greater importance in the United States than it is in West Germany. The selection of the leading personality, however, is influenced by moods and trends in the American public, as shown with the change from Carter to Reagan.

Managing the East-West Conflict

The relationship between the FRG and the U.S. is characterized by political closeness and geographical distance. The relationship between the FRG and the USSR is the reverse. The geographical and political asymmetry of the East-West conflict becomes clearly visible whenever the question of relations with the Soviet Union is raised or the perception of Soviet conduct becomes an issue.

Looking at the United States, for one thing its position as an island-continent, its geo-economic base and its global interests made it a natural competitor of the USSR in efforts to re-shape the international system— and the only country capable of checking Soviet aspirations for primacy in that system. For another, its interpretation of the Soviet challenge after World War II, especially after the Communist invasion of South Korea in 1950, led it to emphasize the military aspect of the competition, so that it established a number of alliances (of which NATO was only one), entered into bilateral security arrangements with over 40 states and became heavily involved in programs to maintain "internal security" in countries such as Angola, Guatemala, Iran and Vietnam. That it also formed relationships on other bases and promoted economic and social programs throughout the world was in part a reflection of its values, in part an accompaniment to the policy of containment.

For the FRG, the Soviet problem consists not only in the difference between notions of political order in West and East, but also, and vitally, in the potential exercise of hegemonial pressure by the USSR in Europe. From the very beginning the FRG was confronted at close quarters with Stalinist fore-field policy, in which much of Eastern Europe was reduced to a condition of dependence on the USSR and established as a shield against Western invasion. The West Germans could never be certain that they were not meant to suffer a similar fate. Throughout the 1950's, the West Germans saw the Soviet Union, with its massive military power, as a permanent threat to German interests and as a potential invader of German territory. Bonn's policy towards Moscow has, then, been characterized by a dialectic approach, in which a trans-bloc security policy and cooperative relations with the opponent are based on firm links with the Western Allies.

A policy of containment has remained the joint basis of U.S. and West German policy towards the Soviet Union for 40 years. There have, however, been regular differences between Washington and Bonn on the question of what constructive, political ties the West or single Western states could and should establish with the USSR.

U.S. experience with the foreign policy of the Kremlin is based not only on European history but also on acute confrontations in different trouble-spots in the world, where the interests of the U.S. and the USSR in their capacities as world powers cut across one another. Europe is one of these trouble-spots, but only one, and the U.S. concern is more about "global power projection" (and about the strategic nuclear balance) than about Europe *per se*. Against this background, the political elites in the U.S. tend to see Soviet policy as expansionist, and the USSR as challenging American political and military positions throughout the world. Moreover, this challenge is perceived as being couched primarily in military terms, and, therefore, as one which must be met by military measures.

Conversely, the political elites in the FRG, on the basis of European history, see the ambivalence of Soviet conduct: defensive in motivation, from Moscow's angle, and yet perceived by its neighbors as offensive. In its perception of Soviet military potential the FRG has always primarily concentrated on the land forces in Europe. Even when the role of these forces is considered that of a police force—without approving this—and even when Soviet defense needs after their experience with Hitler are accepted, Soviet land forces still seem oversized for defense purposes and in relation to those of the West. The magnitude of these forces aroused concern after 1945 that the USSR would go beyond consolidating its forefield, occupied by the Red Army during the Second World War, to attack the West and expand beyond its own bloc—a concern enhanced by the Korean War. The West Germans, though, deem the military threat more latent than overt and—following from that—are worried less about actual aggression than about potentially hegemonial pressure by the USSR on the small and medium-sized Western European states. In contrast to the American public the West German public tends to see Soviet behavior as a political challenge calling for a political response.

In so far as the U.S. actively pursues a policy of détente, it premises it on the East-West conflict and seeks a *modus vivendi*. In the Reagan era, the effect and possibility of détente were initially doubted and the legitimacy of the Soviet regime was fundamentally questioned, i.e., the resolution of the East-West conflict through ending Soviet rule was declared a desirable long-term goal. Scepticism towards the USSR as a partner in political negotiations matched the intention to neutralize the military threat by military means. Towards the end of the Reagan era, however, primacy was given to the diplomatic instrument of policy. Even competitive behavior in the Middle East and a military build-up in the Gulf could not conceal the necessity of regulating the essential security issues with the Soviet Union at the negotiating tables in Geneva, Vienna and elsewhere.

In the FRG the resolution of the East-West conflict is not one of the expectations or goals expressed in *Ostpolitik*. The West Germans believe that this conflict will continue for the foreseeable future. They seek to defuse it by agreements that can create a *modus vivendi*, while taking precautions to make it inconceivable for the USSR to opt for a military solution to this conflict. Thus, successive German governments, starting from the late Adenauer era in the early 1960s, have always defined security policy in terms which permitted cooperation with the other side. They have never tried to do away with the East-West conflict but rather to introduce procedures allowing it to remain competition and not to become war.

While elements of the political elites in the U.S. have sometimes tended towards isolationism and unilateralism, the German actors have always had a broad consensus favoring continued political and military ties with the U.S., on the one hand, and multilateral positions in dealings with the USSR, on the other. Both within the Western Alliance and the East-West conflict system, multilateralism predominates in West German policy. Accordingly, unilateralist U.S. tendencies have always been received critically, just as German *Ostpolitik* has repeatedly caused concern to Americans. Any comparison with the foreign policy of the Weimar Republic is inappropriate, however, seeing that the FRG's integration in the Western Alliance and its special relationship to the U.S. is not in question; no new Rapallo is conceivable. Neither Americans nor West Germans can escape the East-West conflict system today, and so they will have to operate in a dialectic of defense against military pressure and political cooperation with the other side.

Evolving Defense Policy

As noted earlier, Washington and Bonn have a common security interest, that of depriving the USSR of any incentive and temptation to use military power. From the beginning of their collaboration on defense, both sides have seen the advantages of a common policy and from the beginning they have differed as to what that policy should be. The reason for this is not only the differing geopolitical situations of the two countries but also their differing traditions of military and strategic thinking.

In formulating its defense policy the FRG, directly confronted by 30 divisions of the Soviet Army, and only a few years away from the end of World War II, thought primarily in terms of defense and denial. The FRG was not a nuclear power and has not become one; in spite of the *Bundeswehr's* nuclear launch vehicles, the German government has never been able to utter a threat of punishment as a means of deterrence. For this reason, German authorities attach great importance to the U.S. nuclear guarantee as protection against the nuclear arsenal of the USSR; below this level, the West Germans, though they have adopted the concept of flexible response should conventional defenses be breached, have focused all their defense activities on deterrence through denial. Conversely, the United States has sought to deter conventional as well as nuclear attacks by the threat to employ nuclear weapons, though there is some question as to whether this reflects actual policy rather than declaratory policy.

As long, however, as NATO is threatened by massive Soviet/WTO forces there is always the possibility that nuclear weapons may have to be used to bring to a halt a conventional attack; accordingly, the United States has, as discussed in Chapter 2, developed plans for their employment in varying numbers against various targets—in Europe as well as in the USSR proper. This gives the West Germans the feeling that in the event of an East-West war they would not be in the audience but on the stage, since a limited nuclear war would most probably mean the total destruction of Germany. Thus, despite the wish to be covered by the nuclear guarantee, there is a high degree of sensitivity to all scenarios of limited warfare or those which employ short and medium range nuclear weapons deployed in Europe.

Indeed, increased awareness among publics and elites of the consequences of nuclear war has led to both ethical arguments against their use, as in the positions taken by many churches, and to military arguments that dependence on nuclear weapons could lead to crisis instability and that their actual employment could escalate into an all-out nuclear war. Accordingly, Americans and West Germans alike have come to believe that at least the dependence on "early first use" of nuclear weapons should be abandoned.

At the moment, however, the American approach to maintaining the nuclear guarantee seems to be acceptable to the Germans, at least as far as theater nuclear forces are concerned. In the last few years, the United States has agreed to reduce the number of nuclear weapons in the European theater, to de-emphasize some delivery systems and even to trade off most of the intermediate range nuclear forces whose deployment was approved in 1979 for comparable draw-downs in Soviet missiles—all with West German approval. The single current issue is that of whether to modernize the Lance missiles in Germany by extending their range from 70 to some 280 miles—a proposal which the Americans are pushing, while the Germans are dragging their feet. On the horizon, however, is another one: whether to trade off Lance and other short range weapons for their Soviet/WTO counterparts; here, the Germans are leaning toward "triple-zero" (though *not* toward complete denuclearization) while the Americans are resisting.

By and large, however, the Americans have almost completely abandoned their efforts to create NATO theater nuclear forces capable of conducting a wide range of operations more or less independently of those carried out by U.S. strategic nuclear forces. Instead, the United States is attempting to maintain the credibility of the deterrent in two ways:

1. By programs that would make its strategic nuclear forces more survivable, more effective against a variety of targets and better able to carry out a range of missions in a protracted nuclear war;

2. By the Strategic Defense Initiative, a program aimed at developing and deploying some form of ballistic missile defenses, capable at a minimum of protecting missile silos, command control centers and other hard targets and at a maximum of shielding most of the population from direct attack.

Although the German government would prefer arms control to arms build-ups, it has no real quarrel with the U.S. policy of modernizing strategic nuclear forces—especially since the United States also favors reductions in the strategic arsenals of the two superpowers. Nor is there a great clamor within Germany for strategic arms reductions, since these weapons do not touch the same nerves as do those deployed on German soil. And while most Americans also favor cuts in strategic nuclear forces, they have not so far opposed programs for their modernization, which are officially justified as a means of pressuring the Soviets to negotiate seriously, as a hedge against uncertainty and as a way of maintaining a more stable and still credible strategic deterrent.

No such near-unanimity exists with respect to SDI. Many German and quite a few American critics are apprehensive about its potential for triggering an arms race. They are disturbed over the possibility that SDI may interfere with U.S.-Soviet arms reductions, rather than stimulate them, as Mr. Reagan initially hoped. This cluster of concerns has resulted in a cautious and restrained public endorsement of SDI by the Kohl government, coupled with questions and complaints in private, and to a much more vigorous opposition by the SPD, the Greens and even by the FDP, the junior partner in the Christian-Liberal Coalition. American perspectives on SDI are, if anything, even more mixed. While President Reagan and former Secretary of Defense Weinberger continue to endorse the ultimate objective of a shield against nuclear-armed missiles and to push for expanded and comprehensive research on this approach, other officials in the United States government, together with many Air Force officers and civilian analysts, prefer to concentrate on hard point defense. Along with growing doubts about the feasibility of a population shield, there are growing concerns about its costs which, for the full system, could reach an estimated 750 billion dollars over the next 15 years. In a time of enormous budgetary deficits, which are likely to lead to cuts in defense expenditures rather than to further increases, some individuals fear that SDI could be funded only at the expense of other programs which are regarded as more vital, whether these be the maintenance of a global presence or the bolstering of conventional defenses in Europe.

Apart from their differing approaches to nuclear deterrence, one key to understanding the different emphases in American and German defense policy is to be found in differing assessments of Soviet military capabilities. On both sides of the Atlantic, the judgment is that Soviet nuclear forces grew markedly in the 1970s and 1980s. While the balance of power has shifted in the Soviet favor, the West Germans do not see this as giving the Soviet Union a first strike capability, and believe that the existence of a second strike capability on either side means that the capacity for mutual deterrence remains. Conversely, American officials (though not all American analysts) are concerned lest the Soviets be able to knock out key elements of U.S. strategic retaliatory forces through attacks on missile silos, bomber bases and nodes in the system of command, control and communications, thereby degrading the capacity for prompt, controlled attacks against Soviet military targets. As indicated earlier, this concern has led the United States to take extensive measures to strengthen and to safeguard its strategic nuclear forces and is one of the factors behind the support for SDI in official circles.

Judgments concerning the effects of the parallel modernization of Soviet conventional forces are also divergent, partly because the NATO forces were also significantly strengthened over the past decade and partly because of the many, and frequently intangible, variables that affect assessments of net capabilities. Official estimates from Bonn, Brussels and Washington all stress Soviet advantages in tanks, planes, guns and divisions available for combat and on this basis warn that a conventional attack could force NATO to consider the use of nuclear weapons "after days, not weeks." This assessment is not shared by many defense analysts, American and West German, who point to over-estimates of Soviet/WTO readiness for combat, the difficulty of achieving surprise, the inability, because of the terrain, to exploit fully WTO numerical superiority, and so on; in fact, many military professionals on both sides of the Atlantic, speaking unofficially, maintain that NATO can cope with an attack by Soviet first echelon forces and that the mobilization and movement forward of second echelon forces is fraught with difficulty. (Our own judgment is that Soviet/WTO conventional capabilities, while impressive, are not overwhelming but that prudence requires that we take steps to "hedge our bets"—for which see Chapter 9.)

As far as operational doctrine is concerned, both Germans and Americans favor a mobile defense of the forward area, for which their forces are armed, organized and trained; though there are serious questions as to whether such a defense can maintain the depth and the resilience needed while still tied to a relatively shallow defensive zone, there are no indications that either country is prepared to modify its doctrine. There is, however, another approach favored in some quarters in the United States which could, if adopted, lead to bitter disputes, that of the maritime strategy. As noted in Chapter 4, this calls for air and naval operations against Soviet submarines, surface vessels and naval air bases, followed or accompanied by strikes, by carrier-based aircraft against other military targets and perhaps by amphibious and airborne landings at key points on the Soviet coast; the argument is that this would contribute to the defense of Western Europe by drawing off Soviet troops and aircraft to distant regions and would insure that even if this defense crumbled the USSR would not be able to defeat the "island continent" that is the United States. Whatever its merit, adoption of such a strategy would result in a shift of resources and it could lead to a diminution of U.S. participation in air and ground combat on the Central Front and perhaps even to greater detachment from the integrated military structure of NATO; accordingly, it has not received wide support in the Federal Republic.

This situation leads to differing views of the priority to be accorded to different tasks. Although the United States allocates more than half its military budget to forces earmarked for the defense of Western Europe, it gives top priority to the improvement of strategic offensive and defensive systems and argues the necessity for maintaining both powerful naval forces and a capacity to intervene in defense of Western interests outside the NATO area. In contrast, the FRG has always given forward defense in Europe top priority. Since the beginning of discussions on the German contribution to Western defense (Himmerodt, 1950) the motto has been that defense must begin right away and as far eastwards as possible. This was the pattern and mission of the Federal Army and this is what the Germans see as the main goal of joint defense efforts. From the German perspective, the U.S. contribution to joint forward defense—240,000 men in the Seventh U.S. Army and in Air Force units in West Germany—is underestimated in current discussions of security policy and strategy. Its deterrent value is esteemed very highly in the FRG, seeing that any aggressor would be confronted with U.S. soldiers from the first moment and would thus be at war with the United States of America. In German eyes, it has always been wrong to question precisely this part of the U.S. contribution to joint defense whenever tensions arose regarding tasks to be undertaken or burden-sharing between Bonn and Washington. The concern in Bonn is today that the big investments in the SDI program and in the next generation of nuclear missiles might be at the expense of this "conventional presence" in Europe. Bonn is also concerned with U.S. plans to redeploy troops from West German sites in times of crisis elsewhere, thereby jeopardizing the strength of the land forces in Central Europe without a general agreement on troop reductions between East and West having been concluded.

Agreeing to Differ:
Role Conflicts in the Alliance

This brings us at once to the fundamental question of roles and responsibilities within the Alliance. Obviously, decisions on force priorities and resource allocations will require an agreement among the member states which will not be easy to obtain. This is not because NATO lacks mechanisms for the coordination of policy; these include everything from committees of experts to the North Atlantic Council. Part of the problem is that national interests—and hence national policies—are bound to differ.

Another part is that consensus is difficult to achieve, even between husband and wife, much less among sixteen sovereign nations. Largely, however, difficulties arise because the United States and other European countries, notably the Federal Republic of Germany, attach different expectations to the Alliance and have a different sense of the role the United States should play.

The FRG is not the smallest member of the Alliance, nor is it, like France and the United Kingdom, a nuclear power. The FRG is a middle-size member. It has no nuclear weapons, yet it maintains the strongest contingent of land forces in the European part of NATO. Without doubt, its geographical position makes the FRG a strategically important country. NATO is neither an American nor a European organization-it is a North Atlantic one. Both the U.S. and the FRG benefit from membership in it. They have vital security interests in the Alliance. While the U.S. is far less dependent than the FRG in all important political fields, its strategic interests and the security of the American "island" favor active membership in NATO—though some believe that as a superpower it could if necessary uphold those interests on its own or readjust its expectations as to what it hopes to accomplish in the world at large. True, the goal of keeping Western Europe secure is more easily attained through NATO than in other ways but membership in the North Atlantic Treaty Organization brings with it heavy burdens and results in numerous constraints on U.S. freedom of action. When the acceptance of U.S. leadership was not forth-coming, the United States has, on some occasions, ignored both multinational and individual inputs and gone its own way. And though most U.S. publics and elites indorse the official policy of support for NATO, there are elements who would see that organization restructured or even dissolved.

It is all but inevitable that West Germany should have its own view of the role the U.S. should play in NATO. On the one hand, it wants leadership but on the other it wants the U.S. to consider its partially divergent regional interests. It particularly wishes serious consultations before U.S. decisions are taken, in order to present the German view on vital security questions. And it has, as one means to that end, made significant efforts to place intra-Alliance relations on a more equal basis by both joining with and working through separate European institutions, such as the West European Union and the European Community.

Thus, a constant structural problem for the Alliance derives from the dual roles of the U.S. as a superpower and as a member of NATO. NATO is an alliance with a limited mandate and limited regional responsibility. In certain cases, the American "superpower" has requested the aid of European states, e.g., in Middle East crises, and has met with reservations from the European, and particularly the German, side. Washington's argument was that joint interests, as in the Persian Gulf, were being defended and that therefore NATO should give political and if possible, military support. Furthermore, it pointed out that the United States might, under some circumstances, have to withdraw forces from Europe as well as to utilize units in the United States that were earmarked for NATO. In such instances, Americans argued, West Germany should not only facilitate the dispatch of U.S. troops and supplies to the Middle East but also mobilize reservists and/or utilize civilian employees to fill any gaps thereby created.

The German reservations took a variety of forms. First of all, they noted that the Middle East was outside NATO's area of responsibility, so that the Alliance as such could not become involved. Furthermore, they pointed out, the *Bundeswehr* is both assigned to NATO and limited, by the Basic Law, to the defense of the homeland; hence, the Federal Republic could not send troops to the Middle East. Moreover, they argued that Europe was susceptible to pressures of the most varied kind and that if the United States practiced "horizontal escalation" externally (i.e., out-of-area) the Soviet Union could respond by internal escalation, against Europe. In the German view, both U.S. and other Western interests are best served if the Central Region is not drawn into crises in other regions and is, indeed, strengthened rather than weakened in the event such crises occur.

The contributions that the U.S. and the FRG make to the Alliance differ sharply in form and substance. Those differences follow from the factors influencing security policy outlined in Chapter 1. Geostrategic positioning gives the U.S. a base that is relatively secure from conventional attack and is conducive to global power projection, while the FRG is primarily a land power that is potentially very vulnerable to conventional attack. U.S. strategic nuclear forces and global responsibilities contrast with German renunciation of independent nuclear capabilities and primary emphasis on the Central Front in Europe. It is therefore not surprising that the U.S. relegates a larger portion of its national output to defense, distributes that spending more heavily to air and naval forces, and adjusts its defense programs more rapidly to perceived shifts in the East-West military balance, while the FRG, with primarily regional security interests, spends a smaller share of output on defense, relegates a larger portion of defense outlays to ground forces, and tends to sustain defense spending as a more constant share of national output and government outlays over time.

The German view of its own Alliance burden stresses the social costs imposed by its defense commitments, as well as the actual defense outlays. Maintenance of a draft, high concentrations of military forces in a crowded country, and limitations on desired social programs, for example, are seen as important dimensions of that burden. The German view of U.S. contributions to the Alliance places great emphasis on the role of the Seventh Army as an integral part of European defense. West Germans also stress the importance of the U.S. participation in multilateral approaches to the Soviet Union as an Alliance contribution.

The U.S. view of German burdens typically places less emphasis on socio-economic dimensions than on direct military contributions. In particular, capabilities which enhance the potential for a sustained conventional defense on the Central Front receive considerable attention. Rates of increase in real defense spending and the defense share of the GNP are typically used in the U.S. as short-hand measures of defense contributions. There is also a tendency in some quarters in the U.S. to question the importance of the Seventh Army in overall European defense and to stress the relevance to the Alliance of American global capabilities.

These differences in perspective are understandable but they serve, nonetheless, as potential points of friction when either country is called upon for a greater defense effort, whether the pressure is internal or external. And this friction is likely to increase in view of widespread sentiments among Americans that the West Germans are not paying their share of the cost of defending Europe, that they are contributing little or nothing towards the safeguarding of Western interests "out-of-area," as in the Middle East, and that they expect the U.S. to pare down its own socio-economic programs in order to fund defense, while theirs stay untouched.

This feeling has led to calls in the United States for increased defense spending by West Germans (and other Europeans), to threats to draw down American Forces in Europe and even to proposals (as in the Nunn Amendment of 1984) that these be reduced unless the Europeans meet certain prescribed defense goals. Whatever the value of improving the NATO defense posture, attempts to do so in this way are unlikely to achieve much, if anything, and will almost certainly be counter-productive in terms of U.S.-German relations.

More acceptable means of adjusting the burdens of defense are already in effect, in the process for the rationalization of defense programs under way in NATO and in the agreement on increased spending for the NATO infrastructure program. Two further measures are under consideration. One is a shift from defining burdens in terms of defense inputs to measuring contributions in terms of desired military outputs. In this way the issue would be not the percentage of GNP allocated to the military but the number of ADE's (Armored Division Equivalents, a standard way of comparing forces from different countries) on the Central Front. The other, frequently advanced but never adopted, is for role specialization, with, for example, the Federal Republic assuming responsibility for country-wide air defenses while the United States provides more strike aircraft.

Burden sharing will remain an issue for the Alliance as long as the publics in the member states have not learned to recognize the specific burdens of other countries in terms of political and socio-economic criteria. The Alliance will remain in trouble as long as it is not seen as a political institution based on common interests, different views and a difficult—but essential—consensus, in which all members receive something less than their full desires.

Since it is obvious that the present and future economic bases of the industrialized countries do not provide for serious increases in defense spending, it seems worth looking at alternative ways of insuring security. The Soviet Union, the leading power of the WTO, is confronted with similar economic problems and the Gorbachev administration may give us the opportunity to agree on decreasing instead of increasing defense burdens on both sides. The conditions for this will be discussed in the following subchapter.

Continuing the Process: Détente and Arms Control

Probably no issue has so bedeviled American-German relations as that of détente. Even their definitions of the word diverge. To the Germans it is a long-term process leading to enhanced security and to better East-West relations. Though former Secretary of State Kissinger also saw détente as "a continuing process, not a final condition," this was not a common American view; the word has been employed more often to reflect a certain degree of accommodation between the two blocs. When Americans, in all walks of life, found that this accommodation was either non-existent or evanescent, they became bitter and frustrated, whereas the German plodders on the path to peace and security continued to move ahead.

These different interpretations and applications of détente stem from almost every one of the strategic, political and economic influences mentioned earlier. To give one illustration of their application, the United States is not only a superpower but a global power with worldwide interests which are challenged at many points by the Soviet Union and its associates, whereas the Federal Republic is a regional power whose interests are focused on its immediate front, especially on the German Democratic Republic and on the Soviet role as a European superpower. To give another, the scant resource base of the Federal Republic, and the dependency of its economy on imports and exports as well as the assumption that economic interactions will lead to political change, have all encouraged it to promote détente; the United States had no such incentives.

Moreover, the United States always bears in mind that the Soviet Union is the *only* power that can really hurt it militarily and then primarily by virtue of its nuclear capabilities. It has, therefore, tended both to see the Soviet challenge as a military one and, when it did practice "military détente" to focus on arms control measures which could reduce that threat, in particular on strategic arms reductions. West Germany, on the other hand, was keenly aware of the presence of Soviet troops along its Eastern frontier and concerned lest these or other forces be utilized to back up Soviet political pressures. In consequence the West Germans, when they pursued arms control, did so through the CSCE and, to a lesser extent, through the Vienna negotiations on MBFR. Given their senses of the nature of the challenge, the two countries obviously took different routes.

This does not mean that the West Germans have an unrealistic image of the Soviet Union. They have never forgotten that the USSR is an imperial power, ready at any time to exert pressure on the periphery of its empire in order to preserve—and perhaps to expand—its domain. Yet the Federal Republic has always known that the opponent has to be a partner in the security dialogue, for the sake of peace. German policy has thus been characterized by a dialectic, in which cooperative relations with the opponent and the search for a trans-bloc security regime are dependent on firm links with its Western Allies. Conversely, the United States tends to see the Soviet Union through a single prism; that of a challenger with whom it has little in common. Political elites in the United States tend to see Soviet policy as expansionist and Soviet motives, which are derived in part from communist ideology, as the establishment of a new world order compatible with Soviet beliefs and aspirations. It is, therefore, no surprise that many in the United States, even before the Reagan era, doubted that the East-West conflict could be resolved by compromise and cooperation and formed the intention to neutralize the Soviet military threat by military means.

Even though these American attitudes have blurred with time, the American approach to détente remains cautious and largely unidimentional, i.e., it concentrates on arms control. Inducements to move beyond this to a wider range of relations, with more productive possibilities, will not flow from any suggestions that we might make. Instead, such a shift in policy is more dependent on some success in arms control negotiations, some indications that the competition with the Soviet Union in the Third World can be lessened (as by the projected withdrawal of Soviet troops from Afghanistan) and perhaps by the changes in the political atmosphere initiated by Mr. Gorbachev.

This brings us to arms control, where the positions of the two sides are both more mixed and less divergent than is commonly assumed. The United States, for example, agreed recently in the CDE to new confidence building measures. But it came to those negotiations only reluctantly. In MBFR, which one high official several years ago termed "the dullest game in town," the U.S. has sought little and up to 1987 achieved nothing—though the new WTO proposals for asymmetrical reductions on conventional forces are under consideration. On theater nuclear forces, it has signed an agreement which would place severe limits on its own and Soviet missiles in the 300-3000 mile range, an outcome which was sought but not achieved in 1982-83, and both sides may be moving toward the ultimate abolition of battlefield missiles. In the strategic arms negotiations, both the U.S. and the USSR have agreed in principle on a 50% cut in offensive forces, though the form that this will take, and the question whether it will be linked to constraints on the development and testing of SDI, are still at issue.

U.S. positions reflect various motives and influences, ranging from worries about potential anti-Americanism in Europe to concerns about the correlation of forces. In CDE, the U.S. had nothing to lose by signing the agreement, while in MBFR it had to worry both about the problem of verification and the possible effects of reductions on NATO defenses. (One NATO official reportedly said that "no conceivable outcome to MBFR would leave the Alliance better off than it is today"). Intermediate range nuclear weapons, which were installed primarily (and perhaps mistakenly) in an effort to be responsive to the needs of the Allies, are marginal militarily, and their elimination could therefore be accepted, even if not approved, by everyone. The SDI-START combination, however, is regarded in Washington as decisive for future American nuclear policy, for American concepts of deterrence and, if Mr. Reagan is correct, for the question whether deterrence can be replaced by defense and ultimately by disarmament.

The West German position is different. The Germans are strong promoters of CDE, both because of its emphasis on confidence-building measures and because of the forum in which those measures were devised and approved. In line with the other Allies, Germans and Americans were successful in reaching a compromise with the Soviet Union and the GDR on advanced confidence building measures at the Stockholm CDE-Conference, and discussions are to be continued in a second CDE-Conference after the Vienna CSCE-meeting.

Bonn, of course, pushes mutual forces reductions—no matter whether an agreement on this issue is settled in the MBFR or the CSCE framework. As for cuts in INF, which Herr Schmidt and Herr Kohl were both prepared to negotiate away in 1982-83, these are now regarded as perhaps too much of a good thing—if only because all of the political anxiety and unrest attending on deployment has gone for nought; however, Bonn supported in 1987 the "double-zero" solution to INF. (Somewhat ironically, Washington suggested that the INF-mission could easily be taken over by sea-based systems of U.S. strategic nuclear forces, thus reversing the positions of the early 1980s.) In START, the Germans would like to see deep reductions, which could decelerate the arms race and ease concerns about strategic instability. As for SDI, this is something from which they would like to see the United States back off. Most German defense experts would like to see SDI used as a bargaining chip—as would many U.S. experts.

The American disappointment at the lack of results of détente so far is countered by German expectations of the behavior-changing effect of the détente process. The agreement achieved in the Alliance on the 1967 Harmel Report has had a different status in the FRG so far than in the U.S. In adopting the Harmel formula NATO had expressly broadened its mandate from defense to relaxation of tension, the latter even being declared a goal of equal rank. This was the basis for the German policy towards the East and it was in this context that the Germans also saw U.S. arms control, notably the SALT policy. American attempts at the beginning of the Reagan Administration to get NATO to move away from the Harmel formula, because of disappointment at the lack of results, met with resistance from the smaller partners, particularly the FRG. For the Germans, the equal status of defense and détente in NATO has taken on the character of a fundamental belief, even of a basic law.

This more political German approach to détente was matched by a more instrumental American approach, through arms control. Since the beginning of the policy of détente arms control had been seen as a means of reducing the dangerous aspect of the East-West conflict through partial cooperation with the other side. The U.S. governments kept to this policy: at the height of détente diplomacy in the early 1970s the U.S. was also concentrating on the SALT process, while the Germans primarily tried to engender a political framework for a system of trans-bloc security, through CSCE and MBFR. This policy has been continued by successive federal governments in Bonn, even with the change from a Social-Liberal to a Conservative-Liberal coalition. The Reagan Administration originally moved away from this, attempting to consolidate the Western bloc *vis-à-vis* the USSR instead of attempting to build structures that would transcend the blocs. In dealing practically with negotiations on arms control and confidence building the positions of the two governments again approached convergence in the second half of the 1980s. Thus, in the following, final chapter we have to ask ourselves whether taking the way back to Harmel might not open the way forward to a new Alliance consensus based on a productive tension between defense and détente.

9

Defense and Détente:
The Path Before Us

Klaus von Schubert and Joseph I. Coffey

How to Deal with the East-West Conflict

Neither war nor capitulation can be the aim of a defense policy. Survival and self-determination constitute the political aims within which the question of war and peace has always been debated. The nuclear age has not resolved the problem of insuring both survival and self-determination but brought it more sharply into focus. Even though all the traditional elements of rivalry, ideology and power reappear in the East-West conflict, the opponents in this conflict are denied the option—open to previous generations—of resolving the conflict by war. The conventional instruments of power, arms and the military, have become unconventional as a result of weapons of mass destruction. This makes it imperative to solve conventional problems of superpower rivalry unconventionally: arms and the military are not maintained for war-fighting and victory, but for forestalling war. The conflict cannot be ended by a show-down but has to be transmuted into a competition of a different kind.

Equally unconventional are the task and structure of the Atlantic Alliance. It is an Alliance which unites Americans and Europeans, victors and vanquished from World War II. The form of this alliance—a military one—reflects the unsolved task, at the end of that war, of making peace. But it also reflects the solvable task of keeping peace, despite conflict and in conflict. This means first, that no adversary should expect to prevail over one or more of the members of the Alliance. But it also means that the time gained by preventing war must be used to build a peace which is based on understanding and not on threat. This policy is agreed upon by the members of the Atlantic Alliance and is consistent with the basic values of the Western community of nations.

These twin aims of defense and détente stand in a dialectic relationship to one another. This dialectic can lead to disagreements within the Alliance which can paralyze its capacity to act. Yet it can also point a way to the future because it reflects the true nature of the problem. Détente without the capability of self-defense would deprive the Alliance of its reason for being. The citizens of the Western states would not accept a reduction of tensions that could only be bought at the expense of defenselessness in the face of military power. Nor would these citizens accept the abandoning of détente if so doing turned the arms race into an inescapable and unrelenting fate. The Alliance derives its vitality from its ability to bear the tension of this dialectic.

The West also has a dialectic relationship with the East, in that it is simultaneously trying to deter any act of aggression, by means which must seem threatening, and at the same time to improve—and hopefully to transform—relations with the Soviet Union and the countries of Eastern Europe. An intelligent and successful security policy must ensure that these aims do not compete, but complement and reinforce each other.

The basic condition for an agreement with the Soviet Union is a consensus within the Western Alliance about the Soviet Union. The difficulty of the West, remembering that it must deal with the Soviet Union both as a revolutionary regime and as a classic power, has, since 1917, been a central element in the East-West conflict or West-East conflict. We do not, however, claim that the one is independent of the other. The fear of revolutionary expansion, which had haunted Europe ever since the French Revolution, and which was not unfounded, was equally directed against the universalist aspect of Lenin's theory of revolution, which became Soviet ideology. The Sovietization of the East European states occupied by Stalin in the course of the war against Hitler's Germany fostered fear in Western democracies of further expansion of the Soviet imperium.

Even though, after the "hot" phase of the "cold" war, the *status quo* was followed by a tacit understanding between East and West, both sides in the conflict were still secretly worried that the long-term aim of its opponent might nevertheless be the victory of its own order. Yet how can security beyond the boundaries of the blocs be organized in cooperation with one's opponent in the conflict as long as high levels of armament remain and as long as there is doubt about an adversary's true intentions? How can clarity be gained about one's opponent and what must a Western *Ostpolitik* look like for the Soviet Union to respond to Western ideas? How can one prevent one's own behavior from having the opposite effect to what one intended?

First, the Western community should form a realistic picture of Soviet behavior and capabilities. Exaggerations are just as harmful for security policy as understatements. Myths are not a solid base for rational policy. The members of the Alliance must recognize that the Soviet Union has weaknesses as well as strengths, that its policies are not all aimed at the demise of the West and that its objectives, like those of the West, are best secured by peace and cooperation. Indeed, recent developments in the USSR make it clear that only in this way can the Soviet Union hope to solve its problems.

Cooperation presupposes self-confidence on both sides. Over-arming or making threatening gestures are just as little a mark of self-confidence as are subservience or appeasement. As long as the Alliance maintains a situation whereby no one can conduct a successful military offensive against it, the West cannot be blackmailed by military pressure. NATO's strength is revealed in its own policy's openness to cooperation and not in unilateralism, which in reality represents a retreat. Its self-confidence is manifested in the adequacy of its own powers, and not in a striving for superiority, which is in reality a sign of an inferiority complex. The West has sufficient strength to enable it to speak frankly to the Soviet Union.

A self-confident Western stance towards Moscow is marked not only by its avoidance of unrealistic thinking in terms of worst-case-scenarios but also by a realistic assessment of the military capabilities of the Soviet Union and the Warsaw Pact. The West should communicate to the Soviet Union its apprehensions about what it considers to constitute a threat and should in doing so be as frank and as precise as possible. A realistic and non-propagandistic portrayal of the situation by the West would enable the Warsaw Pact to form a realistic and non-propagandistic picture of Western capabilities and intentions, as well as of Western perceptions of the Soviet threat, perceptions which are behind the military activity of the Atlantic Alliance. This mutual realism is an important condition for any arms control policy in the East-West conflict.

Maintaining one's own security presupposes an understanding of the security interests of one's opponents, difficult though that may be. The Soviet Union has always claimed for itself a manifest security interest vis-à-vis the West, producing as historical evidence Napoleon, post-1917 interventions, and Hitler. China on its East is also considered by Moscow to be a potential threat. The Soviet Union feels hemmed in on all sides and believes it necessary to arm against a largely hostile world. This is how Moscow justifies not only the high level of Soviet armament but also its buffer zone policy. The West, on the other hand, sees this as a sign of imperialist policy and of potential—or in the case of Afghanistan actual—expansionism.

If one wishes to react correctly to Soviet security policy—which in some instances is perceived as a threat to Western interests—one must carefully consider the underlying security interests of the Soviet Union. Once this condition has been fulfilled, the West can urge the Soviet Union to respect Western security interests and to enter into the necessary discussion about mutual perceptions of threat. This discussion must open both parties' eyes to the fact that a defensively motivated policy can be perceived as offensive and can therefore lead on the other side to armament instead of disarmament. A realistic assessment of the military capabilities of both sides cannot be done unilaterally, but can only be arrived at by a joint comparison of, and adjustment of, the estimates produced by the intelligence services of East and West.

Threat analysis, on a comparative basis, and finally in discussions between the opponents, can lead to the recognition that absolute security is unattainable and that it is counter-productive to arm against all possible opponents and all conceivable dangers. There are signs from the new Gorbachev administration of a Soviet rethinking of basic security assumptions which might help start a bloc-to-bloc security dialogue; indeed, Mr. Gorbachev himself has suggested this.

If this dialogue leads to recognition that true security can be achieved only by limiting the power of the participants, the East-West conflict would take on a different character: it would be transformed from a confrontation characterized by fear of defeat and hope of victory into a competition of political and economic orders. Khrushchev's characterization of East-West relations as "peaceful coexistence," which implied the continuation of the ideological offensive, should be changed to "peaceful competition," a phrase with a slightly different wording and a vastly different meaning, as indeed the Soviets seem to recognize. All participants could profit from this kind of competition. They would not only save on arms expenditures but they would also gain the freedom to deal with the real problems of the future on a planet with a huge population and limited resources. Then they would be able to see where and how urgent problems like the protection of the environment, the careful utilization of raw materials, the adaptation of technology to human needs and the production of food for the starving could be better solved. Yet participation in peaceful competition means adopting an open-minded attitude to the historical process and accepting a variety of different models and solutions, in other words, giving up the exclusiveness of political ideologies in favor of ideological pluralism. This does not mean giving up one's own view of truth; it does, however, mean leaving the judgment to history.

How to Change Defense Policy

Whenever, in the history of NATO, questions of military doctrine were discussed, the subject of debate was usually the strategy of nuclear deterrence with its weapons and delivery systems. In this context, the principal issues affecting American-German relationships were the maintenance of the nuclear guarantee and the coupling of Europe to the strategic potential of the U.S.A.

These issues were difficult to resolve because, despite the multiplication of nuclear delivery systems within the theater and the various proposals for more flexible nuclear options, few believed that the United States would be more willing to launch a nuclear warhead from Hesse than from Montana and even fewer that the Soviets, in retaliating to any first use of nuclear weapons by NATO, would respond differently in one case than they would in the other. Moreover, to the extent that any action by NATO would prompt a differentiated Soviet response, it was likely to be the employment of battlefield nuclear weapons, which the Germans saw as triggering a limited nuclear war on their soil. Conversely, the employment within the theater of longer-range systems such as the Pershing II and GLCMs, which could reach targets on Soviet territory, would increase the likelihood of large-scale Soviet retaliation. Thus, the nuclear guarantee has the two disadvantages of being uncertain and of being escalatory.

At the same time, the nuclear guarantee cannot under present circumstances be given up. The Allies believe that nuclear weapons deter the initiation of nuclear operations by an opponent, hinder him from freely employing conventional forces and remind him that success on the battlefield heightens the danger of nuclear war. The question is whether a different deployment can reduce the danger of escalation without creating additional uncertainties.

In our judgment, the means for upholding the nuclear guarantee exist in plenty; even though the "double zero" agreement has been signed, the United States will still have battlefield nuclear weapons in and around Europe, nuclear capable aircraft, ballistic missile submarines (part of whose arsenal is earmarked for SACEUR) and the cruise missiles aboard the ships and submarines of the Atlantic Fleet. Over time, the battlefield weapons, which are generally regarded as most vulnerable to attack and most difficult to control, might also be "bargained away," along with some of the forward-based strike aircraft, either against their Soviet counterparts or against WTO armored and mechanized divisions. As the experience with INF showed, there are no intrinsic advantages to, and many drawbacks to, "highly visible" land-based missiles in Europe.

The ultimate result could be a Central Europe largely free of nuclear weapons—but not without a nuclear deterrent. The implementation of the nuclear guarantee in time of need would, as it always has, depend primarily on the fact that a successful Soviet operation against Western Europe would pose a major threat to U.S. interests and constitute a major defeat for the United States and secondarily on the fact that in time of crisis, calculations of capabilities, and even of costs, may count for less with decisionmakers than anger, frustration and a sense of loss; in this respect, the 300,000 U.S. soldiers and airmen in Western Europe may, as the Germans recognize, constitute the best assurance of an American *riposte*. Thus, the emphasis should be on tangible evidence of solidarity on the key issue of precluding Soviet/WTO aggression in Europe, not on new deployments of nuclear weapons.

However, no new formulation of the nuclear guarantee, no fresh assurances as to commonality of purpose, are likely to restore belief in the credibility of the nuclear deterrent against all possible forms of aggression. Public discussion in most of the Alliance countries, including the United States, indicates an erosion of the belief in a defense strategy basically built on nuclear deterrence; President Reagan's arguments in his "Star Wars" speech give evidence of this. Hence, we see a need for a new strategy based on a more robust conventional defense.

In our opinion, and in those of other experts attempting to formulate a new strategy, it should be based on three criteria: no prospect of success for surprise attacks, no incentive for preemption and, above all, stability in a crisis. Crisis situations reveal the true efficacy of a strategic concept.

In such situations it is imperative to maintain one's own position by calm and confident action without having to resort to threats and thus, should these threats not succeed, to escalation to nuclear war.

There are a number of problems in developing a strategy based on these criteria. One is that they are not accepted officially as the principles which should govern doctrine and force posture on the Central Front, where NATO is still wedded to the concept of flexible response. Another is that both the United States and the Federal Republic have, by and large, rejected any major restructuring of their forces or any shift from the current reliance on mobile defense. A third is that current suggestions for improving conventional defenses face serious obstacles; thus increases in the strength of active duty forces are virtually ruled out by budgetary constraints and declines in manpower, and large investments in advanced weapons, such as would be needed to implement the plan for Follow-on Forces Attack, are not only dependent on further increases in defense spending but are open to question on grounds of technical feasibility, as well as because some may deem them "provocative." This being the case, it seems to us that we must look to solutions which do not require major changes in either forces or expenditures.

Without going into details concerning force structure, troop stationing, infrastructure programs, etc., we recommend a reshaping of defense capabilities which would:

1. Preclude the destruction by air attack (or by strikes from conventionally armed missiles, should these not be removed under the "double zero" agreement or any subsequent arrangements) of the NATO air forces now deployed in Western Europe, the air bases from which U.S. and other incoming squadrons will operate, the air fields at which initial U.S. ground reinforcements will land, and the depots from which they will draw their weapons and equipment. Measures to achieve these desirable ends are already under way and while we would prefer the less expensive options (such as building shelters and constructing more secondary fields for dispersal of aircraft) we do not prescribe any particular mix of active and passive defenses.

2. Provide strong covering forces, armed with anti-tank and anti-aircraft weapons, which can meet an aggressor as soon as he crosses the border, delay and disrupt his advance and give time for NATO to mobilize and to occupy its designated defensive positions. Rather than depending, as they now do, on the movement forward of mobile units from the national contingents in West Germany, these covering forces should consist primarily of German troops organized and equipped for territorial defense, screened and strengthened by light mechanized forces from all the armies on the Central Front, so that any attacker would immediately find himself up against all the Allies, not just West Germans.

3. Utilize the mobile units thereby made available, along with West German territorial brigades, to further strengthen the main battle area, with U.S. and British reinforcements, and French troops if available, con-

stituting a mobile operational reserve. The mission of these reserves should, as is now the case, be that of checking any breakthrough and restoring the integrity of the main battle area; "defense in depth," whatever its theoretical advantages, would place at risk too much German territory and offensive operations, whatever their utility in time of war, have political costs which suggest that they should not be planned in time of peace.

4. We believe that forces such as we have described would be capable of conducting a successful defense against the Soviet/ WTO units available for an attack with little or no warning; however, we recognize that this defense could be strengthened if WTO operational reserves and second echelon forces could be delayed, disrupted or even brought to a halt before they could engage in battle, utilizing both conventionally armed strike aircraft and high-technology weapons. These latter, however, should be designed and employed against troops in the combat area rather than against those far behind the lines-a measure which should make them both more cost-effective and less provocative than the weapons and the supporting systems now being developed.

The actual deployment of forces on the Central Front reflects the structure of the Alliance by being visibly multinational and insures that the risk is shared by all. This valid principle does not, however, mean that all members must play the same role. The distribution of responsibility has to take into consideration varying geographic and economic factors, as well as those of size; it is neither feasible nor sensible for each country to maintain its own army, navy and air force, to say nothing of multiple capabilities within each service. In our view, a redistribution of roles and missions, both to countries and within their respective armed forces, is long overdue. Thus, the U.S.A might contribute more planes to the common defense and fewer reserve divisions—though the presence of Soviet troops in Central Europe requires, for the time being, a more than symbolic presence of U.S. troops in West Germany. The Federal Republic of Germany can make use of the advantages of operating in its own country, of its infrastructure and of its military reserves to increase its contribution to air defense and to territorial defense, as with the covering force. In this way, and perhaps only in this way, can an effective defense be maintained at reasonable cost.

It is obvious that decisions on operational doctrine and force postures cannot be separated from those on arms control; that is why the development of a crisis-stable military structure at the dividing line between NATO and the Warsaw Pact must also become the subject of talks between the two Alliances. Hopefully, NATO and the WTO will, through confidence-building measures, gain such trust in one another that they will be willing to discuss those military options which each considers to be the most dangerous, options such as a disarming nuclear strike or a surprise attack by conventional forces. Although no conceivable arms control agreement can eliminate all offensive options, some of these could be reduced, while retaining defensive capabilities, at least against conventional attack. Thus, the Alliance would combine a new operational doctrine emphasizing defense with elements of arms control, military-political confidence-building measures and arms technology adapted to meet its new requirements.

As a means to this end, it seems to us that the West, and West Germany in particular, should put forward more ambitious proposals which would respond to, and test the validity of, the WTO proposals of May 1987 for asymmetrical reductions in forces and weapons particularly suited to offensive operations and capable of initiating a surprise attack and should take up the offer of bloc-to-bloc discussions on military doctrine. Correspondingly, the West should speed up consideration of the "bold, new measures" for mutual force reductions mentioned in the Halifax Communiqué of the North Atlantic Council. As part of these measures the West should consider a thinning out of heavily armed, mobile forces along the frontiers on both sides, and perhaps the establishment of limited nuclear-free zones. Such a move, which would be very much in line with the policy of not deploying in forward areas nuclear systems susceptible to destruction or capture in the very first hours of any war, could be a prelude to, and perhaps facilitate, agreement on the reduction or elimination of battlefield nuclear weapons mentioned earlier. Thus arms control could complement arms policy in establishing a crisis-stable defense of the Central Front, based largely on conventional capabilities, but still under the protection of the "nuclear umbrella."

In this connection, the "nuclear umbrella" might also undergo changes. We agree with the proposal for "deep cuts" in strategic nuclear forces accepted in principle by the U.S. and the USSR; in our judgment, these would enhance stability, improve East-West relations and perhaps lead to mutual deterrence at very low levels of weapons.

This immediately raises the question of the Strategic Defense Initiative, which is intended to facilitate reductions in SNF and, hopefully, to eliminate any possibility of an offensive nuclear strike. It is probably unrealistic to expect SDI to neutralize the enormous nuclear offensive potential of the superpowers but if offensive capabilities could be drastically reduced on both sides, the SDI concept could be meaningful after all. However, the technical difficulties of developing and installing comprehensive missile defenses, the potential vulnerability of key elements of such a system, such as space-based sensors and/or weapons, and the very real possibility that it could, at some stage, make feasible a disarming strike, all militate against it. Moreover, the need for a theater SDI, capable of intercepting short and medium range ballistic missiles, should largely end with the implementation of the "double zero" agreement. We understand the desire to explore technological innovations which could enhance security, and appreciate the need for advanced research as a hedge against an uncertain future. However, our own preference would be to utilize restrictions on the testing of SDI and delays in its deployment as bargaining chips in the current negotiations with the USSR over reductions in strategic armaments, partly because we are persuaded that the larger version of SDI is infeasible and the smaller version unnecessary, partly because we deem it essential to seize this opportunity for arms control and détente.

To recapitulate, we have, in the interest of maintaining crisis stability, strongly suggested both improvements in air defenses covering critical military targets in Western Europe and the exploration of a strategy which places greater reliance on covering forces, makes better use of reserve units and in both these ways frees up mobile units for the limited role of restoring the integrity of the main battle area should that be breached. We have also suggested complementary arms control measures which would reduce capabilities for offensive operations, extend confidence-building activities and eliminate or cut back on medium-range, short-range and battlefield nuclear forces, perhaps including some nuclear-capable strike aircraft. Finally, we have endorsed negotiations now under way on cuts in strategic nuclear forces and suggested that consideration be given to accepting restrictions on SDI, should these be needed to gain acceptance of "deep cuts" in SNF.

Switching strategy will not be easy; as noted earlier, both the United States Army and the *Bundeswehr* are wedded to a concept of mobile operations, for which their forces are organized, equipped and trained. Moreover, both countries are committed to FOFA in principle and the United States has under development some systems intended to implement this concept. Given, however, budgetary pressures in both countries, such programs may be cut anyway and should not, in our opinion, be given priority over more mundane measures for improving defensive capabilities. And through the strength of the American propensity toward "high tech" must be acknowledged, against that can be set German concerns lest some military postures be too provocative in time of peace and too dangerous in time of war.

Moreover, there will undoubtedly be opposition to some of our specific recommendations for arms control. Despite criticism from within and without the government, President Reagan remains firmly committed to SDI and unwilling (at least as of November 1988) to accept any restrictions on research and development and testing of SDI components and architectures. Nor will everyone be comfortable with proposals which change the reliance on nuclear weapons in Europe for deterrence and for coupling; it was only after considerable pressure that Chancellor Kohl agreed to accept the "double zero" agreement. And extensions of this to include battlefield nuclear weapons, like measures to alter the composition and the development of conventional forces, are certain to be resisted by those who are fearful of change, concerned about unforeseen consequences or simply moved by different concerns that we are. We believe we are sensitive to "the winds of change;" we think our ideas as to how the West should ride those winds are valid, but we recognize that not everyone will agree.

By and large, however, our recommendations are consonant with long-term influences on U.S. and West German defense policy. Even with respect to arms control, where elements in the United States have, as part of their general opposition to and distrust of the USSR, opposed arms control agreements, the tide is changing; not only are American publics and political elites overwhelmingly in favor of arms control but the Reagan Administration itself has pushed for reductions in both strategic and theater nuclear forces. As for the predilection to utilize "high tech" to solve defense problems, we do not oppose the policy but seek only a modification of its implementation to emphasize battlefield and very short range conventional weapons.

Finally, it should not be forgotten that the success of any strategy depends not only on budgets, arms and troops; even the best strategy will be futile if the people lack trust in their country's security policy. This trust we would hope to enhance by a greater emphasis on effective defense, based on non-provocative operational concepts and force postures, by arms control, which can reduce the threat, and by détente, which can ameliorate unwarranted fears and assuage untoward concerns. Not everyone will agree with every detail but hopefully a consensus as to the basic thrust can be developed among both publics and elites of the various countries belonging to the Alliance. To this end, the Alliance's operational doctrine must be formulated in such a way that it can be understood by the general public; otherwise NATO will be unable to sustain either defense or détente.

Finding a New Alliance Consensus

Despite the wide gap in power levels within the Alliance, all its members are mutually dependent. Even the United States would find it hard to achieve its national objectives alone and unaided. The Alliance was formed to pursue common security interests in an asymmetrical geographic framework and this has been continued to the present day. NATO's further success depends on its variety—which military experts might deplore—not being seen as an obstacle to common policy and a weakness in the structure of the Alliance but as a wealth of resources and a source of strength. It also depends on whether the geographical asymmetry of its partners does not divide them but enables each to play the specific role suited to it.

These common security interests include meeting the challenge of Soviet power projection without recourse to war, of converting tension to détente and the competition in armaments to an arms reduction process without undermining the capacity for defense. While neither of these goals can be achieved without the cooperation of the Soviet Union and other members of the WTO, Alliance cohesion is vital to success and a consensus on policy is essential to cohesion.

In our opinion, there are a number of issues on which consensus is difficult to achieve, one of them being burden-sharing. While all members accept the principle that burdens have to be shared, they differ markedly over how this should be determined, and as to the weight that should be given to social and political burdens. Projects to more accurately measure budgetary contributions and to allocate a larger portion of them to NATO-

wide construction programs or toward meeting high-priority defense needs
are already under way and we have no new formulae to propose. We do,
however, believe that it is detrimental to Alliance cohesion if burden-
sharing is seen by individual members of the Alliance as an opportunity
to bargain for their own advantages and if it thus fails to achieve its
purpose of optimizing military strength. Of special importance in the
American-German debate is recognition of the role played by political,
geographical and economic factors in affecting contributions—on both sides
of the Atlantic.

Another issue that concerns the Alliance is the policy for dealing with
"out-of-area" threats to Western interests, threats which not only raise
serious questions about the allocation of resources (as to the Central
Command of the United States or the *Force d'Action Rapide* of France)
but also generate disputes among the Allies as to whether, and if so how,
these threats should be met. These disputes are frequently bitter, with the
Americans arguing that the use of the military instrument may be essential
and the Germans favoring the political and economic instruments, with
the Americans stressing the essentiality of Allied support to U.S. military
forces once these are engaged and the Germans holding that any out-of-
area involvement not only weakens the Central Region but relegates the
Germans to the status of "world power fellow travelers." On the other
hand, the West Germans maintain that stability in the central European
region can enable the U.S.—either as a world power or within its Alliance
framework—and even West Germany, as a member of NATO and an
important member of the European community—to intervene more successfully, using political and diplomatic rather than military means. The
best we can do is to reiterate the solution already designed by NATO: that
those members of the Alliance having the means and the willingness to
cope with "out-of-area" threats do so, but that the Alliance, as an entity,
not become actually involved.

A third area on which NATO needs to reach a new consensus is that
of the roles and responsibilities of its members. We have previously pointed
out the advantages of functionalization at the national level; these hold
equally true at the Alliance level, where the Europeans could assume
primary responsibility for the defense of their own territories against
conventional attacks, placing on the United States, as is now the case,
primary responsibility for providing the nuclear deterrent and for carrying
out maritime operations. And though such a realignment could take place
without a re-structuring of NATO, we also endorse the "two pillar" concept,
under which (a more united) Europe would speak with a more coherent
voice on defense policy, on arms control and on détente.

This last area is of primary concern, since the Alliance has been of at
least two minds on the subject. Given divergent U.S. and European views
of the importance of détente, of its separability into regional and global
components and of the preconditions for improvement in East-West relations, this is not surprising—but it is no longer acceptable. If the Alliance

is to take advantage of "glasnost" in all its variations, if it is to deal successfully with Soviet and WTO arms control proposals and, above all, if it is to enhance the security of Europe, it must devise a clearer and more forward-looking policy on détente. In our view, this policy should aim at the establishment of an East-West security regime, premised on the assumption that all parties will recognize the futility of using force or threats of force to achieve their objectives and based on the belief that at least limited cooperation between competing political and social systems is possible.

That reaching a consensus on these issues will be difficult goes without saying. Some of the changes suggested imply both that the United States will play a role that may not accord with its concept of superpower responsibilities and that it modify its conflictual approach to the USSR in Europe. Others suggest that the European members of the Alliance move further and faster toward the abandonment of cherished symbols of nationhood, such as navies, and toward the subordination of their individual views to a larger whole. We cannot say whether this will be possible; we can only point out that it is now time for a major change in past attitudes and old ways of doing business.

To sum up, it is our view that NATO, which will begin in 1989 the fifth decade of its existence, is at a turning point: it can continue to be concerned primarily with military means of enhancing security or it can focus on transforming the situation in Europe in ways such that defense programs, while still necessary, will be much less important than they now are. Given the serious economic difficulties of some member states, the demands on their resources deriving from aging populations, dwindling energy supplies and damaged ecologies, and the larger problems of the globe, to whose solution the industrialized countries must, for their own sakes, contribute, it is obvious that the members of the Atlantic Alliance will increasingly look outward. The only question is whether that Alliance will look outward with them or whether it will remain preoccupied with the relatively narrow concerns of its first forty years.

Bibliography

Books

Adams, S. *The Iron Triangle: Politics of Defense Contracting*. New York: Council on Economic Priorities, 1981.

Adenauer, Konrad. *Erinnerungen, 1945-53, 1953-1955, 1955-1959, 1966 and 1967*. Stuttgart: Deutsche Verlags-Anstalt, 1965-1969.

Afheldt, Horst. *Defense and Peace*. Münich: 1976.

――――. *Defensive Defense*. Starnberg: 1983.

Baring, Arnulf. *Aussenpolitik in Adenauers Kanzlerdemokratie*. Deutsche Gesellschaft für Auswärtge Politik. Münich: Oldenbourg, 1969.

――――. *Machtwechsel, Die ära Brandt-Scheel*. Stuttgart: 1982.

Barton, John H. and Lawrence D. Weiler, eds. *International Arms Control: Issues and Agreements*. Stanford, CA: Stanford University Press, 1976.

Bechhoefer, Bernhard. *Postwar Negotiations on Arms Control*. Washington, D.C.: The Brookings Institution, 1961.

Bender, Peter. *Neue Ostpolitik, Vom Neuerbau zum Moskauer Vertrag*. München: 1986.

Benz, Wolfgang, ed. *Die Bundesrepublik Deutschland: Geschichte in vier Bänden*. 4 vols. Frankfurt: Fischer Verlag, 1989.

Bliss, Howard and M. Glenn Johnson. *Beyond the Water's Edge: America's Foreign Policy*. Philadelphia, PA: J. B. Lippincott Company, 1975.

Bloomfield, Lincoln. *The United Nations and U.S. Foreign Policy: A New Look at the National Interest*. rev. ed. Boston: Little, Brown and Co., 1967.

Bowman, William R. *Limiting Conventional Forces in Europe: An Alternative to the Mutual and Balanced Force Reduction Negotiations*. Washington, D.C.: National Defense University Press, 1985.

Bracher, Karl Dietrich, Theodor Eschenburg, Joachim C. Fest, and Eberhard Jäckel. *Geschichte der Bundesrepublik Deutschland*. 6 vols. Wiesbaden: Deutsche Verlagsanstalt and Stuttgart: F. A. Brockhaus, 1983-1988.

Brandt, Willy. *Begegnungen und Einsichten. Die Jahre 1960-1975*. München: 1978.

Brown, Harold. *Thinking About National Security, Defense and Foreign Policy in a Dangerous World*. Boulder, CO: Westview Press, 1983.

Brzezinski, Zbigniew. *Power and Principle*. New York: Farrar, Straus, Siroux, 1983.

Carstens, Karl and Dieter Mahncke, eds. *Westeuropaische Verteidigungskooperation*. Wien: Oldenbourg, 1972.

Carter, Jimmy. *Keeping Faith*. New York: Bantam Books, 1982.

Cline, Ray. *World Power Assessment*. Boulder, CO: Westview Press, 1977.

Coffey, J. I. *Deterrence and Arms Control: American and West German Perspectives on INF*. Monograph Series in World Affairs, vol. 21. Denver, CO: University of Denver, 1985.

_____. and Alan T. Dieter, Jr. "Allied Perceptions of Threat," *International Forum. Sozialwissenschaftliches Institut der Bundeswehr.* Munich: 1983.

Collins, John M. *U.S.-Soviet Military Balance: Concepts and Capabilities, 1960-1980.* New York: McGraw-Hill, 1980.

Dean, Jonathan. *Watershed in Europe: Dismantling the East-West Military Confrontation.* Union of Concerned Scientists. Lexington, MA: Lexington Books, 1987.

Deane, John R. *The Strange Alliance. The Story of the Efforts at Wartime Cooperation with Russia.* New York: The Viking Press, 1947.

Douglass, Joseph D. Jr. *Soviet Military Strategy in Europe.* New York: Pergamon Press, 1980.

Deutsch, Karl W. *et al. Political Community and the North Atlantic Area.* Princeton, NJ: Princeton University Press, 1957.

Deutsche Gesellschaft für Friedens- und Konfliktforschung (DGFK). Zur Entspannungspolitik in Europa. Baden Baden: Nornos Verlagsgesellschaft, 1980.

Dunn, Keith and William P. Staudenmaier, eds. *Strategic Implications of the Continental-Maritime Debate.* The Washington Papers, No. 10. New York: 1984.

Eisenhower, Dwight D. *Mandate for Change, 1953-56.* Garden City, NY: Doubleday and Company, 1963.

Etzold, Thomas H. and John Lewis Gaddis, eds. *Containment: Documents on American Policy and Strategy, 1945-1950.* New York: Columbia University Press, 1978.

European Security Study Group. *Strengthening Conventional Deterrence in Europe: Proposals for the 1980s.* New York: St. Martin's Press, 1983.

Fischman, L. L. *World Mineral Trade and U.S. Supply Problems.* Washington, D.C.: Resources for the Future, 1980.

Frie, Daniel and Dieter Ruloff. *East-West Relations.* Cambridge, MA: Oelgeschlager, Gunn & Hain, 1983.

Garthoff, Raymond L. *Détente and Confrontation: American-Soviet Relations from Nixon to Reagan.* Washington, D.C.: The Brookings Institution, 1985.

Gilpin, Robert. *U.S. Power and the Multinational Corporation.* New York: Basic Books, 1975.

Golden, James R., Asa A. Clark, and Bruce E. Arlinghaus, eds. *Conventional Deterrence: Alternatives for European Defense.* Lexington, MA: Lexington Books, 1985.

Griffith, William. *The Ostpolitik of the Federal Republic of Germany.* Cambridge/London: 1978.

Haftendorn, Helga. *Abrüstungs- und Entspannungspolitik zwischen Sicherheitsbefriedigung und Friedenssicherung zur Aussenpolitik der BRD 1955-1973.* Dusseldorf: Berklsmann University Press, 1974.

_____. *Sicherheit und Entspannung. Zur Aussenpolitik der Bundesrepublik Deutschland, 1955-1982.* Baden-Baden: 1983.

Halloran, Richard. *To Arm A Nation.* New York: Macmillan & Company, 1986.

Hanrieder, Wolfram F. and Larry V. Buel. *Words and Arms: A Dictionary of Security and Defense Terms, with Supplementary Data.* Boulder, CO: Westview Press, 1979.

Hudson, George and Joseph Kruzel, eds. *American Defense Annual, 1985-1986.* Lexington, MA: D. C. Heath and Company, 1985.

Jacobsen, Hans-Adolf. *Von der Strategie der Gewalt zur Politik der Friedenssicherung.* Düsseldorf: 1977.

―――. *Sicherheit und Zusammenarbeit in Europa (KSZE).* 2 vols. Köln: 1973 and 1977.

Jervis, Robert. *The Illogic of American Strategic Doctrine.* Ithaca, NY: Cornell University Press, 1984.

Kaiser, Karl. *Die EG vor der Entscheidung: Fortschritt oder Verfall?.* Bonn: 1983.

Kaufman, Daniel J., Jeffrey S. McKitrick and Thomas J. Leney, eds. *U.S. National Security: A Framework for Analysis.* Lexington, MA: Lexington Books, 1985.

Kaufmann, William W. *The 1986 Defense Budget.* Washington, D.C.: The Brookings Institution, 1985.

Kegley, C. W., Jr. and P. McGowen, eds. *The Political Economy of Foreign Policy Behavior.* Beverly Hills, CA: Sage Publications, 1981.

Kennedy, Robert and Daniel S. Papp. *The Evolving Strategic Environment.* Strategic Studies Institute, U.S. Army War College, Carlisle Barracks, PA: 1979.

Kissinger, Henry A. *The Troubled Partnership.* New York: McGraw-Hill Book Company, 1965.

Komer, Robert W. *Maritime Strategy or Coalition Defense?* Cambridge, MA: Abt Books, 1984.

Kross, Walter. *Military Reform: The High-Tech Debate in Tactical Air Forces.* Washington, D.C.: National Defense University Press, 1985.

Labrie, Roger P. *SALT Handbook.* Washington, D.C.: American Enterprise Institute for Public Policy Research, 1979.

Link, Werner. *Der Ost-West Konflikt.* Stuttgart: 1980.

Litwak, Robert. *Détente and the Nixon Doctrine.* New York: Cambridge University Press, 1984.

Mackinder, Sir Halford. *Democratic Ideals and Reality.* New York: H. Holt & Co, 1942.

Macintosh, James. *Confidence (and Security) Building Measures in the Arms Control Process: A Canadian Perspective.* Prepared for The Arms Control and Disarmament Division, Department of External Affairs. Ottawa, Ontario: Department of External Affairs, 1985.

Mahncke, Dieter. *Berlin im geteilten Deutschland.* München: 1973.

Mako, William. *U.S. Ground Forces and the Defense of Central Europe.* Studies in Defense Policy. Washington, D.C.: The Brookings Institution, 1983.

McNamara, Robert S. *The Essence of Security.* New York: Harper & Row, 1968.

Morgan, Patrick M. *Deterrence: A Conceptual Analysis.* 2nd ed. Beverly Hills, CA: Sage Publications, 1977.

Neal, Fred W. *Détente or Debacle: Common Sense in U.S.-Soviet Relations.* American Committee on East-West Accord, New York: 1979.

Nixon, Richard. *The Memoirs of Richard Nixon.* New York: Grosset and Dunlap, 1978.

Noack, Paul. *Das Scheitern der Europäischen Verteidigungsgemeinschaft.* Düsseldorf: 1977.

Rielly, John E. ed. *American Public Opinion and U.S. Foreign Policy, 1983.* Chicago, IL: The Chicago Council on Foreign Relations, 1983.

―――. ed. *American Public Opinion and U.S. Foreign Policy, 1987.* Chicago, IL: The Chicago Council on Foreign Relations, 1987.

Russett, Bruce and Harvey Starr. *World Politics: The Menu for Choice.* San Francisco, CA: Freeman, 1981.

Schmid, Günther. *Entscheidung in Bonn, Die Entstenung der Ost und Deutschlandpolitik 1969-1970.* Köln: 1979.

Schmidt, Helmut. *Defense or Retaliation.* New York: Praeger, 1962.

von Schubert, Klaus. *Wiederbewaffnung und Westintegration*. Stuttgart: 1970.
Schwartz, David M. *NATO's Nuclear Dilemmas*. Washington, D.C.: The Brookings Institution, 1983.
Snow, Donald M. *Nuclear Strategy in a Dynamic World*. University, Alabama: The University of Alabama Press, 1981.
Snyder, Glenn. *Deterrence and Defense*. Princeton, NJ: Princeton University Press, 1961.
Steel, Ronald. *Pax Americana*. New York: The Viking Press, 1967.
Stupak, Ronald J. *American Foreign Policy: Assumptions, Processes and Projections*. New York: Harper & Row, 1976.
Tatu, Michel. *Détente and the Atlantic Nations*. Chicago: Chicago Council on Foreign Relations, 1977.
Thompson, Kenneth W., ed. *Sam Nunn on Arms Control*. Lanham, MD: University Press of America, 1987.
Weber, Hermann. *Geschichte der DDR*. München: 1985.
Weigley, Russell F. *The American Way of War*. New York: Macmillan Publiching Company, 1973.
Wettig, Gerhard. *Entmilitarisierung und Wiederbewaffnung in Deutschland 1945-1955*. München: 1967.

Articles

Abshire, David. "A Resources Strategy for NATO," *NATO's Sixteen Nations*, 30 October 1985.
Ball, Desmond. "The Development of the SIOP, 1960-1983," in Desmond Ball and Jeffrey Richelson, eds. *Strategic Nuclear Targeting*. Ithaca, NY: Cornell University Press, 1986.
von Baudissin, Wolf Graf. *"Kernwaffe und das Arlantische Bundnix,"* in Dieter S. Lutz, ed. *Sicherheitspolitik am Scheideweg?* Bonn: Schriftenreihe der Bundeszentrale für Politische Bildung, 1982.
Bertram, Christoph. "European Security and the German Problem," *International Security*, 4, 3, Winter 1979/80.
Bloomfield, Lincoln. "Crisis Management Outside the NATO Area: Allies or Competitors?" in Frans A. M. Alting von Geusau, ed. *Allies in a Turbulent World*. Lexington, MA: Lexington Books, 1982.
Borawski, John. " 'Next Steps in Conference and Security' Building Measures," in Stan Windass and Eric Grove, eds. *Common Security in Europe 1988*. The Foundation for International Security. Adderbury, England: 1988.
Brill, Heinz. *"Konferenz über Vertrauens- und Sicherheits-bildende Massnahmen und Abrüstung in Europa,"* *Europaische Wehrkunde* 2, 1984.
von Bülow, Andreas. "Defensive Entanglement: An Alternative Strategy for NATO," in Andrew J. Pierre, ed. *The Conventional Defense of Europe: New Technologies and New Strategies*. New York: New York University Press, 1986.
Bundy, McGeorge. "To Cap the Volcano," *Foreign Affairs*, 48, 1, October 1969.
Bundy, McGeorge, George F. Kennan, *et al.* "Nuclear Weapons and the Atlantic Alliance," *Foreign Affairs*, 60, 5, Spring 1982.
Connel-Smith, Gordon. "President Reagan and the Caribbean Crisis," *Washington Quarterly*, 7, 4, Fall 1984.
Cordesman, Anthony H. "An Exclusive Interview with General Bernard W. Rogers," *Armed Forces Journal International*, 120, 2, September 1983.

Dean, Jonathan. "MBFR: From Apathy to Accord," *International Security*, 7, 4, Spring 1983.

De Rose, Francois. "NATO's Perils—and Opportunities,"*Strategic Review*. XI, 4, Fall 1983.

Dettke, Dieter. "Security in the Context of an Enlarged European Community," in Carl F. Pinkele and Adamantia Pollis, eds. *The Contemporary Mediterranean World*. New York: 1983.

Dick, C. J. "Soviet Doctrine, Equipment, Design and Organization: An Integrated Approach to War," *International Defense Review*, 16, 12, December 1983.

————. "Soviet Operational Maneuver Groups: A Closer Look," *International Defense Review*, 16, 6, June 1983.

Donnelly, Christopher. "Development of the Soviet Concept of Echeloning," *NATO Review*, 32, December 1984.

Duchêne, Francois. "*Die Rolle Europas im Weltsystem: Von der regionalen zur planetarischen Interdependent*," in Francois Duchêne and Wolfgang Hager, eds. *Zivilmacht Europa—Supermacht oder Partner?* Frankfurt: 1973.

Dunn, A. "Considerations After the INF Treaty: NATO After Global 'Double Zero,' " *Survival*, XXX, 3, May/June 1988.

Dunn, Keith A. and William O. Staudenmaier, "Competing Strategic Concepts: The Need for a Unified Military Strategy," in Stephen J. Cimbala, ed. *National Security Strategy: Choices and Limits*. New York: Praeger Publishers, 1984.

Erler, Fritz. "*Sicherheit und deutsche Einheit II*," SPD-Pressedienst, 4 April 1955. *Zweite Republik*. Stuttgart: 1974.

Fialka, John J. "Europe Debates Missile Pact's Aftermath," The *Wall Street Journal*, 7 December 1987.

Flynn, Gregory. "Public Opinion and Atlantic Defense," *Occidente*, 1 January 1984.

Gallois, General Pierre. "U.S. Strategy and the Defense of Europe," *Orbis*, 7, 2, Summer 1963.

Garrett, James M. "Conventional Force Deterrence in the Presence of Theater Nuclear Weapons," *Armed Forces and Society* 11, 1, Fall 1984.

Gelb, Leslie H. "The Mind of the President," *The New York Times Magazine*, 6 October 1986.

————. "Reagan's Military Budget Puts Emphasis on a Buildup of Global Military Power," *The New York Times*, 7 February 1982.

Goloshubov, Yury. "High time to Convene the European Conference," *Soviet News* (from *Pravda*), 22 January 1974.

Gordon, Michael R. "Technology and NATO Defense: Weighing the Options," in James R. Golden, Asa A. Clark and Bruce E. Arlinghaus, eds. *Conventional Deterrence: Alternatives for European Defense*. Lexington, MA: Lexington Books, 1985.

Gouré, Daniel and Jeffrey R. Cooper, "Conventional Deep Strike: A Critical Look," *Comparative Strategy*, 3, 1984.

Gray, Colin S. and Jeffrey G. Barlow. "Inexcusable Restraint: The Decline of American Military Power in the 1970's," *International Security*, 10, 2, Fall 1985.

Gross, Richard C. "Pentagon Drafts Plan to Upgrade Strength," The *Washington Post*, 18 March 1983.

Growlich, Klaus W. "Eureka-eureka?" *Aussenpolitik*, 37, January 1986.

Hacke, Christian. "*Parlamentarische Opposition und Entspannungspolitik-Die Position der CDU/CSU zur KSZE*" in Helga Haftendorn *et al.* eds. *Verwaltete Aussenpolitik*. Köln: *Wissenschaft und Politik*, 1978.

Halloran, Richard. "Pentagon Draws Up First Strategy for a Long Nuclear War," *The New York Times*, 30 May 1982.

_____. "Two Studies Say Defense of Western Europe Is Biggest U.S. Military Cost," *The New York Times*, 20 July 1984.

_____. "New Weinberger Directive Refines Military Policy," *The New York Times*, 22 March 1983.

_____. "Weinberger Angered by Reports on War Strategy," *The New York Times*, 24 August 1982.

Hassner, Pierre. "Détente and the Policies of Instability in Southern Europe," in Johan Holst and Uwe Nerlich, eds. *Beyond Nuclear Deterrence*. New York: Crane, Russack, 1977.

Hermann, Charles L. "Defining National Security," in John F. Reichart and Steven R. Sturm, eds. *American Defense Policy*. 5th ed. Baltimore and London: Johns Hopkins University Press, 1982.

Heyhoe, D. C. R. "The Alliance and Europe, Part VI: The European Programme Group," *Adelphi Papers* No. 129, London: The International Institute for Strategic Studies, 1979.

Hoagland, Jim. "Rhetoric From Bonn. Why Is the German Foreign Minister Saying Nice Things About the Soviets?" *Washington Post*, 18 August 1988.

Hughes, G. Philip. "Cutting the Gordian Knot: A Theater Nuclear Force for Deterrence in Europe," *Orbis*, 22, 2, Summer 1973.

Huldt, Bo. "Considering the East-West Military Balance," in *The Conduct of East-West Relations in the 1980s, Part III. Adelphi Papers*, No. 191, London: The International Institute for Strategic Studies, 1984.

Huntington, Samuel. "Conventional Deterrence and Conventional Retaliation in Europe," *International Security*, 8, 3, Winter 1983-84.

Husbands, Jo L. "Definitions of Security," in Charles E. Pirtle, Supervising ed. *International Security: Concepts and Approaches, an Introductory Course*. Center for International Security Studies, University of Pittsburgh, 1979.

Jacchia, Enrico. "What Was Bothering Andreotti?" *International Herald Tribune*, 22-23 September 1984.

Jaszunski, Grzegorz. *Zycie Warszawy*, 15 May 1973.

Jung, Ernst F. "Conventional Arms Control in Europe in Light of the MBFR Experience." *Aussenpolitik* English Language Edition, 39, February 1988.

Kaiser, Karl. "The U.S. and the E.E.C. in the Atlantic System: The Problem of Theory," *Journal of Common Market Studies*, V, 4, June 1967.

_____. "Warning: Security of West at Stake," *International Herald Tribune*, 9 March 1979.

Karber, Phillip A. "In Defense of Forward Defense," *Armed Forces Journal International*, 121, 10, May 1984.

Kass, Ilanna and Michael J. Deane. "The Role of Nuclear Weapons in the Modern Theater Battlefield: The Current Soviet View," *Comparative Strategy*, 3, 1984.

Kelleher, Catherine McArdle. "The Defense Policy of the Federal Republic of Germany," in Douglas J. Murray and Paul R. Viotti, eds. *The Defense Policies of Nations: A Comparative Study*. Baltimore, MD: Johns Hopkins Press, 1982.

Keller, Bill. "As Arms Buildup Eases, U.S. Tries to Take Stock," *The New York Times*, 14 May 1985.

Kennedy, Robert. "Soviet Theater Nuclear Capabilities: The European Nuclear Balance in Transition," in Robert Kennedy and John M. Weinstein, eds. *The Defense of the West*. Boulder, CO: Westview Press, 1984.

Kiep, W. Leisler. "*Auch in Helsinki die deutsche Frage offenhalten*," *Die Zeit*, 25 July 1975.

Kirkpatrick, Jeane. "Grumbling About Reykjavik," *Washington Post*, 27 October 1986.

Kissinger, Henry A. "Détente with the Soviet Union: The Reality of Competition and the Imperative of Cooperation," in Robert J. Pranger, ed. *Détente and Defense*. Washington, D.C.: American Enterprise Institute, 1976.

————. "NATO's Future," Reprint of a speech given in Brussels, Belgium, *The Washington Quarterly*, 2, 4, Autumn, 1979.

————. "A Plan to Reshape NATO," *Time*, 5 March 1984.

Kohl, Helmut. "*Wir haben mehr Kontakte möglich gemacht*," *Süddeutsche Zeitung*, 13 September 1984.

Komer, Robert W. "Maritime Strategy versus Coalition Defense," *Foreign Affairs*, 60, Summer 1982.

————. "Prospects for Allied Cooperation Outside the NATO-Area," in James A. Thomson, ed. *NATO: Agenda for the Next Four Years*. Santa Monica, CA: The RAND Corporation, January 1982.

————. "What 'Decade of Neglect'?," *International Security*, 10, 2, Fall 1985.

Laird, Melvin R. "A Strong Start in a Difficult Decade: Defense Policy in the Nixon-Ford Years." *International Security*, 10, 2, Fall 1985.

Landry, John R. *et al.*. "Deep Attack in Defense of Central Europe: Implications for Strategy and Doctrine," in *Essays on Strategy: Selections From the 1983 Joint Chiefs of Staff Essay Competition*. Washington, D.C.: National Defense University Press, 1984.

Lebow, Richard Ned. "The Soviet Offensive in Europe: The Schlieffen Plan Revisited?," *International Security*, 9, 4, Spring 1985.

Leicht, Robert. "*Deutsche Verantwortungsgemeinschaft*," *Süddeutsche Zeitung*, 11 September 1984.

Liko, Karl. "*Von Madrid nach Stockholm*," *Österreichische Militarische Zeitschrift* 1, January/February, 1984.

Löwenthal, Richard. "Vom Kalten Krieg zur Ostpolitik," in R. Löwenthal and H. P. Schwarz. *Die Dritte Republik*. Stuttgart: 1974.

Luders, Carl. "*Ideologie und Machtdenken in der sowjetischen Aussenpolitik*," *Aus Politik und Zeitgeschichte*, *Beilage zur Wochenzeitung Das Parlament* 37, 1981.

Luttwak, Edward. *Washington Post*, 29 November 1987.

McCartney, Robert J. "Bonn's Defense Minister Cautious on Arms Talks," *Washington Post*, 17 June 1988.

McFarlane, Robert C. "Time Out on Defense," *Washington Post*, 3 January 1988.

McNamara, Robert S. "The Military Role of Nuclear Weapons: Perceptions and Misperceptions," *Foreign Affairs*, 62, 1, Fall 1983.

Mearsheimer, John J. "Nuclear Weapons and Deterrence in Europe," *International Security*, 9, 3, Winter 1984-85.

Mertes, Alois. "Outlook for the Conferences on Confidence Building and Disarmament in Europe," *Aussenpolitik* (English edition), 1, 1984.

Meyer, Stephen M. *Soviet Theater Nuclear Forces: Part II: Capabilities and Implications*, Adelphi Papers, No. 188, London: The International Institute for Strategic Studies, Winter 1983/4.

Monnet, Jean. "Memorandum of 3 May, 1950," in Gilbert Ziebura. *Die deutsch-franzosischen Beziehungen seit 1945—Mythen and Realitaten*. Pfullingen: Neske, 1970.

Newhouse, John. "The Diplomatic Round," *New Yorker*, 22 July 1985.

Neuchterlein, E. "National Interests and National Strategy: The Need for Priority," in Terry L. Heyns, ed. *Understanding U.S. Strategy: A Reader.* Washington, D.C.: National Defense University Press, 1983.

Nunn, Senator Sam. *The New York Times,* 21 June 1984.

Nye, Joseph S., Jr. "U.S. Power and Reagan Policy," *Orbis,* 82, 3 Summer 1982.

Odom, William E. "Trends in the Balance of Military Power Between East and West," *The Conduct of East-West Relations in the 1980's, Part III,* Adelphi Papers, No. 191, London: The International Institute for Strategic Studies, Summer 1984.

Osgood, Robert E. "American Grand Strategy: Patterns, Problems, and Prescriptions," *Naval War College Review,* 36, 5, Sept.-Oct. 1983.

Peterson, Philip A. and John G. Hines. "The Conventional Offensive in Soviet Theatre Strategy," *Orbis,* 27, 3, Fall 1983.

Pond, Elizabeth. "Kohl Hails Thaw in West German, Soviet Relations," *Christian Science Monitor,* 15 January 1988.

Posen, Barry R. "Measuring the European Conventional Balance," *International Security,* 9, 3, Winter 1984-85.

_____, and Stephen van Evera. "Defense Policy and the Reagan Administration: Departure from Containment," *International Security,* 8, 1, Summer 1983.

Putnam, Robert D. "Summit Sense," *Foreign Policy,* 55, Summer 1984.

Record, Jeffrey. "Jousting with Unreality: Reagan's Military Strategy," *International Security,* 8, 3, Winter 1983-84.

_____. "NATO in 1984-An Update," in Barry M. Blechman and Edward N. Luttwak, eds. *International Security Yearbook 1984/85.* Boulder, CO: Westview Press, 1985.

_____. "The Impact on NATO of Security Requirements Outside the Treaty Area," in Joseph Wolf, ed. *Strengthening Deterrence: NATO and the Credibility of Western Defense in the 1980s.* Cambridge, MA: Ballinger Publishing Co., 1982.

Reifenberg, Jan. "Watershed in Arms Control: Now for the Future," *Frankfurter Allgemeine Zeitung,* 11 December 1987, translated and reprinted in *The German Tribune,* 20 December 1987.

Reubard, Karl-Heinz. "Rearmament, NATO and the *Bundeswehr* Seen Through the Eyes of West German Citizens," in Wolfgang R. Vogt, ed. *The Military as Counterculture? Armed Forces in a Changing Society.* Opladen: 1986.

Rogers, Bernard W. "The Attack of Warsaw Pact Follow-On Forces," *Military Technology,* May 1983.

_____. "The Atlantic Alliance: Prescriptions for a Difficult Decade," *Foreign Affairs,* 60, Summer 1982.

Rosenau, James H. and Ole R. Holsti. "U.S. Leadership in a Shrinking World: Emergence of Conflicting Belief Systems," *World Politics,* 3, April 1983.

Rosenberg, David Alan. "U.S. Nuclear War Planning, 1945-1960," in Desmond Ball and Jeffrey Richelson, eds. *Strategic Nuclear Targeting.* Ithaca, NY: Cornell University Press, 1986.

Rühl, Lothar. "Franco-German Military Cooperation: An Insurance Policy for the Alliance," *Strategic Review,* XIV, 3, Summer 1988.

_____. "*Im Schatten der roten Raketen,*" *Die Zeit,* 4 March 1977.

_____. "*Sorgen um die Graue zone,*" *Die Zeit,* 16 December 1977.

von Sandrart, General Hans-Henning. "Forward Defense—Mobility and the Use of Barriers," *NATO's Sixteen Nations,* 30, Special Issue 1/85.

Schlemmer, Benjamin F. "Soviet Technological Parity in Europe Undermines NATO's Flexible Response Strategy," *Armed Forces Journal International,* 121, 10, May 1984.

────── . "Successful Blitzkrieg Possible in 15 years if NATO Doesn't Produce Better," *Armed Forces Journal International*, 122, 12, July 1985.

Schlesinger, Arthur, Jr. "Foreign Policy and the American Character," *Foreign Affairs* 62, 1, Fall 1983.

Schmidt, Peter. "Public Opinion and Security Policy in the Federal Republic of Germany," *Orbis*, 28, 4, Winter 1985.

von Schubert, Klaus. "Conditions of Survival," *Aus Politik und Zeitgeschichte: Das Parlament*. Bonn: 10 March 1980.

Scott, william F. "Soviet Concepts of War," *Air Force Journal*, March 1985, reprinted in *Current News, Special Edition*, 1276, March 1985.

Seignious, George M., II and Jonathan Paul Yates. "Europe's Nuclear Superpowers," *Foreign Policy*, 55, Summer 1984.

Shulman, Marshall D. "Toward a Western Philosophy of Coexistence," *Foreign Affairs* 52, 1 October 1973.

Shuster, Alvin. "Soviet Gives Way on Europe Parley," *The New York Times*, 28 May 1973.

Sienkiewicz, Stanley. "Observations on the Impact of Uncertainty in Strategic Analysis," in John F. Reichart and Steven R. Sturm, eds. *American Defense Policy*. Fifth ed. Baltimore, MD: The Johns Hopkins University Press, 1982.

Sinnreich, Richard Hart. "Strategic Implications of Doctrinal Change: A Case Analysis," in Keith A. Dunn and William O. Staudenmeier, eds. *Military Strategy in Transition: Defense and Deterrence in the 1980s*. Carlisle Barracks, PA: Strategic Studies Institute, 1984.

Smart, Ian. "Future Conditional: The Prospect for Anglo-French Cooperation," *Adelphi Papers*, No. 78, London: Institute for Strategic Studies, 1971.

Smoke, Richard. "The Evolution of American Defense Policy," and "A Summary of Developments Since 1975," both in John F. Reichert and Steven R. Sturm, eds. *American Defense Policy*. 5th ed. Baltimore and London: Johns Hopkins University Press, 1982.

Sommer, Theo. "*Entspannung hat ihren Preis*," *Die Zeit*, 21 September 1973.

Stewart, James Moray. "Conventional Defense Improvements: Where is the Alliance Going?," *NATO's Sixteen Nations*, 30 March 1985.

Stratmann, Peter K. "Prospective Tasks and Capabilities Required for NATO's conventional Forces," in European Security Study Group. *Strengthening Conventional Deterrence in Europe: Proposals for the 1980's*,. New York: St. Martin's, 1983.

Stucklen, Richard. "*Konferenz der Unsicherheit*," *Bayernkurier*. 19 October 1974.

Sutton, Boyd D. *et al.*., "Deep Attack Concepts and the Defense of Central Eruope," *Survival*, 16, 2, March-April 1984.

Tankman, Philip. "The Schultz-Weinberger Feud," *The New York Times Magazine*. 14 April 1985.

Tatu, Michel. "*Europaische Verteidigung—einegemeinsame Aufgabê?*," *Dokumente*, 22 January 1983, Special Edition.

Tebbe, Wolfgang. "The Transatlantic Dialogue and the European Defense Industry," *NATO's Sixteen Nations*, 30, October 1985.

Thurow, Lester. "A Time to Dismantle the World Economy," *The Economist*, 9 November 1985.

Treverton, Gregory F. "Defense Beyond Europe," *Survival*, 25, 5, Sept./Oct. 1983.

Urban, Mark L. "Major Reorganization of Soviet Air Forces," *International Defense Review*, 16, 6, June 1983.

Voigt, Karsten. "German Security Policy and European Security Needs," *AEI Foreign Policy and Defense Review,* 3 & 4, March 1983.

Vorkotter, Uwe. "Europe looks towards New Technology Horizons," *Hannoverische Allgemeine,* 22 July 1985. Translated and reprinted in the *German Tribune,* 1189, 28 July 1985.

Watkins, Admiral James D. "The Maritime Strategy," *Naval Institute Proceedings.* Reprinted in "From the Pentagon, An Ultimate Battle Plan," *The New York Times,* 12 January 1986.

von Weizsäcker, Carl Friedrich. *"Über weltpolitische Prognosen,"* *Europa-Archiv,* 1, 1966.

West, F. J., Jr. "Maritime Strategy and NATO Deterrence," *Naval War College Review,* 28, 5, September-October, 1985.

Wetterhahn, Armin. "The Soviet Guided Missile Cruiser *Slava,"* *International Defense Review,* 1, January 1984.

Wettig, Gerhard. "The Garthoff-Pipes Debate on Soviet Strategic Doctrine: A European Perspective," *Strategic Review,* XI, 2, Spring 1983.

Whit, Flora. "Nuclear War Escalation Seen Likely," *Washington Post,* 14 March 1983.

———. "Weinberger: Star Wars' Defense Plan is No Fantasy," *Washington Times,* 12 April 1983.

Wickham, General John A., Jr. "Light Infantry Divisions in Defense of Europe," *NATO's Sixteen Nations,* 30, Special Issue 1/85.

Yankelovich, David and John Doble. "The Public Mood," *Foreign Affairs* 63, 1, Fall 1984.

Zimmermann, Dr. Friedrich. *"Pflicht zur Verteidigung des Westens,"* *Das Parlament,* Bundestag, Bonn, 17 March 1979.

Anonymous. "Americans Assess the Nuclear Option," *Public Opinion,* 5, 4, Aug./ Sept. 1982.

———. *"Bonner Appelle an den Senat,"* *Süddeutscher Zeitung,* 9 December 1987.

———. "Bonn's 'Star Wars' Role Draws a Soviet Protest," *The New York Times,* 5 April 1986.

———. "Defense and Offense," *Public Opinion,* 6, 2, April/May 1983.

———. "Eurofighter," *The Economist,* 7 September 1985.

———. "Foreign Affairs: What's Past is Prologue," *Public Opinion,* 6, 4, Aug./Sept. 1983.

———. "Interview with Mr. Weinberger," *USA Today,* 11 August 1983.

———. "Mertes in Stockholm: *Vertrauen allein starkt nicht die allgemeine Sicherheit"* *Frankfurter Allgemeine Zeitung,* 5 May 1984, 2.

———. "The New Trade Strategy," *Business Week,* 7 October 1985.

———. "Pentagon Spending is the Economy's Biggest Gun," *Business Week,* 21 October 1985.

———. "President's Speech on Military Spending and a New Defense," *The New York Times,* 24 March 1983.

Speeches and Interviews

Adenauer, Konrad. *"Rede des Bundskanzlers Konrad Adenauer auf einer Kundgehung der DEU in der Universität Bonn vom 28.3.1952"* in Klaus von Schubert, ed. *Sicherheitspolitik der Bundesrepublik Deutschland. Dokumentation, 1945-1977,* 2 Vols. Bonn: Schriftenreihe der Bundeszentrale für Politische Bildung, 1978.

Brezhnev, Leonid. "Helsinki Final Act Was Major Event in History of Post-War Europe," *Soviet News*, 5 August 1980 (from *Pravda*, 30 July 1980). "Remarks of Secretary of Defense Harold Brown at the U.S. Naval Academy given May 30, 1979." Reprinted in the Department of Defense *Selected Statements* 79-4, 1 July 1979.

Carter, Jimmy. "Speech on the Anniversary of the Signing of the Helsinki Accords, August 6, 1980," *America Digest*, Bonn, 1980.

––––––– .*1980 State of the Union Message, 23 January 1980*. Washington, GPO: 1980.

Genscher, Hans-Dietrich. "Comments on the Anniversary of the Signing of the Helsinki Accords, 31 July 1980," *Bulletin* 89, 5 August 1980.

Haig, Alexander. "Relationship of Foreign and Defense Policies." *Current Policy*, 302, Bureau of Public Affairs, United States Department of State. Washington, D.C.: 30 July 1981.

Honneker, Eric. Interview with *Neues Deutschland, Berliner Zeitung* and Press Agency ADN, 18 August 1984.

Kissinger, Henry A. "Prepared Statement," in *The INF Treaty*, Part 4, Hearings before the Committee on Foreign Relations, U.S. Senate, 100th Congress, 2nd Session, February 22, 23, 24, and March 3, 1988. Washington: GPO, 1988. Press Conference of Secretary of State Henry A. Kissinger, 22 July 1974, reprinted in Roger P. Labrie, *SALT Handbook*. Washington, D.C.: American Enterprise Institute for Public Policy Research, 1979.

Kohl, Helmut. "Freedom Is The Prerequisite for Peace," policy statement to the *Bundestag*, 21 Nov. 1983. Translated and reprinted in the *Bulletin*, 20 Dec. 1983.

––––––– . Statement on the Signing of the SALT II Agreement, CDU *Pressemitteilung*, Bonn, 18 June 1979.

Mitterrand, Francois. "*Rede in Bonn am 20. January 1983 anlasslich des zwanzigsten Jahrestages der Unterzeichnung des Vertrages uber die deutsch-franzosische Zusammenarbeit*," *Europa-Archiv*, 10 March 1983.

Reagan, President Ronald. "Peace and National Security," Televised Address to the Nation, Washington D.C., 23 March 1983, reprinted in U.S. Department of State, *Realism, Strength, Negotiation: Key Foreign Policy Statements of the Reagan Administration*, May 1984.

"Press Conference, 31 March 1982," *The New York Times*, 1 April 1982.

Rostow, Eugene V. Testimony. *Hearings before the Committee on Foreign Relations on the Foreign Policy and Arms Control Implications of President Reagan's Strategic Weapons Proposals*, Part I, Nov. 3, 4 & 9, 1981. Washington, D.C.: 1981.

Schmidt, Helmut. "Speech before the Annual Meeting of the IISS," *Survival*, 1, January-February 1978.

Schultz, George. "Security and Arms Control: The Search for a More Stable Peace," *Department of State Bulletin*, June 1983.

Speidel, General Hans. "*Rede des Befehlshabers der NATO-Landstreitkrafte in Mittleuropa*, General Hans Speidel, vor der Association of the United States Army in Washington am 8.8. 1960," in Klaus von Schubert, ed. *Sicherheitspolitik der Bundesrepublik Deutschland. Dokumentation 1945-1977,.* 2 Vols. Bonn: Schriftenreihe der Bundeszentrale für Politische Bildung, 1978.

von Weizsäcker, Richard. Interview with the Radio Station *Deutschlandfunk*, 20 August 1984.

––––––– . Speech on the occasion of Taking Office as President of the Federal Republic of Germany, *Bulletin des Presse- u. Informationsamtes der Bundesregierung*, 80, 3 July 1984.

Official Documents and Reports

Communiqué of the Franco-German Consultations in Paris on February 5 and 6, 1981, in *Bulletin des Presse und Informationsamtes der Bundesregierung* 1 February 1981.

Conference on Security and Cooperation in Europe. *Final Act*, Cmnd. 6198, London: Her Majesty's Stationery Office, 1 August 1975.

Congressional Budget Office. *Modernizing U.S. Strategic Offensive Forces: the Administration's Program and Alternatives.* Washington, D.C.: May 1983.

Department of Defense. *Statement of Secretary of Defense Robert S. McNamara before the House Armed Services Committee on the Fiscal Year 1969-1971 Defense Program and 1967 Defense Budget.* Washington, D.C.: 8 March 1966.

Statement of Secretary of Defense Melvin R. Laird on the Fiscal Year 1972-76 Defense Program and the 1972 Defense Budget, 9 March 1971. Washington, D.C.: GPO, 1971.

Report of Secretary of Defense James R. Schlesinger to the Congress on the FY 1976 and Transition Budgets, FY 1977 Authorization Request and FY 1976-1980 Defense Programs, 5 February 1975. Washington, D.C.: Department of Defense, 1975.

Report of Secretary of Defense Donald H. Rumsfeld to the Congress on the FY 1978 Budget, FY 1979 Authorization Request and FY 1978-1982 Defense Programs. Washington, D.C.: Department of Defense, 1977.

Annual Report, Fiscal Year 1979, Harold Brown, Secretary of Defense. Washington, D.C.: 2 February 1978.

Report of Secretary of Defense Harold Brown to the Congress on the FY 1980 Budget, FY 1981 Authorization Request and FY 1980-1984 Defense Programs. Washington, D.C.: 20 January 1979.

Report of Secretary of Defense Harold Brown to the Congress on the FY 1981 Budget, the FY 1982 Authorization Request and FY 1983-1988 Defense Programs. Washington, D.C.: 1980.

Report of Secretary of Defense Harold Brown to the Congress on the FY 1982 Budget, FY 1983 Authorization Request and FY 1982-1986 Defense Programs. Washington, D.C.: January 1981.

Report of Secretary of Defense Caspar W. Weinberger to the Congress on the FY 1983 Budget, FY 1984 Authorization Request and FY 1983-1987 Defense Programs, February 8, 1982. Washington, D.C.: GPO, 1982.

Report of Secretary of Defense Caspar W. Weinberger to the Congress on the FY 1984 Budget, FY 1985 Authorization Request and FY 1984-88 Defense Programs. February 1, 1983. Washington, D.C.: 1983.

Report of Secretary of Defense Caspar W. Weinberger to the Congress on the FY 1985 Budget, FY 1986 Authorization Request and FY 1985-89 Defense Programs, 1 February 1984. Washington, D.C.: GPO, 1984.

Report of Secretary of Defense Caspar W. Weinberger to the Congress on the FY 1986 Budget, FY 1987 Authorization Request and FY 1986-90 Defense Programs, February 4, 1985. Washington, D.C.: GPO, 1985.

European Community, "Declaration on European Union," *Europa-Archiv* 15, 1983.

The Federal Minister of Defense. *White Paper 1983, The Security of the Federal Republic of Germany.* Bonn: Federal Ministry of Defence, 1983.

_____ . *White Paper 1985: The Situation and Development of the Federal Armed Forces.* Bonn: Federal Ministry of Defense, 19 June 1985.

German Information Center. *Germany's Contribution to Western Defense.* New York: German Information Center, 1984.

Larson, David L. ed. *The "Cuban Crisis" of 1962: Selected Documents and Chronology.* Boston: Houghton-Mifflin, 1967.

Meissner, Boris. ed. *Die Deutsche Ostpolitik 1961-1970. Dokumentation.* Köln: 1975.
NATO Information Service. *Harmel Report. Report on the Future Task of the Alliance.* Brussels: 1969.
———. *NATO and the Warsaw Pact, Force Comparisons.* Brussels: 1984.
NATO Senior Consultative Group. *Report to Ministers,* 8 December 1983.
North Atlantic Assembly, Subcommittee on Détente. *Détente: Results and Prospects.* Brussels: October 1979.
North Atlantic Council. *Report of the Committee of Three on Non-Military Cooperation in NATO,* 1956.
North Atlantic Treaty Organization. "Communiqué of the Special Meeting of NATO Foreign and Defense Ministers," Brussels, 12 December 1979.
———. North Atlantic Treaty. Paris: 1949.
OECD, *Economic Surveys, 1983-1984: Germany .*
Organization of the Joint Chiefs of Staff. *Statement by General George S. Brown, USAF, Chairman, Joint Chiefs of Staff to the Congress on the Defense Posture of the United States for 1978,* 20 January 1977. Washington, D.C.: 1977.
———. *United States Military Posture FY 1981,* Washington, D.C.: 1981.
———. *United States Military Posture for FY 1984.* Washington, D.C.: 1983.
Rogers, William. *American Foreign Policy: Innovation and Involvement,* in *United States Foreign Policy 1971: A Report of the Secretary of State.* Washington, D.C.: 1971.
Strauss, Franz Josef. *"Artikel des Bundesministers der Verteidigung Franz Joseph Strauss zu Fragen der Westlichen Strategie vom August 1961,"* in Klaus von Schubert, ed.
Sicherheitspolitik der Bundesrepublik Deutschland. Dokumentation, 1945-1977. 2 vols. Bonn: Schriftenreihe der Bundeszentrale für Politische Bildung, 1978.
U.S. Congress, House of Representatives, Committee on Foreign Affairs. "Appeal to All European Countries adopted by the Political Consultative Committee of the Warsaw Pact, Budapest, 17 May 1969" in *Conference on European Security,* Hearings, April 25; May 10; August 10, 17; September 7, 27, 1972. Washington, D.C.: GPO, 1972.
———. "Declaration Issued at the Close of the Meeting of the Political Consultative Committee of the Warsaw Pact on the Strengthening of Peace and Security in Europe. Bucharest, 5 July 1966.
———. "Final Communiqué issued after the Ministerial Meeting of the North Atlantic Council Brussels: 4 December 1970." U.S. Congress, Senate. 95th Congress, 2nd Sess. "Concluding Document of the Belgrade Meeting 1977," Report No. 95-773, *Belgrade Conference on Security and Cooperation in Europe.* Washington, D.C.: GPO, 2 May 1978.
United States Department of Commerce, Bureau of Economic Analysis. *Business Statistics 1982.* Washington, D.C.: 1983.
United States Department of Labor. *Abstract of the United States Census.* Washington, D.C.: Bureau of Labor Statistics, April 1980.
United States Government. *Treaty between the United States of America and the Union of Soviet Socialist Republics on the Elimination of Their Intermediate-Range and Shorter-Range Missiles.* Washington, D.C.: December 1987.
Weinberger, Caspar W. *Report on Allied Contributions to the Common Defense: A Report to the United States Congress.* Washington, D.C.: Department of Defense, March 1985.

Miscellaneous

Arkin, William M., Robert S. Norris and Thomas B. Cochran. "Implications of the INF Treaty," Nuclear Weapons Databook Working Paper 87-3. Washington, D.C.: National Resources Defense Council, 1 December 1987.

The Arms Control Reporter, 1985. Brookline, MA: Institute for Defense and Disarmament Studies, 1985.

Chicago Council on Foreign Relations. *Détente and the Atlantic Nations.* Papers from the 1976 Atlantic Conference. Chicago: 1977.

Department of the Army. *FM-105, Operations.* Washington, D.C.: 1982.

——. U.S. Army Operational Concepts and Doctrine Command. *The Airland Battle and Corps 86.* Pamphlet 525-6, 1981.

Deutsche Gesellschaft für Auswärtige Politik [DGAP]. Jahrbuch 1979-1980, Zur Entspannungspolitik in Europa, Baden-Baden: 1980.

——. *Jahrbuch 1982-1983. Zur Lage Europas im globalen Spannungsfeld.* Baden-Baden: 1983.

Ehmke, Horst. "European Self-Assertion," Paper delivered in Bonn, January 1984.

Freie Deutsche Partei (FDP). *Ergebnisprotokoll Arbeitskreis ll Rustungskontrolle/ Abrüstung, Provisorische Materialsammlung,* (Munster, 27/28 April 1979).

——. *Provisorische Materialsammlung vom verteidigungspolitischen Kongress der FDP-Munster,* FDP, Bonn, 1 June 1979.

"FDP Executive Committee: No Role in SDI without European Partners," *The Week in Germany.*

Grabendorff, Wolf. "The Role of Western Europe in the Caribbean Basin," in Stiftung Wissenschaft und Politik (SWP). *Die Europaisch-Amerikanischen Beziehungen bei Sicherheitsfragen in der Dritten Welt.* Ebenhausen, FRG: Publication SWP-K 2378, December 1983.

Hubel, Helmut. *Turkei und Mittelost-Krisen,* Paper, Research Institute of the German Society for Foreign Affairs, Bonn: August 1984.

The International Institute for Strategic Studies. *The Military Balance, 1984-1985.* London:August 1984.

——. *Strategic Survey 1983-1984,* London: 1984.

Kaiser, Karl, Winston Lord, Thiery de Montbrial and David Watt. *Western Security: What Has Changed, What Should Be Done?* London: Royal Institute of International Affairs, 1981.

Kohl, Helmut. Remarks to Robert Bosch Fellows, *Bundeskanzleramt,* 11 September 1984.

Krause, Christian. "Do the Russians Threaten Us?" *Paper No. 10, Study Group on Security and Disarmament,* Friedrich Ebert Stiftung. Bonn: March 1985.

Lapins, Wulf-W. *"Zur einschatzung sowjetischer Bedrohung in der westdeutschen Uberregionalen Tages- und Wochenpresse"* Dissertation, Bonn: 1983.

Litwak, Robert. "Persian Gulf Security and European-American Relations," in Stiftung Wissenschaft und Politik (SWP) *Die Europaisch-Amerikanischen Beziehungen bei Sicherheitsfragen in der Dritten Welt.* Ebenhausen, FRG: Publication SWP-K 2378, December 1983.

Lunn, Simon. *Burden-sharing in NATO.* Chatham House Papers No. 18, London: 1983.

Palme, Olaf *et al. Common Security : The Palme Report,* London: 1982.

Pierce, William R. "Factors Impinging on U.S. Defense Policy." Internship Report, Graduate School of Public and International Affairs, University of Pittsburgh, June 1984.

Rummel, Reinhardt. "The Arab-Israeli Conflict," in Stiftung Wissenschaft und Politik (SWP). *Die Europaisch-Amerikanischen Beziehungen bei Sicherheitsfragen in der Dritten Welt.* Ebenhausen, FRG: Publication SWP-K 2378, December 1983.

Schmidt, Helmut. "*Letter an Herrn Bundeskanzler Dr. Helmut Kohl*," 23 May 1985. Xerox.

Scowcroft, Lt. Gen. Brent, USAF-Retired. *Report of the President's Commission on Strategic Forces.* Washington, D.C.: April 1983.

Sloan, Stanley R. "The Alliance and the Third World," in Stiftung Wissenschaft und Politik (SWP). *Die Europaisch-Amerikanischen Beziehungen bei Sicherheitsfragen in der Dritten Welt.* Ebenhausen, FRG: Publication SWP - K 2378, December 1983.

Sozialdemokratische Partei Deutschlands (SPD). "*Entspannung, ein langfristiger Prozess*," *Sozialdemokratische Sicherheitspolitik* 8/9, November 1980.

————. *Für Sicherheit und Frieden*, Security Conference, Bremen, *Bundestagsfraktion* SPD, Bonn: 19-20 May 1979.

Statement of the Parliamentary Group of the SPD on President Reagan's "Strategic Defense Initiative," Friedrich Ebert Stiftung. Undated Xerox, released in April 1985.

Stratmann, Peter K. *NATO Doctrine and National Operational Priorities: The Central Front and the Flanks*, SWP-LN 2447, Ebenhausen, FRG: Stiftung Wissenschaft und Politik, September 1985.

Woopen, Herbert J. P. "Legal Restrictions on the Deployment of European Forces Outside the NATO-Area," unpublished paper, Washington, D.C., 1983.

Anonymous. *Entspannung: Der Sowjetische Standpunkt* Moscow: *Novosti*, 1977.

————. "NATO Long-term Defense Program, 1978," in *The Military Balance 1979-1980.* London: International Institute for Strategic Studies, 1979.

Index

ABM Treaty. *See* Anti-Ballistic
Missile Treaty
Abshire, David M., 184, 185
Acheson, Dean, 77
Acheson-Lilienthal plan, 45
Achilles, Theodore, 207
"Active defense," 118
Adenauer, Konrad, 72, 73, 76–77, 78,
79, 80, 81, 82, 85, 86, 87, 88,
89, 93, 203, 270, 274
Afghanistan, 5, 9, 35, 55, 57, 159,
190, 201, 206, 208, 209, 210,
231, 232, 236, 247, 264(n12),
283, 288
Afheldt, Horst, 127, 129, 144(n102)
Africa, 214–215
Agreement on the Prevention of
Nuclear War, 231
Air-Land Battle doctrine, 119–120,
180–181, 183
Airland 2000, 12
Algeria, 42, 207
Allende, Salvador, 14, 17, 217
"Alliance for Progress," 37
Alliances, 2, 3, 36–37, 272. *See also*
entries for individual
organizations
"All-Volunteer Army," 53
Altenburg, Wolfgang, 129
"Alternative strategies," 135–137
Anaconda Copper, 14
Andreotti, Giulio, 254
Andropov, Yuri, 254
Angola, 5, 9, 17, 40, 63, 101, 215,
231, 272
Anti-Ballistic Missile (ABM) Treaty,
53, 54, 261
Anti-Communism
in FRG, 72
in United States, 25–26, 31(n23),
60

Anti-Submarine Warfare (ASW), 39
Apel, Hans, 133
Arab-Israeli conflict, 41, 42, 53, 54,
105, 212–214
Arbatov, Georgi, 136
Arias Peace Plan, 218
Arms control, 5, 19, 26, 27, 138,
155, 189, 282, 283–284, 292–
293, 294–295, 297
under Carter, 35, 54, 246–247
détente and, 230–231, 233–254
under Eisenhower, 46–47
under Ford, 54
FRG and, 136, 137, 242–243, 245–
246, 247–248, 249, 250–251,
253–254, 284
under Kennedy, 49, 50, 63
NATO and, 188–189, 240–242,
243, 244, 246
under Nixon, 52, 53–54, 63
under Reagan, 58, 61, 63, 247–
248, 249, 251, 252–253, 255,
260, 285, 295
WEU and, 78
Arms race, 38–39, 48, 60, 228, 244,
276–277
Aron, Raymond, ix
"Assured destruction" policy, 51, 56,
62, 66(n33), 109, 112, 124, 127,
138
ASW. *See* Anti-Submarine Warfare
Australia, 47

Bangemann, Martin, 259
Baruch plan, 45
Belgium, 157(table), 199, 207, 239,
245, 246
Berlin agreement, 190
Berlin Conference, 79
Berlin Crisis, 50
Berlin Wall, 80, 229